Teaching children in the first three years of school

Teaching children in the first three years of school

2nd edition

Freda Briggs and Gillian Potter

 LONGMAN

Longman Australia Pty Ltd
Longman House
Kings Gardens
95 Coventry Street
Melbourne 3205 Australia

Offices in Sydney, Brisbane, Adelaide, Perth, and associated companies throughout the world.

Copyright © Longman Australia Pty Ltd 1995
First published 1990
Reprinted 1991
Second edition 1995

Designed by Rob Cowpe Design
Set in 10.5/12pt Goudy
Produced by Longman Australia Pty Ltd
through Longman Malaysia

National Library of Australia
Cataloguing-in-Publication data

Briggs, Freda.
Teaching children in the first three years of school.

  2nd ed.
  Bibliography.
  Includes index
  ISBN 0 582 91045 5.

  1. Education, Primary. 2. Education, Primary – Aims and
  objectives. 3. Primary school teaching. I. Potter, Gillian
  K. II. Title.

372.1102

Contents

Preface

This book is about teaching young children in their first three years of school. It will help student teachers to develop the skills needed for teaching practice in infant and junior primary classrooms. It is also a book for recent graduates and experienced teachers, especially those who were not trained in current early childhood education methods and now find themselves teaching young children and supervising student teachers on their practicum.

A realistic view of teaching has been adopted throughout the book. Infant and junior primary classes in Australia, New Zealand and the UK have long been recognised as the great innovators in educational practice. While teaching in these schools provides exciting challenges, enjoyment and a sense of achievement, the work also makes stressful emotional and physical demands on committed teachers.

The role and the responsibilities of the early childhood educator have changed substantially with the realisation that societal and economic pressures impinge on the lives of children and affect their capacity to learn. Teachers now recognise and take steps to alleviate the stresses that affect children when parents separate, change partners, suffer unemployment and other problems. Increasing numbers of children start school with some background of pre-school/daycare experience of varying quality because their mothers have maintained their professional careers or returned to the workforce to support their families. Teachers who have not previously encountered poverty may now experience the effects of material deprivation on the children in their classes.

Teachers recognise that, at stressful times, the school may provide the child's only stable environment. Furthermore, when young children are anxious and confused, they turn to trusted teachers for help. The importance of teachers in child protection has been acknowledged by education authorities with the introduction of personal safety curriculum to schools, such as Protective Behaviours in Australia, Kidscape in Britain and Keeping Ourselves Safe in New Zealand.

Schools for young children have been at the forefront in responding to rapid social and technological changes in our multicultural society. They have responded to changes in employment patterns, providing services to meet community needs such as before-school and after-school care programmes, support groups for single parents and fathers who take on the caregiving role. Some schools have initiated groups to raise the self-esteem and job potential of unemployed dads and they encourage classroom involvement for all parents. In all of these school–community services, there is recognition that families and children are inseparable and to help the child, it may be necessary for the school and community to support the parents. Education has become a team effort.

Attitudes to children's learning have also changed. Although early educators, such as Dewey, focused on the uniqueness of the individual, the dynamic nature of learning and the need for concrete experiences within a total learning environment, theory has only recently been put into practice with any substantial degree of commitment. Now, we rarely see the sterile and traditional infant–junior primary school in which it is assumed that children of the same age have the same needs and learn in the same way at the same time in a near-silent, highly-structured, teacher-dominated classroom.

Teachers of young children have many factors to consider as they plan and implement a curriculum which is relevant to individual children in a complex and rapidly changing society. They aim to develop positive attitudes to learning and create opportunities for children to acquire skills which they will need in the world of today and the unpredictable world of tomorrow.

Teaching children in the first three years of school brings together the many and varied aspects of working with young children, families, community and colleagues. In chapter 1, we examine the bridge between life as a student and life as a teacher. We talk about the feelings we may have when we enter a school building for the first time since our own school days, now with a different role to play. We examine reactions to commonly experienced situations and how to manage them. We discuss the tricky ethics involved in teaching and the need to be aware of legal responsibilities to children in our care. It is important for teachers to be reminded of their own feelings as they make transitions in their lives so that they can better appreciate the similar feelings experienced by parents and children, especially five-year-olds starting school.

Transition from home to school is discussed in chapter 2, stressing the need for continuity of experience when the child moves from one setting to another. We identify the common causes of anxiety for school beginners and discuss ways in which teachers can facilitate a happy start to formal education. When students and teachers are reminded of the nature of children's experiences in their pre-school years, they are better able to assist them and plan an appropriate transition curriculum.

It is important for teachers to understand the individuality of each child as a reflection of his or her genetic and environmental experiences. However, it is also important to be aware of the more general developmental characteristics of five to eight year olds to place their behaviour in a wider context and to understand their idiosyncrasies. In chapter 3 we discuss many aspects of children's development, using separate age-groups to create a general picture of the child in the classroom. It is especially important for teachers to gain insights into the dramatic changes that occur between the ages of five and eight when classes cater for mixed age-groups. It is important to note that this chapter is not intended to replace formal study in child development.

With some understanding of the characteristics of the developing child, the reader moves on to chapter 4, which provides the strategies for organised observation. It is crucial for teachers to note individual learning styles, needs and behaviours which provide the foundation for an individually based curriculum. Without a basis of observation, we cannot judge our effectiveness as teachers. How can we be sure of what children have learned or failed to learn? How can we tell that a child has understood? How can we tell whether the children were interested in what we had to offer? In chapter 5, we begin the discussion which spills over into chapters 6, 7 and 8, on how to use the knowledge gained from observation to cater for children as individuals.

Children clearly learn most when they are interested in what they are doing, can appreciate its relevance and can discover and solve problems for themselves in 'hands on' situations. In chapter 5 we have suggested ways of assigning work to children, developing their independence and involvement through learning centres, contracts, assignment cards, peer and cross-age tutoring and working with parents.

In chapter 6, we discuss the organisation of the classroom and grouping systems which can, if properly managed, assist children to achieve their potential. In chapters 7 and 8, we further this discussion by examining the importance of environmental influences on young children's learning. It is widely accepted that a positive learning environment which aims to develop self-esteem, caring relationships, mutual respect and safety, reaps maximum benefits for teachers and all children. We suggest ways in which the classroom can be organised. We show how to develop a 'feeling environment' and how to use the outdoor environment to advantage.

The concepts of effective education and equality of opportunity for all children are discussed comprehensively in chapter 8. We consider many environmental factors which negatively affect children's learning and suggest ways of identifying the responsible factors and offering the necessary support. We have provided behavioural indicators for the diagnosis of child maltreatment and suggest strategies for protecting children.

Chapter 8 also discusses equity for all children in an inclusive classroom. It examines some of the special needs of disabled children in the mainstreamed classroom, children under stress, those with learning difficulties, those with English as a second language and the special needs of highly gifted children.

Curriculum planning is discussed in broad terms in chapter 9. As there are many variables which influence actual curriculum content and implementation, we make no attempt to examine these aspects in detail. We identify the variety of factors to be considered in planning curriculum, the influences that affect teachers' decisions, the planning process and the recording of information. For students, we offer suggestions for the format of their lesson plans for teaching practice and checklists to gauge their progress.

Through many years of working with students and beginning teachers, the authors have found that major concerns revolve around 'discipline' or classroom management. In chapter 10, we explore techniques of attracting and maintaining children's attention, how to keep children on task and how to manage several groups engaged in different activities simultaneously. We emphasise the importance of planning and preparation with the specific aim of reducing the potential for problems. If ideas in chapters 1 to 9 are implemented, misbehaviours will be reduced to a minimum. However, even the most experienced teachers encounter children who defy their most successful strategies and we provide further suggestions for handling serious misbehaviours and aggression.

Early childhood educators recognise that they are not merely working with children but working with families too; they cannot effectively teach children out of context of the family influence, parental attitudes, culture, language and socio-economic factors. Parents are highly significant to children's development and well-being and, in the early years, they are their children's prime educators. To do justice to all children, teachers must develop sound and supportive relationships with their parents. Chapter 11 addresses the issue of parent participation in the classroom and explains what the school, teacher, child and parent can gain from such participation. We also offer suggestions for ways in which parent participation can be facilitated.

Teaching practice is recognised as the most important part of the student-teacher's pre-service training. In chapter 12, we address some of the issues associated with teaching practice that are fundamental to the teaching profession as a whole. We look at problems which are commonly experienced by students and acknowledge the work of Turney *et al.* (1982) who have initiated training programmes for teacher and lecturer supervisors.

We recognise that this book is only an introduction to teaching and, in the final section, we offer checklists for the self-evaluation of teachers and suggestions for further reading, emphasising the need for continuous professional development. Throughout the writing of the book, we have consulted practising teachers working in 'good schools' in all socioeconomic areas, from educational priority to independent schools. We have circulated chapters to education authorities in England, Australia and New Zealand and have adopted their suggested amendments to the text in an earnest attempt to meet the needs of students and teachers in Early Childhood Education in all three countries.

Acknowledgments are due to Monica Love for drawing the illustrations. We would also like to thank the following people:

- Janne Berg of East Adelaide Junior Primary School, South Australia; Caryl Hamer and colleagues, New Zealand Education Department, Wellington

and former colleagues in Sheffield, Nottingham and Derbyshire for reading the manuscript of this book and contributing their comments.
- the staff, parents and children of Scotch College and Swallowcliffe (Elizabeth) Junior Primary Schools, Adelaide, for the provision of photographs (figure 5.3).
- the Messenger Press for allowing use of a photograph (figure 5.2).
- the parents and staff of Hendon, Mansfield Park, Swallowcliffe (Elizabeth) and Fraser Park (Murray Bridge) Primary Schools, South Australia.

Freda Briggs
Gillian Potter
Adelaide 1995

An introduction to working with children in their first three years of school

Back to school

The emotional reactions of new students and teachers to the schools in which they are about to work

When we visit schools that we are about to join as members of staff, we invariably experience feelings of apprehension as well as excitement. 'Am I really sure that this is the right job for me?' and 'Am I really capable of meeting the demands that will be placed upon me?' are the questions we commonly ask ourselves.

We all went to school and, for good or ill, our school experiences had a significant impact on our lives. As a result, returning to school as an adult produces a variety of powerful emotional responses, ranging from wholly positive to wholly negative. These reactions are likely to relate to some aspect of our own childhood.

Student teachers visiting school for the first day of teaching practice face an environment that is entirely new. They don't know their way around the building, they don't know the teachers and they don't know the children or their parents. They don't know about the school's philosophy or procedures. They feel uncomfortable in the staff room, afraid of sitting in someone's regular chair and using someone else's cup. Students worry about whether they will like the children and whether the children will like them. A much greater worry is whether they will like the teaching staff and be liked by them. Early childhood students have an additional anxiety; will the supervising teachers be sympathetic to early childhood methods which they have learned and are expected to practise?

All students worry about whether they have been adequately prepared for the reality of the classroom. Unlike children, they cannot expose their feelings of insecurity. They know that first impressions are all important for the

Figure 1.1: Am I really sure that this is the right job for me?

development of parents' and teachers' confidence. First impressions are also important for their assessment by examiners and, ultimately, for the acquisition of a job. They try to appear competent and professional whether they feel it or not.

In the classroom, neither students nor new teachers know where things are stored. They may have been given a conducted tour of the premises but, tense and anxious, they are unlikely to remember low priority instructions. As a result, the unexpected keeps happening. Student teachers are highly vulnerable to their own inevitable feelings of inadequacy. A visit to one school does not necessarily provide relevant experience for teaching in another. Schools are as different as the people within them but most staff are sympathetic to the new arrival's predicament.

Students and new teachers do things that don't work. Students who have previously practised teaching in preschools are likely to underestimate the capabilities of older children. They may find it difficult to challenge and motivate them and boredom usually brings behaviour problems. Those who have worked with older children may find, conversely, that they overestimate children's capabilities and provide activities that leave a sense of failure and frustration. These problems may also occur when teachers move from middle class to low socio-economic areas and vice versa. This merely emphasises the importance of being able to provide a selection of open-ended materials that can be extended to provide learning experiences across a wide ability range, such as construction kits, opportunities for scientific and mathematical exploration and dramatic play which may lead to the development of language and literacy skills.

When students and teachers fail to achieve their goals, they often become depressed and negative about teaching. When they plan an activity for children that is greeted with 'I don't want to do that', they feel inadequate and rejected. We have to receive positive feedback to make our work worthwhile and that means providing opportunities for children to feel positive.

Students who lack confidence or knowledge tend to copy their class teachers' mannerisms and behaviour in every detail. They choose the same books, the same lessons, the same school materials. They dare not use their own initiative because they cannot risk failure. When teachers appear to be successful in maintaining law and order, anxious students think, mistakenly, that copying them will guarantee a safe, if dull, life. Students who set out to become clones of their supervising teachers are often horrified to find that cloning doesn't work, especially if the teachers they are reproducing lack lustre. Children are very sensitive to the symbols of control and power. Teachers are ascribed authority because they are teachers; they may be boring, they may use inappropriate methods of control and may 'get away' with bad teaching simply because they are teachers and that role gives them power. The student teacher has no power. As a consequence, methods that produce law and order for teachers do not necessarily work for students. Students have to adopt sound teaching strategies to survive.

Control problems are often viewed as the final confirmation of inadequacy. The difficult lesson for students to learn is that they have to develop their own teaching styles; they have to maintain order by providing interesting learning experiences that are relevant to individual children, irrespective of the models they see in the classroom.

Class discipline is the nightmare of students and new teachers alike. They encounter many problems for which their training did not provide the answers. What should they do when one child hits another and claims that the victim struck the first blow? What should they do when a child deliberately pours paint over the clothing of another and swears that it was an acci-

Figure 1.2: At what point should the student call for the help of the classroom teacher?

dent? When should a student intervene? At what point should the student call for the help of the class teacher and will the teacher interpret the call for help as a sign of weakness? Students dislike having to ask questions. They are afraid of seeming ignorant and incompetent. There is so much that they need to know to operate effectively that if they do not ask questions and remember the answers, they are likely to make many mistakes during their first weeks in the classroom. Most supervising teachers are sympathetic providing that students learn from their mistakes.

Students' defence mechanisms

It is a very uncomfortable feeling when we are uncertain of ourselves, especially when we are in situations that involve the judgement of our capabilities. Teaching practice is a crucial part of students' training and the stepping stone to their chosen career.

Most schools welcome students and new teachers with considerable sensitivity and warmth. Some schools receive so many students and new teachers into their midst that scant attention is paid to their arrival and the motto tends to be one of 'sink or swim'.

When adults try to hide their negative feelings, they set up a series of defence mechanisms to protect themselves. The most common form of defence is attack. Uncomfortable students may become highly critical of their supervising teachers, commenting only on negative aspects of their relationships with children, their management techniques and the curriculum they use.

A second common defence mechanism for the uncertain student and beginning teacher is avoidance of new or difficult situations. Students often tell their teachers that they cannot possibly organise a maths or science session because their training taught them nothing about science and maths in the previous two or three years. They tend to occupy themselves with 'busy work', writing up their observations and lesson plans in the classroom, tidying up and doing the easy, familiar, non-threatening tasks. When they have to teach they choose rigid, formal lessons that require children to sit still and copy-write. These are the methods with which they are most comfortable because they are the familiar ones from high school, and possibly their own primary school days. When they read stories, they play safe and choose the storybooks already in the classroom. Uncomfortable students know that they are inadequate but blame everyone else for their problems.

A third common defence mechanism commonly used by student teachers in crisis situations is to resort to the behaviour models that they experienced in school. They make frequent and monotonous pleas for 'sh-sh-shush', which are so repetitive and boring that they have the opposite effect to the one desired. They use punitive measures to maintain absolute silence, calling 'Hands on heads' or 'Fingers on lips' (sometimes simultaneously!). Punishment often relates to the adults' problems and their own childhood experiences in school rather than the gravity of children's offences.

Uncomfortable students who hide and fight their feelings sense a loss of control and everyone else is held responsible. In despair, they may ask for a transfer to another school on the basis of a personality clash or they may resign, convinced that they have chosen the wrong career.

It's normal to feel uncomfortable in new situations

Students and teachers have to understand that feelings of discomfort are normal and natural. Some newcomers disguise them with brashness and over-confidence, determined that no-one will suspect that this highlight in their career has nightmare potential.

In new situations, everyone has to face a sense of inadequacy. It is important that we realise how we feel, why we feel uncomfortable and how we are reacting to other people. We need to ask how many of our self criticisms are justified and how many constitute our own defence against these inadequate feelings. There is always something to learn in a classroom. There is a great deal to learn from the children. If we concentrate on our own feelings, we are unlikely to be able to respond to them.

Students and new teachers have to accept that they cannot possibly be prepared for all the eventualities that may occur in a classroom. No-one can provide a recipe book that gives all the answers because no two situations are ever exactly the same.

Teachers have to weigh up the circumstances of the moment with their knowledge of the individual children, their personalities and backgrounds, before they reach decisions and act. That involves practice and experience, both of which take time. Teachers are always learning; there is never a time when they can say 'I know everything I need to know'.

The supervising teacher's defence mechanisms

Another difficulty for students is that their supervising teachers may not know what is expected of them. Some may have been trained to work with older children and they are unfamiliar with the ideology and pedagogy of early childhood education. Some teachers take their responsibilities seriously, attend meetings about the teaching practice and understand what is expected of them and their students. Others do not. Some are highly conscientious, taking time to explain and demonstrate the curriculum, their teaching strategies and their evaluation of students' efforts. Some do not.

The teachers responsible for students have the dual advantage of being on 'home ground' and being in charge. Many go through the same feelings of discomfort, however, and experience personal concerns. They may ask, 'What sort of student will they send me? Suppose that we don't like each other. What if I don't like sharing my class with another adult? What if the student is older and tells me what to do? What will I do if the children like the student better than me? What if the student is the opposite sex? What if the student fails?'

We must acknowledge our inadequate feelings before we can feel comfortable about them. No-one should expect a student or new teacher to be as competent as someone who has several years of experience. Self-understanding is vital for teachers of young children because teaching is both tiring and emotionally draining. Teachers are accountable to and under the jurisdiction of changeable school and department administrators. They relate to other staff as well as to children, parents, school management and other professionals. It is important that teachers understand their feelings and respond in constructive ways to emotionally demanding situations. They are better able to understand children if they can understand themselves.

The relevance of our own early experiences

Most adults are influenced by the way they were reared in childhood. That influence is especially relevant when we are living and working with young children, whether they are other people's or our own. The way in which our parents and teachers responded to our needs may still affect the way we think, feel and react. Few of us had the good fortune to be handled by perfect care-givers who satisfied all our needs for security and attention in early child-hood. Hostility and resentment are normal parts of the growing-up process. The problem is that we may identify ourselves with individual children and feel the necessity to protect or punish them for reasons that relate to our own early experiences. If we were victimised by school bullies, we may respond very negatively to children who remind us of them, imposing a system of jus-tice in the classroom that is more relevant to our own experience than to the current circumstances (King 1978). Recognition that our past experiences affect our responses enables us to look more objectively at the activities we offer children. If our memories of music lessons, art or physical education are negative and bring back reminders of derision and failure, we are not only likely to avoid teaching them, we are likely to transmit our dislikes to children.

To work effectively with children we need to examine our own school and family experiences, identifying what we liked and disliked and how those feelings continue to affect us. If negative feelings are not recognised and understood, they are likely to emerge in ways that we find difficult to identify and deal with. The children with whom we work will be the ones who suffer. Strong, negative feelings about any aspect of school life may be indicative of pent-up emotions from the past. Some people become very resentful and respond quite irrationally when they see other adults condoning behaviour that, in their own childhood, resulted in punishment. We bring our personal values to the classroom and to child-rearing and need to be aware of what these values are, how we acquired them and how they affect us.

Managing stress

Causes of stress

Teaching is reputed to be one of the most stressful occupations in present times. Stress is an intense degree of nervous tension caused by anxiety. The most difficult situations to manage are those in which our efforts appear to be unappreciated and life seems to be out of control.

The high rate of burn-out among teachers can be attributed to many factors:

The personality of the sufferer. People react differently to stressful situations. Some see them as a challenge and they create the additional energy that is required. Others feel inadequate and increase their stress levels.

Students and teachers in the wrong career. Students and teachers join the teaching profession for many different reasons, some of which have nothing to do with children. Female students sometimes enter teaching to fulfil their parents' expectations. Some enrol because they don't know what else to do with their lives. Some choose teaching because it fits in with married life and parenthood. Some teachers choose teaching young children because they find it difficult to relate to older children and adults. Stress arises when students and teachers realise that they have chosen the wrong career but, for reasons of pride, parents' expectations, family sacrifices and a lack of alternative choices, they feel that they cannot turn back. There may be massive verbal denial that a mistake has been made but their behaviour in school indicates otherwise.

Unrealistic expectations
* *The job is much more difficult than expected*
  Entrants to a teaching career often underestimate the physical and emotional demands that children make on them. They become aware of the wide variations in children's interests, abilities and needs and worry about their ability to meet them.

* *Time is the enemy*
  Stress arises when there is too much work to be done within the time available. The greater the stress, the greater the chaos, the less we achieve. Stress has a cyclical effect. Stressed students and teachers often fail to plan their time appropriately. Insecure mature-age students often do much more than is expected of them, conscious of their need to 'do well' and reward their families for their sacrifices. Others are often carried away by their own successes and do not discipline themselves to work effectively in terms of time and effort.

Anxieties about job prospects
In an employers' market, students and contract teachers often become over anxious about their job possibilities. This can have two extreme effects: Some students become hyperactive in their desire to compete and win while others become negative and 'switch off', saying 'What's the use of trying—we're not going to get jobs anyway'. Students may become so negative that the quality of their work diminishes to the extent that they have to leave the course. Anxieties are especially high in the final year of teaching practice when so much appears to be at stake.

Problems with interpersonal skills
While lecturers urge early childhood education students to cater for individual differences and create positive self-concepts, this behaviour must be mod-

elled to be effective. Students easily succumb to feelings of low self-worth, triggered by insensitive peers, supervising teachers and lecturers, all of whom need positive feedback from each other. Without mutual support, there is little likelihood of job satisfaction and a high risk of stress.

Inadequate physical working conditions

Poor working conditions matter when there are concurrent stresses from other sources. Drab schools in depressed areas can provide a challenge to energetic and self-confident teachers. They are likely to add to the stress of new teachers and students who are already experiencing other concerns. Inadequate resources can be stressful to the most enthusiastic teachers. It is always infuriating when we plan a lesson requiring a film only to find that every video or projector is broken and long-promised repairs have been overlooked by administrators. The lack of basic equipment in schools can affect the quality of teaching adversely, especially if the shortage is due to mismanagement. On the other hand, teachers in impoverished schools with supportive staff are often ingenious in their creation and use of improvised learning materials.

Stress management on teaching practice

If students and teachers mismanage stress, it worsens and can result in physical ill health, insomnia, constant tiredness, migraine headaches and depression. The difference between gaining satisfaction from a challenging job and becoming stressed by it, is the way in which challenges are met. To reduce opportunities for stress on teaching practice:

- Students should ensure that assignments for other subjects are completed before teaching practice commences. It is difficult for students to give full attention to children if they are worrying about essays and their due dates.
- Job and social commitments should be reduced to a minimum for the duration of the practice.
- Finances should be put in order before teaching practice It can be devastating to find that car registration is overdue or repairs are necessary and there are no funds to pay for them.
- Lessons should be planned at least a day in advance so that students can check on the availability of teaching materials and audio-visual aids.
- Students' ideas should be discussed with the class teacher or lecturer so that problems can be identified and avoided.
- Materials should be prepared the night before they are required so that the student is not rushed in the morning. A last-minute check should be made to ensure that everything is available, including teaching plans.
- The classroom should be prepared before children arrive.
- Lessons should be evaluated with the teacher after every session. Were the objectives achieved? What went well? What would the student change if

the session were repeated? How could unwanted interruptions have been avoided?

- Students should try not to panic when the lecturer arrives. Lecturers rely substantially on teachers' evaluations of progress and students are not failed if they have a bad day. We all have bad days. Lecturers only become worried when students do not realise that there are problems!
- When students feel stressed, they should ask themselves. 'Who owns the problem?' If it is the student's, it helps to write down what can be done to change it. It may be necessary to talk to the lecturer, student counsellor, a fellow-student or a family member. Is there any way in which other people can provide support? If students have allowed themselves to fall behind in their work, they should list the tasks to be done in order of importance and complete the most urgent. Deadlines should be set and adhered to.

If the stress problem is really owned by someone else, it should be handed over to the person or persons responsible. If lecturers assign tasks without considering teaching practice commitments, students should make appointments to see them, ensuring that they can show conclusively that the workload is unrealistic. If lecturing staff are unsympathetic, students should talk to their counsellors.

Students should feel free to say 'No' to extra commitments during teaching practice. If they take on too many responsibilities, they end up doing none of them well and that results in guilt, low self esteem, loss of confidence and more stress (Read 1976).

Professional ethics and legal responsibilities

Professional ethics

Teaching children of five to eight years is both a rewarding experience and a serious responsibility. Teachers are often unaware of the extent of their influence, for good or ill. How children perceive their school may affect not only their own educational progress but the progress of their own future children and, through them, the progress of subsequent generations. Such influence brings serious responsibilities.

Young student teachers are often in the process of asserting their independence, developing individuality and fighting the values of their parents' generation. They demand that society should not judge them by their appearance but by what they really are. Sadly, they can ill afford such luxury until they have proved their competence. Teaching practice is seldom long enough for staff and parents to judge student teachers on the basis of their hidden qualities. They are assessed by their demeanour as well as by their personalities and professionalism. Although this assessment may be highly subjective, it is the reality of the workplace.

As professionals, teachers are expected to dress and behave in a way that inspires the confidence of parents who trustingly leave children in their care. Parents of children in private schools pay fees for their children to be educated by people with specific values and philosophies. School managements reserve the right to reject students who do not conform to those expectations.

In fulfilment of their ethical and professional obligations, educators must act impartially, regardless of their own prejudices and religious or political beliefs. They must treat children equally, irrespective of their race, colour, creed, sex, country of origin, religion, social class or cultural background. Each child and each parent is entitled to courtesy and consideration regardless of personality traits, socio-economic status, morals, values or personal inadequacies. This is not easy. Teachers find that some children are more likeable than others. The children they like are usually the ones who respond positively to them. Children compete for adult attention and it is sometimes difficult for students and teachers to be impartial. In the first three years of school, children recruit their parents as allies in their cause. It becomes even more difficult when the most likeable children also have the most likeable and supportive parents. We all need to be liked and receive approval for the work we do. It is all too easy to do favours for those who give positive feedback. Teachers' pets are a reality to others in the class as well as to parents.

When children conform and are consistently reliable, pleasant and hard working, teachers often ascribe attributes to them that they do not possess. They are often mistakenly referred to as 'bright' when, in fact, they have only average ability but a strong motivation to please. Children sense their own superiority from teachers' attitudes and praise. This can be damaging when the children move into the next class, are assessed more realistically and the deficiencies in their basic concepts become apparent. These children can become frustrated, resentful and lose confidence and interest. Some may never recover.

Teachers must take action to discourage the peer group competition triggered and maintained by enthusiastic but misguided parents. This can be overcome by encouraging children to beat their own best efforts, praising them for progress and individual effort rather than achievement, while simultaneously communicating with parents about what is happening in school and why.

In the privacy of staff rooms, some people talk about individual children in a disparaging way. Such conversations violate children's rights to privacy, are unprofessional and may bias other teachers who come into contact with them.

The tendency to mainstream children with disabilities in 'ordinary' schools means that most teachers have these children in their classes early in their careers. The rationale for this practice is that both disabled and 'normal' children benefit from shared learning experiences and social interactions. Disabled children are particularly vulnerable to unethical practices and special consideration has to be given to their needs, especially their emotional needs.

In conclusion, the classroom should have a democratic atmosphere in which children sense that they are treated fairly and equally. All children should be encouraged to express their views and feelings. School must never be used as a platform for the teacher's own religious, sexist, racial or political beliefs. On controversial issues, both sides of the argument should be presented for children to consider.

Confidentiality

Children and parents who reveal confidential information to teachers should have their confidentiality respected. It would be unethical for teachers to reveal it to other people in the staffroom or outside school. This leaves teachers with the dilemma of how and what information should be recorded on children's record cards and whether parents should have open access to them.

There are some exceptions to the confidentiality rules. For example, all education authorities usually expect teachers to report suspicions of child abuse to state social welfare authorities. Teachers find it difficult to report cases when victims request secrecy before making their disclosures. It is also devastating for children who have been assured of confidentiality to learn that their teachers told others. The maintenance of confidentiality by teaching staff allows abuse to continue unchecked and amounts to collusion with the offender. In these circumstances, teachers have a responsibility to explain to children that they have the right to be safe, that what is happening is wrong, that children are never to blame for what adults do and that it is necessary to tell special people who will help to make them feel safe again. Teachers have an ethical responsibility towards victims of maltreatment. Students and teachers must make enquiries about laws relating to children and reporting procedures in their regions. It is particularly useful for teachers to meet with local health, welfare and child protection professionals working with the families in their catchment area.

Legal responsibilities

Students and teachers need to be aware of their legal rights, responsibilities and liabilities. As laws vary from state to state, they should contact their local education departments and teachers' unions for up-to-date information.

School personnel are responsible for the protection of children while they are in school. When accidents and injuries occur, students and teachers may be held responsible if it can be shown that there was an element of carelessness or negligence. Such negligence has been proven for instance when:

- Children were allowed to leave the classroom two minutes before the appointed time and were injured by motor vehicles while crossing the road. Their parents argued that, had the children been released at the appointed time, they would have been met and the accident would not have occurred.

- Teachers failed to check the safety devices on climbing apparatus erected by children, resulting in accidents.
- A teacher confiscated a car aerial from a child in the school play area for safety reasons. When she returned the aerial to its owner, he injured another child with it, resulting in permanent brain damage. It was argued that the teacher should not have returned a potentially dangerous instrument to a child.

In all of these cases, the teachers were successfully sued by children through their parents. In determining negligence, a court considers whether or not the person in charge of the victims exercised reasonable care and acted sensibly.

Education authorities are insured against third party claims. Teachers' unions usually provide protection for their members. Further protection from liability is available through private insurance. Students should be cognisant of safety, risks and protection. They should not take groups of children outside the school unaccompanied by a qualified member of staff. Most authorities stipulate minimum adult:child ratios for excursions.

Teachers are often uninformed about what they can and cannot do. Broadly speaking, teachers of children aged five to eight years are deemed to be *'in loco parentis'*, that is, they are expected to behave in the same way as responsible parents. The detail of what this implies should be investigated before embarking on teaching practice.

Corporal punishment is now banned by many authorities. Students and teachers should check the local situation with their own education authorities. Corporal punishment is inappropriate for children aged five to eight years and there are better alternatives for handling behaviour problems. The children most likely to drive teachers to violence are those who already experience a great deal of corporal punishment at home and are smacked indiscriminately.

Copyright laws

Copyright laws are complex, containing prohibitions on the photocopying of printed materials and the copying of audio and video tapes.

For purposes of photocopying, students and teachers need to know what proportion of a book or article they are allowed to copy and for what purposes the copy may be used. When the reproduction of materials is prohibited, it is often worthwhile to seek the publisher's permission to copy pages for educational purposes. American publishers are known to be expensive in their charges but there are exceptions. A New Zealand teacher wrote for permission to copy a video and received the response that, in view of that country's anti-nuclear policy, the video could be copied and used throughout New Zealand free of charge.

In general, photocopying is allowed if the reproduction is likely to have no effect on the sale of the book. Teachers are only permitted to copy worksheets if the publisher has stipulated, in writing, that the page in question may be reproduced for classroom use.

This section has amassed information which could present a depressing view of teaching. Most students embark on teaching practice in a state of great anxiety. Within a few days, they experience tremendous satisfaction from working with children and become so attached to the class and school that they continue to visit long after the practice is over.

TASKS FOR STUDENTS

Before starting teaching practice:

1 Identify your feelings and list
    • the aspects of teaching practice that worry you most;
    • the aspects of teaching practice that please you.
    Compare your anxieties and anticipated pleasures with those of other students in your group.
2 What do you consider to be your greatest strengths for working with the five to eight year age group?
3 In what areas of your development do you think you will need the most help? Why?
4 What will you need to know about the school, classroom, teacher and children that has not yet been made available to you? List the queries appropriate for your lecturer and your supervising teacher.
5 Recall and record some things that happened to you when you were about the same age as the children you are going to teach.
    • What were the adult's expectations of you?
    • What form of 'discipline' was used?
    • What did you like and dislike?
    What significance do you think these aspects of your own childhood have for you as a practising teacher?
6 List some of the things that children, teachers and parents do that irritate you in school. List some of the things that give you pleasure. How do these relate to the likes and dislikes that you had in childhood?
7 On your first day in school, consider and record your negative criticisms of the class teacher and school programme. Keep these until your last day, then check to see whether your impressions have changed. If they have, why did these changes occur?
8 Which school subjects did you enjoy as a child? Which do you enjoy teaching now? Which school subjects did you dislike most in childhood? Why? What do you dislike teaching now?
    Note any relationship between the subjects you liked and disliked in childhood and what you enjoy or dislike teaching now.
9 What aspects of the curriculum or day-to-day routine do you find

yourself avoiding? How do you avoid them? Why is this happening? What would be the long-term effects on children of your avoidance?

10 What qualities and skills do you expect to find in a 'good teacher'?

11 Check the laws in relation to your legal rights and responsibilities in and outside school when working with children.

12 Obtain a copy of professional ethics from your teachers' union and discuss their relevance to present-day teaching.

13 Check the interpretation of '*in loco parentis*' with both the union and your Education Authority. What are the implications for you as a practising teacher?

14 How many pages of a 12-page article and a 120-page book are you allowed to photocopy without the publisher's written permission?

15 Identify and record a recent, stressful experience. Whose problem was it? How did you deal with it? What was the result? With the benefit of hindsight, how could you have handled the situation better? How could you have reduced the level of stress?

CHAPTER 2

Transition from home and pre-school to school

Starting school

Starting school is a major milestone in the child's life experience. It is often associated with change from dependence to independence and from the right to play to the need to 'work'. It marks the beginning of 'growing up'.

Parents, early childhood educators, child care personnel and primary school teachers all have a major responsibility to make the transition from home or pre-school to school as smooth as possible. This is a goal that requires careful thought and planning.

In recent years, education authorities throughout Europe, Australia and New Zealand have been increasingly concerned about the family's initial contact with school, its importance to future relationships, parent involvement and children's long-term educational progress.

What is continuity in experience?

Prominent educationalist John Dewey (1963) spoke of continuity as an experiential continuum. He said that 'the principle of continuity of experience means that every experience both takes up something from those which have gone before and modifies in some way the quality of those which come after'. In other words, continuity in early childhood education means that we must take account of the child's past home and pre-school experiences and modify the new school experiences to minimise change and reduce stress.

The importance of continuity of experience was emphasised in the Council of Europe's Declaration on Pre-School Care and Education in December 1979 following a ten-year study programme relating to the care and education of pre-school children. The first section of the Declaration states that:

> All services with a contribution to make to the development of young children—especially health, education and social services—should

work with and through the family to provide continuity of experience for the child (p. 155).

The final section focuses on the 21 member countries of the Council, emphasising that each regional and local authority guarantees continuity of experience for every child (Roberts 1981).

New Zealand's concern was such that in 1977 the New Zealand Council for Educational Research (NZCER) undertook a five-year study of starting school which involved questioning 300 pre-school teachers, 300 parents whose children attended the pre-schools and 300 primary school teachers who were about to teach the new entrants, as well as the children themselves (Renwick 1984a)

In England, the Department of Education and Science also sponsored a research project entitled 'Continuity of Children's Experience in the Years Three to Eight', which was carried out by a small team from the NFER between 1977 and 1980. The report examined the variety of children's pre-school experiences in playgroups, daycare centres, childminders/family daycare givers, nursery schools/classes and their implications for the child starting school. The research revealed similarities and differences in provision and showed how children's experiences are likely to be interrupted when moving from home and pre-school to school.

Although much is made of 'starting school', for most Australian and New Zealand children it is neither their first experience of separation from a parent nor their introduction to an educational setting. In both countries, the majority of young beginners have had some experience of kindergartens, child care centres or playgroups of some kind. In New Zealand, a large proportion of Maori children start school after attending Maori language Teo Kohanga Reo child care centres. This has particular significance for continuity of language experience in the primary school.

Most educational authorities now espouse continuity in transition in their policies and highlight the importance of liaison between pre-school, home and school. In practice, the quality of transition depends largely on the quality of the physical environments provided by those authorities and on the quality of the teachers who are directly involved; that is, the early childhood teachers who receive the new entrants and the pre-school personnel responsible for the children in transition.

What do we mean by continuity in relation to early childhood experiences?

The concept of continuity in early childhood arises from the undesirability of sharp divisions and abrupt changes in the child's life. If changes are inevitable, efforts should be made to minimise the adverse effects (Roberts 1981).

Continuity is seen to be particularly important in terms of the child leaving home and family for a prolonged period of time. Emphasis is placed on the child being introduced gradually and carefully to the new environment. Roberts confirms that children should not be separated from regular caregivers but parents or parent replacement figures should remain in school until the children have 'settled' and show that they are confident and relaxed. The younger the children, the more important it is that they are received into the new situation sensitively and given opportunities to develop relationships with members of staff in small, family-sized groups.

Children need time to build new, stable, emotional relationships; the smoother the transition, the less vulnerable they are to the trauma of change and subsequent emotional disturbance. The work of James and Joyce Robertson on Young Children in Brief Separation showed the importance and feasibility of continuity in the child's experience. Their films about children in hospital and residential care demonstrated that professionals were often ignorant of children's most basic emotional needs and the damage caused by separating them suddenly from familiar surroundings and trusted adults. Any abrupt change in the pattern of care and early learning can adversely affect growth, emotional stability, social and intellectual development. Children in separation can go through a mourning process that is akin to the experience of grief through bereavement. Children starting school not only have to cope with separation, they also have to adapt to sharing one adult with a large group of children. A teacher cannot give much personal attention to a child when there are 30 others in the class.

Commenting on the school staff:child ratios, Margaret Roberts says:

> This is clearly one example of a break-down in continuity of life experience which is unfortunately characteristic of too many institutions providing care and education for young children. There are too many children in the care of too few adults to be able to build up necessary emotional relationships, or give time and thought to mental companionship relevant to the child's level of development (1981, p. 16).

Children need time to assimilate their new environments before they are required to accommodate to new routines and new demands. For a child starting school, these new demands may mean dressing and undressing in a crowded room without help, queuing to wash hands and use toilets as well as the rituals of large school assemblies, lining up, being required to put up a hand for permission to speak and many more things that do not happen at home or in early childhood centres. These activities represent discontinuity in transition from home and pre-school to school.

Some schools now make concessions in relation to the length of the day for school beginners, the timing of recess periods for the use of the playground and the provision of access to parents. Success in transition will also depend upon the teacher's expectations of both children and parents.

Problems which may result in discontinuity spring from two main sources:

- dramatic changes in the child's physical and emotional environment; and

- the failure of adults to understand and/or respond to the needs of new entrants.

Dramatic changes in the child's physical and emotional environment

Teachers in large schools face a particularly difficult task when they try to match the physical environment of the school to the child's previous experiences.

Although many British nursery classes are attached to the main infant/primary school buildings, most Australian and New Zealand pre-schools are separate. For British children, the need for adjustment may come one or two years earlier when they leave home to join the nursery class. Nursery teachers try to protect their charges from the milieu of older children. Nursery classes usually have their own separate entrances and play areas and nursery children engage in outdoor play when older children are in class. While their adjustment to pre-school may be much more traumatic than the adjustment of their Australian and New Zealand peers, their move to primary school is likely to involve proportionately fewer changes. The British nursery school is an enlarged version of the Australian and New Zealand kindergarten, both of which may be at some distance from the junior primary/infant school and reception classroom.

To understand the problems of children entering primary school from home or pre-school, we must compare their physical environments.

Early childhood centres in Australia and New Zealand aim to provide a setting that complements the home; schools do not. Early childhood centres emphasise cosiness and caring. They offer high staff and adult:child ratios which ensure that children have help readily available when it is needed. There is a strong emphasis on socialisation. Snack times are civilised. Bathrooms are not quite like those at home but expectations are not that different. These pre-schools are usually housed in small, attractive buildings surrounded by gardens that parents tend at weekends. Parents know each other and children know them; they often socialise together. The environment is conducive to a variety of freedoms, such as the freedom to choose activities, use initiative and develop independence. Early childhood teachers are trained to maintain order without raising their voices and, as a result, pre-schools usually give the impression of being happy places where people care for each other.

Parents enrolling their children for school may be entering a primary school for the first time in ten or more years. There is rarely anything homely about the larger schools, either within or without. Some Australian schools are identifiable by loudspeakers and sirens that pollute the neighbourhood. Before school begins, up to 1000 pupils may be milling around the school yard, waiting for assembly and the signal to move inside.

When entering any large primary school to search for the principal's office, the parent seeking to enrol a child may be daunted by the sight of seemingly endless corridors flanked by identical classrooms on either side. In a large primary school, visitors may hear at least one teacher who tries to restore order by shouting at non compliant pupils. Although parents may have experienced similar behaviour in their own school days and survived, parents of new entrants feel apprehensive in their desire to protect their young.

Children starting school often experience anxieties because of the:

- scale and size of school buildings, which are often vastly different from pre-school settings;
- confusing range of the children's new territories and the proximity or distance of hygiene facilities such as toilets, washing facilities, libraries and play areas;
- new organisational constraints on the children's movement around the territory and within the classroom;
- the large numbers of bigger and older children in the playground; and
- the cacophony of new sounds.

Changes are greatest for children transferring to extensive buildings with corridors or open-plan designs and congested activity areas. New entrants to school may feel confused and afraid of getting lost. They sometimes find it difficult to be regimented into lines and tiptoe silently. After the comparative freedom of the pre-school, limitations on space and movement may be irksome and children often experience difficulties in sitting still. Others, accustomed to quiet corners and the opportunity to escape to comparative privacy, feel hemmed in by the lack of personal space available in the typical school classroom.

Small country schools and infant/primary schools staffed by early childhood educators tend to provide a more welcoming environment than primary schools. Their days may be numbered however, due to administrative and economic pressures to amalgamate them with larger schools under the management of head teachers who may be unfamiliar with the ideology and practice of early childhood education.

Two other physical aspects of school life that cause concern to both parents and children involve hygiene facilities and lunchtime arrangements.

Anxieties relating to personal hygiene

Research in New Zealand, England and Australia shows that a major anxiety of staff, parents and the children in transition relates to hygiene. There is a stark contrast between bathrooms in homes and pre-schools and facilities in schools.

Primary school toilet blocks are often out of doors, unpleasant and at some distance from the classroom. Throughout the history of education, school beginners have set out on the long journey to the toilet and have decided to return home instead. The school toilet block may also be the child's introduction to the segregation of the sexes and whereas the child at home or pre-school was able to use the toilet when necessary, the large school requires children to publicly disclose their natural urges or restrict their bodily functions to allotted times on the timetable. The presence of outdoor water troughs also presents a completely alien concept of personal hygiene to children accustomed to hand basins and towels.

The new entrants' dislike of toilet arrangements often results in attempts to postpone usage until they return home from school. Postponement inevitably results in accidents that cause embarrassment and anxiety to both the children and their parents.

Renwick, interviewing 300 New Zealand primary teachers responsible for new entrants, found that they placed a strong emphasis on toilet training. In one instance, this went so far as to suggest that children should practise conforming to school routines and timetables at home.

It is important to note that, when the parents of these school beginners were asked about their children's proficiency in personal hygiene, 99 per cent claimed that they were completely toilet trained. This was confirmed by their kindergarten teachers who said that toilet accidents were not a problem in pre-schools, even though the children were considerably younger at the time of entry. They attributed this difference to the fact that toilets were close to the main area of activities and children were able to use them whenever they felt the need, without having to ask permission. Renwick concluded that, while she appreciated how vexing toilet accidents could be to busy teachers, 'the problem is often a product of the school system rather than an inadequacy on the part of the child' (1994, p.15).

Similarly, the major concerns of Melbourne teachers interviewed by Shepherd, Cullen and Moore (1978) were identified as children's ability to cope with toilet routines unaided (100 per cent). The second area of concern was that children should be able to eat their lunches without assistance (84 per cent). The researchers noted with interest that although these teachers saw themselves as caregivers with responsibility for children's wellbeing as well as their education, they were greatly concerned that they should not have to undertake chores relating to the parental role.

Toileting matters are clearly a source of concern for all parties involved in transition to school. If education authorities are serious in their support of 'continuity' in transition from home to school, this is one aspect of school life that requires their prompt attention. No young child should have to wait until recess or walk alone in inclement weather to use a toilet block that is large, distant and communal and involves confrontation with big, confident and often aggressive strangers from other classes.

A survey conducted by Davies and North (1990) in the Hunter Region was designed to ascertain the effects of a change in enrolment policy by the New South Wales Education Department. This also gained data on the five skills that teachers felt were essential for children entering school. It was indicated that:

- independent toileting,
- working co-operatively with others,
- independent dressing,
- recognising and caring for personal belongings and
- listening and communication skills

were top priorities. Once again, teachers were not concerned with cognitive and fine motor skills which are pre-requisites for formal work.

Anxieties relating to lunch-time arrangements

Another major change for most children starting school is the necessity to eat lunch on school premises. Meal times, in common with sleep times, are emotionally sensitive periods for young children who associate them with home and a one-to-one relationship with a parent. Recognition of this is implicit in the persistence of Australian Greek women who visit school every day bearing hot lunchtime meals for their children or grandchildren. They hover discreetly but protectively, ensuring that the children eat in as civilised a fashion as the school yard permits. Even in British schools where meals are usually served in somewhat better circumstances, new entrants are often terrified by crowds, the clatter and the fact that the food and service are entirely different from mealtimes at home.

Australian and New Zealand parents are often concerned that, while the home and pre-school try to teach table manners and associated hygiene, the school does not. New entrants are often bewildered by the contrast as they consume their sandwiches, often without washing their hands.

The effects of anxiety when starting school

Why are these physical aspects of school life so important? When young children experience difficulties in coping with physical changes, anxieties may be manifested in complaints of feeling sick, headaches, abdominal aches and vomiting, sleep disturbances and nightmares. After an initial period of apparent acceptance of school, distressed children may make excuses to stay at home or may complain of feeling sick to ensure that they are sent home before lunchtime. Other anxiety traits may be evident, such as thumb sucking, eye twitching, stuttering, clinging behaviour or withdrawal, excessive passivity and resistance to joining groups. If the problems are unresolved, the illness is real.

Children who lack confidence may take several weeks to pluck up sufficient courage to protest about what is happening to them. This can be confusing to both parents and teachers who misinterpreted the child's earlier compliance as 'settling down'. Children find it very difficult to express disappointment when they have had high expectations of starting school.

Lunchtime and hygiene arrangements present major concerns for parents, teachers and new pupils. Continuity of experience is often restricted by the

Figure 2.1: Children who lack confidence may take several weeks to pluck up sufficient courage to protest about what is happening to them

physical layout of school buildings which are the responsibility of education authorities and school management. If the school premises inhibit continuity of experience in transition from pre-school to school, it is the responsibility of the school management to press for the necessary changes, especially if 'continuity' is espoused in the education authority's policy.

When adults do not understand and/or respond to the needs of new entrants

One of the most interesting research projects relating to school entry was that undertaken by the Curriculum Research branch of the Victorian Education Department in Melbourne in 1978 (Shepherd *et al.*). Although samples were small and limited to Melbourne schools, the findings were relevant to educationalists elsewhere.

The researchers found that children's perceptions of school are influenced by the type of information received from peers, older siblings, parents and other adults as well as stories and television. These, in turn, are affected by personal values, experiences and attitudes transmitted by both verbal and nonverbal communications. A child's expectations may include stereotyped notions of 'hard work', bad-tempered teachers and head teachers or principals who beat children with canes.

Most pre-school children perceive school attendance as enhancement of their status. Their self-esteem grows as they associate themselves with the mature world. This notion of growing-up tends to come from pre-school teachers who, looking at the children in transition, view them as comparatively mature, big people. Renwick (1994) found that teachers of New Zealand reception classes were less aware of the importance of school entry as a step in the child's maturity, probably because five year olds are the least mature people in the school world.

Unfortunately it is not unusual for well-meaning parents to use impending school entry as a threat when children are misbehaving: 'Just wait until you start school...you won't be allowed to do that...you'll have to work'. School is then presented as a strict place with punitive, authoritarian figures in charge. Although the harassed parents of bored five year olds may resort to such threats lightly, they can jeopardise a smooth transition from home to school by creating needless apprehension.

Renwick found it difficult to extract information from near five year olds about their expectations of school and she sought information from parents and teachers. Those children who had a clear idea of what was ahead anticipated that school would be an enjoyable place where they would read, play, stay all day and eat lunch. Having experienced kindly early childhood teachers and positive child management techniques, children took it for granted that they would be accepted and cared for by kind school teachers who would like them and be their special friends.

The most confident school entrants were sure that everyone would be pleased to see them, that there would be lots of things to play with and that friendship with other children would be instantaneous. School was perceived as an extension of their pre-school experience providing limitless play and the introduction of reading for sheer pleasure. They looked forward to sharing experiences with an enlarged circle of new friends and former kindergarten friends who had already achieved the magic age of five.

Children's high expectations are seldom met. If the first day is not great fun, full of friendship and affection and children have not learned to read by home-time, disappointment can be overwhelming. Parents greet their new entrants enthusiastically with, 'How was school? Did you have a lovely time?' Confused children feel compelled to say 'yes', feeling inadequate and quite convinced that there must be something wrong with them.

The Melbourne researchers found that few children had realistic expectations of school. Only 12.5 per cent of respondents (25 per cent of pre-schoolers) gave responses which projected minimally into the first year of schooling in a meaningful way. These expectations centred exclusively on school routines, the notion of eating lunch at school and playing in a huge playground. There was no spontaneous discussion about what they hoped or expected to learn. Expectations relating to numeracy and literacy had been implanted by members of the family.

Children are under enormous social pressures prior to school entry. Parents buy them uniforms and lunch boxes. Children act out 'going to school' with their new possessions, not because they are looking forward to school but because they are apprehensive. Familiarisation through dramatisation helps them to come to terms with their anxieties.

Learning to read is commonly associated with the aura and magic of starting school. While children have great affection for their pre-school teachers, they give primary school staff far higher status because they are associated with learning to read. Not surprisingly, Renwick found that most parents had the same values and expectations as their children. One New Zealand teacher went further and not only equated school entry with reading readiness but went so far as to suggest that, if children were not ready to read, they should not be admitted to school (Renwick 1984a, 1994).

With such views, there is little wonder that reading looms foremost in the minds of school entrants. Aware of the consequences of these expectations some New Zealand primary schools invite parents and children to school for the all-important first day. Early in the morning, each child is asked to choose a small 'reading book'. The parents are taught to introduce the captions, relate them to pictures and let their children repeat them. At the end of the day, the children go home triumphantly bearing their books to show their siblings that they can read.

Teachers in Melbourne, where there was no specialist undergraduate teacher training for the 5–8 year age group, believed that children were automatically ready for reading, writing and mathematics when they started school. This was not borne out by the abilities and expectations of the children or the expectations of their parents.

The researchers found an interesting difference between the perceptions of parents whose children had, and those who had not, attended a pre-school prior to school entry. Children who had no previous pre-school experience were all deemed by their parents to be 'happy at school', compared with only 46 per cent of those who had been to pre-school. The researchers said that this result was indicative of the lack of a basis for comparison when children have no early childhood education experience. Parents of new entrants recorded a wide range of their children's positive and negative reactions to school, including changes to eating habits and general tiredness.

Shepherd et al. (1978) found that Melbourne parents expected children to enjoy their first year in school and, for the most part, they did. The majority of these parents also expected to find some element of continuity between pre-school and the school programme. They wanted children to continue their creative activities because of the pleasure they derived from them. Only one-third of the multi-racial parent sample expected the school programme to be markedly different from the pre-school. Those parents perceived pre-school to be for playing and primary school for 'learning'.

Most of the Australian parents defined 'learning' as writing, spelling, reading and other undefinable but highly structured academic tasks requiring pencil, paper and sitting at desks. 'Teaching' was synonymous with learning.

Unless teachers were giving formal lessons in basic subjects, parents did not think that they were teaching.

The response of the Melbourne teachers and parents revealed an implicit belief that children were ready for formal lessons at the age of five. This was not due to their ignorance of child development; both parents and teachers were aware of individual differences in children's development, abilities and life experiences but parents did not expect teachers to cater to them. Children were all expected to work at the same level at the same time. If individual children did not make progress, the teachers had a responsibility to make sure that they 'caught up' with their peers. Furthermore the teachers did not anticipate that there would be any difficulties for children exposed to this type of teaching. The quality of their responses indicated a sad ignorance of early childhood education in the state of Victoria. The researchers were alarmed that teachers and parents frequently used the same terminology but meant completely different things in relation to children's care and education. They concluded that, in all aspects of the study, neither parents nor children could provide informed statements about what children could realistically expect to experience at the beginning of the school year.

Parents were uninformed about the nature of the school curriculum, the emotional needs of their children, their intellectual capabilities or how children learn. As a result, they tended to expect teachers to adopt the same teaching methods that they had experienced in school.

Children based their expectations on hearsay rather than direct experience gained from visits or teacher exchanges. As a result, no realistic, informed expectations were held by any of the parties involved in school entry. The level of co-operation and support would, of necessity, be limited by the lack of communication and understanding. With increased awareness of the importance of continuity of experience in transition, school entry could have been more positive and successful.

The recommendations of the Australian researchers incorporated better liaison between school and pre-schools, pre-enrolment programmes to enable parents to understand the significance of child development, introducing reading, and the concept of learning by activity methods, etc. They also recommended that playgroups should be attached to schools where no pre-schools exist and that bilingual staff should be available to help migrant parents. The researchers did not suggest who should teach the parents about continuity in transition from home and pre-school to school; clearly the task could not be left to school staff.

Parr, McNaughton, Timperley and Robinson (1993) conducted a research project in the four city areas of Greater Auckland to determine how primary schools, particularly at the school entry level, are negotiating the process of parent-school collaboration. They found that Junior school classroom teachers seem to have an open door policy and perceive contact with parents as being necessarily direct. Parents however, are not regarded by the professionals as equal partners and conversely, parents see teachers as the experts.

Parents are seen as having little to offer to discussions about curriculum or pedagogy. Parr *et al.* (1993, p. 41) concluded:

> The latter is particularly disturbing in view of the cultural composition of our schools...It is particularly important in the transition to school year to ensure that, as far as possible, classroom culture melds with that of the home on pedagogically important and effective variables. Parental collaboration would seem a logical first step.

In Britain, Potter (1987, p. 73) found that Nottinghamshire mothers experienced the same anxieties as Australian parents about the inadequacies of iaison between pre-school and school. As one parent explained:

> It's a big step [for children]. It's a frightening step but if they went with their nursery teachers and realised that school is just another step, it would help that transition and make it natural. I think it's easy for one institution [the school] to labour under a misapprehension about another institution [pre-school] and complain. If there was more communication and greater understanding, this wouldn't happen.

All the parents in Potter's sample were highly conscious of the difference between pre-school and school. 'School is more structured, more rigid, less individualised and there's less sense of being cared for and more of being told what to do.' They expressed concern about the reduction in opportunities for creativity and freedom of choice. 'They don't have time to play now that they're at school,' parents bewailed.

Some factors contributing to discontinuity in transition from pre-school to school

The British National Foundation for Educational Research has identified features in pre-school and school curriculum which are 'critical' to continuity of experience in transition to school (Cleave 1982). The major features are:

The perceived aims and functions of staff in the pre-school/school services, their influence on the range of materials provided and how they are used. NFER found that adults in different pre-school settings had different aims. Daycare givers emphasised childcare and family support while trained playgroup leaders and teachers referred to social development and practice in basic skills. The chief goal in most centres was to encourage social independence. This is clearly not the major goal of school teachers responsible for new entrants in Britain, Australia and New Zealand.

Financial and spatial constraints, reflected in the provision of educational materials. British state pre-schools offered a much wider range of indoor and outdoor equipment and activities than either daycare or schools. The latter usually offered some of the basic pre-school elements such as a corner for domestic play, sandplay and floor toys. Where school classes were vertically grouped with two or three age-groups together, the range of materials available was often too narrow and the new entrants tended to be disadvantaged. Also, when classrooms had limited space, there were few play materials for the new entrant.

Hours of attendance. School attendance required considerably longer hours of attendance than pre-schools, excepting daycare centres. Children who attended sessional pre-schools were often exhausted by the extended school day. On the other hand, school hours were much shorter than many children experienced in daycare, and this presented problems for working parents.

Access to educational play materials. Children in all types of pre-school provision had complete freedom of choice in what they did for at least half of the day. Choice reduced dramatically to 25 per cent when children started school. It diminished further when they adapted to the routine. NFER found that access to play materials in schools was restricted by artificially created segments of time labelled 'work' and 'play'.

Organisation of the day. Schools were unique in creating compulsory breaks in the programme for playtime/recess when children converged in the playground simultaneously. This often unwanted interruption to concentration and activity was criticised by British teacher-educator Alice Yardley more than 20 years ago. Schools also set specific times for activities such as physical education, assemblies, music, television and, when specialists were involved, art. To function effectively, children had to learn both the order of the day and the procedures for moving from place to place for different lessons. By comparison, pre-school programmes were flexible, incorporating both indoor and outdoor activities simultaneously.

The range of activities available. School activities were markedly different from those available in pre-schools of all kinds. Schools showed a drastic reduction in opportunities for gross motor activity and a considerable increase in occupations involving sitting down quietly for numeracy and literacy. Discontinuities were greatest for:

- children who had experienced only a limited range of activities in their pre-school years, for example, children who went to school directly from home; and
- children who had been taught to count, read or write using different methods to the class teacher.

Some factors which contribute to continuity in transition

There are many strategies available to facilitate continuity.

Pre-school personnel should recognise that some children are ready for more complex tasks. They should introduce activities similar to those that will be encountered at school.

All personnel should be prepared to mix school attendance with pre-school when children are not completely ready to make the break. In centres attached to schools, it is relatively easy to exchange teaching staff from time to time when transfers of children are imminent.

School teachers can help by introducing children to morning-only or part-time attendance. They should ensure that pre-school personnel and parents are aware of basic teaching methods to be used when children start school. Many parents try to teach children to form letters and numbers and some introduce reading materials. Guidance is needed to avoid later confusion for their children.

School teachers can combat fatigue by allowing children to have 'naps' on beanbags or portable beds and by alternating restful and energetic activities. They should also provide some of the familiar pre-school activities of water-play, dressing up, sandplay, painting, etc.

Friendship can be encouraged by inviting established children to befriend new ones until they are confident in class procedures. Confidence will grow with the gradual introduction of new and strange activities, allowing children to watch until they feel safe enough to join in.

Teachers should also be conscious of young children's learning styles and use appropriate activity methods.

Teachers should allocate time to chat to parents of new children because the information they receive is important. Class teachers need to know about ill health, dietary problems and some aspects of the family history, who to contact if the child is ill and where parents work. Much depends on the teacher's skill in establishing a rapport with the parent and child in the early stages. NFER found, however, that children need more than friendliness on the first day of school. In particular, they need a homely, attractive setting and an atmosphere of calm. Frequent but short bursts of individual attention are needed with lots of reassurance. The newcomer is at great risk of losing face by doing the wrong thing at the wrong time. Support from adults and peers is essential to maintain self-esteem.

Parents of children not at pre-school can help the transition process by giving their children plenty of paper, crayons, paints, textas, scissors for cutting out, adhesive, empty cartons and magazines etc. for free play. They should be encouraged to read stories for pleasure to interest children in the written word. Parents can also help their children to read by pointing out letters and words that they see on outings to shops etc.

Enrolment and admission to school

Booklets on preparing children for school

There is evidence of concern for harmonious entry to school in the proliferation of free guidebooks available for parents on 'starting school'. In the foreword to an Education Department of Victoria's booklet *Preparing for School*, the Director described school entry as 'the first and most dramatic of social transitions' in human experience and emphasised that success or failure at this stage can determine success or failure throughout the early childhood years at school and beyond.

Education authorities recognise that most parents wish to help their children but not all parents know how to do it. Some parents believe that it gives children an advantage over their peers if they are taught to read, write and 'do sums' before school entry, not realising that pressures of this kind and inappropriate timing can be harmful. The Victorian publication listed the physical and social skills and stages of intellectual and emotional development necessary for the child's effective functioning at school. Parents were made aware of their responsibilities to ensure that their children could manage personal clothing and possessions, blow their noses, use and flush toilets, manipulate taps and wash hands, handle packed lunches, take turns and co-operate, express their needs and cope with separation from parents for a prolonged period of the day. In other words, the Education Department expected five-year-old new entrants to be socialised for school routine before they arrived so that teachers could get on with the more important task of teaching the 3 Rs.

In contrast, Renwick's guide to New Zealand parents, *Going to School* (1984a), was more realistic in its expectations. She wrote of the teacher's responsibility:

> I feel very strongly about school readiness. It's the teacher's attitude that matters. She must find out where the child is at and work on from there. She must accept the child as he is...not as some theoretical school starter. She must respect the child and let him know that he is part of the class. That is how children adjust readily to school (p. 7).

New Zealand teachers also stressed that, although some social skills were desirable, they were not as important as children's curiosity, interest in the world around them, and eagerness to learn.

It was considered to be 'nice for all concerned' if new entrants could blow their noses and attend to personal hygiene without assistance, but the New Zealand teachers accepted that not all five-year-olds are independent and `it would be foolish if such unrealistic expectations caused anxiety in the home'.

As Renwick points out, real preparation for school takes place over a period of years and no last-minute panic measures can suffice. She stressed the importance of the child being accepted and loved, being given a wide range of stimulating experiences and having opportunities to mix and converse with adults and other children. She also emphasised the importance of exposing children to books and stories. Children lucky enough to have this kind of background should take school in their stride. However in every class there will be some children who have not been loved, who have been exposed to too many adults or none at all, who have been 'talked at' rather than 'talked with', who have been maltreated and malnourished in a physical or a psychological sense, or both.

Most school booklets emphasise the importance of parents exhibiting a positive attitude, referring to the first year of school as a happy time, offering opportunities for new achievements. They give advice on the value of pre-enrolment visits, familiarisation with public transport, and familiarisation with lunchtime routines. As Renwick points out, travelling to school by bus figures quite prominently in children's comments on what they like or dislike about school. For some children, independent travel and paying for a bus ticket can represent a milestone in growing up; others react adversely to the noise and aggression of older children and the sparseness of adult supervision.

Ideally, the school booklet should help parents through the most commonly experienced difficulties, including children's disappointments and reactions when the initial excitement wears off and children resist attending all day every day. The booklet should discuss coping with child fatigue, health and parents' own problems of adjustments to an empty house as well as how they can participate in the educational programme.

The task of writing a single booklet suitable for all ethnic groups and parents with widely differing backgrounds and educational experience is awesome. To be effective, the booklet must avoid the use of educational jargon but it must not patronise the reader. It must emphasise the importance of the impending social transition but, simultaneously, should not cause anxiety or invite over-emphasis of the event ahead. Fortunately, it is just one aspect of the enrolment and admissions programme.

Pre-enrolment

It is valuable for the school to have some indication of anticipated enrolment numbers during the previous year. This information can be obtained by inviting contact from parents through:

- the local community press;
- local pre-school centres of all kinds;
- school newsletters;
- health authorities organising clinics for mothers and young children;
- posters and advertisements in supermarkets, chemists' shops, doctors' surgeries etc.; and
- ethnic press, ethnic radio and interpreters to produce suitable advertising material.

Access to projected enrolment figures facilitates the provision of appropriate staff and accommodation and allows time for the school to arrange meetings with parents and children.

Enrolment involves the completion of admission forms and the collection of information from parents relating to the child's age, health factors (such as illnesses, allergies, medications needed, speech, sight, hearing problems or other disabilities), general behavioural characteristics, pre-school experience, parents' whereabouts in case of emergencies, their addresses and telephone numbers. When children have separated parents, step-parents, etc., it is important to establish who has the right to collect the child from school.

Each school and education authority establishes procedures most suitable for its needs within the community it serves. The South Australian Educa-tion Department stresses that 'it is in the interests of all concerned that the day of entry into the classroom is NOT the first contact between home and school'. Furthermore, it suggests that the first visit to the school should not be monopolised by form-filling and interviewing the parent. 'In fact, many parents would prefer to complete such documents in a non-threatening situa-tion at their own pace, either in school or on a home visit.'

Much valuable information is exchanged at the first interview and most schools now ensure that appointments are made to provide adequate time, free of interruption. In multi-cultural areas, it may be necessary to arrange for an interpreter to be present and teachers are usually careful to ensure that the interview is non-threatening. The teacher must address the parent directly, avoiding the temptation of speaking to the interpreter. The teacher may also decide that a second interview is necessary to discuss personal family matters or the child's problems without the interpreter being present. If a parent is anxious about the visit to school, he or she is unlikely to absorb a great deal of information and arrangements for other visits should be made.

Some schools ensure that parents and children meet their new class teach-ers at the end of the day when they are not likely to be distracted by others in the class. This is a good time to let new entrants see the range of toys and equipment that will be available to them. It also enables the teacher to give each school entrant individual attention. If the child is overwhelmed, it may not be the appropriate time to take him or her on a tour of the whole school, to show the toilet facilities and playgrounds, nor may it be the most expedi-ent time to acquaint the parent with the school's policies, procedures and aims. Other appointments should be made.

School booklets should include the school philosophy, school address, telephone number, contact persons, times, routines, term dates, holidays and functions. Parents will wish to know about the special arrangements made for new entrants, canteen facilities, procedures for absence, notifiable infections, drop-in centres and the school's expectations about their involvement in the transition programme. It must always be borne in mind however, that some parents will not speak or read the English language and communications must not depend on the written word.

Many schools invite parents and children to attend a half-day session or more before the school year begins.

A variety of other methods are used by individual teachers to make newly enrolled children feel welcome. They may send welcoming letters, cards or drawings from class members to make new children feel important and increase their interest.

Methods of entry

A variety of admission programmes are used throughout the UK, Australia and New Zealand. There is no 'ideal' system; each has advantages and disadvantages for the child and the teacher. Some schools accept children in the term before their fifth birthday. Others accept children on the first Monday after their fifth birthday. In Australia and New Zealand, parents are not compelled to send children to school before the age of six but most seek entry at five years. Entry after the fifth birthday means that new children join an established class throughout the school year. This, of course, necessitates planning for individual children and increases the importance of record-keeping and providing activities to cater for a wide range of abilities and experiences. The advantage to teachers is that they only receive one or two new entrants at a time. They can look to established students for support while they give individual attention to new arrivals. Other children are usually extremely happy to introduce new arrivals to class routines. However, some teachers find this entry mode stressful and prefer new intakes to be limited to the beginning of term.

Another popular entry system is referred to as 'scattered entry'. Small groups of children arrive in the first week of school, followed by other small groups in weeks 3 and 4 and others in weeks 7 or 8. Again, this provides children with the opportunity to have attention from the teacher, enables established children to assist in the settling of others and the teacher is never faced with a large number of unhappy little individuals who all seek care and attention simultaneously.

Some schools accept termly intakes and others enrol only once a year at the beginning of the school year. This has caused concern because very young and immature children under the age of five years join the same class as those who are a year older.

Routley and de Lemos (1993) conducted a study in Melbourne on the changing trends in school entry age. The study aimed to examine the trend for parents from middle class backgrounds to delay their child's entry to school, particularly in the case of those children who are under the age of 5 at the time that they are legally entitled to enter school. They found that since 1984, there has been a clear trend for an increase in age of entry to school and that this is most marked in the more affluent middle class suburbs. The tendency to defer entry to school is more marked for boys than for girls and is also related to socioeconomic level. Why do these parents feel that delayed entry is better for their children? How can schools more effectively respond to the needs of the very young child in the early years of school?

Whichever system is pursued, most new entrants are allowed to arrive at school a little later than their peers and to leave early in the afternoon to pre-

Modes of entry

Please identify and note the advantages and disadvantages of the following methods of entry to school.

Mode	Advantage	Disadvantage
4-term system—Groups enter at the beginning of each term		
Scattered entry—a few new entrants arrive each week		
Beginning of academic year only (group)		
Entry on 5th birthday		
A separate reception class		
A new reception group constituting only half of the class		

vent undue fatigue. Every entry mode has advantages and disadvantages and no system is ideal. Teachers and management need to consider carefully their educational philosophies in choosing the mode of entry that best suits their school community.

Look at the Modes of Entry chart above and complete it.

Reducing the risk of distress in the early days at school

Teachers and parents can do much to reduce the level of stress and distress experienced by children during their first days at school.

Distress is most likely to occur in classes where there are large numbers of new and insecure children, a high level of noise and congestion, and where new entrants have to wait for attention. Children are less likely to be distressed when admitted one at a time in a calm, unhurried atmosphere, when parent and child are welcomed personally as very special people and separation is not enforced (Cleave 1982). Children's sense of belonging can be encouraged by having their coat-pegs and personal drawers or trays clearly labelled with their names and pictures for ease of recognition. New arrivals can be invited to spend the first half of the day exploring and playing with toys in the company of their parents.

Parents become embarrassed and feel totally inadequate when their children become hysterical at the school door and refuse to enter the classroom. This can be handled in several ways. Firstly, children are less likely to scream if their parents stay with them in the classroom. When children are thoroughly absorbed in activity, their parents should tell them very quietly and succinctly that they are going shopping or that they are going home to prepare their evening meal and will be back at 2 o'clock, when the big hand is at the top of the clock and the small hand is at 2. Teachers should never allow parents to 'sneak out' when children are absorbed because, when they become aware of their parents' absence, children are likely to feel even less secure than before. Children must learn that they can trust their parents in relation to both separation and collection. Teachers and parents must work together to that end.

Because of their subconscious desire for reassurance that they are needed and will be missed, some parents hover around the classroom door, provoking their children's distress. The teacher may need to have a chat to the parent who disturbs the already settled child with prolonged assertions of affection and demands for assurance. 'I'm going now...say goodbye to me...you'll be a good boy while I'm gone won't you...give me a big kiss...no you can do better than that...let me kiss you. Wave bye-bye now, I'm going' etc.

The parent calls from the doorway for further demonstrations of affection and may even repeat the process at the classroom window. Only when the child panics and weeps does the parent disappear, satisfied that she or he is indispensable.

When children arrive at school distressed, parents should be asked to take them for a walk around the school grounds and return when they have settled down. A teacher aide should accompany them whenever possible to help parent and child relax and talk about attractive features of school life. Suggestions for activities may be made. If parents nag or threaten children, their fear of school increases. If children do not settle, they should not return to the classroom because of the risk of disrupting others.

Continuous school refusal may indicate that a child is not ready for school and needs longer at pre-school. An unhappy child will not benefit from what the school has to offer. Sometimes children return to pre-school on a part-time basis and continue to attend school part-time. They usually make their own decisions to terminate pre-school attendance, announcing 'I don't want to go there today'.

Catering for minority groups

In England and Australia, many migrant school entrants have to absorb a new culture and use the English language for the first time. Maori school entrants in New Zealand may have spoken the Maori language at pre-school and at home. It is imperative that bilingual teachers or aides are obtained to advise on the provision of continuity of experience in the classroom for children of different ethnic and cultural groups. In addition to this obvious link, there is a need to provide other kinds of cultural continuity in the curriculum.

Critical social changes for new entrants

Children starting school are joining a society that is very different from any previously encountered. At home and at pre-school they have had ready access to adults. In school they may suddenly find that they have to share a single adult with large numbers of other children. The presence of large numbers imposes organisational constraints on teachers. These have serious implications for new children. Some of the 'critical features' identified by NFER are:

Contact with crowds of children. New entrants are often the smallest as well as the youngest in school. Other children are not only bigger and noisier, they are stronger, confident and more aggressive and can present a threat at lunchtime and other breaks when everyone is obliged to go outside into the playground. Numbers in pre-school settings range from one, two or three children at home to 25 in a centre. In school, a five-year-old is likely to be thrust into crowds of 200 or more children, three or four times a day. It is not surprising then, that children's anxieties and fears revolve around schoolyards

The lack of familiar adults when children are in the most anxiety-provoking situations. There are few familiar adults present when recently-enrolled children are outside their own classrooms. This makes children feel insecure, nervous and lonely.

Waiting and taking turns. Organisational procedures often require children to line up, stand still, and wait. New entrants in English schools were found to spend three times more time than pre-schoolers on these laborious and often unnecessary routines. The increase is sometimes explained by the need for large populations to move around buildings in an orderly manner without disturbing other classes. The authors have observed that the adoption of 'lining up' often dates back to the teachers' own school experiences and is used more from habit than necessity. More efficient classroom organisation could eliminate the need for queues.

Competition for adult attention. The difference in adult: child ratios between pre-school and school limits opportunities not only for gaining attention but also for modelling language and having one-to-one conversations. British pre-schools offered an average ratio of 1 adult to 11 children, while teachers of new school entrants had 30 or more children in their classes.

British (Tizard & Hughes 1984) and New Zealand research (Smith 1985) showed that the increased presence of adults in pre-schools does not necessarily result in more dialogue with children. NFER found, however, that one-to-one conversations occupied only a small proportion of time in both schools and pre-schools. Contacts in both situations were brief and mainly managerial in content. Children engaged in more conversation at home with parents and childminders where there was less competition for the adults' attention.

Loss of individuality. School life is more impersonal than pre-school. The child becomes one of a class or one of a group, often given the title of a native animal such as a kiwi in New Zealand, a koala or kangaroo in Australia and a robin in England. These groups sometimes denote status, such as 'top' readers or poor readers. At home and with childminders, children are addressed individually. Children address teachers one at a time, but teachers address them as groups.

When children start school, they have few opportunities for individual interaction with their teachers. New entrants have to become accustomed to a loss of individuality. This makes it difficult for young children to express their confusion, concerns and anxieties at the very time when they should be expressed. Some new entrants fail to respond when instructions are given to the whole class.

Restrictions on children's interactions with each other. Schools house large numbers of children and have small activity areas. As a result, children transferring from pre-school to school suffer a reduction in their opportunities for interaction with peers.

NFER researchers found that after children's transition to school there was a marked increase in parallel behaviour, compulsory grouping and class activities in which children participated alongside peers but remained passive towards them.

Time constraints. Imposition of organisational constraints on time resulted in new children being left behind, being last and failing to complete designated tasks. This was found to be particularly apparent in routine domestic tasks such as dressing and undressing for physical education, eating lunch and toileting.

Discontinuity is worst for children transferring from home or small pre-school with good child–adult interaction to a large school where they experience a loss of individuality and become one of a large crowd. This kind of discontinuity can be absolutely overwhelming for the school beginner.

Strategies for minimising disruptions to the socialisation of new entrants

According to Cleave (1982, p. 163), schools should:

- recruit and utilise the presence of the new entrants' willing siblings or acquaintances already established in school, especially for help at lunchtime and other times in the playground;

- ensure that the reception class is kept separate and intact, especially in open-plan schools where the need for a safe home-area is crucial;
- allow new entrants to enter school immediately on arrival, irrespective of assembly arrangements for the masses;
- allow new entrants to start school and leave school at times to miss the big rush of older children, if this can be arranged with parents;
- arrange for new children to have their mid-morning and afternoon break at different times from the rest of the school;
- if school toilets are at a distance, arrange for regular supervised visits to reduce risks of queues at recess and lunchtime;
- supervise hygiene routines, sending only small numbers to the water troughs or handbasins at any one time;
- gradually introduce new entrants to crowded events;
- involve new entrants' parents or family representatives in the classroom;
- change any classroom organisation that results in queues of children at the teacher's desk;
- question why children are regimented, consider what children are learning from such school experiences and query whether that learning is worthwhile and appropriate. Time wasted on unnecessary routines can be used more productively;
- provide safe space for new entrants in the classroom and designate 'reception class only' playground space for children who need it;
- ensure that the reception class teacher is close at hand when the class is in a larger group;
- seat the new entrants near the teacher's desk;
- introduce the entrants by name and tell others about their interests, pets, brothers and sisters etc.;
- allocate teacher aides to work with new entrants, especially in situations where they might get lost or be left behind.

There are many more ideas that can help to reduce discontinuity for children starting school. British researchers confirmed that mid-morning, lunchtime and afternoon breaks provided the most powerful forces for distress. These were the major changes in the patterns of life from home and pre-school to school. Compared with the pre-school garden with its wheeled toys and equipment, the schoolyard is often like a busy highway. New school entrants are mystified or terrified by the seemingly aimless rushing around that passes for 'play'. If children know the teacher on duty, they cling to that teacher for safety. Without the presence of a known teacher, young children spend their break-times in passivity, trying to avoid the oncoming hordes. Unfortunately, contrary to the hopes and expectations of new entrants, school life is not a maze of new friendships and loving people. NFER found that new entrants are slow to form friendships and tend to seek out old acquaintances and siblings. Older brothers and sisters may be caring for a while but the demands of younger children can become an embarrassment to them in their peer group. The long, comparatively empty lunchtimes can result in boredom and loneliness for young children. Some teachers pair them off so that experienced children can look after younger ones. This should be by negotiation.

Difficulties at lunchtime are often related to formal routines and pressures. NFER recommended that children should have some control over their meals, with minimal constraints on what they eat. It was also suggested that new entrants should not stay at school for lunch during the first fortnight.

Although Australian and New Zealand children are not constrained by the formality of lunches and one could criticise the level of informality adopted, children are not always pressure-free. Larceny from lunchboxes is not uncommon. Some teachers put pressure on children to consume food that they do not like or do not want. Mealtimes are emotional times for adults as well as children. A teacher in the multi-cultural Melbourne suburb of Preston, complained that the predominantly Greek boys in her class were overweight, lethargic and made excuses to miss physical activities. Lunchtime revealed that the teacher had been conditioned to 'remember the starving children in India' and the feelings of parents who had so lovingly prepared the food. She routinely insisted that children must eat everything in their lunch boxes, ignoring pleas that they were 'full'. Brief communications with parents disclosed that they were packing more and more food each day because, no matter what they sent, the lunchboxes were always returned home empty. Parents were alarmed by the apparent increase in their children's appetite and it never occurred to them that their children were being force-fed. So often, a simple communication between teacher, child and parent can resolve difficulties which, if ignored, dominate children's nightmares and result in a resistance to attend school.

Discontinuity in pedagogy

As we have seen, the smooth transition of children from pre-school to school is often marred by differences in the philosophies, aims, pedagogies and physical environments between the two sectors of education.

When Margaret McMillan (1912) introduced the British nursery school, it was intended to be quite separate and different from the primary school. The first pre-school teacher education courses, worldwide, were separate and different from school teacher-training.

When British pre-school education expanded in the early 1930s and again in the 1970s, local authorities favoured the provision of nursery classes attached to infant and infant/primary schools. Those who promoted the departure from the traditional nursery school model were motivated by economic and financial constraints, supported by the argument that the physical link between pre-school and school would promote continuous educational development.

Pre-school teachers expressed fears that the exposure of three- and four-year-olds to the primary school environment would merely increase the trauma for children at an earlier age. They also suspected that, under the direction of primary-trained head teachers, pre-school personnel would be pressured to modify their practices and philosophies to match those of the primary school. In other words, pre-school would become just a watered-down version of the traditional primary classroom. Derbyshire school log books confirm that when there was a shortage of teachers in the primary school, it was customary to transfer the nursery teacher and replace her with an unqualified aide, confirming the comparatively low value of pre-school education in relation to the primary sector (Briggs 1978).

The concept of the pre-school as the bridge between home and school implied that the nursery offered many of the physical amenities and some of the atmosphere of the caring home; it was small, welcoming and comfortable, providing a range of education and socialising experiences involving parents at a time when the primary school was neither physically nor psychologically hospitable to them. In Australia and New Zealand, pre-school education was introduced by voluntary organisations in small purpose-built and homely kindergartens. They, too, adopted the role of the bridge linking home and school and the philosophical differences between pre-school and primary became more apparent. Early childhood teacher-training in both countries was, and still is, distinct from primary school training.

The responsibility for pre-school education has been allocated to education authorities in Britain, New Zealand and most Australian states. In New Zealand there is a national authority, responsible for all types of education and pre-school care. In Britain, nursery schools and classes are the responsibility of local authorities.

Administrative arrangements can facilitate or impede the communications that are needed for continuity in education. New Zealand and South Australian experiences show that a single employing authority or a shared site do not guarantee a single philosophy of early childhood education for the five-year-old child. A pre-school centre can be isolated, regardless of its location, if the philosophies of pre-school and primary school staff are so different that they preclude the necessary mutual respect, communication, co-operation and interchange.

Early childhood educators and primary school teachers have traditionally adopted substantially different philosophies and teaching methods. Pre-schools emphasise the development of the whole child as an individual while primary schools concentrated on academic subjects, intellectual development and 'the class'. This difference in focus has been investigated by the countries making up membership of the Council of Europe (Woodhead 1979). A survey of provision undertaken by the British Department of Education and Science in 1982 further confirmed that the transfer of children from pre-school to infant/primary schools brought even more dramatic changes than was found previously, including a reduction of free choice for children in their activities from 62.9 per cent to a mere 12.1 per cent (Curtis 1982).

Although the children were often of the same age, teachers in the two sectors held quite different aims, expectations and priorities, adding to the discontinuity of the children's educational experience.

The British research also suggested that the child's confusion increased when the reception class was housed in an open-plan unit with a philosophy of open education. Curtis (1982, p. 5) commented:

> These units may offer excellent ways of utilising space and providing the facilities for a stimulating environment but they are not the best places to give the youngest children the sense of security they need.

Curtis concluded that young children interact more in a close, homely environment, and teachers and schools should take account of this in making their classroom arrangements.

The Conference of the Council of Europe (1979) concluded that if:

> any curriculum is to be meaningful to a young child, it must be embedded in his total life experiences and take into account not only his own values and expectations but also those of his peers, family and community at large...in this way, there is less likely to be a mismatch between home, pre-school and school.

The importance of teacher training

Bearing the different philosophies in mind, it is easy to see why the attitudes of teachers to new entrants depend substantially on the type of training that they experienced as well as their personalities and whether they are in the role by choice or because their options were restricted. Ronald King (1978) in his book *All Things Bright and Beautiful?* showed not only that pre-school and primary school teachers were markedly different in their philosophies but that there were further distinctions between teachers trained to work with infants (5–8 years) and those trained for primary school in general. These differences were revealed in the way that teachers behaved and talked to children as well as their attitudes to discipline.

The early childhood educator who has been trained to work with the child from birth to eight years or three to eight years is clearly in the best position to offer continuity of experience from pre-school to school, because initial training involves teaching in both sectors. In addition, early childhood teacher education in any country involves a curriculum based on a knowledge of child development, differing substantially from primary teacher training with a class and subject focus.

Students on teaching practice invariably experience a wide variety of teacher attitudes to new enrolments. Some primary-trained teachers undo the work of the pre-school in relation to independence, free choice, the use of initiative and open communications. This undoing is viewed as essential to the establishment of authority and discipline. Such attitudes can spring from training that fails to take account of children's individual learning styles and needs.

Continuity of experience in education and smooth transition requires a degree of similarity between the methods and philosophies used in the pre-school and reception class in early childhood and primary education. King (1978) confirmed that pre-service teacher education produces markedly different methods and different attitudes to children in the first three years of school.

Most reception class teachers are kind and considerate to new arrivals and their parents but their role requires much more than kindness. If education authorities adopt policies stressing the importance of continuity of experience in transition from pre-school to school, (and most have), then they must also recognise the importance of the teacher who is responsible for introducing new entrants to school. It follows that they must also appoint only the most suitably qualified and experienced teachers for this responsibility.

TASKS FOR STUDENTS

1 What is the school's policy in relation to continuity of experience in transition from home and pre-school to school?
2 How does this policy compare with the policy of the education authority?
3 How is the policy translated into practice in that particular school?
4 What arrangements are made prior to school entry for:
   • the child to visit the school with the parent?
   • the child to visit the school with the pre-school teacher?
   • the reception class teacher to visit the home?
   • the reception class teacher to visit the pre-schools and daycare centres feeding the school?
5 How far away are toilets and handbasins from the reception class?
6 What arrangements are made for new entrants to use toilets at school?
7 What special arrangements, if any, are made to protect new entrants in the school playground?
8 What arrangements are made for school enrolment?
9 If possible, obtain copies of school letters and leaflets given to parents enrolling their children. How are parents expected to prepare their children for school?
10 Are parents allowed to stay with new arrivals in the classroom? If YES, for how long? If NO, what is the rationale for their exclusion?
11 How far does the reception classroom resemble the local pre-schools feeding the school? How does it differ?
12 What arrangements are made for entry to the school? What are the

advantages and disadvantages to teachers, and children, of this method?

13 Ask new entrants what they like best about school, what they don't like about school, what they are learning.

14 Ask parents of pre-school children what they expect children to learn in the first year of school.

15 Ask parents of pre-schoolers how they prepare children for school.

16 Ask teachers of new entrants which aspects of school life cause the greatest problems and anxieties for new arrivals.

USEFUL REFERENCES

Davies, M. & North J. 1990, 'Teachers' Expectations of School Entry Skill, *Australian Journal of Early Childhood*, vol. 15, no. 4, December.

Hains, A. *et al.* 1989, 'A Comparison of Pre-school and Kindergarten Teacher Expectations for School Readiness', *Early Childhood Research Quarterly*', vol. 4, no.1, March.

Katz, L.G & McClellan, D.E. 1991, *The Teacher's Role in the Social Development of Young Children*, ERIC Clearing House on Elementary and Early Childhood Education, Urbana, Ill.

National Association for the Education of Young Children (NAEYC) 1990, Position Statement on School Readiness, 1509 16 St., NW, Washington DC.

Children in the first three years of school

Although all children are different and develop at different rates, teachers often identify certain trends and similarities among children of similar ages. Between the ages of five and eight, there are many developmental aspects each with individual variations. These differences have serious implications for teachers in their curricula planning, their choice of teaching methods and the most effective forms of classroom management. As it is now common practice to place school entrants in mixed classes, it is essential that both teachers and parents have realistic expectations of children's behaviours and achievements.

This chapter provides information relating to children from five to eight years in the classroom. It is intended to help practitioners in the field but should never be used as a replacement for in-depth studies in child development.

Adjustment to school

If children are well adjusted at home and pre-school, they may be ready for the experience of joining a school group that is supervised by a caring early childhood trained teacher. The change from home life is challenging and sometimes frightening but exciting and rewarding. Children usually want their parents to accompany them to the classroom on the first day or two, perhaps with support diminishing thereafter. Confident children accept and enjoy school. Entrants enjoy making new acquaintances and having older children to imitate. Exposure to a variety of models is important. Their basic standards are those absorbed from parents but, at school, these are modified and adapted to their own emerging personalities (Lee 1990).

School attendance sometimes brings a change in children's behaviour. Those who have acquired the reputation for being troublesome at home often become compliant and co-operative in class. When the opposite occurs, it is

Figure 3.1: Dressing is much more difficult than undressing

indicative that they are not yet ready to adjust to a large group situation. It is advisable to allow such children to remain at home or at pre-school for a longer period of time, making the introduction to school more gradual.

The recent school entrant is usually capable of entering the school building, finding the classroom and teacher, placing lunch and personal possessions in the appropriate places, all without assistance.

In bad weather, five- and six-year-olds will need help to remove and store raincoats and boots. Children who drop their clothing on the floor need encouragement to pick it up because others will walk over it. Dressing is much more difficult than undressing. Without adult help children will wear clothes inside out and become frustrated if they have to take them off and start again. They seldom recognise their own shoes or socks alongside others. This has significance for teachers who allow children to undress for water play or physical activity. Name tags are vital to avoid confusion and distress.

Some will need a nap during the day and classrooms should have beanbags or sunbeds readily available for tired children.

They need the security of routines and clear, sensible rules. They not only obey them, but remind others about what they are allowed or forbidden to do. Five-year-olds like to conform and they become upset if they are rejected by others. They accept new rules as absolute and worry if they are broken. They fear terrible consequences if they make mistakes, for example by not returning equipment to the appropriate storage place. These troubles clear up if parents and teachers work at them together. Well adjusted five-year-olds are fundamentally loving and trusting. When happy and occupied, they are independent and confident but when over tired, unhappy or sick they behave like infants and turn to teachers for comfort (Lee 1990).

The curriculum for five-year-olds must take account of their individual competencies, need for variety, comparatively short concentration span, and inability to sit still for any length of time. They need teachers who use activity methods and seize opportunities to extend learning through children's current interests. They need teachers who are fair and consistent in their relationships with children but flexible in their planning and implementation of lessons. They need a programme that varies in pace and intensity of activity.

Given adequate warning, five-year-olds complete tasks and return materials to the appropriate shelf or cupboard, albeit untidily.

Five-year-olds are very vulnerable to seasons and weather. Teachers often complain that their classes are uncontrollable when it is windy or when children have been kept indoors for several days because of rain. Since fives need opportunities for movement, it is helpful to have a large area available in which energetic activities can be carried out regardless of inclement weather. British schools are much more likely than their Australian and New Zealand counterparts to have space designated for physical exercise, equipped with climbing ropes, climbing frames, large mats, planks, jungle gyms, balls, skipping ropes and hoops which can be stored in the room and set up easily. Corridors and porches can be used in inclement weather for large blocks, portable swings and messy play.

For disadvantaged children, a secure, well-conducted classroom provides a haven that may be the only stable part of their troubled lives. Five- and six-year-olds often view their understanding teachers as auxiliary mothers or fathers who look after them rather than teach them. Teachers never replace primary caregivers but they should endeavour to provide a homely and secure environment that emulates the loving home. Children derive new confidence from the daily welcomes, protection, assurances and from the sheer satisfaction of broadening their experiences (Gessell, Ilg & Ames 1968). Once a pattern is set, typical five–six-year-olds do not wish to deviate from it. They like social routines and the pleasant rituals that are repeated regularly because they feel confident in handling them. Confident children talk a lot and ask many questions, especially those involving 'Why...?'. They like to see their teacher in the classroom when they arrive at school and are apt to worry if the teacher is late or absent. As they are constantly making new discoveries and have to assimilate so many new experiences, they prefer school and home situations that remain relatively stable.

After a few months, some children are less willing to come to school than they were previously. There may be occasional difficulties about leaving parents or main caregivers. The mother says 'I don't know what's wrong. He used to like school'. Sometimes, this occurs because the child has encountered a problem at school: he doesn't like lunchtimes or someone upsets him in the playground. Sometimes, the reluctance to come to school merely indicates that the child has only just found the confidence to protest and has previously conformed reluctantly because it was expected of him. School refusal often reappears a year later when children are six.

Most school entrants can use toilets without help although 15 to 20 per cent continue to wet their beds at home. Anxiety about starting school may bring a return to bed-wetting in children who were previously dry. New arrivals are likely to need a companion to accompany them to toilets situated at a distance from the classroom. Accidents occur when children find school facilities unpleasant and they attempt to postpone toileting until they return home. Another problem for this age group lies in the tendency to become engrossed in activities to the extent that children ignore their natural urges. They wriggle and hop and clutch their genitals but wait for the teacher to suggest that they should visit the toilet. Some five-year-olds still need help to wipe themselves clean (Harris & Liebert 1992). When children become confident, they use visits to toilets as an excuse to escape from boring sessions. This is a particularly attractive alternative if it involves an interesting outdoor walk out of the teacher's sight. However prepared they are for school, children are usually exhausted at the end of their day and need a quiet snack and the attention of a parent when they return home from school.

Attitudes to self and others

School entrants sense that they have come a long way along the road to maturity by starting school. It is an important milestone for children and their parents. Adults have different expectations of them; they are no longer babies and they like to be treated as 'grown up'. They are almost independent in most of their home routines and, with care and strong support, stable children are usually ready to accept some responsibilities in the community life of the classroom.

Fives can be much more self-contained as individuals than they were at four. They often behave and sound like miniature adults. They are serious about the acquisition of skills and their ability to take 'grown-up' responsibilities. They enjoy dressing up and pretending to be adults, using adult language and correcting each other about minor details of procedure. They give advice on how plumbers or electricians or motor mechanics do this or that. They can often be heard 'talking themselves through' a task.

They are serious about themselves and try to understand what it feels like to be adult when they teeter around the classroom wearing high-heeled shoes, carrying adult-sized handbags.

Five-year-olds are rightly considered to be mature by pre-school staff. They are increasingly aware of how their actions affect their environment. They are often shy in their approach to new people but they build up slow, steady relationships which make them popular with teachers. They ask teachers for permission, often when permission is unnecessary. Parents and teachers

Figure 3.2: Boys and girls try to understand what it feels like to be adult

receive a considerable amount of affection from five-year-olds, but primary caregivers remain their favourite people. Children are often proud of their parents' achievements and brag about them.

Although five-year-olds are comparatively fearless (Briggs & Hawkins 1993), they like to stay close to the familiar base, whether that base is at home or the classroom at school. This has implications for open-plan schools and their organisation (Briggs 1991).

Fives show a remarkable memory for things that occurred when they were two or three years old. They hoard thoughts and experiences as well as things. Through questioning other people, they acquire an impressive store of information. They require a degree of orderliness in their lives but live in a 'here and now' kind of world which makes it difficult for them to wait for anything, least of all wait for promises for tomorrow, next week, next birthday or next Christmas.

In their first year at school, children show a better ability to play with others, share and take turns. They are less bossy than they were a year earlier. However, life is not always smooth with siblings. Indoor play presents more problems than outdoor play, especially if there is limited space. Five-year-olds can also be jealous of the attention given to other children and they may derive pleasure from telling tales and blaming others for their own misdemeanours.

Most fives play well with and alongside children of their own age but they are most interested in themselves and what they want to do. They realise that other children are useful to their ends and they are willing to be useful to others in exchange but they are more rivals than collaborators (Lee 1990). Most are beginning to choose friends of their own gender but some still play with members of the opposite sex who share their interests. Because they are home-based, children of this age need friends who are readily available in their neighbourhood. They are incapable of playing at the team games enjoyed by older children but concentrate hard on the skills they want to acquire such as riding a bike or scooter or skipping with a rope. Children of this age play best in pairs. When three are present, two tend to gang up on the third. Friendships are fickle but very important. Some children use emotional blackmail very effectively, threatening to withdraw their friendship if someone does not conform to their demands. Teachers and parents often encounter very distressed children whose special friends have, on the spur of the moment, declared 'I won't be your friend any more'. If given support, the natural, egocentric side of the five-year-old reasserts itself. Fives are likely to choose new friends for their various abilities, such as 'I'll come to sit by you. You're a good painter'.

Children of this age are often boastful, fearless and they seem to 'show off' very frequently. Adults often find this tiresome but teachers recognise that it is a rational outcome of their self confidence and cope with it good humouredly, encouraging their real achievements (Lee 1990). A wise parent only allows a five-year-old to invite one child at a time into the home until

Figure 3.3: Five-year-olds enjoy dramatisation and puppetry

he or she is mature enough to cope with the hazards of group play. This kind of maturity is rare before seven or eight years of age. Sometimes the five-year-old will play well with older children, accepting a junior role in dramatic or domestic play. The excessively bossy child will be happiest with younger children who are willing to be directed. Bossy five-year-olds will, however, take turns if others agree to play their way for part of the time. Some pairs of children are incompatible between the ages of five and eight and become good friends thereafter. Putting children together before they are ready merely highlights their lack of common ground except for arguing and fighting. Some amenable fives need to be protected from exposure to certain social situations for prolonged periods of time. They easily become fatigued and, when tired and frustrated, may explode in a disconcerting way.

Many children can read the most obvious signs associated with other people's emotions such as anger, sadness, fear and happiness. Not until they are about 8–9 years can they detect false displays of emotion. Children may feign emotions for fun from the age of two and as they get older, they also become more proficient at concealing their true feelings. This is because their socialisation process teaches them that they have to keep their emotions under control to become acceptable members of society. By the time they reach school, children are expected to know that it is not acceptable to make hurtful comments to others. They also learn to suppress their feelings when they have to say 'thank you' for something they do not like or want. Social pressure to regulate the use of language comes before pressure to control facial expressions. As a consequence, children's real feelings are more likely to be expressed in their body language rather than words (Gnepp & Hess 1986; Harris & Liebert 1992).

Children of 5–8 years tend to view people distinctively. They remember negative behaviours rather than positive ones and fail to recognise that people have good and bad traits. They cannot reconcile contradictory information about the same person (Harris & Liebert 1992). If a person appears to be kind, she is perceived as kind (Briggs 1991). If someone gives a child a present, that person is categorised as good, even if the gift was stolen or it was given as a bribe. Young children are unable to recognise hidden motives.

The development of self-awareness proceeds at the same rate as knowledge about other people. At 5–8 years children's descriptions of themselves are likely to concentrate on their physical characteristics, activities and possessions. At around 7–8 years, children begin to identify themselves with age-mates and use these comparisons to identify their own characteristics. They talk about what they're 'good at' and 'no good at'.

It is interesting to note that, the more contact girls and boys have with each other, the more they avoid each other's company. Children who have been placed in mixed groups become less willing to work in such groups. The more girls work with boys, the stronger their negative stereotypes become (Lockheed & Harris 1984). Maccoby (1990) suggests that the major factor is the gender difference in interaction styles. Boys in groups concentrate on competition and dominance. They interrupt each other, boast, give commands and make threats if things don't go their way. Girls tend to make polite suggestions, co-operate, avoid conflict and take turns (Maccoby 1990). These different styles lead to difficulties when male and female children try to work together. School-age girls are unlikely to be able to influence male peers. If their wishes are to be taken seriously, girls have to become more aggressive in male company. Interestingly, boys do not moderate their aggression when they join female groups; they become more dominant and aggressive (Miller, Danaher & Forbes 1986). Not only do boys dominate girls in mixed sex groups, they get more of the teachers' time by calling out and using other attention seeking behaviours (Morgan & Dunn 1988; Kelly 1988). International research shows that while boys play in groups and learn to utilise team support, girls play in pairs. Girls' friendships are generally more exclusive, more possessive and more intimate. Boys reveal less of themselves to friends, possibly because of their concern for dominance (Maccoby 1990; Rubin 1980; Maccoby & Jacklin 1987).

It is useful for teachers to know which of their peers children would choose to play with. Some children will be ignored. They are often shy and lonely or introverts who are not troubled by their lack of friends. Some children will be rejected. Rejected children are likely to remain so throughout their school lives. They tend to be low achievers who lack social skills and communication skills in particular. Rejected children are often used as scapegoats by their peers. Some are classed as 'provocative victims', provoking classmates into picking on them and retaliating aggressively (Kupersmidt 1989, cited in Harris & Liebert 1992). In some cases, children are rejected because of their physical traits. On the other hand, good looks don't guarantee popularity. Social rejection is complex and self perpetuating. Negative behaviours can be the result of rejection. Being rejected reduces opportunities for practising social skills. Furthermore once a child is branded as 'bad' or 'mean', it is difficult to overcome the negative stereotyping. At the same time, the rejected child expects hostility and distrusts friendly overtures (Hymel 1986; Waas 1988).

The most successful intervention programmes have involved pairing a rejected child with one or two more popular classmates for a specific time each week. These sessions are accompanied by positive reinforcement for desired behaviours and effort (Harris & Liebert 1992).

School aged children choose friends who are similar in age, sex, socio-economic status, race and achievement. From seven to eight years, children may decide to choose the advice of friends rather that parents and they may be more afraid of the disapproval of peers than the disapproval of parents (Utech & Hoving 1969; Perry, Perry & Weiss 1989).

Physical development

Most five-year-olds have acquired a high degree of physical control by the time they start school. Their control over large muscles is likely to be much better than control over their finer movements. Fives like to climb on jungle gyms and climbing frames of different kinds. They may move from one piece of apparatus to another with comparative ease and confidence. They run along beams and scramble under them. Most are capable of jumping from a height of about a metre on to a soft mat. Gross motor activity is well developed at five. Children can usually walk in a straight line, run lightly on their toes, march in time or dance to music. They can descend stairs and skip using alternate feet. Most can stand on one foot for eight to ten seconds and hop on each foot for several seconds. The alternating mechanism is practised and strengthened in their play. Five-year-olds love riding tricycles and become adept in their manipulation, making sudden stops, reversals and fast cornering. They are interested in stilts, roller skates and skateboards but cannot sustain their balance for very long.

When kicking balls, five-year-olds may throw and kick simultaneously. Their eyes and head move with greater synchronisation as they turn to look at the ball. They face things squarely and are direct in their approach. They like to throw things such as soft balls and beanbags, and begin to use their hands more effectively for catching things.

The economy of movement seen in five-year-olds is in marked contrast to the expansiveness of the pre-school child. Fives seem more restrained and less mobile, maintaining concentration for increasing periods of time. They are, nevertheless, extremely physical and the restraint has to be self-imposed. They become very restless when left in a sedentary position for any length of time. When they have nothing to do other than listen, they wriggle, scratch themselves, poke their clothing or their bodies or other children, creating what teachers euphemistically call 'discipline problems'.

Most five-year-olds can sit upright. Their approach, grasp and release are firm and precise although hand–eye co-ordination is still inaccurate and subject to further development. They continue to utilise pre-school toys but much more skilfully and purposefully than before, making more intricate structures from engineering, building and construction kits. They continue to play with large building-blocks, but there is a growing appreciation of smaller and more intricate construction equipment with which they may attempt to copy diagrams or models, building bridges, forts, roads and railways, steps, farmyards and zoo buildings which they use with miniature people, cars and animals.

Most five-year-olds like playing with jigsaw puzzles. They complete familiar puzzles faster than adults, manipulating pieces at mercurial speed. Puzzles need to be numerous and graded for difficulty. Less confident children tend to complete the same puzzles repeatedly, knowing that they are not risking failure. Teachers may have to persuade them to move on to new and more difficult puzzles, giving discreet help and praise for effort.

Some fives are already adept with their hands and like to practise intricate skills such as fastening accessible buttons and shoelaces. They may also like to participate in elementary weaving and sewing with darning needles and wool.

Children of this age often watch others engage in physical skills and then attempt to copy them. They will trace and repeat patterns, letters and numbers. Most fives can copy geometrical shapes such as squares and triangles as well as the easier letter shapes, including V, T, O, C, and U. These are likely to be large and irregular in size, drawn in several disconnected parts. Some fives print letters on pages at random with no thought for spacing, starting at the top or even maintaining the same direction. Letters may lie flat in a horizontal position and there is sometimes a reversal, often termed 'mirror writing', at this age. There is considerable variation in the ability to write numbers. Those who can write beyond 10 often reverse the second digit. Writing ability will depend on the child's physical development, motivation and earlier experiences. Some children will have enjoyed the use of writing and drawing materials in their own homes, some will not. Some children will write their own forenames spontaneously, others will not. Some will have weak finger muscles that make it difficult to grasp and control a pencil. Left- or right-handedness is usually well established at five. Children approach their tasks with the dominant hand, although both hands may be used for building purposes. There is often no longer a tendency to transfer crayons, pencils or paintbrushes from one hand to the other.

Figure 3.4: South East Asian children often demonstrate the ability to draw fine detail and perspective at a very early age. This scene, drawn with coloured textas, depicts life in the village of the five-year-old artist. Children began to include aerial warfare in their pictures when television was introduced to the village

Figure 3.5: Young children draw their homes as boxes with chimneys, irrespective of where they live

Most five-year-olds like to draw and paint, experimenting with a variety of materials. For painting, they continue to use thick paint brushes, large paint pots and easels. Some children like painting on the floor on large sheets of paper. South-East Asian children, especially those from Indonesia, are often exceptional in their ability to create small, detailed drawings. Children of European descent tend to draw recognisable but primitive human shapes with disproportionate head, trunk, arms and main features. They recognise that the people look 'silly' and they laugh at their own efforts. They draw simple, oblong houses with a door, two windows, a roof and a chimney. It is interesting to note that this type of house is drawn identically by children living in high-rise flats in central London, caravan dwellers in Australia, residents of two-storey houses in the USA and even Balinese children living in bamboo shelters in compounds. Many fives enjoy colouring-in pictures with outlines, the challenge being to control the crayons or textas within the limits of the lines and provide a variety of colour. Most can name four primary colours and match up to twelve.

Six-year-olds are characterised by their restlessness. They run indoors and outdoors, never quite sure where they want to be from one moment to the next. They continue to dig in sand and soil. They fill and empty wheelbarrows and carts. Most are now skilled at riding tricycles at speed, often cornering on two wheels, braking sharply and swerving to avoid other children and hard objects. Sand, water and mud continue to keep them occupied. This age group has a great interest in reality. They ask 'Is it true?'. Their fantasy play has strong elements of real life, showing evidence of careful observation. In dramatic play they like to have a coherent story running through the play and they like to perform with an informal audience.

Most six-year-olds like to help adults with domestic tasks. They will fetch and carry and take messages. They will set tables in a routine fashion. Sixes are always active, even when they are supposed to be sitting still. They seem to be all 'arms and legs', and need plenty of opportunities for movement. Teachers who are foolish enough to keep them sitting on the floor for more than 15 minutes at a time find that they fidget and touch other children as they stretch their limbs. Restless, the recipients of knocks respond with pushes and shoves and there are usually protests that disrupt the concentration of others. Even on chairs they wriggle, tilt the chair legs and fall off. If children are not allowed frequent opportunities for movement, teachers can expect problems.

Sixes engage in a great deal of oral activity. Some grimace and place their tongues between their teeth when they concentrate. They bite their tongues or cheeks accidentally. Some bite nails, chew their pencils or anything that comes to hand. Some sixes will balance their bodies in space whenever the opportunity arises. They run downhill, feeling as light as air and, with the wind behind them, sense that they are travelling at great speed. They swing high without assistance. They like to crawl through spaces, climb over and up and slide down large structures and ropes. They climb higher than ever

Figure 3.6: Sand, water and mud are popular, especially when given a variety of substantial materials such as drainpipes, tubes, hosepipes, funnels and barrels that provide opportunities for adventure as well as learning

before, experiencing new and tantalisingly different views of their world from these higher perspectives.

Some children enjoy helping with physical tasks at school, such as sweeping, dusting or cleaning blackboards. They mop tables and floors after painting but they are not very thorough and, unless supervised, may block sinks, splash and make more mess, especially if they have been deprived of waterplay in the first year of school. Six is the age for boisterous wrestling and vigorous play which often ends up in tears because they don't know when to stop. There may be a need for regular reminders about the individual's right to say 'No' and children's responsibility to stop when others no longer wish to participate in vigorous play.

Six-year-olds recognise the value of their hands as tools but they continue to feel awkward when faced with tasks requiring fine motor skills. They are challenged by toys that create demands on these skills. Interest is often less in making an end product than in mastering equipment. For this reason, when a major construction has been made, the architects often destroy it, gaining satisfaction from the power of destruction as well as the capacity to create. Adults are often surprised to find that building is more erratic at six than it was at five. This is because hand and eye co-ordination is slower and less accurate, and children become clumsy. Girls like to dress and undress dolls and boys will do so if not inhibited by sex-role conditioning. This can involve

Figure 3.7: Sixes need space for play

some very fine movements if there are zips and fasteners to manipulate and clothes are turned inside out.

Sometimes, sixes stand up to write but rest their bodies across the table or lay their heads sideways on their upper or lower arms. With practice, pencil grasp is less awkward than at five but the performance remains laborious. Pencils are held awkwardly with changing grasps and body positions as well as a tilted head. Sixes hold their pencils close to the points and exert a tremendous amount of pressure, resulting in broken lead. They enjoy spending prolonged periods of time at pencil-sharpeners creating substantial and often unnecessary waste. Rules for the use of sharpeners may be necessary to prevent children from wasting time and causing disruption to others.

At six years, children show an interest in lower-case letters as well as capitals. They may mix them up in the words they write without differentiating them by size. Six-year-olds commonly print some in reverse, especially 's', 'b', 'd', 'p', and 'q'. Some will write from left to right but correct it when the mistake is pointed out. With adult guidance, letters such as 'a' and 'h' may now be drawn with one continuous stroke. The size of letters is inconsistent, tending to increase towards the end of the line. Similarly, six-year-olds can rarely write in a straight line or write vertically. Depending on their experience, many will be able to write both their forenames and surnames but not their addresses. Some will write numbers up to twenty but, again, there is a strong tendency to reverse the second digit.

Six-year-olds prefer free drawing and painting but continue to colour in pictures that provide detail, variety and challenge. Their own efforts are still crude, boys concentrating on transport while girls tend to focus on houses and domestic scenes. Both boys and girls draw people in their pictures.

Six-year-olds like to touch and handle everything, asking questions about how things work, what they are made of and 'What happens if...'. Good teachers harness this curiosity for learning. They provide construction kits and activities that involve cutting and pasting, making sculptures, using different textures in collage and working with wood, clay and block salt. Adults never have all the answers to children's questions, but must help them to find books that will provide the answers, teaching children how to obtain information for themselves. This contributes to the skills of independent learning. One irritating aspect of six-year-olds is that they have little idea of time. They are so curious and interested in everything that they appear to 'dawdle' and 'mess about' when the adult expects them to 'get on with the job' (Lee 1990). The problem is that six-year-olds often seem so competent and sensible that we expect them to be more mature than they really are. We must also remember that we often keep them waiting, letting their eagerness drain away. At this age, they are questioning their earlier belief that unbearable rules govern life; asking 'Why?' more urgently.

Sixes can move their eyes from one place to another and back again with great dexterity but most find it difficult to copy anything from a blackboard

Figure 3.8: Children can display endless patience and concentration. Making a rabbit hutch

onto paper. Teachers often underestimate the complexity of this operation which necessitates visual retention of the image on the board while looking at the paper at a different eye-level. Six-year-olds are easily distracted and their hands may continue in activity while their eyes watch what others are doing.

In woodwork, children need supervision and assistance although they may reject the latter. They show endless patience and concentration in trying to master the skill of hitting nails straight into the wood. They pull out the bent nails and repeat their efforts until satisfaction is achieved. Teachers may like to give children practical tips on how to hammer a nail without bending it. They can also help by providing suitably soft timber for the purpose. Saws bend and stick in the hands of young carpenters. They will spend hours struggling to saw a piece of wood in two. Once this is achieved, they will move forward to make crude structures which, to them, are swords or aeroplanes. If dowelling, primer, paint and adhesive are available, they will make colourful boats with funnels and aeroplanes and propellers. Children of both sexes benefit from these experiences and teachers should give strong encouragement to reluctant participants.

Within the patterns of physical development described here, there are huge individual variations, depending on social pressures and conditioning, motivation, experience and the development of large and small muscles.

After the overactivity and exuberance at six years, the **seven-year-old** is often viewed as much calmer, more civilised and easier to live with. Sevens are still very active and energetic but periods of high activity are offset by periods of immobility and absorption. Although most sevens enjoy balancing, climbing, dancing, using bats and balls and riding two-wheeled bicycles, they exhibit an unaccustomed caution in many of their gross motor activities. They may develop an awareness of heights and danger and begin to consider the risks.

Most enjoy physical education classes and games at school and, by eight years, their bodily movement tends to be more rhythmic and graceful with a sensitivity and control of posture that was previously missing. Sevens like to perfect their physical skills and will repeat their efforts until they are entirely satisfied with the results. Because of this concern for proficiency, their activities and interests are apt to change quite rapidly. When they sense that they can do something well, they move on to another experience and another challenge.

Seven-year-olds like to get involved in activities with a strong motor component. At this age, girls often want to join callisthenics or dancing classes. Most boys and some girls like to engage in carpentry, using a wider range of adult tools such as hacksaws, tenon saws and screwdrivers. In the playground, 7–8-year-olds skip or jump over ropes and play hopscotch and group games.

Most seven-year-olds read sentences and recognise familiar words out of context. There may be substantial differences in reading ability, with some

Figure 3.9: Sevens make canals and drainage systems

children now fast and competent and others just starting. Girls tend to read more frequently and more enthusiastically than boys. Differences in abilities relate to conditioning, the nature of the teaching approaches and materials used, motivation to read, self-confidence and home experiences as well as children's abilities to memorise and recognise minute differences in letter and word shapes.

Sevens may use rulers to mark the lines they are reading. Although some may read in a dull, stilted fashion, the more competent are now gaining understanding from content. As a result, they tend to predict new words, relying on the first two or three letters, their knowledge of similar words, the semantics, the syntax and the illustrations. They prefer to be told difficult words rather than labour over them and risk an interruption to the flow of the reading. The most troublesome words tend to be those which adults mistakenly assume to be easy, words such as 'and', 'the', 'this' and 'that', which have no distinctive pattern and no pictorial meaning. Some will reverse words, perceiving 'was' as 'saw' and 'pot' as 'top'. It is also commonplace for children to interpret one letter incorrectly, thereby changing the meaning of the word.

By **eight**, many can run into a moving rope, skip and run out again without stopping the rope. Some try to handle footballs and junior cricket bats and balls. They develop greater accuracy in throwing, kicking and catching balls. By eight, they are enjoying the variations of footwork involved in soccer. They also like to play with kites, home-made paper or balsa-wood aeroplanes and other games that require throwing and chasing. Children of both sexes create their own competitions to see who can jump the highest or the farthest or run the fastest. By eight, they are very dramatic in their activities.

Hand and eye co-ordination improves with practice, and the use of tools becomes both more intense and more persistent. Pencils are still held tightly with the hand close to the point. Print reversal is now much less common than hitherto, and can usually be remedied with a little assistance. Children are likely to be capable of printing several sentences with letters reducing in size towards the end of the line. Some children continue to prefer large letters while others use small ones. Horizontal control improves substantially during the year. Towards eight, there are fewer errors in writing numbers up to and beyond twenty. Figures become more uniform and, with practice, are reduced in size. Eight-year-olds are usually capable of writing all the letters of the alphabet correctly, maintaining some uniformity of size, slant and spacing. They can make a specific effort to write neatly but, on most days, are in too much of a hurry to worry about tidiness in print. Most eights have increased the speed, accuracy and smoothness of hand–eye co-ordination. They hold pencils, paintbrushes and carpentry tools with comparative ease and control. There is still a gap between what they want to do and what they can do with their hands and this causes frustration.

By **eight**, the mechanics, content and therefore comprehension in reading are in better balance and children may stop to discuss illustrations or talk about what they have read. Towards eight years, children often relate their reading choices to their level of maturity, and 'easy' books are rejected as babyish. Reading is now more relaxed and books are held comfortably on the lap, using an occasional finger to focus on difficult words. Confident children are often happy to read easy, short stories to younger children or listen to less competent readers, thereby reinforcing their own skills.

Gender differences in physical development

Gender differences in height and weight are negligible at five years. The average 6–7-year-old boy is slightly taller and heavier than the average six-year-old girl but by the end of middle childhood, the situation is reversed. Girls tend to lag behind boys in most measures of athletic ability and strength, including running, long jump and grip strength (Harris & Liebert 1992). The biggest gender differences involve catching and throwing. In both skills, boys out-perform girls throughout early childhood. In throwing speed, three-year-old boys throw balls significantly harder than three-year-old girls and the differences widen with age (Thomas & French 1985; Harris & Liebert 1992).

One obvious factor in determining proficiency is the amount of practice children get in these activities. From preschool onwards, boys in Western culture spend considerably more time than the girls engaged in running, jumping and using balls in activities outdoors (Harper & Sanders 1978). Boys are

Figure 3.10: Girls and boys must be given equal opportunities

also more competitive, pitting themselves against each other in strength, speed and agility (Stoneman, Brody & MacKinnon 1984). In addition, in mixed groups, girls are reluctant to compete with boys but will compete vigorously against other females (Harris & Liebert 1992). Girls tend to be better than boys at activities requiring fine eye–hand co-ordination, balance or flexibility and girls are more proficient at hopping (Williams 1983).

Emotional development

Most of the anxiety traits exhibited by five-year-olds relate to going to bed. Some children still fall asleep sucking their thumbs and starting school may increase the habit temporarily. Others return to their old comforter blankets and favourite soft toys. Anxieties about school sometimes result in night fears and bedtime problems. The hand-to-face emotional response is manifested in nose-picking, nail-biting and face-scratching, all of which are commonly encountered at five. Nose-sniffing also often causes adult concern. Children who do not show signs of tension release in the classroom are likely to do so in their interpersonal relationships, especially with their main caregivers when they arrive home. Once they leave school premises, they can become stubborn, resistant, cranky and aggressive, resorting to the excesses of their pre-school years. The quiet, compliant child at school may change character completely, becoming noisy, demanding, destructive, rude and overactive (Gessell, Ilg & Ames 1968).

At five, children are quite co-operative in group situations and seek permission before they act. They may begin to enjoy caring, protective relationships with younger siblings who previously aroused strong feelings of jealousy. However, they need a lot of help to adjust to the arrival of new babies. This help may include the provision of soft family dolls for the safe release of feelings of hostility. Therapeutic play activities, such as sand, fingerpainting, water, woodwork and clay, should be available. Parents often forget that nine months can be an eternity in a child's life. With the early confirmation of pregnancy, parents sometimes tell their children of impending family additions long before young children are ready to receive the information. By the time the new babies arrive, their siblings are often tired of hearing about them. Teachers and others should avoid adding to this by asking the repetitive question, 'Hasn't your new baby arrived yet?'. They should also avoid any inference that the five-year-old is lucky to have a new baby brother or sister. Few 5–8-year-olds regard themselves as fortunate when their position in the family is displaced forever by a crying, demanding, useless infant who cannot communicate and is neither a doll nor a playmate! Family life changes to fit the routine of a new baby. Older brothers and sisters are often asked to remain quiet to allow baby to breastfeed and sleep in peace. Family friends, neighbours and relatives come to admire and make cooing noises at the pink, wrinkled little creature. They bring gifts and often ignore older siblings. Their disappointment, sense of rejection and confusion commonly result in reduced concentration and regression in school, a return to babyish or attention-seeking behaviour and complaints of headaches, stomach-aches or sickness so that they can remain at home with a parent.

Five- to eight-year-olds may worry that younger siblings are receiving treats from their parents while they are at school. They are concerned about equal rights and equal shares. They relate material possessions, such as the gift of a postage stamp and the largest slice of cake or piece of chocolate, to favouritism and affection. If these early days are not handled well by caring adults, antagonism towards siblings can be lifelong.

Some young children give adults the impression that they are devoted to their new baby brothers or sisters but are merely behaving as the adults expect them to behave. Their emotional frustration is released when no-one is watching, by nipping or pinching and making the baby cry. They need someone to express reality for them: life is different and it will never be the same again. Their parents and their siblings are lucky to have them around to help with the chores but they don't have to feel lucky or even happy about the change. They need to be given opportunities to show off the new baby in the classroom so that they can take pride in being a brother or sister. Teachers can invite new parents to bring their babies into school to be bathed and fed. The five-year-old siblings need extra and special attention from teachers, parents and other people to adapt to their new circumstances.

Five- and six-year-olds need some advance warning to prepare for anticipated events, and it is often difficult to achieve the balance between enough warning and too much. Their eating and sleeping patterns become disturbed by the prospect of a school outing, or they may become excessively shy or overactive when the long-awaited day arrives. Excitement of this kind can spoil a school outing if it results in sickness. Many an exhausted 5–6-year-old sleeps throughout a long-awaited visit to the circus.

Five-year-olds are much less brash than they were at four and there is much less 'showing off' in company. This new, inhibitory poise creates a new kind of determination to get their own way. They may become dogmatic, indicating that they alone know what is right and how to do things. It is important to recognise this as a temporary phenomenon and growth trait. If adults try to correct them or widen their knowledge, five-year-olds argue interminably, often until they, or the adults, become angry. They will often express their frustration in name-calling. If addressed sharply, they usually cry. For the most part, however, five-year-olds will hold their ground and are less likely to seek comfort from blankets and toys than they were a year earlier. Nevertheless, they need help to maintain self-control.

Some five-year-olds function badly unless they get a good start to the day. Adults can help them to adjust to less popular demands by using flexibility and imagination, enabling children to carry out the adult's wishes while incorporating their own ideas.

Fears

Frightening robber–stranger–monsters dominate the fears and dreams of children from 5–8 years. (Briggs & Hawkins 1993). Everyday bedroom furnishings, lampshades and even dressing-gowns hanging behind doors become animated when drowsy children peer through the darkness. Shadows often assume human shapes. The rustling of leaves and branches of trees touching walls give the impression that robbers are coming to steal them.

When children go to bed unaccompanied, they may peep under their beds or in their wardrobes when no-one is watching. These investigations require a great deal of courage because the children have to steel themselves to the possibility that someone might be hiding. At five to six years, children commonly talk in their sleep and sleep disturbances may result in sleep-walking. Nightmares are often repetitive, involving being chased by imaginary creatures and humans. Few children realise that they could ask for a low-watt shadow free night light or torch. These facilities increase children's confidence substantially.

Fears increase when children reach the age of six years. In a study of 378 Australian and New Zealand children, Briggs (1991, 1994) found that 69 per cent of children were most afraid of ghosts, monsters and strangers/robbers. They were also very afraid of 'people who dress up as monsters and wear sheets and masks'. This has particular significance for schools planning Halloween activities. Although children enjoy dressing up and frightening or teasing others, they are often terrified of television programmes or real-life situations in which people peer through masks which present an evil appearance and prevent recognition (Briggs & Hawkins 1993).

At six years, 69 per cent of Australian and New Zealand children were afraid of violence. One-third referred to domestic violence and fears of family breakdown as well as peer and sibling violence, violent strangers and corporal punishment. Two-thirds of Australian 5–8-year-olds referred to their fear of strangers but when asked to define a 'stranger', they described men of evil appearance who steal children and take them home in their cars (Briggs 1991, 1994). The same children revealed that they trusted people according to their appearance. They trusted women with children, women who resembled their grandmothers and men with kind faces. On the other hand, they feared disabled adults and people who differ from the norm. Adults need to understand that children are fearful when they are not sufficiently mature to handle new situations. Parents and teachers should confer to ensure that sensitive and fearful children are not exposed to inappropriate academic, social or sporting pressures.

From 7–8 years, some children are fearful of situations in which they may feel inadequate and embarrassed. They are afraid of rejection by peers, parents and teachers. They are afraid of failure and may fear new situations such as moving to the next class. They still suffer from fears of the dark.

Eights try to control their fears by acting them out in their play. They enjoy playing games such as Hide and Seek which allow them to startle and alarm others although they are still afraid of being startled. Children in this age group are easily influenced by their parents' fears and television news reports which could relate to their neighbourhood or street. Multi-cultural New Zealand children referred to their fear of rape, knife fights and murder, some referring to events in their own families (Briggs 1991, 1994). Children's television viewing should be monitored by parents. This can be difficult when there are older siblings who have an insatiable appetite for violent and 'spooky' films. From time to time, adults need to encourage discussion to help children to differentiate what is real and what is imaginary. Children contribute valuable insights to these discussions.

Developmental changes at six to seven years

At around six years of age, most children undergo substantial changes in their development and behaviour. Whereas five-year-olds were comparatively well-organised at home and at school, sixes are often brash and defiant, alarming parents who don't understand what is happening. Sometimes six-year-olds give the impression that they are at war with the whole world. Overdemanding, explosive and belligerent behaviour is interspersed with dawdling hesitation and indecision as well as extremes of affection and rejection, dependence and antagonism.

The sixth year brings fundamental changes in both physical and psychological development. The milk teeth are shed and adult teeth begin to appear. The body chemistry undergoes subtle changes, with greater susceptibility to prevailing ailments such as ear, nose and throat infections, mumps, chickenpox, sickness and diarrhoea. Other major developmental changes affect the whole neuromotor system. These changes manifest themselves in psychological traits which appear at around five-and-a-half years of age. At six, children are not just bigger and stronger, they are different. Parents often complain that they 'don't know what's got into him/her recently' as new impulses, feelings and actions surface with the underlying development in the nervous system.

Some conflict is a normal accompaniment to developmental change and sixes are likely to go to extremes, especially when attempting to use their newly acquired powers or when subjected to stress. Simple decisions that would not trouble the five-year-old become complex issues involving new emotional factors (Gesell, Ilg & Ames 1968). As a result, even a choice of activity, the selection of a chocolate bar from a display in the supermarket or the choice of flavour of an ice-cream can become a major decision that results in frayed patience. 'If you can't make up your mind, you can do without. We can't wait all day', is a cry commonly heard in shopping centres. Once their selections have been made, six-year-olds are still likely to change their minds and throw temper tantrums because they think, in retrospect, that they made the wrong choice.

At Christmas, six-year-olds want many presents but may be undecided about what they want. They are often rudely rejecting when they receive something that does not meet their precise specifications. Birthday and Christmas parties are often disastrous because the eagerness and self-centredness of six-year-olds makes them vulnerable to stressful social situations with their peers (Gesell, Ilg & Ames 1968). Hosts often pounce on their birthday presents, expect to win all the prizes and then sulk, whine or throw tantrums if they don't. Many six-year-old hosts find themselves confined to their bedrooms while the party proceeds without them.

At six, children cry easily but, just as easily, the tears can be turned to laughter. The relationship of children to adults is much more ambivalent than previously, swinging from love to hate and back again with greater rapidity and frequency than before. Six-year-olds are often self-centred, obsessive, irritable, rebellious and negative as well as co-operative, energetic, adventurous and enthusiastic. They continue to be intensely curious and become easily frustrated, finding failure hard to accept (Lee 1977). Violent threats are often made at times of frustration. At the same time, six-year-olds are often madly in love with their teachers and make promises to marry them when they grow up. What the teacher says is right and teachers' standards are accepted over and above family standards.

Children's irresponsibilities should be discouraged appropriately, recognising that their aggression relates to new feelings and experiences. At this stage

SUMMARY OF STAGES IN CHILDREN'S GROWTH AND DEVELOPMENT

Physical development at about 5 years

Weight about 19.5 kg (42 lb).
Height about 107 cm (42 in).
Is agile and energetic.
Can dress and undress himself.
Can run, skip, climb, dance, jump, swing, throw a ball, and catch it fairly well, build with big boxes, planks, barrels.
Rides a tricycle very fast and can use a scooter skilfully.
Draws people, houses, aeroplanes and vehicles recognisably.
Sleeps about 10 hours in 24.

Feelings at about 5 years

Self-confident.
Boasts, shows-off, threatens but also shows friendliness and generosity.
Shows desire to excel and can be persistent and purposeful in learning a new skill.
Shows good degree of control of emotions and on the whole is stable.

At about 6 years

Vigorous and adventurous.
Uses body actively.
Enjoys using large apparatus for climbing, swinging by arms, hanging by knees.
Can somersault, skip with rope, run and jump, use climbing ropes.
Begins to use a bat adequately.
Moves to music with understanding.
Throws and catches more skilfully.
Loss of milk teeth begins.
Permanent teeth begin to erupt.

At about 6 years

More unstable than at five years
Swings from love to hate and back again rapidly.
Tends to be self-centred, obsessive, irritable, agressive rebellious.
But can also be loving, fiendly, enthusiastic, cooperative.
Intensely curious.
Finds frustration and failure difficult to accept.

At about 7 years

Active and energetic.
All physical pursuits becoming popular.
Can walk along narrow planks, balance on poles, use bats and balls well.
Dances with pleasure.
Enjoys physical education periods at school.

At about 7 years

More stable than at six years.
Independent and may be solitary for short periods.
Self-critical.
May be moody and dissatisfied at times but gradually becomes more self-reliant and steadier in all emotional expression.
Fact usually distinguished from fantasy.
Lacks control of his own energy and will become overtired and irritable.

From eight years upwards

Period of great agility and vitality.
All physical activities carried out with grace, economy and co-ordination.
Games requiring exactness such as hopscotch, conkers, marbles, fivestones, jacks, complicated ball and skipping games, roller-skating, juggling, rounders, are increasingly popular.
There is a good deal of group wrestling and skirmishing.
Hiking, swimming, running, climbing hills are enjoyed.
General health is good.
Appetite sound and food is enjoyed.
Energy tends to flag suddenly but a short rest and more food restores it easily

From eight years upwards

Emotionally independent of adults to great extent.
Need for acceptance by peers.
Deep satisfaction in intellectual pursuits.
Joy and delight in physical prowess and skill.
Usually good control of strong emotions except in mob situations.
Anxiety aroused by ineffectual adult management of environment.

Social Behaviour at about five years	Needs at about five years
Vocabulary can be up to 3000 words. Asks many questions. Often content to play alone for long periods, mastering a skill, but also plays with other children, especially in building and imaginative play. Prefers games of rivalry to team games. Group games often need adults to arbitrate. May be nervous of active older children in playground. Basically dependent on adults—parents and teachers—and needs their approval. Enjoys stories about strong and powerful people (e.g. Samson and Batman).	Calm, reasonable approach from adults who can control his rivalry, encourage his serious attitude to achievements and counter his showing-off with affectionate banter. Play material as for four-year olds. Books, stories, songs, music. Support of parents on beginning school. Skilful introduction to school life by teachers. Accurate answers to questions.
At about six years	**At about six years**
Talks freely and is still interested in new words. Is usually beginning to read. Begins to move away from dependence on adults but needs unobtrusive help, and demands praise. Is often quarrelsome with other children but shows need of their co-operation in his play. May have a particular friend. Tenacious of his own possessions. Teacher's standards often accepted, rather than mother's. Father's authority usually unquestioned.	Much patience from parents and teachers. Firm control over daily routine within which he can be allowed much freedom to enquire, experiment and explore. Environment at school and at home rich and stimulating. Encouragement for his efforts and praise for his achievements. Play material which requires skills—Meccano, Lego, train sets, dolls' dressmaking, knitting, cooking, puppet-making, drawing, painting, modelling. Arrangements for adequate rest and sleep.

At about seven years	At about seven years
Reads a good deal, enjoys writing his own stories. Watches television with comprehension and appreciation. Depends less on adults except for specific help in work. Make-believe play becoming dramatic play. Can plan and carry out projects with other children but still needs some arbitration by respected adults.	Same as for six-year-old. Protection against overtiredness.

From eight years upwards	From eight years upwards
Membership of group of own age now important. Individual desires submerged for benefit of group. Weak adults and nonconforming children despised and ignored. Mob violence may erupt if excited by irresponsible leaders. Team games, camping, collecting are popular. Boys and girls mix fairly well except for more masculine boys and more feminine girls who tend to make their own separate groups. Towards the end of this period sexes tend to separate. Rebellion against authority shown by rejection of adults, tricking them, complaining, dodging unpopular jobs, verbal battles. Competent adults are, however, respected. Towards the end of this period the child is friendly, matter-of-fact and co-operative with adults.	Opportunity to learn accurately about real world. Rich academic environment. Books, music, creative materials. Reliable, confident adults and reasonable, consistent standards set and demanded. Independence and trust. Undemonstrative, steady affection at home. Matter-of-fact, straightforward information in reply to questions. Opportunities for games and physical activities.

Summarised from Lee, C. M. 1977, *The Growth and Development of Children*, 2nd edn, Longman, London.

they need protection from themselves because they are often their own worst enemies, defining what not to do by going ahead and doing it.

At six, children are inept in handling human relationships. Behaviour with siblings and peers may change suddenly from very good to awful and from hurtful to contrite. They charge about, slam doors, bump into things, drop things on the floor and walk over them, break things and become bad-tempered and frustrated. At the same time, they are capable of intense concentration, enthusiasm and effort which teachers can channel into learning. They aspire to independence but require unobtrusive help when they take on more than they can handle. They respond well to praise and classroom management based on positive reinforcement, daily routines with freedom to enquire, experiment and explore.

Sexual development

Five-year-olds tend to ask fewer sex-related questions than they did at four. Their sexual interest revolves around having babies, especially if someone they know is pregnant or a relative has had a new baby. The question 'Where do babies come from?' may have already been answered, but the question is repeated. It is a difficult question to answer satisfactorily because references to seeds, eggs or sperm are confusing. Five-year-olds accept that babies grow in their 'mummy's tummy' and will repeat the information, without any measure of understanding, often at inappropriate moments.

Some children cling to the notion that they were 'bought at the hospital', and persist in repeating this explanation even when they are told otherwise. Some will have seen childbirth scenes on television and girls in particular may share half truths and garbled information. Many continue to proclaim that babies emerge from the mother's mouth or navel or that the abdomen is cut open and stitched up again. Few children can comprehend the mechanics of the birth process until they see the birth of pets or farm animals.

Five-year-olds are interested in babies and they love to talk about what they were like when they were babies. Girls talk about having babies when they grow up. Without adult intervention, boys will play with dolls, 'feed' them, make up their cots and change nappies. They perform domestic chores without pretending to be either mothers or fathers.

School librarians should stock books to explain sexual differences and childbirth to young children. It is important that when questions are asked in class, adults should provide honest answers without embarrassment. Books on sex education and child protection should be available for parents. Boys are curious about their own bodies at an early age and it is important that parents talk to them about masturbation and erections because of the tendency of boys to encounter highly sexual peer group environments (Briggs 1995b).

At the age of five, children have usually been taught by well intentioned adults that nudity, underwear, genitals and toileting matters are all 'rude', and 'rude', in turn, is recognised as naughty and punishable. New Zealand children said that they could not complain to their parents about other people's rude behaviour because their parents would 'go mad' and blame them. Why did they think that their parents would react so strongly? 'Grown ups like rude behaviour but they want to keep it to themselves' was the most common explanation (Briggs 1991, 1994).

Children of seven and eight said that if someone behaved rudely, they would feel embarrassed and guilty and blame themselves. This has serious implications for child protection curriculum.

Some children show a reluctance to undress in school. This may be a temporary whim. At worst, the refusal to undress can be a sign of sexual molestation. At an appropriate, private moment, the teacher should encourage the child to discuss his or her feelings about removing clothes.

When gender differences are exaggerated by school toilet arrangements, children's curiosity is intensified. After using unisex toilets at home and in preschools, children conjecture about what goes on behind the walls that now separate them. Six-year-old boys may pluck up the courage to chase girls into the female toilets, hoping to gain an insight into the secrets of the opposite sex. Teachers' reprimands merely confirm that there is something different and even wicked about children's bodies now that they are five. It may help to dispel myths if new entrants tour toilet arrangements for both boys and girls on their first morning at school.

At six, children are taking more interest in their anatomical structure but the emotional aspects of sexual relationships are beyond their comprehension. Sixes giggle and tell silly jokes about underwear. They feel daring when they use words associated with excretion and genitals. Teachers should take the rude words out of the closet and provide children with the correct vocabulary. Traditionally, parents have given children the appropriate terms for all body parts except their genitals and breasts. Some migrant parents give children ethnic words to ensure that no-one will understand them if they refer to genitals in public. Some parents provide pet names such as 'winkle' and 'pee-pee' instead of penis. Because female genitals are hidden, many parents never refer to them at all. This omission ensures that children lack the language to report sexual misbehaviour if it occurs. By their omission, parents are telling children very clearly that they cannot cope with information about the human body. This makes it impossible for children to seek help when they are worried about sexual matters.

The correct vocabulary should be introduced at pre-school level but can be taught formally in school when children draw around body shapes and label parts, or they encounter anatomically correct dolls.

At six or seven years, children are likely to indulge in harmless games of 'You show me yours and I'll show you mine', with others their own sex or with members of the opposite sex of the same age. This kind of behaviour is particularly prevalent in and around outdoor toilet blocks. Other children sometimes take advantage of the six-year-old's interest in anatomy, involving them

Figure 3.11: At eight, groups of children gang up against others

in hospital play or 'mothers and fathers'. This can be avoided by close supervision of toilets and frequent visits to playrooms, especially when children become unusually quiet.

Sixes are interested in love and propose marriage to adults of the opposite sex. There is a vague notion that marriage results in children but they rarely know how it happens. Children of this age like babies and pressure their mothers to have more, even though they may already have babies in their families. They are not very interested in pregnancy but may be fascinated by the birth of puppies or kittens.

Children in the 5–8 age group may use well established sex-role stereotyping regardless of their home circumstances. When asked about the roles of mothers and fathers, a five-year-old boy insisted that mothers stayed at home to wash dishes, cook and look after children. He had been reared by his sole-parent father-caregiver.

In a study by Martin (1989), children heard stories about a girl who liked to play with transport toys and a boy who liked domestic play. When asked if they could guess what other toys these fictitious children might like, respondents of 4–6 years based their assessment on gender stereotypes: the boy would like transport toys and the girl would like dolls. From seven years upwards, children began to realise that there could be other alternatives.

Harris and Liebert (1992) noted that some parents and teachers now make efforts not to pressure children to conform to gender stereotypes. The ideal is for people to have the positive attributes of both genders: the independence and assertiveness associated with males and the expressiveness and sensitivity of females. However, studies show that only masculine traits contribute to self-esteem, suggesting that aggression, assertiveness and dominance are still valued by society. As a result, more pressures are placed on girls to acquire male assertiveness than are placed on boys to acquire feminine characteristics (Alpert-Gillis & Connell 1989, discussed in Harris & Liebert 1992).

As a consequence, between the ages of seven and eight, boys and girls tend to stop playing together. Some boys reject all girls and any activities associated with them. At seven there may be some mutual exploration, experimentation and sex play, either with the same sex or the opposite sex, but this is less common than at six. Sevens sometimes engage in boy–girl love affairs that are based on fantasy and the notion of marrying when they grow up.

Children may be aware of their sensitivity to touch and tickling in the genital area and they are curious about anatomical differences. There is more interest in crude jokes, most of which refer to excretion. These excite because they are daring: adults are cross if they hear them. They belong to the child culture and are handed on from one generation to the next.

Eights are more curious about sexual development, taking greater interest in toilet notices and adult products in shops. It is not unusual for children in this age group to repeat obscenities to provoke a reaction from adults or to impress peers with their pseudo-sophistication. Most children inquire, 'What does...mean Mummy?' especially if obscenities are seen in graffiti or heard in the peer group but not used in the home.

There are clearly many complex changes in the development of children between the ages of five and eight years. It is vital that teachers have a sound theoretical knowledge and understanding of these changes and needs so that they can provide an environment which will meet children's needs.

TASK FOR STUDENTS

ESSAY TOPIC

There are substantial changes in children's development between the ages of five and eight. Discuss some of the major differences and their implications for the teacher of a vertically grouped class with a mixed age range.

USEFUL REFERENCES

Berk, L.E, 1991 *Child Development*, 2nd edn, Allyn & Bacon, USA.

Briggs, F. & Hawkins, M.F. 1993, 'Children's Perceptions of Personal Safety Issues and their Vulnerability to Molestation', *Children Australia*, vol. 18, no. 3, pp. 4–9.

Clay, M. 1990, 'A Portrait of a Five Year Old', *Independence*, vol. 15, June, no. 1.

Russell, E. 1990, 'Teaching the Young Child to Draw and Paint', *Independence*, vol. 15, no. 1, June.

Schiller, W. & Veale, A. 1989, *An Integrated Expressive Arts Programme*, Australian Early Childhood Association, Watson, ACT.

Observing children as individuals

CHAPTER 4

The need to observe children as individuals

Why observe?

As we noted in chapter 3, there are often extreme differences in the development of children of the same age and even greater differences in the three-year span between five and eight years. Some five-year-olds may be as tall as six- or seven-year-olds and vice versa. Some six-year-olds may operate at the same level as seven-year-olds in some areas but not in others. Children who are able to handle sophisticated intellectual challenges do not necessarily progress at the same pace in their emotional and social development. Some children will take longer than others to develop their finger muscles for finely co-ordinated work. Some will be proficient in language skills, while others will be able to read fluently but lack number concepts.

Physical differences, abilities and children's past experiences vary so enormously that common sense decrees that we cannot and should not attempt to teach all children the same things at the same time in the same way. However, a visit to any vertically-grouped school often reveals teachers using the same teaching materials, the same tasks and the same time-spans for an entire class of five- to eight-year-old children. It follows that only a small proportion of these children will learn what the teacher wants them to learn. Some will lack the necessary experience and skills to benefit from the tasks, while others will have progressed beyond the selected stage of operation and, with insufficient challenge to their intellectual capacities, become bored and troublesome. Teachers choose this teaching method because it is the easiest, requiring comparatively little imagination, preparation, planning and supervision. As they fail to meet the needs of about one-third of the class, they need stricter and more punitive controls to maintain law and order in the classroom. Another reason for engaging children of different ages in the same activity is the teacher's lack of knowledge about child development, child observation and individual differences. It is widely known that these subjects are neglected in some teacher education despite the fact that a sound knowledge of children's developmental stages, developmental needs and observation skills are crucial for the planning and implementation of appropriate learning experiences for children of vastly different abilities and characteristics.

Child observation by teachers is a process of systematically looking at, and recording, the behaviours of children in relation to their own behaviour. It is an ongoing, day-to-day task, necessary for making decisions about all matters relating to teaching. These decisions relate to:

- all aspects of the learning environment;
- the learner;
- the teacher;
- other learners;
- others in school; and, when necessary,
- family members.

The decisions relating to teaching include:

- what learning experiences to offer children;
- when to offer them;
- how to offer them;
- what materials and equipment to use;
- what limits will be set and how much freedom children will have within those limits;
- how to organise the child's day to advantage;
- how to involve parents in the classroom;
- how to group children for different activities; and
- how to evaluate their own performance and the responses of children.

For teaching to be successful, teachers need to know:

- what individual children are capable of achieving so that they can be appropriately challenged and guided;
- what individual children enjoy doing so that their interests can be utilised for teaching purposes;
- which strategies are most appropriate for individual learning styles.

To cater for individual differences, teachers must note evidence of children's:

- individual learning problems;
- understanding and misunderstandings;
- attitudes and behaviour;
- responses to the teacher's behaviour;
- responses to different teaching materials and teaching styles;
- stress and anxiety traits;
- family, peergroup and child–teacher relationships;
- developmental stages: social, emotional, physical and cognitive development including creativity.

To individualise learning, it is necessary to observe and note each child's performance in order to plan appropriately and select the most effective learning materials. It is widely known that children respond to some teaching methods and educational materials better than others: most learn best through activity and by being challenged and guided to find things out for themselves.

When teachers are in the habit of monitoring children's progress and behaviour on a day-to-day basis, they are able to detect the onset of learning problems and health problems and make an accurate assessment of children's individual capabilities. Minor problems identified and treated in the early stages are less likely to become major problems later in the child's school life.

Specific uses of child observation

Knowing individual children and understanding their behaviour

When children are anxious or distressed, their anxieties are likely to affect their behaviours, especially their capacities to socialise, concentrate, and meet intellectual demands. When teachers are aware of the symptoms of anxiety, they must look for the possible causes and work out an appropriate response within the curriculum and by involving parents and outside professionals as necessary. Teachers who do not observe children carefully often label them inappropriately, attributing poor performance to lack of ability. In addition, teachers need to be aware of children's interests so that they can call upon them to extend the children's learning.

Awareness of progress

The typical child does not progress evenly across physical, emotional, social and cognitive development. Children go through periods of marking time or even regressing before moving to the next stage. Growth will be made in one area but not in another. It is the responsibility of early childhood teachers to provide activities to develop specific areas and move children on to the next stage when they show signs of readiness. When we look closely at the diversity of skills and abilities in any single age-group, we realise the futility of trying to teach the same lesson to all the class, presuming that they are all ready to learn the content simultaneously.

Evaluating the effectiveness of teaching techniques, resources and organisation

When teachers constantly observe children, they become aware of individual reactions to different teaching strategies. Some children will respond well to problem-solving methods while others are still at the stage where they want precise instructions for everything that they do. Some children may be ready to leave the classroom to search the library for information while others lack confidence and self-esteem and need help to develop both. When teachers note, through the observation of children's reactions, that their approaches, teaching aids, materials or methods are inappropriate, modifications must be made and monitored.

Behaviours and inference

All people 'behave' in some way or other all of the time. Behaviours are triggered by many things. They are the result of past experiences and past conditioning as well as current circumstances and personality traits. In other words, something happens to trigger a particular response in an individual and it emerges as a form of behaviour. Behaviours, then, are the observable products of certain characteristics of individuals or of certain processes going on inside those individuals (Cartwright & Cartwright 1974).

Personality traits and characteristics influence children's behaviours. Such traits produce a predisposition to act in a certain way in certain circumstances. Some children appear to have been born more placid and patient than others. Some are more cheerful. However, apart from inheritance, they are exposed to life experiences that influence their personalities and responses. Some characteristics hinder while others help the learning process.

There are many possible reasons for behaviour but those reasons are rarely observable; teachers note specific behaviours and events directly preceding them but they often have to infer the processes and characteristics that triggered them. A sound knowledge of child development enables them to draw inferences, reach conclusions and act upon them. In other words, even though they did not see the preceding process, they can make an informed judgement on the basis of the child's behaviour and their own knowledge. Successful observation, then, depends upon accuracy of interpretation which, in turn, requires an up-to-date theoretical knowledge of child development. Teachers can never be sure of the accuracy of conclusions based on inference, but they are more likely to be right if the inference was reached after careful observation of behaviour.

Observers' biases

The strongest criticism of observational techniques is that they all involve a certain amount of subjectivity. When we are working with young children, however, there is no better way of gathering essential information about learners, teachers and events. There are certain known tendencies and biases that observers need to consider before embarking on observation.

Perceptions tend to change after events. Delays in recording often result in inaccuracies. Notes should be made as soon as possible after the child has been observed. This may necessitate carrying a pocket notebook and pencil around the classroom.

There is a tendency to give a higher rating than is deserved when the observer approves of the behaviour of the child. This is often referred to as 'the halo effect'. It leads teachers to judge children mistakenly as highly intelligent or dull when they merely conform or fail to conform to the teacher's values and expectations relating to their dress, self-expression, family background or willingness to undertake tasks. Furthermore, teachers who view children in positive terms tend to dismiss deviations as occasional, atypical occurrences that can be ignored. Because they do not look for deviant behaviour, they do not see it when it is present. Looking back to their own schooldays, most readers will recall the 'teacher's pets' who were presented as the epitome of perfection for everyone to emulate. The rest of the class was all too aware of the imperfections of these individuals and realised that the 'halo' effect was the result of the teacher's myopia.

For the same reasons, there is a tendency for teachers to give a lower rating than is deserved if the observer dislikes some aspect of the behaviour, appearance or background of the child. This often leads teachers to mistakenly attribute a lack of ability to children on the basis of their disruptive behaviour in class, their dirty clothing or poor family circumstances.

Similarly, in the collection of anecdotal records, some observers only record approved behaviours exhibited by children they like and negative behaviours exhibited by those they dislike. These errors may occur subconsciously because the recorder is editing the observation and evaluating the behaviour simultaneously. Observers have to be sensitive to their own behaviours and modify them as necessary.

Divergent thinkers are often discredited if they show creative thinking in response to questions when teachers have only considered one answer as the 'right' answer.

Teachers often reach overgenerous conclusions when they are assessing the impact of their own work, especially if they want to find that the method they use is successful. Similarly, they tend to be unduly severe when observing and inferring the effectiveness of methods that they do not like. This trend is especially prevalent when teachers are pressed into using new equipment, new curriculum or new teaching methods.

The fact that the observer approves or disapproves of some aspect of the child's behaviour can influence the observation and the recording. Observers may think that some behaviours are more important than others, and these value judgements affect the checklists.

There is a tendency for teachers to make errors by relating unrelated characteristics. If a child has a history of excelling in one area, the teacher may view other aspects of the child's performance unrealistically. In other words, observers sometimes have preconceived ideas about relationships between characteristics.

If observers are in a bad mood, the observations are more likely to be negative and subjective than if they were collected on a good day.

Teachers' observations and inferences may be influenced by their expectations and impressions. Unbeknown to a class of tertiary students, one of the authors asked a colleague to come into the seminar room for two minutes. The colleague carried a pile of papers in her hand and complained, at some length, of the inefficiency of the administration. She wore a distinctive apricot coloured dress and her dark-brown hair was worn in a soft, casual style. When she left the room, students were asked to record their observations. In every case, the students edited them and made inferences. They assumed that the lecturer was the senior academic when, in fact, she was the junior. This assumption was based on the confidence with which she entered the room, her middle-class mode of dress, the criticisms they had overheard and the pile of papers in her hands. Their perceptions of a strong personality influenced their visual memories and they recorded that she was dressed in strong colours, predominantly purple, and had red hair tied back in a severe style.

To ensure objectivity in observations, teachers should involve other people in checking their findings from time to time. They can involve colleagues sharing an open work area, teacher aides, student teachers or suitable parent helpers.

Teachers often fall into the trap of observing and evaluating only certain types of learning, that is, those easiest to assess. The result is that teachers are usually able to produce information about children's test results but lack information about social interaction, numeracy and language development. Comprehensive information is only possible when a variety of recognised observation procedures is used.

Students often underrate the value of observation and record-keeping. They complain that they 'don't have time to write it down'. Apart from the difficulty of retaining large quantities of detailed information, unless observation is undertaken in a systematic and disciplined way it loses its accuracy and usefulness. Biases cannot be eliminated entirely in child observation but they can be controlled if observers are aware of them.

Observing children

One of the most difficult skills for the teacher to learn is the ongoing observation of children while in charge of the class. Although there is some emphasis on observation during training, the observation role is not left behind at graduation but continues throughout the teaching career. Good teachers are those who can distance themselves from what the children are doing and see themselves as others might see them. They ask themselves frequently, 'What am I expecting these children to learn right now? Why do I want them to learn this? Is it worth learning? Is it appropriate to their various levels of development? Where does this activity fit into the individual child's learning process? Which children are interested and working to capacity? Which chil-

Figure 4.1: Students are often asked to observe children out of context

dren are not? Why aren't they?'. These kinds of questions have to be asked daily to avoid the purposeless 'busy work' that occupies and wastes so much time in junior classrooms.

Good teachers not only observe the children in their class, they observe the responses to their actions and adjust them as necessary. They have the flexibility to change their plans when they don't work or when an opportunity arises for spontaneous teaching.

Student teachers complain that they find observation 'boring'. That is because they are often asked to sit in a corner of the room and observe children out of context with no opportunity to plan or implement a programme based on their observations; in other words, they are asked to observe for observation's own sake. When we encourage such practices at pre-service level, students are apt to make the mistake of thinking that their ability to observe is all that matters. The reality is that observation without action is futile.

Practising teachers do not have the time to withdraw to a corner of the classroom to write observation notes. They observe while they teach, jotting information on small pads in their pockets or on record cards in their files so that at the end of the week, the month or the term, they can see quite clearly how a child is progressing and which skills need strengthening. One of the problems for the student is to 'unlearn' the pupil perspective in order to make the transition to the teacher role. The latter sees the class quite differently to the pupil. Children face the problems of performing to the requirements and expectations of their teachers. The major element, for them, is to react to what they perceive to be the adults' demands. As we have already noted, these demands may be oblique or they may be stated clearly. For children, the classroom is a social situation marked by constraint. In the early stages, the pupil's task will be to test out the precise nature of the controls to see how much freedom there is within the adults' framework.

The teachers' problems are quite different. They have to define the situation and set the pace, making sure that what they want to happen actually happens. The initiative is in their hands. To succeed, they have to know whether the material they planned to teach has actually been taught. Teachers cannot assume that exposing children to information results in learning. In practice, nothing has been taught unless it has been learned.

Fortunately, observation skills improve with practice. Once teachers have acquired the observation habit, it becomes second nature. They need to decide which observation technique will facilitate the collection of the required information. Teachers of young children cannot learn all that is necessary by asking questions, nor can they use the personality tests and questionnaires favoured by some teachers of older children. The most practical technique for the day-to-day gathering of information involves on-the-spot recording of what children are doing and saying and how they feel about their world and their place within it. Teachers need to know how children function. They need to understand the quality of their interpersonal relationships as well as their capacity to work with different materials. They need to understand how and why children behave in specific ways and say specific things. Innate characteristics are a predisposition to certain behaviours in certain circumstances. Teachers cannot directly observe the predisposition but they can observe the behaviours. The knowledge gained about children's characteristics can be useful in making decisions about what they do in the classroom.

The observer observed

Students and teachers intent on observing children must always remember that they, too, are being observed. Irrespective of status, age and gender, our presence in a classroom creates an impact on the occupants' perceptions of us, each other and themselves. When we first enter a classroom, children are primarily concerned about who we are and why we are there. In other words, they are concerned with our status. Students and lecturers are often mistaken for relatives of the teacher or other class members. 'You're like my granny', said a six-year-old, greeting the author warmly. 'She's like my granny, too', chipped in a second child, not to be outdone. The comments lost some of their charm, however, when the first child added, 'My granny's dead'. The second one added, 'So is mine'.

In the long term, who and what we are is secondary to our personal identity. Long-term ripples are caused not by our status, but by our own attitudes and behaviours. These, in turn, affect children's perceptions and responses. It is important for students and teachers to sense children's responses to different aspects of their own behaviour and personalities, monitor the events that precede negative feelings and examine possible changes. In other words, when we talk about observation, we do not simply mean watching children and recording their behaviour in the classroom. We need to consider the possible causes and attempt to understand our own related feelings and responses. We have to admit that we become angry and frustrated in specific situations. We have to identify the children that we particularly like and dislike and the range of behaviours that please and irritate us. Only by making these admissions can we modify our own behaviour to change relationships. 'Sensitivity to the way in which children, their parents and teachers respond to our presence can be the key to the underlying structure of the situations themselves' (Walker & Adelman 1975, p. 9).

Entry into classes will have varying levels of effect. The variation can be attributed to differences in teaching methods, the personalities of teachers, social factors, children's previous experiences and our own behaviour. We modify the way in which we present ourselves on a day-to-day basis according to the situations we face and our notions of the expectations of others. We may talk to children differently depending on whether we are being overheard by other teachers, parents or senior staff. These adjustments are usually made subconsciously. Students and teachers have to be sensitive to their own behaviour and consciously make adjustments, monitoring their effect and modifying them as necessary.

Some precautions for preliminary observations

Generally, it is best for student teachers to position themselves unobtrusively where children's faces and teachers' faces are visible. This enables students to note the nonverbal communication, eye-to-eye contact and children's reactions. Some observations are best acquired out of sight. For example, children playing in a home corner or pretend shop will talk freely if they are not aware of the observer's presence; children also modify their language and behaviour when supervised. It is usually possible for observers to sit behind screens where they can hear children but not influence their conversation and behaviour.

While learning about teachers' methods of control, it is best for observers to place themselves in positions where they can scan the room and listen closely to one group. During any activity, the drift of conversation and involvement gives a good indication of whether children are stimulated and interested and whether the requirements are appropriate or too difficult. It is important that observers do not intrude and influence communications and activities by inhibiting conversation and movement.

Eye-to-eye contact is highly significant as a means of communication in the classroom. It is efficient as a means of encouraging and restraining individuals without disrupting the rest of the class. Students can establish a teacher presence quite quickly by mastering the technique of scanning the class and fielding long, stern glances at those indulging or contemplating indulgence in undesirable behaviour. When used appropriately, eye-scanning gives children the impression that students, like teachers, see all and know everything. Intrusive and influential eye communication should be avoided, however, when observers are recording the behaviour of individuals.

We have already noted that personal values often influence the observations of students. 'Many adolescent tertiary-level students start teaching practice with strong, rigid, moral and political beliefs which are so close to their emotional selves that they find it difficult to separate them' (Walker & Adelman 1975, p. 11). Some students are unable to tolerate the value systems associated with private, fee-paying or denominational schools and view the entire experience in negative terms, allowing their personal views to affect their observations. Others, attuned to middle-class morality, behaviour and values, are shocked by disadvantaged schools.

It is difficult for mature adults to recall how emotionally demanding teaching practice can be for adolescent students who know only their own environments and view the world in terms of black and white, right and wrong. Unless students and teachers are aware of their own prejudices, their observations and subsequent responses will be inaccurate and unproductive, if not damaging. Students often make inappropriate judgement about families when their views of human behaviour are narrow and inflexible. Parents may be branded and dismissed as feckless and uncaring on the flimsiest of evidence. Many cries for help from young victims of sexual molestation are ignored on the assumption that 'it must be that kind of family' or 'it couldn't happen in a professional family'.

Fieldwork should be viewed as a time for gathering data, not only about children but about the adults too. This is especially necessary when students are encountering a variety of new situations involving different behaviours, expectations, morals and values. Teachers and lecturers can help by giving students encouragement to discuss their feelings about their contacts and new experiences and how these feelings affect their body-language and behaviour. Did they shrink from the dirty, unkempt child or provide the needed attention? Did they avoid contact with the mother who is known to be a prostitute, or feel uncomfortable with the father who has been in jail? How do their feelings about parents' values and lifestyles affect their feelings towards their children? Do students feel differently about the children of professionals? How are these different feelings manifested in the classroom?

These aspects of observation and teaching should be discussed openly with supervising teachers or lecturers. It also helps if diaries are kept as part of the teaching practice documentation. The important thing, however, is for students to have the freedom to analyse their feelings as part of the normal observation procedure, without guilt or fear of failure. No student is perfect.

No teacher is perfect. Improvements are made by recognising imperfections and using them creatively.

Checklist for preliminary observations of the physical setting

To use the classroom effectively, students and new teachers may have to make changes to the physical setting, bearing in mind that what works for one class teacher does not necessarily work for anyone else. The following is not a finite checklist; students and beginning teachers may wish to add further suggestions. Many potential problems can be avoided by changing settings.

Location of classroom. Is it adjacent to a corridor? If so, are there distractions in the corridor? Are the partitions made of clear glass that enable children to be distracted by occurrences outside? What can be done to change this? If the classroom is in an open-plan unit, is it central or peripheral? How is it separated from other class areas? Does the noise level of other classes impinge on your class? What effect will this have on quiet work, such as stories and group discussion? Which of your activities will need to be moved to other areas to avoid interrupting neighbouring classes? What alternative areas are available? If other teachers and other classes are extremely noisy, how do quiet teachers maintain quiet classes?

Materials and facilities. How far distant is the classroom from a 'wet' or 'messy area' with water, painting easels and cleaning-up materials? Can children reach these areas without supervision? Can they walk there without disturbing other classes? If not, what arrangements are made?

What materials are readily accessible to children? Where are they stored? Are storage cupboards kept locked? What are the routines for cleaning-up?

What materials are available for use from the school store? What are the procedures for obtaining them?

Check on the availability of visual aids and teaching materials. How many hoops, skipping ropes and balls are there and where are they stored? Note the availability of outdoor and indoor apparatus for climbing and balancing.

Note the whereabouts of adhesives and brushes, cooking equipment (gas or electric?), refrigerator, waste products for collage and sculpture, scissors, woodwork, musical instruments and art materials. Are there cameras, televisions and videos, slide projectors or overhead projectors?

Check on the availability and whereabouts of games, puzzles and reading books.

Are there special rooms for special purposes? Are there specialist teachers for certain subjects? Are there times when all the classes merge for a common purpose (such as television or exercise)?

Note the availability of posters, pictures and other exhibits. How long have the pictures been on the classroom wall?

Are there pets in and around the classroom? Who is responsible for their maintenance? Do children take them home at weekends? How is this arranged?

What are the routines for hygiene, especially at lunchtime? Do children have to seek permission to visit toilets? How far distant are they from the classroom? Where are handbasins in relation to toilets? Do teachers supervise their use at recess/playtime?

Shape and size of classroom. Note the overall shape and size of the classroom and the location of fixed furniture, lights and electrical points.

Is the chalkboard sited in a position where everyone can see it or will it be necessary to move some tables and chairs? Is there sufficient floor space for activities or will more space be required? Can the adults and children see each other clearly or is there something impeding vision? Some classrooms are cluttered with artwork hung from the ceiling and adults have to bend their heads to avoid a jungle of bric-a-brac. In general, children tend to ignore exhibits after a day or two.

Emergency procedures. Note emergency procedures in case of fire as well as the whereabouts of first aid materials and routines for accidents.

Environment. Note the classroom temperature, provision for sunlight and artificial lighting and the provision for ventilation, heating or air-conditioning.

Uses of space. Students should note how the teacher uses different parts of the classroom, corridor and outdoor area for different purposes. Could this use be extended further? How does the teacher supervise children working in these different locations? Note the arrangements and rules for using different special areas, for example the library, the communal 'wet area' and quiet rooms.

Checklist for general observations of children

1 Note the names and ages of children in the class.
2 Request details of children with known 'special needs' so that these can receive your attention.
3 Note who arrives first and last and with whom.
4 Note friendship groups. Do these children sit together? Do they play together at home? If not, how were the friendships formed?
5 Who are the withdrawn and isolated children? Does the teacher know the history of the isolation? What attempts have been made to draw these children into groups? Which methods have been most and least successful?
6 Who are the class clowns? Are they bored? Do they complete tasks slowly or quickly? Observe their concentration span when occupied in self-chosen tasks.
7 Which children always raise their hands when the teacher asks a general

question? Do they have the answers or are they merely putting up their hands to appear attentive?

8 Which children never raise their hands? Does the teacher address questions to them individually? Do they know the answers when questioned?

9 Who always sits at the back of the group on the carpet for a story? Are these the children who also sit at the back of the room? Observe their behaviour. Do they concentrate on what is happening? Do they respond to questions? Do they distract others?

10 Which children always sit close to the teacher? Do they touch the teacher? Do they concentrate?

11 Which children 'tell tales' more than most? How does this activity relate to their sociability and achievement in class?

12 Which children are asked to bear messages for the teacher? Are the same children chosen consistently or are roles shared?

13 Is there any negotiation over the allocation of communal tasks? How does the teacher decide who helps to mop up the floor and wipe down tables? What efforts are made to ensure that jobs are not allocated on sexist lines?

14 Are there any official or unofficial sub-groups within the class? On what basis have the groups been formed? Do they relate to parent friendship groups, social class, shared interests or the teacher's perceptions of ability and achievement? If children are allocated to different groups, how is that allocation made?

15 Who are the classroom bullies? How does the teacher manage and discourage bullying?

16 Which children claim territorial rights over certain areas? Do some children try to restrain certain others from playing in their groups or with specific materials? Do girls have the freedom to join boys when they play with blocks and wheeled vehicles? Are boys encouraged to join in doll and domestic play and dressing-up? If not, how might these situations be changed?

17 Who are the leaders in the class? How is their leadership exhibited? How does the teacher allocate leadership roles to children?

18 Which children always turn to an adult for help and reassurance, even when help is not necessary?

19 To which children are you attracted more than others? Why? Which children do you like least? Why? How far do likes and dislikes relate to your own values, differences in social class and expectations?

20 Which children exhibit poor concentration?

21 Which children are known to have special needs? Some schools exhibit their photographs in the staff room. Teachers can then see at a glance which child suffers from haemophilia, allergies, epilepsy etc. and what steps must be taken if problems arise. Enquire which children, if any, are debarred, by court order, from access to a parent following divorce. This information is necessary because of the risk that banned parents **may** approach children while they are at school.

General observation of teachers by students

1 Do teachers arrive before the children? How do they greet each child and parent on arrival? What do children do immediately after being greeted? What do parents do? Does the greeting provide a genuine and warm welcome? Are children allowed to enter the classroom directly or do they have to line up outside at the sound of a bell? How does the latter affect the teacher's capacity to welcome individuals? Note the types of instructions given to children entering school. What do they tell you?

2 Does the teacher seem to be a different person when he or she talks to children? Analyse the differences.

3 Ask to see the teacher's plans for the week and the term.

4 Ask to see the teacher's records of individual children's progress.

5 How does the teacher encourage children's independence and self-discipline?

6 Note whether the teacher uses predominantly positive sentences and positive behaviour management techniques or negative ones?

7 How does the teacher handle the situation when a child gives a wrong answer to a question?

8 How does the teacher handle the unexpected occurrence?

9 How does the teacher attract children's attention and lower the noise level? Does he or she use positive or negative punitive methods? Note the method used and the effects.

10 Note the occasions when teachers settle disputes in such a way that both parties emerge with dignity.

11 How does the teacher use quietness or silence as a method of communication?

12 Note how questions are used to ascertain whether children have learned what the teacher aimed to teach.

13 Note the teacher's varied use of voice for communicating excitement, approval, sympathy, disapproval, anger. How do children respond?

14 Assess the complexity of the vocabulary and grammar used by the teacher, especially when giving instructions. How does this compare with the language used by the children?

15 Does the teacher use particular gestures or postures indicating an expectation of change in children's behaviour?

16 Can you discern, from the use of voice and facial expressions, which children and parents the teacher likes most and least?

17 How does the teacher use children's interests for spontaneous teaching? Note examples.

18 Note examples of teachers using positive child management techniques to change unwanted behaviour.

19 Note examples of teachers referring to children's emotions and show the circumstances in which these references were made.

There are many other aspects of teaching that are worthy of note and emulation. Students should be capable of observing the effects of what is said and done in the classroom, rejecting the negative and learning from the positive.

Methods of collecting observational information about children

There are several ways of recording children's behaviour, depending on the purpose of the observation and the situation observed.

Log books or diaries

At intervals during the day, the teacher makes records of outstanding occurrences. Comments are likely to include the activities selected by different children. This is necessary for several reasons:

* to ensure that certain children do not choose the same activity repeatedly, avoiding other experiences;
* to take note of how many activities are chosen by children, especially those who have short spans of concentration;
* to become aware when a child chooses an activity for the first time;
* to note signs of emotional disturbance;
* to become aware of individual problems and achievements in the development of literacy and numeracy, science, etc.

Some situations will require attention to the duration of certain behaviours. It is important, for instance, to know how long an emotionally disturbed child remains in therapeutic activity such as water-play. It may also be important to know how many times a child does something within a specific period of time.

At the end of the day or week, the teacher transfers information to children's individual record cards.

Specimen descriptions

These are records of continuous behaviour sequences which include not only the child's behaviour but the physical setting and the outside influences on the child. Such a technique can be helpful when a teacher must focus on one child or a small group of children who display behaviours which need thoughtful management.

Event sampling

This is an observational method that looks in detail at the events which occur, usually within groups of children. The teacher decides ahead of time which event will be observed and establishes focal points for obtaining more detail. Checklists can be part of this method, which may be especially useful if the teacher wishes to monitor the participation of boys or girls in a particular activity, such as construction play, transport equipment or domestic play.

Description of life setting

These are descriptions of observed behaviour as affected by environmental settings. Comparisons are made of children's behaviour when they change from one setting to another or when the teacher changes his or her behaviour or teaching method.

Collections of work samples

Many teachers keep files on individual children, collecting samples of their work to demonstrate their progress, abilities and levels of understanding. The file contents are dated and shared with parents, either informally or at formal parent-teacher sessions.

Counting behaviours

This method is useful when behaviours can be clearly defined and clearly seen. For counting, the teacher and student need to draw up a frequency record along the following lines.

NAME OF CHILD ....

DATE OF BIRTH ....

BEHAVIOUR OBSERVED: Incidences of excessive clinging to the teacher

Date	Tallies	Total
April 1	IIII	4
April 2	IIIII I	6
April 3	IIIII II	7
April 4	IIIII IIIII	10
April 5	IIIII IIIII II	12

Such a tally might show that the frequency of behaviours increases on certain days of the week, and this helps the teacher to investigate the possible cause.

Time sampling

For behaviours that occur frequently, it will be necessary to observe them carefully at certain times, perhaps for ten minutes in the morning and ten minutes in the afternoon. It may be possible to observe a child over short but regular periods of time and make predictions about total behaviour from the findings. It is vital that timing is accurate and consistent.

NAME: ....

BEHAVIOURS OBSERVED:...

Date	Timespan of behaviour From — To	Total minutes
April 1	9.30—9.55 11.00—11.15 2.00—2.15	55
April 2	9.00—9.17 10.00—10.10 11.01—11.20	47

Observation involving timespans enable teachers to see patterns of children's behaviour. Some behaviours occur more frequently early in the morning while others, due to fatigue, are likely to occur later in the day.

Bar charts and graphs

Information gained from tallies is interpreted on a graph or chart which is clearly labelled. The horizontal line provides the number of observations and the vertical line indicates the number of behaviours counted. (Graphs provide immediate information relating to the increasing or declining frequency of specific behaviours.) Bar charts can be used instead of graphs for easy identification of behaviour patterns.

Number of behaviours

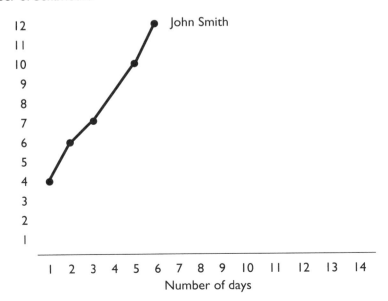

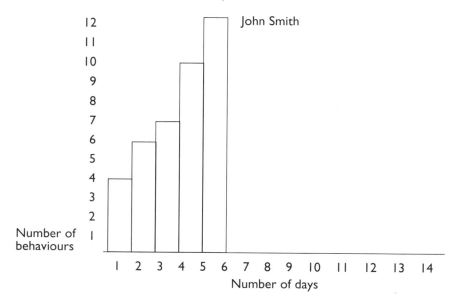

Charts and checklists

These are usually quick and easy to carry out. Teachers can adopt the list best suited to a specific teaching situation. They help teachers to remember which children have taken turns at different activities, such as woodwork, science experiments, construction work, etc. They help teachers to know which children have reached a specific stage in their physical skills, numeracy and reading. In other words, checklists indicate whether or not something has been completed by each child. They do not necessarily indicate the quality of the work or the level of understanding.

All these techniques are useful for particular purposes. The teacher decides that he or she is going to observe and then decides which technique is most appropriate for that particular situation. Most teachers use a combination of techniques to gain a thorough understanding of children's needs.

Checklists to show the activities and progress of individual children can be made in a variety of ways. By using checklists, teachers can see at a glance whether children are learning and gaining a balance of experiences.

Similarly, checklists for literacy and numeracy will provide the teacher with a clear understanding of children's stages of development.

Teachers will make lists according to their objectives and their expectations of children's progress.

A participation chart may be useful to check which children engage in particular activities, for example building blocks and construction play, play that encourages language development and creative activities. A standard checklist can be readily made for all these activities.

NAME OF CHILD ....

ACTIVITIES SELECTED: WEEK COMMENCING..

Activity available	**Number of occasions that the child engaged in the activity**
Balancing materials	
Balls	
Bats	
Books	
Building blocks	
Cardboard boxes	
Card games	
Cars	
Clay	
Climbing	
Collage	
Computer activities	
Construction kits	
Counting games	
Craft activities	
Crayons	
Digging	
Doll play	
Domestic play	
Drawing	
Dressing-up	
Fantasy play	
Finger-painting	
Listening posts	
Mathematics exploration	
Musical instruments	
Painting	
Puppetry	
Role-play	
Ropes	
Sand	
Science experimentation	
Sculpture	
Swings	
Telephones	
Textas	
Water	
Woodwork	
Wheeled vehicles	
Writing	
Other: (please stipulate)	

EARLY READING CHECKLIST (Adapted from Schickedanz & Molina 1979)

NAME OF CHILD ....

Progress	**Date behaviour observed**
Child understands that books have specific stories in them.	
(Child uses strategies to get adult to read so that he/she can master the story lines.)	
Child sees self as a 'reader'.	
Enjoys books.	
Child thinks you can make up a story to go with print or books: does not yet know that each book has a specific story.	
Child is beginning to understand that each book has a certain story, that print is conventional—you can't completely make up what it says.	
Child understands even more that the print in each book is specific, that print is conventional—each book has its own story and its own words.	
Child can find the page where the story talks about _____	
Child asks you questions about story or pictures.	
Child spends time in the library area reading to him or herself.	
Child reads to friends or to dolls.	

PARTICIPATION CHART

ACTIVITY ....

WEEK COMMENCING ....

Name	NUMBER OF OCCASIONS Participating
G. Adams	IIIII I
C. Bentovin	I I
A. Kornblum	III

All the names of class members will be printed on these forms.

Anecdotal records

Anecdotal records for observational purposes are brief accounts of events that are meaningful to students or teachers in relation to the education and behaviour of children. Anecdotal records can be seen as 'word pictures' of incidents, behaviour or events that occur in certain circumstances. It is important to emphasise that records must be factual descriptions of occurrences. Summaries and conclusions are only drawn from a series of such records over a period of time.

It has already been shown that there are methods of recording observations and some are more appropriate than others for particular purposes. Anecdotal methods are most useful for recording children's spontaneous and unexpected kinds of behaviour, for which checklists and charts are not available.

As we are dealing with spontaneous behaviour, the recording method is relatively unstructured. This lack of structure, in turn, necessitates a greater degree of care and self-discipline. Anecdotal records are devalued only when observers fill them with trivia or make their own subjective inferences as they record. Each anecdotal record should relate to one specific event. If more than one child is involved in the incident, separate records are necessary for each child. The incident is then considered along with the child's other behaviours and it can be interpreted in the light of the overall pattern of behaviour. Such records may reveal that the child previously perceived as a victim is, in fact, the instigator of incidents, or alternatively, that the same child is victimised repeatedly. This leads the teacher to examine the aspects of the individual's behaviour that contribute to victimisation and how these behaviours can be changed.

Because teachers observe 'on their feet', it is rarely possible to make the anecdotal record as it occurs but notes or cassette tape-recordings should be made as soon as possible afterwards. Anecdotal records are the most vulnerable to observers' biases, especially when selections are made for recording. Students and teachers must constantly monitor their own feelings to ensure that they are not directing their attentions on behaviour or children that particularly displease them and behaviours that are not typical for that observed child.

The dangers of anecdotal records lie in the bias of the recorder and the ways in which incidents are perceived. Their advantage lies in the fact that they require no formal preparation.

How to avoid subjectivity in recording

1 Choose words, carefully avoiding personal interpretation and the use of adjectives, for example:
   - 'Kim was playing alone in the construction area' is ACCEPTABLE, whereas

- 'Kim was playing quietly and happily in the construction corner' is subjective and UNACCEPTABLE. It is unacceptable because it involves an interpretation or misinterpretation of Kim's feelings at the time. Similarly,
- 'Kim said, "Give that to me"' is ACCEPTABLE, but
- 'Kim was angry and shrieked "Give that to me"' is NOT ACCEPTABLE.

Other descriptive words such as 'whispered', 'sulked', 'chattered', 'screamed' and 'shouted' should also be avoided, especially if they are not relevant to the observation.

Children's subjective comments should be recorded exactly as they were said with no additions or subtractions, such as 'I'd like to put Tim in the garbage bin and put the lid on him'.

The interpretation of anecdotal records should be kept quite separate from other recordings. Interpretation is most meaningful when there are a number of recordings to consider, for example:

NAME: Julie Wang

DATE: 2/5/89
INCIDENT:
Julie selected the puzzle that she completed yesterday. She placed all the pieces in the correct order then pulled it apart and completed it again, repeating the process several times.

DATE: 3/5/1989
INCIDENT:
Julie selected the same puzzle as yesterday and repeated the pattern of making it, destroying it and remaking it.

DATE: 4/5/89
INCIDENT:
Julie selected the same puzzle as yesterday. I invited her to try a new puzzle. She said 'No'. I took a new puzzle from the shelf and asked Julie to help me make it. Julie said 'No' and returned to her own puzzle.

Interpretation: To reach any satisfactory interpretation, it will be necessary to observe Julie more systematically and closely. Is she physically or emotionally unwell? Does she lack the energy to respond to new challenges across the curriculum? Is there a general pattern of avoiding new activities? Does this relate to a lack of self-confidence in general? When more data is collected, the teacher should plan and evaluate changes of approach, which may include contacting parents.

Reviewing several anecdotal records made over a period of time for the same child, teachers are in a better position to judge their importance and assess whether they represent typical or atypical behaviour. It is difficult and often unwise for observers to attempt to interpret separate incidents. Summaries, interpretations, actions and results should be stored in children's personal files.

Students tend to waste time recording children's conversations and incidents that are trivial and useless. Some selection has to be made about what to record and selection should limit records to matters affecting decisions about:

- what and how to teach individuals;
- signs that the activities provided are appropriate or inappropriate; and
- signs of social, emotional or physical ill-health and adjustment problems.

Students and teachers sometimes reject individual record-keeping as unnecessary and onerous. The task of recording observations for a whole class may indeed seem insurmountable but it imposes a discipline on students and teachers alike, forcing them to look carefully at both children and their own behaviour. Without this form of discipline, observations are often spasmodic and subjective and teachers find, at the end of the year, that, among other things, they know little about the quiet, compliant children who have made no demands on their time and they have no clear perception of their own effectiveness as professionals (Cartwright & Cartwright 1974, chapter 5).

There are a number of texts available dedicated to the acquisition of observation techniques. Most were published in the 1970s. Student and teachers interested in gaining more information should consult the following:

Cartwright, C.A. & Cartwright, G.P. 1984, *Developing Observation Skills*, 2nd edn, McGraw-Hill, USA.

Cohen, D. & Stern, V. 1978, *Observing and Recording the Behaviour of Young Children*, Teachers College Press, NY.

Moyer, J. 1986, 'Child Development as a Base for Decision-Making', *Childhood Education*, May/June, 1986.

Nicolson, S. & Shipstead, S. 1994, *Through the Looking Glass: Observations in the Early Childhood Classroon*, McMillan, New York.

Walker, R. & Adelman, C. 1975, *A Guide to Classroom Observation*, Methuen, London.

Wragg, E. 1994, *An Introduction to Classroom Observation*, Routledge, London.

TASKS FOR STUDENTS

1 Draw up a participation chart for the children in your class, listing all available activities in which there is free choice.

2 Draw up a progress chart for a five-, six- or seven-year-old to show individual progress in the development of mathematical concepts.

3 Collect a series of anecdotes for a child who is thought to be lacking in self-confidence. Summarise, interpret them and make recommendations. Discuss your efforts with the class teacher.

4 Collect a series of anecdotes about a teacher and summarise them. When possible, share your interpretations with colleagues or lecturers to see if there is basic agreement on the findings.

Catering for children as individuals

A classroom which facilitates individual learning must be consistent and well-organised. Each child needs to know what is expected of him or her, how much time is available and what he or she must do when the task is completed. The teacher who makes these lesson plans and implements them must be cognisant of individual concentration spans, capabilities, needs and interests so that children are challenged appropriately and can work independently at their various levels. The teacher decides how work is assigned to children, how completed tasks will be checked and how children's on-task application can be maintained. The teacher must therefore have a realistic understanding of how much work a child can be expected to complete in a day, what resources will be necessary and how these resources might be best arranged for easy access and minimal confusion.

Whatever organisational procedure is adopted, it is imperative that all children are familiar with it. It is also important that the teacher monitors the success of the procedures through careful and systematic observation and record-keeping, as discussed in chapter 4.

Setting children to work

Teachers usually have specific tasks for children to do, for example a science experiment or some research on a particular topic, as well as more general work which carries with it greater freedom of choice. In the first instance, teachers may assign specific work tasks by blackboarding instructions, distributing instruction sheets, displaying work charts or simply making an announcement. A daily bulletin board is an effective way of assigning both specific and general work tasks to competent readers, while individual instructions may be given to each child at the conclusion of his or her work conference with the teacher. Where children have folders or assignment books, directions for further work may be written or individuals may have a notebook where daily records and instructions may be kept. Some classes make good use of 'pigeon holes' or mail boxes where the teacher may leave personalised instruction sheets or a note identifying specific tasks to be undertaken, completed or re-done by a child. With this organisational procedure, the teacher identifies the specific tasks for the whole class or individuals with learning objectives clearly in mind and necessary learning materials close to hand. Individual children will respond to the tasks according to their ability, taking the required amount of time. It is imperative for the teacher to constantly monitor the group, offering the necessary guidance to keep children on task, to assist where problems arise, to extend where necessary or to modify where the appropriateness of the task is questionable. Knowledge of each child's development and interests is therefore fundamental. As there are a variety of activities being undertaken at any one time, the teacher must keep precise and informative records. These may be in the form of a checklist for each child, with room for a qualitative comment. Certainly a class checklist is helpful to indicate, at a glance, which tasks have been completed by whom.

When assigning general work tasks the teacher may choose to use one or more of the following strategies:

- The children are required to complete some writing, maths and reading on a daily basis but the precise details of the activities are not specified and there is a strong element of choice.
- The children may be set requirements for one week; for example, they might have to complete one of the three science experiments available, finish reading their library book, make two entries in their journal and finish two maths assignments.
- The teacher may wish to vary the aforementioned procedure and require that children complete a certain number of assignments in each curriculum area in the week. This means, in practical terms, that a child could work all day on one curriculum area to complete the requirements, before moving on to a different set of assignments.
- When working with eight-year-olds, the teacher may wish to determine the amount of time that is spent on all curriculum areas, allowing the children to schedule their own day. However, the keeping of daily records by the children is imperative and the monitoring of this system by the teacher is not without its problems.
- The teacher may draw up an activity wheel and, by spinning the wheel, small groups of children may be set to work on different areas of the curriculum at the same time. At a predetermined time, these activities will then be changed around. A free activity time is part of the cycle so that all children have free choice on a daily basis. This procedure enables the teacher to plan to work with all students at given times during the week. Its disadvantage is that children do not have any choice nor, because of the time constraints, do all children find their activity continuing and flexibility in the day is lost.
- The teacher may select a focus for the week and offer a variety of activities

which directly relate to it. For example, a teacher may wish to emphasise aspects of social education and so structure the learning environment to that end. Other areas of the curriculum may be dealt with in a similar way.

These strategies are useful to avoid chopping up the child's day into separate, unrelated compartments. They also encourage integrated learning. However, teachers must establish procedures and methods which best suit their own children and circumstances. They must also evaluate them regularly.

Using learning centres

Learning centres can take various forms but they require an area of the classroom where children can go to look, touch, talk, play, write and problem-solve alone and together. The centres may have riddles to solve, questions to answer, experiments to do, worksheets, job cards, kits, bulletin boards or displays. Regardless of the form, learning centres provide the means for developing the ability to solve problems creatively through individual exploration. Learning centres allow the classroom to be child-centred rather than teacher-centred. When teachers provide self-help learning materials, they choose them for a range of activities which are designed to facilitate the development of specific learning concepts. For children, the situation has many of the characteristics of self-chosen play, as they linger or return to the materials which the teacher has chosen to arouse their curiosity. These materials must be designed to focus on the children's learning needs and interests while facilitating their explorations and problem-solving skills. As the children work with the materials in a learning centre, the teacher can interact informally with individuals, observing their reactions and questioning them to encourage problem-solving.

How to set up a learning centre

First, identify the reason for establishing a centre. It will be directly related to the needs and interests of the children, for example topics within the current theme, reinforcement of some concepts in maths, science or social education, activities associated with a current event or a special time of the year. Through careful discussion with the children, the teacher can begin to design the shape, position and content of the centre (see figure 5.1). Careful choices must then be made:

- Where will the centre be?
  - In a corner, on a window ledge, at the back of the cupboards, in the corridor, or behind a screen?
- What activities and materials would best meet the needs and interests?
  - Manipulative tasks like jigsaws, sorting and matching, games like bingo or snap;

Figure 5.1: A learning centre

    – Concrete experiences like building, experimenting, estimating?
- What materials can be made by the children?
    – Goods to sell in shops, post box, posters?
- How can the activities and materials be displayed and stored?
    – In pocket charts, files, boxes, folding screens, mobiles, tins, on a table?
- How can the instructions be given clearly?
    – On work cards, tape recordings, prior discussion, pictorial representation, bulletin boards, assignment charts, overhead projector sheets?
- How can progress be checked?
    – Self-checking devices, peer checking, centre leaders, teacher conference, check lists?
- How can children be encouraged to contribute their own thoughts to the centre?
- How will children record their responses to the activities? Will they share them with the others at any time?
- How will the teacher keep records on individual children's participation and learning?
    – Will each child have a card with all the activities listed and space for ticks and comments?
    – Will each activity have a class card upon which each child's name is written to be checked off on completion?

Figure 5.2: The Dairy Board sponsored a breakfast learning centre, which all children could use. The press provided publicity which did not damage the dignity of any families.

- Will it be appropriate to provide a series of pockets containing cards for each activity alongside each child's name?
- Will the teacher direct the children as to who will work on what activity and keep personal records of children's involvement and progress?
- Will the children have a contract of work to be completed in a day or a week?

A learning centre in action

Swallowcliffe (Elizabeth) Junior Primary School, South Australia provided a choice of twelve different learning centres to each class from 9 a.m.–12.30 p.m. daily. The centres were planned and prepared by a group of teachers, led by the deputy principal. At the beginning of each day, class teachers discussed the challenges that would be available and children made their personal choices. Each child was responsible for a personal file which acted as a record of completed tasks. The teacher ensured that children experienced a wide range of activities during the course of the week.

Children checked into their chosen learning centre by clipping their personal, named peg onto the number assigned to each learning centre. Group membership was limited to four pegs a centre at any one time.

Learning Centre Number 1 was the ever-popular food centre. Children

Figure 5.3: Four pags at learning centre No. 3 and face painting is underway

made toast, scrambled eggs and learned about nutrition in a programme designed to alleviate the effects of poverty in a low socio-economic area.

Centres offered a wide range of activities involving music, literacy, numeracy, science, creativity, computers, craftwork, drama, etc.

At the end of each session, the teacher and children discussed what was achieved during the morning. Children's records were checked. Learning centres have been found invaluable in Educational Priority schools. Since their introduction, children have developed greater levels of self-discipline, self-motivation and concentration.

The centres help to individualise learning for children by enabling them to pace themselves, selecting activities and completing them at an appropriate rate. When children experience success in solving problems or mastering skills, it enhances their self-esteem, which is a strong motivation in learning. Learning centres allow for active participation by children and therefore are a natural extension of children's play. Young children do not learn best by being told but by building up understanding through active participation and appropriate questioning. They may be encouraged to become more independent in their learning by having some control of their choices and setting their own goals. The use of learning centres is said to have a humanising effect on difficult classrooms because they are variable and readily adaptable to children's individual differences in learning style. Centres permit freedom of physical movement about the room for children, and this is a distinct advantage for those in this age range who find it very difficult to sit still for prolonged periods of time. The use of such centres enables children to work in varied social groupings in and out of doors. Finally, the use of learning centres can reduce discipline problems because the method is generally well suited to the ways in which children characteristically play and learn.

Using contracts

Contracts or work agreements can be used to both integrate learning across the curriculum and to eliminate or at least modify the typical time schedule. The teacher determines the unit of work, decides the learning objectives and then clearly describes the work to be covered by individual children. Instructions are usually given on a contract form which has space for the date set, due date for work and signatures of teacher and child. Such contracts resemble programmed learning and may be on a daily or weekly basis.

On the other hand, the individual child may participate in the negotiation of a contract which could be used for specific tasks such as might be expected in maths or science, or which could be used for work to be completed in a week. The level at which a child will negotiate with the teacher largely depends upon his or her previous experiences. At one end of the continuum, the teacher may decide on the topic, make some suggestions as to how the topic may be explored, ask some open-ended questions and identify ways that the information may be reported. The child may then begin with this contract and modify it slightly as personal questions and interesting digressions arise. At the other end of the continuum, a child may wish or be encouraged to explore a topic of interest, pose his or her own questions and decide how to answer them and report back. For example, if a child shows interest in a television programme relating to flight, wild animals or other suitable topics, these interests can be developed by contract work. The teacher is a guide and resource person. Such contracts must be discussed with the teacher before work begins to ensure that the questions posed are worthy of investigation and to identify related aspects of the topic which have not been considered by the child. When using contracts in the classroom, teachers must be skilful in observation, conferring and record-keeping, as individual children respond in different ways. The inexperienced child or unmotivated child, for example, may think that the minimum tasks outlined are the only tasks that must be done in a week. Teachers must be careful, too, that contracts address integrated learning across the curriculum rather than focus on 'reading, writing and arithmetic'.

Very young children are likely to need far more support than older children where their literacy levels are lower, their awareness of time is more confined to the present, their organisational abilities are still in need of fine-tuning and their management of independence requires much adult guidance. Teachers who want to use contracts must be sensitive to the devel-

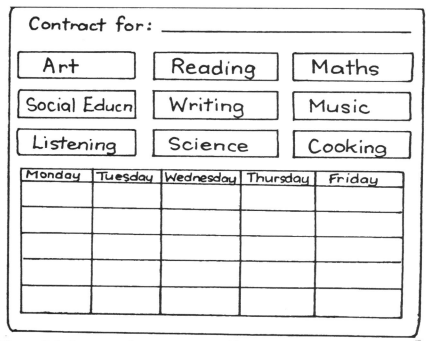

Figure 5.4: A contract for a seven-year-old

opmental levels and consequent needs and abilities of the children with whom they are working.

Using assignment cards

Some teachers use cards suggesting activities to be undertaken, either as part of their teaching programme or to be undertaken when other tasks are complete. The cards may be prepared for any aspect of the curriculum and must be clearly set out so that children can follow the instructions and work independently. For very young children graphics are crucial, giving support to a minimum of words.

The basic aim of assignment cards is to offer children learning experiences which will reinforce concepts that have previously been introduced. The questions need to be open-ended to encourage and extend thinking and problem solving. However, if an activity has one and only one answer, questions may be written on the back of the card so that children are self-sufficient in terms of checking their work. Teachers may like to put extension questions beneath the answers to encourage further exploration. The types of activities appropriate for activity cards are many and varied. Where the focus is on specific concepts, then puzzles, riddles, brain teasers or experiments may be relevant. Where specific information is required, the teacher needs to ask closed questions which may be answered by simple research of readily accessible resources, for example: how many people live in London? Which city has more people—Auckland, New York or Sydney? How long is the life cycle of a butterfly? What are the stages in that cycle? Who wrote the story *The Wind in the Willows*? When and in what country was the book published?

Activity cards should be laminated and made as attractive as possible, written boldly and succinctly with pictures or illustrations as a contextual support. All cards should have a title, for example 'Experimenting with Mirrors' or 'Making a Mask'. Those relating to the same topic or area of the curriculum may be colour-coded. This facilitates easy filing, checking and referencing for children and teachers. Cards must be accessible so that individuals can make their own choices. When teachers wish to develop a topic or concept sequentially, cards need to be clearly numbered. It is most useful to leave some blank cards in the file so that children can enter their own additional activities.

Assignment cards are a valuable and flexible resource to use when catering for the needs of individual children, either as an integral part of the programme, or as an extension or for remedial work. They can be used by individuals, pairs or small groups or they may be the basis of free activity. Assignment cards offer children opportunities for active participation (or interactive participation where groups are concerned) in their learning, free choice and independence. The use of cards is a fine way to develop children's initiative, resourcefulness, curiosity and interpersonal skills.

Using children's interests

Teachers and students should seize upon evidence of children's interests and use them for learning purposes. For example, a six-year-old boy revealed that he had watched a television documentary about eagles in the Andes. He referred to the programme in his journal and asked the teacher how to spell 'wingspan'. With the teacher's encouragement the boy found more information about eagles from library encyclopaedias and books on birds. He looked at their whereabouts on the globe and found more information about their habitat. He then made his own book about eagles, which he used for home-reading.

Sometimes, groups of children reveal a common interest. A head teacher decided to get to know the junior classes by reading Bible stories. He started with the story of the prodigal son and soon found that six-year-olds were incapable of making value judgements and sympathised with the son who left home and squandered all his money. Interest was only aroused when the feckless son went to a farm to look after pigs.

'My uncle keeps pigs', interjected one boy. 'My grandad has a farm', said another. 'My dad works in a bacon factory', said a third. During the weeks that followed, they embarked on a project about pig-farming. They visited the piggery and the bacon factory, learned all about pig products and completely forgot about the prodigal son! Spontaneous teaching of this kind requires the courage, flexibility and imagination to postpone plans and seize opportunities for expanding children's interests while enthusiasm is high.

Using peer tutoring and cross-age tutoring

Children learn a great deal from each other. Cross-age tutoring was founded upon the notion that peers are natural teachers. It presumes that young children will respond positively to older children placed in roles of guidance and authority. Most children enjoy helping younger children as well as their peers. The benefits are social and emotional as well as intellectual.

A programme of Year 5 and 6 children together with Reception children provides a good mix, and a 45–60 minute session time once per week or fortnightly is quite manageable. Cross-age programmes function best on a regular basis since the children learn to trust and grow in their knowledge of each other through a regular routine. Young children like routines and they like to know what activities lie ahead.

Class groups which have some prior experience of cross-age work should respond comfortably to older children from Years 10, 11 or 12. Sessions with this age mix can be more product-based, if that is the teacher's need, since the older children possess more highly developed skills. Book production is appropriate with these age groups, as are large-group activities such as drama or physical education. Occasionally work with cross-age groups finds an unexpected bonus, for example, a socialisation programme for a group of under-achieving boys resulted in greater confidence and enjoyment at school after a lengthy cross-age tutoring programme with a group of five- and six-year-olds.

Carefully planned cross-age programmes demonstrate that the learning process takes many forms. Given the relation of trust with an older child, a young child will learn new skills and make progress in ways not imagined by the teacher. Obviously the extra time and assistance in a one-to-one situation, where young children receive attention from a non-threatening authority figure, is a source of pleasure to them. Here they can share their achievements and talk about their new skills with older children.

For the older child, cross-age work can be a refresher course in behaviour management. Often junior primary children are more open, their messages clearer and more succinct. They can be very frank in expressing their needs. The older children have to cope with this as quasi-teachers, not as children. Nevertheless the older children are empowered through their new roles. They are working in partnership with adult teachers to foster learning via a co-operative model.

The older children who come to assist have often been 'labelled' in some way by other teachers. Through cross-age tutoring, they are offered a chance to begin again, to be a different person and create a new label. There is also the opportunity for the older children to confirm their own knowledge. Someone who is struggling with maths and spelling can learn and relearn much basic information by sharing it with and explaining it to a beginner.

School should be a happy place and learning should be fun. Too often, for older children the joy of the junior primary class has been forgotten. In cross-age tutoring it can be rediscovered.

Preparation

The in-servicing of older children and staff supporting the scheme is of critical importance, so that the goals and rules of the programme can be clearly identified and understood. The charting and display of ideas is an excellent way of promoting the scheme and this helps to dispel the 'first-time' nerves of the participants.

Simple tasks to initiate the building of relations between children include conventional classroom chores such as cleaning bird cages and fish-tanks— tasks which normally require adult help or close supervision. With success it is easy to move to other curriculum areas, providing that older children have been sufficiently prepared. It helps to include social outings in the programme so that the children have many and varied interactions with each other. A group barbecue is normally a big success, with the advantage of having additional help from the seniors. Visits to the beach and the museum are also productive.

The teacher should anticipate possible problems. Older children must be careful about the way in which they present themselves to younger children since they are role models. They must take special care when speaking to younger children. They must not use name-calling, silly teasing games or 'put-downs' as these damage the trust upon which cross-age work depends. Older children must be brought to some understanding of equal opportunity so that there is no differentiation between the sexes. Older children may have the notion of young children as 'cute', as human toys to be played with rather than taught. In the preparation process it might be useful to draw up a 'bill of rights' so that all children understand what is unacceptable behaviour. Cross-age tutoring sessions need to be supervised carefully because some secondary school children monopolise activities. Some very young children will not work co-operatively with older children who use an authoritarian manner. Teachers have a role to play in the development of skills; peer tutoring does not merely provide an opportunity for adults to sit back and rest. Peer and cross-age tutors can be valuable in maths activities and games, listening to readers, creative writing, making personalised books, research and many other situations requiring discussion and concrete experience. As with parent involvement, however, instructions must be given to older children clearly and succinctly so that the objectives are understood and realised.

Using parents and other adults

Parent participation in the education programme will be discussed at length in chapter 11. It is sufficient to say that teachers who care about catering for children as individuals recognise that the success of their work very much depends upon the support of their children's parents. This is especially important in the teaching of child protection curriculum (Briggs & Hawkins 1994). Active co-operation between teachers and parents is fundamental to success. Not only can parents be a valuable resource in and out of the classroom but parent participation in the programme facilitates the reinforcement of learning at home and influences attitudes to school. It reduces opportunities for misunderstandings while building partnerships between children's co-educators. Children need to be able to see a unity between the two very significant groups of people in their lives.

Creating a positive learning environment

The term 'learning environment' must apply to the 'feeling environment' as well as the 'physical environment', both of which are developed as a result of the teacher's attitudes towards and beliefs about the education of young children. So important is the effect of the environment on the individual's learning and development that it will be discussed at length in chapters 7 and 8.

Summary

Catering for the needs of individual children is a fundamental responsibility of all students and teachers. Children have vastly different backgrounds and life experiences; their learning has been an implicit part of these experiences since birth. If any school programme is to be effective, it must acknowledge each child's individuality and build upon skills, knowledge, interests and attitudes. It must aim to assist each child to feel happy, secure and successful as a learner and to foster special curiosity. Teaching a class as a whole, with all children doing the same thing at the same time in the same way cannot be justified. Only by observing, listening and talking with the children can a student or teacher hope to recognise the child's individual learning strategies. Only by offering a wide selection of materials and activities can a teacher develop children's interests and motivation for learning, their ability to make decisions and choices, along with independence, problem-solving skills, responsibility, initiative, self-expression and confidence, all of which are basic to success in school and life. All this can only occur within a well-planned, stimulating learning environment.

TASKS FOR STUDENTS

Visit a classroom catering for children in the five- to eight-year age group. Observe and note the following:

1 Which of the activities available appear to be most successful in absorbing children's attention and interest? What are the children doing? What are the children learning? Why are they so absorbed? What is the teacher doing to extend children's learning? How is learning made enjoyable in these particular activities?

2 Observe and describe an example of a teacher involved in spontaneous teaching, for example, by asking questions or providing extensions for learning when a child has made a discovery.

3 Note any activity that does not seem to maintain children's interests for long. Can you account for this? Could the activity be made more challenging? If you were responsible for this class, what would you do to rectify the situation?

4 Plan an integrated learning centre to cater for the interests of some of the children in the class that you have just visited. What factors influenced your decisions in the choice of activities to be presented, materials selected, challenges to be offered, and method of presentation?

How classrooms are organised

Open education

Open education and open-plan schools

Parents and students are often confused by the terms 'open education' and 'open-plan school'. The two are not synonymous.

Open-plan schools may or may not offer open education while open education is not restricted to open-plan buildings. An open-plan school is one in which classrooms are not separated by walls and corridors. Open-plan schools were the creation of British architects in the 1960s, and as the open buildings were made available before the concept of open education, there is reason to suspect that their introduction related to building costs rather than a revolutionary educational philosophy.

The teachers allocated to the new types of school were left to experiment with different organisational and teaching methods to maximise the use of the buildings imposed on them. The designs were copied in Australia and New Zealand in the 1970s at a time when the British were moving back to smaller units.

Education authorities did not provide in-service training to enable teachers to work effectively in their new school buildings because there were no experts available. The state of Victoria introduced open-plan designs in the mid 1970s, but the nearest expertise on their use was an hour's flight away, in Adelaide, South Australia. Some teachers resisted change, improvised walls from bookcases and screens and continued to use traditional methods. Others devised completely new ways of teaching, none of which were ideal.

Most open-plan schools incorporate a quiet area for reading, a closed area for noisy activities such as music and dance and a 'messy' area for painting, cookery and creative activities. Each class has its 'home-base' and its own teacher. Some schools incorporate all age groups from pre-school to Year 6. Variations come with the organisation of the day, the role of the teacher and the freedom of children to make choices.

Two organisational systems evolved, the first of which gave children complete freedom to select their own Teaming activities. At some English primary schools there was complete freedom of movement for all pupils aged from three to twelve years. This freedom increased the responsibilities and demands made on teachers for the following reasons. Teachers:

- were allocated to specific work areas for prolonged periods of time to listen to children read or provide maths activities, art and crafts, cookery, music etc. With less variety and contact with large numbers of children across the primary school age range they gained less job satisfaction than before;
- had to cater for the needs of children with widely different abilities (aged from three to twelve years) using work areas simultaneously;
- did not get to know children because of the large numbers involved.

In addition, the organisation was complex and often chaotic, resulting in high levels of teacher burn-out and staff turnover. Younger children were often insecure and fretful and, in their wanderings, they disturbed older children at work. Parents became anxious when they found that their children were spending an inordinate amount of time engaged in their favourite activities. Some found that their sons regularly missed reading and their daughters avoided maths. Because of the numbers they were seeing each day, teachers were unaware of these deficiencies.

To overcome the problem of avoidance of curriculum, staff had to introduce a detailed system of recording. Initially, children were encouraged to maintain their own records of work but, of course, some cheated and checks became necessary. Teachers had to keep records to show which children had worked in their areas of supervision each day and what they had done. This proved to be a major task as each member of staff saw dozens of different children daily for varying periods of time. For records to be useful, subject teachers had to pass the information on to the class teachers so that they could review the progress of children in their class or home group. This became too cumbersome and time-consuming. Many dissatisfied parents moved their children to traditional schools.

A second system was then tried. Instead of children circulating freely, they were given contracts to complete specific work projects to a certain standard within a given period of time. Thereafter, they could engage in free play. The system failed because of the tendency of children to rush through their contract work at breakneck speed to acquire their freedom. Speed resulted in error which, in turn, brought frustration.

Schools began to experiment with different methods. A third system required the teachers to circulate to different work areas with their classes. It also necessitated timetabling the use of work areas, thereby removing the element of choice in activities.

Some authorities realised the shortcomings of the design and moved to double units, separate classrooms with sliding partitions and shared creative activity areas that enabled teachers to 'team-teach' and offer an integrated curriculum while providing scope for noisy and quiet activities. These designs appeared to lower teachers stress levels and provided a more popular and workable alternative for children in the five- to eight-year age group.

Open learning environments

Open education is unrelated to open-plan schools in that it can take place in any type of building. Some open-plan schools are open only in the architectural sense. We appreciate the need for open learning environments when we accept that children's learning is not restricted to the hours of 9 a.m. to 12.30 p.m. sitting behind tables or desks in classrooms, while the rest of the day is allocated to ('non-learning') play. Adults often have problems in identifying what constitutes 'learning'. Learning is something that only the children can do: teachers do not teach anything until it is learned. Children learn all the time but they do not necessarily learn what teachers are trying to teach and want them to learn.

Children learn to identify letters of the alphabet from cereal cartons and shop signs. Learning to read from supermarkets is probably more valid as an educational experience than connecting a series of dots with a pencil on a duplicated work sheet. To be successful, teachers must realise that the more authentic the learning situation, the more lasting is the learning that takes place. Children will remember and write what is relevant to them long before they reproduce the words in the vocabulary-building exercises in reading schemes.

When we visit an open learning environment, we expect to see a classroom and adjacent area that caters for exploration and discovery, articulation and recording. Such an environment is crucial to the sound development of basic skills in literacy and numeracy which, in turn, are necessary for further growth.

An open learning environment caters for all the ability levels of children in the class. It recognises that children proceed at different rates and that progress may be completely unrelated to their chronological ages. The open environment is designed to encourage children's natural curiosity and eagerness to learn. It recognises the value of relating learning to individual interests. A variety of creative approaches may be used, including the integrated curriculum (see p. 217).

The development of children's initiative and self-reliance is encouraged in an atmosphere of structured freedom. The capacity to choose, within limits, gives children the message that they are worthwhile and valued people. The teacher encourages the discussion and evaluation of these choices so that children think about what they do and what they gain from their activities.

Any early childhood learning environment should be a comfortable place in which children and adults can live and work together in harmony. Reading corners should be cosy and inviting with comfortable chairs, thick rugs, bean-bags or large, attractive cushions. Books should be displayed with their covers attracting potential readers. Popular but disintegrating books should be replaced. Large books should be stored so that they are easily retrievable. The interior of the reading bay should be carpeted and partitioned to keep out noise.

Learning centres provide the core of a learning environment (see p. 103). Any programme for five- to eight-year-olds must allocate time for the child to pursue an interest without being stopped by a bell. There is nothing more exasperating than to be engrossed in meaningful discovery or creativity only to be told that 'it's time to pack up and put everything away' because of some restriction created by the school timetable. It is particularly frustrating if the child is told to pack away merely to be projected into the school yard where there is nothing to do. Some teachers allow children to take a break whenever they feel the need, providing balls and play materials for what might otherwise be an empty play area. This is practicable when there are parents or students available to supervise the outdoor environment and the staff coffee facility is flexible.

The recess-free, continuous session was tried with success in the 1960s and recommended by Alice Yardley, author of the *Young Children Learning* series. It was practised in a few innovative schools such as Lincolnville, Victoria in the late 1970s. Most schools returned to traditional practices because, although young children preferred not to be in the yard with older children, teachers needed a coffee break and found it beneficial to mix with their colleagues.

Open environments flow from one physical space to another, using corridors and the outdoors. Learning can be spontaneous. For example, children began to make a 'big snake' from building blocks. It grew longer as more children became interested and joined in. When they ran out of classroom space, the snake began to wind its way along the corridor. When they ran out of materials, the children declared that this was the longest snake in the whole world. This was challenged by their teacher. How did they know that the snake was the longest? How long was the longest snake in the world? Where did it live? What was its name? The children were encouraged to visit the library and find reference books providing details of the longest snake, its length and habitat. They then measured their own snake, firstly by using 'giant strides', then using their feet. When they made comparisons with the book, they discovered that they needed to measure in metres, that a ruler would not suffice, and they needed a builder's tape. All their findings were recorded and their interest was extended by a visit to the reptile section of the zoo and the production of their own book about snakes. This is what we mean when we say that learning is most successful when it arises from children's immediate interests.

To the observer, the open environment is one that makes the most of the outdoors as well as the classroom. There may be flower or vegetable patches that children supervise. There is likely to be a class-made bird table and possibly a nesting box. There will be children feeding, cleaning or playing with rabbits, guinea pigs or white mice. There may be a box of eggs being hatched by the warmth of an electric light. A seven-year-old may be teaching a five-year-old how to feed the goldfish and other water creatures. There may be a small uniformed group working in a 'police station', filing pictures of wanted 'criminals' with their names in alphabetical order, typing reports on their 'crimes'. Some will be taking fingerprints and others will receive and record lost property. In role-play, they sell licences for money and keep records of their sales. They take telephone calls and write down messages. They use maths and language, reading and writing, counting and recording, sequencing and dramatisation. They may even take black and white photographs of their 'prisoners' and develop them in the school darkroom.

Another child brings in a creature to show an adult. The child is encouraged to count the legs, describe the patterns and colours on the wings and point out other features. The child is then referred to a book about insects to see if it can be identified and is encouraged to be kind to the insect and take it back to where it was found.

Children in open learning environments are not just practising basic skills and memorising facts. They are acquiring independence by finding out how to obtain information for themselves. They learn to question and discover. They are treated as people who want to learn and respond as responsible, productive, self-motivated and co-operative people. The only time that children have to be prodded to learn is when the teacher's goals are in opposition to their own. Most children are reasonable when presented with explanations as to why the teacher's goals must take precedence over their own at a particular point in time. Their co-operation is greatest when they have the facility to achieve their own goals for most of the day. Successful teachers find out what their goals are and use them to extend learning (Spodek 1971).

Varied amounts of structure for each child

Just as each child in the class is developing differently, so each child varies in his or her ability to handle openness in the classroom. As in many other aspects of children's development, teachers often mistakenly assume that children possess identical abilities in handling freedom.

An environment that is emotionally and physically safe is the only one that fosters learning. Some children cannot cope with physical openness because they are emotionally disturbed and/or come from insecure family environments. Some children are entirely lacking in self-discipline and need a more structured day.

The open classroom is democratic. Its members discuss and agree on a few reasonable rules. The creation of rules and penalties cannot be left to children, however, because they have a harsh sense of justice that leans towards 'an eye for an eye and a tooth for a tooth'. Rules should be few and clear. 'Do not move or damage someone else's construction' is essential. Children can also see the sense of 'Do not throw anything in the classroom'.

It is useful to encourage discussion on how they can make sure that no-one accidentally knocks down their construction when walking past. This usually results in the creation of a 'safe' construction area away from access routes.

Children can also be encouraged to discuss how irritating it is to be disturbed when they are reading. This calls for suggestions on how and where they can create a quiet, peaceful and attractive reading corner.

They can be involved in the formation of fair and efficient rules for clearing up.

Open classrooms have boundaries and structures, but the boundaries are shown to be there to benefit children rather than to restrict them.

In-depth learning experiences

It seems that one of the hardest teaching skills to acquire is the capacity to make learning meaningful and extensive, not just keeping children happy and skimming over information superficially. Checks for ensuring this in-depth quality are:

Encourage children to observe fine detail. When a child brings an interesting object to show to adults, encourage close observation, including the use of a magnifying glass. Help the child to describe the object in terms of patterns, colours, shades, textures, shapes etc.

Provide extensive opportunities for reading and writing. Children can listen to stories and tell stories using tape recorders. Group stories can be told or written. Teachers can provide short stories with 'What do you think happened next?' for children to complete and tell. Wall stories, large group story pictures with captions, home-made class books and personal books all provide opportunities to read to and listen to others. Children can keep records, personal diaries and write experience stories relating to 'how I made a…'. Children can make labels for artwork and construction. They can create their own books using filmstrips, overhead projectors, matching pictures, word games and crossword puzzles. Teachers can make co-ordinating listening tapes for favourite books.

Challenge children to better their own best efforts rather than compete with other people.

Challenge children to find out more about items of interest. Migrant children may return to their countries of origin for holidays with their parents or grandparents. When they are back at school, use the visits for learning, stimulating interest with 'Let's find out where he went…let's find out about how people dress and what they eat in that country…let's find out about their music'. Teachers in multi-racial cities are likely to find shops that sell international foods. Children's parents or older siblings may like to join in and help a group of interested children to find out more about their country. Assistance may also be obtained from embassies and multi-cultural centres.

Reference books should be readily available in the classroom as well as in the school library. Children should be shown how to use encyclopaedias and other reference books so that they learn to go directly to the sources. There is much greater satisfaction from finding out things for ourselves than being told by a teacher, especially if the finding-out process is introduced as exciting and 'grown-up'.

The role of the teacher

The role of the classroom teacher is that of facilitator of learning rather than the source of all learning: in open education, the child is the main source. The teacher has the responsibility to provide the resources to initiate and extend children's skills and thinking. The teacher is no longer the fount of all knowledge and children the passive listeners who write what they are told and draw according to instructions. The teacher provides the appropriate opportunities and materials to extend each child to the next stage of development. Appropriate timing is crucial to success.

The teacher in the open classroom is likely to be inconspicuous, working at child level from small chairs or the floor. The teacher moves around the room from child to child, indoors and out-of-doors. The teacher questions and challenges, encourages problem-solving and communication. The teacher requires a good imagination to stimulate and extend children's ideas, prod and stretch each child's intellect with demands that are within his or her capabilities.

Streaming by ability

The term 'streaming' is used to describe the method of separating children into classes (or groups within classes), according to perceptions of their academic abilities. This separation may be the result of tests of various kinds or at the whim of teachers. Separation and labelling can be fixed and remain with the child throughout the school, such as the separation of children into ability groups labelled as class/grade/standard 1A, 1B, 2C etc. with the 'brightest' children in the A classes and those labelled as slow learners in C grades. A more common method is to divide the children into sub-groups within a class, sometimes referring to them as 'top table' or 'bottom table' but, more often than not, disguising the children's status by the use of ingenious nomenclature, such as Eagles or Blackbirds. These names fool no-one, least of all the children allocated to those tables.

Streaming does not remove the differences between pupils' abilities in the classroom, but those who advocate the practice believe that the ranges are reduced to more manageable proportions for teachers. Schools commonly streamed children according to perceived ability until the mid 1960s. In deciding which children should be allocated to which classes, teachers gave them tests, often of their own making.

It was the British Hadow Report of 1931 that recommended streaming by ability as an appropriate method of organising the primary school. It also recommended that a primary school curriculum should be seen in terms of activity and experience rather than learning to read, write and cipher. The two recommendations were fundamentally disparate because, on the one hand, the Hadow Committee saw all children as being educable and able to profit from learning by experience but, on the other hand, it introduced a form of internal organisation that reflected Cyril Burt's notion of intellectual potential as fixed and predetermined by genetic endowment.

A preference for the latter resulted in the perpetuation of formal teaching methods and a rigidity in organisation that prevented the introduction of activity methods for another 35 to 40 years.

In the early 1950s the procedure of dividing children into A, B and C ability groups within classes and schools came under criticism when it was realised that the differences between children's abilities were actually increased by the way in which the school was organised. Researchers found consistently that children from disadvantaged homes were placed in classes labelled as 'low ability' while children of professionals were placed in 'top ability' classes. School streaming reflected the social and educational differences of children's parents and exaggerated differences in intellectual development.

The danger of streaming children in schools was exposed in Britain and the USA in the mid 1950s. P. E. Vernon (cited in Jackson 1964) recorded that children:

> relegated to a low stream to suit their present level of ability are likely to be taught at a slower pace whereas the brighter streams, often with better teachers, are encouraged to proceed more rapidly. Initial differences become exacerbated and those duller children who happen to improve later fall too far behind the higher streams in attainments to be able to catch up. They lose their chance to show their true merits (pp. 123–4).

Streaming received a great deal of attention throughout the late 1950s and early 1960s when researchers showed that education confirmed and perpetuated social inequality. J. S. Blandford's (1958) research confirmed that streaming by ability depresses the attainment levels of children in the lower groups.

Children are often allocated places according to which reading book they are given. Ambitious parents urge their children to read better and faster to get on to the top table. 'Have you heard the good news?' asked a proud mother, patting her daughter's head. 'The teacher told us that she's going onto the top table next week.' 'Is the top table being enlarged?' the author asked, 'Or is some other child being demoted?'. The mother did not comprehend the reason for concern. 'It isn't called top table', interspersed the six-year-old brightly. 'All the tables have different names. The dunces are called Turtles.'

J. C. Daniels (1961) compared streamed versus unstreamed classes over a four year period and found that the level of attainment of children was highest when they were unstreamed. Evidence showed that, in non-streamed schools, teachers were much more enthusiastic and more interested in their work than those responsible for streamed classes. The average IQ score of children increased by three points and there were similar improvements in reading, maths and English. There was a reduction in the range of ability in nonstreamed classes. The slow learners and children of average ability gained most from being in a mixed-ability group and their progress was markedly better than when segregated with others branded as 'C' or 'D' stream.

In 1962, investigations undertaken by Goldberg and others in New York favoured classes with a broad ability range. They also found that learning was influenced more by the quality of the teacher than the streaming that had taken place.

A more meticulous American study by Borg in Utah in 1966 showed that pupils in unstreamed groups developed better work habits, healthier self-concepts, a better feeling of belonging and fewer personal problems than their counterparts in streamed schools. These improvements were most marked with slower pupils.

Nils Eric Svensson (1962) confirmed that the more academic Swedish children were not disadvantaged in unstreamed classes but set the pace for the whole class.

H. Clarke (1956) found that grading by perceived attainment discriminated against younger children. They tended to be placed in the lowest streams and remained there. Although most schools using streaming claim that children can move up to higher grades, in practice they rarely do. The reason for this is that the gaps between upper and lower groups widen as they move higher up the school, and it becomes impossible to transfer children who were misplaced at the age of five.

In England, J. W. B. Douglas (1964) found substantial performance differences between the upper and lower groups after four years at streamed schools. He found that potentially bright young children were depressed by the fatalistic atmosphere of the lower grades. Teachers had low expectations of them because they were viewed as having unchangeable, low intelligence. Because teachers treated the children as dull no-hopers, they behaved as such. Researchers found that children performed according to teachers' expectations.

Sir Alec Clegg, investigating teachers' attitudes (1963), found that both children and teachers were blighted by feelings of inferiority when placed in low status groups. The 'A' grade children were invariably selected for classroom and school responsibilities and were given the leading roles on formal occasions. They were selected to represent the school. Lower group children were branded as 'stupid' by staff, peers, family and neighbours and their position in the school hierarchy was an embarrassment to them at home as well as at school. Lower-grade children complained that when anything went wrong in school, they were always suspected and questioned first. When anything went well, the top grades were given most credit.

Brian Jackson (1961) found that teachers were also streamed according to the grade they taught. 'A' grades were given the most highly qualified teachers who were ascribed the greatest prestige because they were responsible for children from the highest socio-economic group. Newly-qualified graduates and those with comparatively poor qualifications were assigned to C and D streams.

In England, the most extensive investigation on streaming, involving 7200 children, was undertaken by Joan C. Barker Lunn and Elsie Ferri (1970) for the National Foundation for Educational Research (NFER). They found that bright children developed favourably, irrespective of the type of class they were in. On measures of social and emotional development however, some relevant differences appeared. As in the research involving New York schools, the attitudes of average and below-average children deteriorated consistently in schools streamed by ability. When schools were unstreamed, children classed as average and below-average made gains in emotional and social development. Children were always aware of the streaming process and their relative positions in the hierarchy.

There was clear evidence that streaming affected their motivation toward school work. In streamed schools, pupils' attitude to school and their relationships to teachers depended on the classes or streams they were in, whereas all children related to their teachers in unstreamed classes.

The NFER research showed that the crucial factor is the teacher's attitude towards streaming. Teachers who approve of it typically emphasise academic success, irrespective of the ages of the children they teach. They also communicate their dislike of below-average pupils to others. Children who work with these teachers also show the least desirable attitudes, irrespective of the organisational policy of the school.

In New Zealand, NZCER (1984) reported that the question of whether to stream or not to stream dominated debate. A 1962 survey of Auckland teachers showed that 81 per cent were willing to classify children by perceived ability at nine years of age. Most thought that streaming would raise all attainment levels, cause children to work harder and decrease the incidence of undesirable behaviour, resulting in greater satisfaction for teachers, parents and children. In a second New Zealand study, Watson (1969) found that 75 per cent of the parent sample favoured streaming by ability, and only 4 per cent opposed it. All except two of the forty-five schools catering for these families used ability grouping.

In the New Zealand secondary schools that she studied, Cora Vellekoop (1969) also found that streaming reproduced the different socio-economic backgrounds of children's parents. In the report, *Education in Change*, published by the Curriculum Review Group of the Post-Primary Teachers' Association, the point was made that low-ability pupils benefit most when first placed in mixed-ability groups and that high-ability pupils benefit by helping others and teaching themselves how to learn when the teacher is occupied with the slower achievers. Teachers in unstreamed classes are more likely to make the effort to cater for individual differences (NZCER 1984).

From the mid 1950s to late 1960s most student teachers were acquainted with these research findings, and streaming by ability was replaced by vertical grouping. When the practice of primary school streaming stopped, lecturers removed the topic from teacher training curriculum.

Why is it a matter of concern to educators several decades later?

In recent years, teachers have not been informed of the dangers of streaming children by ability, and some are now returning to it, imagining that they are introducing a completely new concept.

Streaming is also being promoted (as a means of benefitting 'gifted' children) by administrators who are seemingly unaware of its history and disadvantages.

New Zealand Council for Education Research reached the following conclusions (1984):

1 Streaming children according to their perceived ability does not promote their academic achievement.
2 The social and emotional development of children is enhanced by placement in nonstreamed classes. Children in mixed-ability groups show healthier self-concepts, more positive attitudes to schools and participate in more activities. Placing children in lower streams results in earlier school leaving and delinquency. Anti-social subcultures flourish in these environments.
3 Streaming *per se* is less important in influencing children's development than the attitudes and practices of teachers. School policies and the physical organisation of classrooms are more readily changed than teachers' attitudes and habits. When teachers are placed unwillingly in mixed-ability classes and continue informal methods of segregation that emphasise intellectual skills, the results are the same as those from streamed classes.
4 Teachers of streamed classes do not adjust the content of instruction to suit different abilities and rates of children's development. Research studies showed that all classes were attempting to cover the same ground in much the same way.
5 Low-stream children suffer most from streaming. A common explanation for this relates to the attitudes and professional skills of teachers assigned to these classes. NZCER commented that 'This situation is in marked contrast to that of the medical world where the most difficult cases are assigned to the most highly skilled professionals'.
6 There are strong sociological reasons for mixing ability groups. If schools represent a microcosm of society, all abilities should have the chance to mingle freely. Streaming creates an undesirable elitism in schools.
7 Mixed-ability teaching is demanding because work needs to be individualised. Experienced teachers find that the strain diminishes with practice and all children benefit.

In conclusion, there are many disadvantages for children in streamed schools. Disadvantages are also apparent when teachers with pro-streaming mentalities are responsible for classes in schools that claim to be unstreamed or mixed-ability. We need to carefully examine the grouping methods used in our classrooms to ensure that we are not labelling some children as bright and superior and others as unintelligent, slow and inferior.

Teachers not exposed to early childhood ideology often fall into the habit of ascribing intelligence to children in such a way that it becomes a compliment rather than a description of only one part of their total development. This assumes that intelligence is all that we need to function effectively in society.

Traditional grouping

In a traditional school, the new entrant joins a class which consists of up to 30 or more new entrants of roughly the same age. They may have joined the class simultaneously, they may have joined on their fifth birthdays or at the beginning of the term before or after the fifth birthday. Transfer to the next class takes place at around the age of six, when most or all of the first year in school has been completed.

There are many variations of this pattern. Some authorities require children to spend three years in the lower school and others do not. The younger children may only experience a short period of time in the reception class before moving on. Sometimes all the children move into the next class at the same time or, alternatively, they may transfer in small groups at the end of a term. There is no ideal system. Each has its advantages and disadvantages.

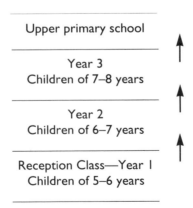

Traditional school in which the child progresses through several classes according to ability

The reception class presents a bewildering scene for the new arrival. There are new routines to learn, new rules to remember, new restrictions, new rights and privileges. New arrivals are often overwhelmed by the number of children, all of whom may be seeking help from the teacher. They all need help to learn routines. Many lose their personal clothing and their personal equipment. They may need help to find the toilet, fasten shoes or replace clothing. Some will cry for their mothers and if one new arrival shows signs of distress, others tend to follow.

New Zealand research shows that boys take much longer to settle than girls. They are less likely to possess reading and writing skills than girls and even less likely to express themselves clearly. Only half of male school entrants were 'easily understood' and three times more boys than girls had 'speech which can be understood only with difficulty' (Renwick 1984b, pp. 16–17).

Typically, new male school entrants look forward to school but have few skills to help them adapt quickly. They may recognise their own names but only 59 per cent of New Zealand boys could write them when they started school, compared with 82 per cent of girls. Boys were four times less likely than girls to recognise any of the letters of the alphabet. They could use the toilet and blow their noses (but found sniffing easier!) and had greater difficulties than girls in getting dressed.

About 85 per cent of girls had achieved independence in dressing when they started school and 60 per cent recognised, recited and counted numbers up to 10. These findings have a double significance for the reception class teacher. First, new male entrants are likely to need a considerable amount of attention to bring them to the level of the girls in terms of social skills, language arts and basic numeracy. If all the children are at the same stage of development at the same time, it becomes extremely hard and time-consuming work as teachers help to fasten a dozen or more pairs of shoes before and after lessons.

A major problem for children in traditional classes relates to change. With each long school holiday and class change, children may lose up to three months of their earlier learning. At the commencement of any academic year, teachers commonly complain, 'I don't know what they were taught last year—they don't seem to know anything'. The previous teacher affirms that when the children left her, they were competent in skills which they have now forgotten.

Holidays are responsible for some regressions but there are additional problems caused by the trauma of moving class. As when children start school, there is a great deal of peer group and family-inspired gossip about the habits and expectations of the teacher responsible for the next class. Children often enjoy alarming younger siblings with stories of hard work and horrendous punishments. Even when children are positive about the move, they have to face another classroom, seats at different tables, different routines and rules, different clothes pegs and storage facilities, different expectations and more demanding tasks.

Transfer time has been rightly referred to as the annual upheaval of 'moving up'. It imposes a serious strain on both children and teachers (Ridgway & Lawton 1969, p. 16).

There are often strong pressures from home to 'move up' regardless of the child's social and emotional development. Remaining in the same class (when the main peer group moves on) is synonymous with failure and disgrace and is only advantageous if particular attention is given to the pacing and presentation of appropriate curricula (Kenny 1994). Transfer from one class to another provides status, but when the time for change comes, there is an inevitable uncertainty, an unspoken unease. 'Shall I like the teacher? Shall I be able to do the work? I don't want to leave my present teacher. I might not like my new one.' Suppressed curiosity about what they do in the next class and what the teacher is like is mixed with apprehension about different expectations and whether the child will be competent to handle them. Parents add to the tension in much the same way as they add to the tension of starting school. 'When are you going up? If you don't work hard, you'll be kept down. You'll have to work a lot harder in the next class.'

In the traditional school, the child experiences trauma associated with major changes not once, but four times in the years from five to eight.

Some children may lose up to a whole year of learning as a result of transfer-related tension and resultant retardation. If we remember that this is also the period when children are most likely to suffer from a range of common illnesses, the potential loss becomes substantial. By the same token, any system that reduces the number of transfers must be advantageous. That is one of the first arguments for vertical grouping (or multi-age).

What is vertical grouping?

Instead of a school having three classes catering for five-, six- and seven-year-olds respectively, a school with vertical (or multi-age) grouping will have three classes, each with children of five to seven years. At the end of each academic year, one third of the group moves on. At the beginning of each year, a new intake of five-year-old school entrants arrives, constituting one-third of the entire class. This arrangement has been commonly practised in South Australia since the early 1970s but it was only introduced in Victoria in 1993.

Class A children	Class B children	Class C children
10 aged 7 years	10 aged 7 years	10 aged 7 years
10 aged 6 years	10 aged 6 years	10 aged 6 years
10 new entrants	10 new entrants	10 new entrants

The organisation of a junior primary/infant school with an annual intake of 30 new entrants

Arguments for vertical grouping

Continuity

The first and most obvious benefit of vertical grouping is that, for a child who has made the enormous adjustment from home to school, life can go steadily forward, the child growing in confidence physically, intellectually, socially and emotionally without unnecessary checks or tensions relating to 'moving up'. The teacher gets to know children better, and can recognise when they are going through unstable periods and need help.

Social development

One of the greatest advantages of vertical grouping is that children help each other. Older children stimulate the younger ones to learn and move on to the next stage. They show what can be done and set the pace. Older, confident children stimulate the development of spoken language, ranging from the incidental overhearing to deliberate teaching and reproduction. Older children read to younger ones and demonstrate the sounds associated with different letters. When young children can read, older ones are happy to listen to them and praise them for effort.

Older children teach new arrivals about class routines. They help them to pack away at the end of lessons, showing them where things go and how to clean up the tables. They tell new arrivals when it's time to go to another room for television. When young children experience difficulties in practical tasks, older children are usually happy to intervene and advise the strugglers on alternative methods.

With sound teacher models, older children develop gentle, caring attitudes towards younger children. This is especially beneficial for those who have no younger siblings at home. They patiently teach new entrants how to fasten their shoes and put them on the right feet. They help them when they put their clothes on inside out. Responsibility develops naturally and is rewarded. Older children look forward to the arrival of new five-year-olds and treat them with great patience, kindness and consideration (Ridgway & Lawton 1969).

Maturity comes from the free interchange between children. The younger ones become independent more quickly than in traditional classes, where all the children are roughly the same age. In vertically grouped classes, they copy the models they see and rapidly acquire social skills and social maturity.

Because of the help that children give each other and because the new entrants never constitute more than one-third of the vertically grouped class, pressures on teachers are substantially reduced. The five-year-olds, relaxed and confident, can play with each other and are not too numerous to receive the individual attention that they need from time to time.

When young children start reading, they want the opportunity to practise, their skills. Enthusiastic new readers should be heard daily. It would take a teacher in a traditional class of 30 children five hours a day to hear each child read for only ten minutes. In vertically grouped classes, children read to each other and listen to each other. There are no queues of children waiting to be heard at the teacher's desk. The strain is eased for the teacher when only one-third of the class is requiring special help at any one time. The purposeful learning of the more mature children can be harnessed for longer and more profitable periods of time.

Children progress at their own pace

One of the advantages of vertical grouping is that young, gifted children have the facility to move at their own pace and progress faster than in a traditional classroom. The teacher has a wide range of learning materials to cater for the breadth of abilities. There is less likelihood of the teacher holding a child back because 'he/she isn't supposed to do that until the next class'. Ideally, the slow learner should feel more comfortable in a vertically grouped class because, for three years, there will be other children present who are working at a slow pace. The teacher of a vertically grouped class has to take account of individual differences but can do so more readily when the ability range is normally very wide.

Boys who are slow to settle in school clearly benefit from the stability of the vertical group. Teachers are well aware that chronological and mental ages do not necessarily correspond. Young, bright children are sometimes emotionally or socially immature. Other children of average intellectual ability have excellent social skills. In a mixed-age and mixed-ability group, children have much to offer each other. Those with uneven development merge inconspicuously in work and play groups that suit their personal needs. There is no restraint and no scope for interpersonal competition.

School/home relations

As teachers relate to children for a prolonged period of time in vertically grouped classes, there is more incentive for teachers and parents to get to know each other. Teachers learn about the families' joys and problems and, over time, parents are likely to feel more comfortable in their involvement with school and classroom. Children always benefit from the knowledge that their parents have confidence in their teacher and school.

Children with special needs

Children who have a speech or hearing impediment or a physical disability, benefit from staying with teachers who know and understand them. The effort of adjusting to new teachers, new classrooms or new companions is even more difficult for such children. Traditional schools cope with the problems of disability by keeping the children in the same class for a longer period of time. This can stigmatise children and make them feel inferior. The trend to mainstream special children in ordinary schools and classrooms makes vertical grouping particularly valuable.

Arguments against vertical grouping

Cost

One of the strongest arguments against the introduction of vertical grouping to traditional schools is the fear that more equipment will be needed to provide for the wider age range in each classroom. Initially, the cost is likely to be more than the cost of equipping a school with horizontal grouping. Most traditional schools only provide large equipment for the reception class. In a vertically grouped school, at least three classrooms will require ready access to reception-class equipment such as water play and sand play areas, painting easels and building blocks. Each classroom will need jigsaw puzzles for all the stages of development. Similarly, story books, readers and number equipment will be needed for every attainment level in every class. Once the initial outlay has been made, the cost of maintenance is no different from that of the traditional school.

Vertical grouping is more demanding on the teacher

Criticism: Vertical grouping necessitates accurate record-keeping relating to the detail of each child's progress.

Response: Efficient teachers keep records irrespective of the type of school they work in.

Criticism: Teachers have to have a bigger repertoire of songs, stories and ideas to ensure that children do not become bored over a three-year period.

Response: They do.

Criticism: The teacher has to plan very carefully to ensure that activities are appropriate for all attainment levels.

Response: All teachers should plan for children's different levels of ability.

Clashes of personality

Criticism: Clashes of personality are more damaging if children spend three years with the same teacher.

Response: There will always be clashes between children and teachers. It would obviously be unwise to place a child with a teacher he or she disliked. Vertical grouping makes it easier to move children to an identical class without difficulty.

Vertical grouping is often resisted by teachers who argue that it could result in two or more members of a family being placed together in the same class. Although some siblings benefit from togetherness in the same class, others do not. With three classes available to choose from, there is no reason why siblings should be placed together if remaining together is not advantageous to all concerned. Sometimes it is beneficial for twins to be separated to enable them to develop as individuals. This is possible when there are three identical classes from which to choose.

Criticism: Teaching a wide age range is more difficult than teaching children who are at much the same developmental level. It is argued that it is more difficult to teach music, physical education and other lessons involving the whole class than teaching a traditional class.

Response: The difficulties are not insurmountable and there can be advantages. This was the frequent argument of teachers involved in the introduction of 'multi-aged grouping' to junior schools in Victoria in 1993. Their concern revolved around the inadequacy of the child development component in primary teacher education in Victoria, the scarcity of early childhood specialist programmes for the 5–8 year age group and the lack of in-service education to bridge the gap in knowledge relating to children's development.

The personality of the individual teacher

There are no perfect teachers because there are no perfect people. Teachers have strengths and weaknesses, likes and dislikes which affect their teaching skills. A teacher who takes a class for three years has tremendous influence over the children. Ideally, the teacher has to have a balance of interests and abilities to share with the children. When the teacher lacks interest in a particular field of learning, it is customary to team teach or exchange classes.

Stability of staff

Antagonists claim that vertical grouping fails when schools have frequent staff changes. Vertical grouping may be less successful if staff change but the children remain comparatively stable. They occupy the same classroom for three years even though they may have different teachers.

Parents' views of vertical grouping

In changing from horizontal to vertical grouping, school staff may meet bewilderment, anxiety and even hostility from parents whose ideas on schooling relate to the limitations of their own early learning experiences. In the interests of everyone, full explanations of any proposed major change in the educational programme must be given to parents. Parents should also be included in the evaluation of progress in the months that follow change. Parents need to understand the philosophy of the school, the reasons for the change in organisation and the anticipated results.

They are usually concerned that staying in the same class with the same teacher will impede their children's progress and that their children will receive less attention than before due to the presence of more demanding younger (or older) pupils.

The Directorate of School Education, Victoria, released a video, *Making the Move,* about the planning and implementation of a multi-aged structure at Cowes Primary School (1993). This is available from the Education Shop, PO Box 645, Carlton, 3053 and is useful for parents and school staff.

The widespread and long term adoption of vertical grouping indicates that experienced teachers realise that children have a better potential for learning if they are not grouped into homogeneous age or ability groups. Improvement is not, however, automatically consequent on reorganisation. As the British Plowden Report (1967) warned, 'a mere change in organisation, unaccompanied by a serious attempt to change teachers' attitudes, beliefs and methods of teaching, is unlikely to make any difference to either attainment or to the quality of teacher–pupil relationships' (vol. 2, app. 11, para. 3.4).

Summary

Thirty years after vertical grouping was introduced to British and South Australian primary schools, it is still widely used and was recently introduced in the state of Victoria in 1993. No school makes radical changes to grouping without considerable thought and discussion.

Victoria's Education Department found that rearranging a school already well established in horizontal age grouping can be profoundly disturbing to staff and parents. Some teachers had already turned to vertical grouping spontaneously, without realising that it is a system that has been regarded as controversial. Some offered variations, mixing reception children with grade two children. This is thought to assist teachers in developing children's social skills but does not necessarily provide continuity for all children.

The popularity of vertical grouping can be attributed to a variety of factors. First, it is the most appropriate form of division for activity-based classrooms. The advantages for teachers include:

• less pressure to listen to early readers: there are always responsible children available to help;

- teachers start with smaller classes at the beginning of the school year and the group gradually increases in size, giving more time for individual new entrants as they arrive;
- less time is spent on routine matters because there are few new entrants;
- new arrivals settle down more quickly in a mixed-age class;
- teachers can give attention to older children when younger ones are playing;
- a mixed-age group is easier than teaching thirty or more 'big rampageous boys' (Ridgway & Lawton 1969, p. 158).

Teachers of five- and six-year-olds in horizontally grouped classes often feel that their children are just beginning to make really satisfying progress when it is time for them to move on to the next class. Vertical grouping provides teachers with opportunities to witness much greater development over a longer period of time and that, in turn, provides greater satisfaction.

One aspect of vertical grouping that is often mentioned is the 'family' atmosphere in the classroom. It is 'a more natural way of making the dramatic change from home life to school' (Ridgway & Lawton 1969 p. 158).

Vertical grouping fails when teachers continue to teach as if all the children in the class are the same age and at the same level of development at the same time. Failure is also apparent when teachers divide children into formal age groups within the one class. Sadly, in some schools, groupings have changed but attitudes have not. Six-year-olds in a vertically grouped class gleefully informed the author that the sad child she had being talking to was a 'stupid dummy' who had failed and been 'kept down' and was having to repeat the reception-class curriculum all over again. The teacher confirmed that the child had 'started again' with the new entrants. Her traditional ideas were so entrenched that she had completely ignored his progress during the previous year and he was once again classed as a school beginner. Teachers who have been trained with a 'whole class' and subject focus are at greatest risk of continuing horizontal grouping methods and ideas in situations that require catering for individual needs. They set up artificial barriers in the classroom. There was a great deal of teacher resistance to vertical grouping when it was adopted statewide in 1993. However, school principals who supported it sometimes did so on organisational rather than educational grounds. They told the authors that when five-year-olds constitute a minority in a class, they are more amenable to organisational structures intended for older children. They make 'less fuss' during the first week of school when required to attend lengthy whole school assemblies and they adapt more readily than reception class children to 'going with specialist teachers' to specialist classrooms. In other words, administrators like vertical grouping because it enables them to impose inappropriate structures on school entrants with fewer protests than hitherto.

TASKS FOR STUDENTS

Visit a classroom catering for children aged five to eight years.

1   Describe one activity that provided opportunities for integrated learning across the curriculum. What were those opportunities?. How, did the teacher utilise them to teach literacy, numeracy, science, etc?

2   List the learning experiences that should be incorporated in: a cookery session with children, and a woodwork activity. Show which aspects of mathematics, science, physical activity, hygiene, social skills, reading and writing etc. can be involved.

3   How are the children grouped in the classroom? Enquire what criteria the teacher used for placing individuals in these groups.

4   Could you identify slow learners in this class? How?
Looking back on your own childhood experiences, how did you know which children in your class were 'slow learners'? How were they treated by the teacher? How were they treated by other children? How did this affect their social relationships? How would this affect their self-esteem? How do you think they felt about school? How might this affect their progress and chances in life?

5   Discuss the following. Some teachers and some parents appear to value intellectual development and academic achievement to the exclusion of all other aspects of children's development.
Can you provide evidence of this from your own experience? Were the intelligent children aware that they were valued more highly than others? How did they know? How did this affect them? How did the less favoured children respond?

6   Parents and teachers who support grouping children according to their perceived abilities often argue that life is competitive and 'the sooner children learn to cope with competition the better'. Plan a ten-minute talk to present to a parents' meeting to account for your own unstreamed, multi-aged classroom organisation. Ensure that you use everyday, jargon-free language so that you are clearly understood by 'average' parents.

7   You have accepted the position of teacher responsible for a class of 30 children in a state school. The class consists of 10 new entrants and 20 six- to seven-year-olds. Plan how you will cater for this wide range of abilities during your first week in school.

Creating a positive learning environment

The school learning environment directly reflects the teacher's level of understanding about children's needs and how they learn. The way in which the environment is planned is a powerful regulator of the children's behaviours.

The learning environment consists of several aspects which are interdependent. These can be categorised as:

- the physical environment (including out-of-doors);
- the teacher–child relationship;
- the peer relationships.

The last two contribute to what can be called the 'feeling environment'.

Physical environment

Children and teachers operate best in a comfortable physical environment. It must be practical and workable, interesting, stimulating and above all, safe.

At the beginning of the school year, the teacher organises the room so that it appeals to new children joining the class. The teacher sets standards and chooses interesting displays but, as the term progresses, children are given more opportunities to make contributions of work, art, personal items, pets, plants etc. and offer suggestions for room changes. They may also be involved in the rearrangement of furniture to create different functional areas. Early in the term, children should be included in discussion about the purposes of different areas in the room and the basic rules associated with use. The more that children are involved in developing the learning environment, the more they will value it.

Every classroom environment can be seen in terms of what Dr Elizabeth Jones (1973) describes as dimensions. The first dimensions are referred to as 'hard' and 'soft' dimensions. These can be viewed in terms of a continuum with a hard environment at one extreme and a completely soft environment at the other. A hard environment is typified by the old traditional classroom with hard wooden floors, desks in rows, neatly organised and locked cupboards and a blackboard at one end of the room. In these schools, windows were at a high level so that the children were not distracted by the world outside. At the other end of the continuum is the classroom which resembles a home with comfortable, cosy furniture, cushions, beanbags, adult laps to sit on, soft floor coverings and open shelves with an inviting array of activities from which to choose. The teacher's attitudes to children's learning are reflected in these contrasting situations. The teacher in the hard, traditional environment chooses to be removed from the children, intent on group control. The teacher in the soft environment encourages children's independence, decision-making and social interactions in pleasant surroundings while showing a responsiveness to their needs for acceptance and security.

A second dimension is the level of openness and closure within the classroom. Open materials include water, paint, sand, clay and others that do not impose restrictions on children; in other words, there is no single correct method of use. At the opposite end of this continuum are workbook tasks, duplicated sheets, exercises, puzzles and tracing patterns. In the first instance, the number of options open to the child are limitless while in the second, there is only one correct answer or method of completion. Some activities fall between the two extremes of open and closed, for example, building blocks and farm animals.

Where materials are visible and readily accessible, the teacher's organisation could be described as open. A closed organisation is typified by high shelves where visibility and access are restricted for the children or where locked doors prevent access.

It is imperative that teachers find a happy balance between these two dimensions. Closed activities must be selected very carefully to ensure that they are appropriate in terms of learning. Before presenting such activities, teachers need to ask themselves what the children will learn when using these materials and whether that learning is worthwhile. All too frequently, these tasks are given as 'busy work' to keep children occupied.

Open activities are important for children but they must extend or challenge thinking to be educationally useful. Teachers' attitudes are reflected in the way that they either leave children to work freely or intervene inappropriately. For example, where block play becomes very adventurous and the construction tall and shaky, the completely open-minded teacher lets the child continue to experiment without intervention. The close-minded teacher, on the other hand, gives precise instructions for building and dismantling. Between these two extremes, there is the balanced teacher who allows freedom, offering subtle guidance relating to important matters such as safety and weight distribution and what might happen if building blocks fall down. Clearly the child will learn most with this teacher.

The third dimension that Jones (1973) identified relates to the intrusive or seclusive nature of the environment. Within any classroom it is necessary to have areas where children can be alone or work in small groups as well as areas where they come into contact with each other. The construction of the classroom, its size, shape etc., will have some influence on these intrusive and seclusive areas. Where there is a large space, quiet areas can be created easily. The basic arrangement of furniture can determine whether the environment is intrusive or seclusive. Secluded or partially secluded areas may be created by using mobile pin-up boards, mobile book shelves or easels as screens. A relatively large degree of seclusion may be created for quiet reading, listening posts, small group discussions, writing centres, small puzzle and construction work. It may be appropriate to soften such secluded areas with the addition of beanbags and cushions. For total seclusion, a cosy, soft corner big enough for one or two children, may be created with their help. This could be a cave, a cottage, a cubby or a miniature castle and would no doubt change during the year. Cosy places can be created indoors or outdoors from large building blocks and empty refrigerator cartons available from shops.

Many young children need a quiet, private time at some stage during the day to rest, think, work or simply be alone. Teachers need to plan their learning environment so that these needs can be met. Similarly, if small groups of children need to work together, a partially secluded space will foster sustained interaction, limiting outside intrusion while enabling the teacher to monitor the group. It is common in classrooms to have these partially secluded areas set up as learning centres or curriculum focus points for maths, language, science or social education. This provides for practical and efficient use of space.

An open area is necessary for children to gather together simultaneously. Often this area has cushions as well as a large rug or mat. Such a large area may be used quite flexibly. Teachers could use the area for assigned work, story time, shared book experiences, shared writing time, language time or music and some may use it for free activity. It is inappropriate to use this intrusive area for individual assigned work where the teacher does not want talking, helping or copying. It places enormous strain on young children to have to cut themselves off from the stimulation of their friends. Teachers often find themselves imposing rules such as 'don't talk', 'keep your eyes on your own work' etc. and although children learn to obey these rules, the effectiveness of this teaching mode must be seriously questioned in the light of knowledge relating to children's learning styles. If a child has a difficult task to do, the environment must be free from intrusion.

The extent to which teachers themselves are intrusive is reflected in the amount of talking they do, the amount of directing of activities that occurs, the number of choices they permit and the level of independence they encourage in the children. Where the teacher constantly intrudes there is often too much stimulation, with one group of children impinging on another. There may be a lot of noise and confusion, with the teacher's input not necessarily being simply in response to children's needs. A seclusive environment in which the teacher withdraws for prolonged periods of time is

Figure 7.1: A cosy outdoor place

boring and suitable only for periods of rest. Clearly, the type of environment created must be sufficiently flexible to meet the changing needs of children.

The fourth dimension can be viewed in terms of mobility. An environment which encourages high mobility is one that focuses on large muscle development. The playground, the gymnasium or multi-purpose room where there are large climbing frames, ladders, and ropes are examples of such environments. A low-mobility environment facilitates only fine motor co-ordination development through more sedentary activities, and is more typical of primary and infant school classrooms.

Opportunities for mobility need to be planned, particularly for young children who find it difficult to sit still. The efficient use of appropriate soft or secluded areas, and rugs, walls, pin boards, table tops and the outdoors, offer variety and facilitate choice and independence.

The fifth and final dimension identified by Jones (1973) refers to the simple or complex nature of the environment. A simple environment is uncluttered, unstimulating and has few distractions for the child, resulting in frequent activity change, short attention spans and a need for adult direction and assistance. A teacher who favours this dimension offers closed or semi-closed activities where instructions are given clearly and the answers checked carefully with ticks and crosses. In the simple outdoor environment, children play repetitively on basic swings and climbing frames, and in the sandpit.

A complex environment, on the other hand, has a wide variety of materials, activities and opportunities which stimulate innovation, initiative and decision-making. Too much stimulation can, however, result in confusion, frustration and behaviour problems, and again we see the need for a balance and careful planning.

Teachers should never expose all the play materials simultaneously: changes are necessary to revitalise activity and develop new interests. Teachers may 'complicate' and extend the environment not only by adding to it but by offering ideas or by participating in activities themselves. They need to decide whether children will be allowed to make tasks more open-ended and complex by introducing their own ideas. Will the children's suggestions be encouraged or squashed?

The organisation of the physical space in school directly impinges on how children feel and behave while they are there. A carefully arranged environment adds a significant dimension to a child's educational experience. It can:

- encourage movement and interaction;
- encourage deep involvement;
- promote independence and self-direction;
- encourage the use of skills;
- lengthen or shorten the attention span;
- contribute to co-operative learning;
- stimulate curiosity and problem-solving.

Figure 7.2: In a complex and open learning environment, the adult is the resource person who listens to children's ideas, challenges their thinking and points them towards resources and further opportunities for learning

When the environment is not carefully considered and planned it can cause frustration, discomfort, confusion and dissatisfaction, all of which are likely to result in behaviour problems.

Organisation of the physical space

The organisation of the physical space must be convenient and helpful for individual children who need:

- good light to enable them to see what they are doing;
- fresh air and appropriate temperatures;
- personal space and social space;
- storage space that facilitates self-service and the replacement of play materials;
- ready access to reading and writing materials;
- ready access to all relevant resources for play and learning;
- variation of learning materials to stimulate interest;
- displays, instructions and information at an appropriate level for reading;

- child-sized furniture;
- room to move around freely, particularly when using a wheel chair, callipers or a walking frame;
- a clear view of the blackboard when necessary;
- a well-organised, vibrant and functional room;
- the choice of activity areas;
- clear instructions, limits and routines.

The teacher must distinguish and separate noisy and quiet activities, messy and clean tasks and active and inactive areas to reduce the likelihood of behaviour problems. Where the teacher has not identified the major traffic paths in the room and has placed furniture, resources or activities inappropriately, frustration will occur. Children become distressed and angry when their constructions are accidentally knocked over or when paint or water is splashed on drawings.

Where materials and resources are inaccessible to children, frustration and boredom may result. All learning materials and displays must be at the children's eye level.

Materials must be thoughtfully stored, stacked and labelled to facilitate easy access for their use and return. Children should develop responsibility towards maintaining this organisation for the benefit of their peers. The teacher can encourage this by labelling all containers and shelves to show where materials belong. If many materials are clustered together, congestion and arguments can occur. If similar materials are placed side by side, young children will undoubtedly replace the wrong thing in the wrong place, causing frustration for the next user. It is much easier to remember where things belong if they do not look alike. However, where materials are expected to be used in conjunction with one another, as for example coloured stringing beads or blocks with design cards, then the cards should somehow be stored in the big box with the beads or blocks. Similarly, jigsaw and other puzzle pieces should be coloured on the back so that odd pieces are easily identified and replaced. In the painting area, there should be an obvious storage arrangement for paint, brushes, sponges, paper, card, paper towels and cleaning materials.

Teachers need to consider how they place everyday materials. Children constantly need lead pencils, coloured pencils, scissors, glue sticks, pencil sharpeners etc. These things are often found in a central storage area where teachers can monitor their use. Centralised storage of materials results in the constant movement of children with the risk of overcrowding, queues, collision and discipline problems. To avoid congestion and interruptions, materials can be placed in several places around the classroom so that children do not need to move far to reach them. Consideration also needs to be given to the distribution of paper, reference books, dictionaries, materials for counting, posters, alphabet charts and equipment useful for stimulating children's interests or reminding them of ideas and concepts.

When central storage places are used, children are likely to be distracted as they look up from their tasks to see who is passing. This kind of movement is both unproductive and disruptive.

Children also need personal storage space. In many schools, children are allocated individual trays which slide into storage units. To avoid delay and congestion, particularly at going-home time, storage units should be placed in several strategic areas around the room.

Summary

A positive learning environment is one which motivates children to learn. The careful arrangement of the physical space contributes substantially to children's endeavours. By balancing the many dimensions of the environment thoughtfully, arranging furniture, display units and storage facilities to form varied functional work areas, and distributing materials efficiently around the room, children can work alone and together on various activities. The products of their efforts can be displayed in an attractive way which not only contributes to the visual appeal of the environment but emphasises the value that teachers place on the children's efforts. In turn, the children feel a pride in ownership of their class environment as well as their own contribution to the class.

Careful planning is needed to reduce the risk of frustration from overcrowding, jostling, accidental damage of creative efforts, loss of concentration, disruption and other hazards that lead to tension, anger and negative behaviour.

Using the outdoor environment

Within the concept of open education, children are given the freedom to extend their learning activities into corridors, school libraries and appropriate outdoor spaces and places. Teachers who appreciate the value of real-life experience for children's learning organise excursions that take them beyond the school boundaries. These visits may simply involve a walk to a park, building site or shopping centre or involve bus, tram or train travel, any of which can be new to the child who is driven everywhere by car. Some suburban children have never been to a city, visited a department store or travelled on a lift or escalator. Others may have spent their family holidays in exotic far-flung places but may never have visited the fish market, fire station or cathedral. Before students and teachers plan excursions, they need to know something of the children's experiences so that plans produce maximum learning benefits.

What can children learn from excursions?

Children learn most by having opportunities to see things for themselves, touch, taste and smell, hear them, and talk about their findings with the guidance of a well-prepared teacher. Excursions offer experiences to stimulate interest in a specific subject as well as to extend learning. They should be fun and add variety to the school programme. They should also be relevant to the needs and interests of the particular group of children. Before deciding on the location for the visit, students and teachers should take account of children's interests and maturity levels, and what kind of experiences will provide greatest benefit, given the aims and objectives of the programme.

Excursions can be useful for developing children's powers of observation and skills in interpretation. The adults should encourage children to notice small details and differences in detail which might otherwise be overlooked. They may need pointers to the differences in sounds and other factors necessary to help them to appreciate their environment. Children can be encouraged to observe and feel the changing seasons, for example by observing the activities of nesting birds, examining, feeling and smelling buds, leaves and flowers and comparing the trees. They can acquire the concepts of language, mathematics and science from their environment. With a sensitive teacher, they will become aware of natural and artificial patterns and shapes, textures, numbers, measurement and spatial concepts. They will gather natural objects during a walk in the park or on the beach, talk about their appearance and their purpose in life. Some will wish to find out more about these objects and will need direction to appropriate resources. Others will count them, sort them, match them up, paint them, use them in collages and write about them. Excursions followed by the provision of related books can combine to make a highly effective, integrated unit of work.

Social studies can be enriched by field excursions. Children begin to appreciate the contributions that different human beings make to their world when they see people at work. When children deliberately blocked a school drain with paper to create a flood, the class was allowed to meet and talk to the plumber. He gave them a tour of the school water supply and explained the waste disposal system. He showed them how the water reached the tap and where it went when they removed the plug from the sink. Such was their interest that the teacher seized this opportunity to expand the children's knowledge of public hygiene. They embarked on a project with the co-operation of the health authorities, resulting in an unusual but rewarding visit to the sewage treatment plant.

It is important for children to learn of the valuable contributions that people make to society, be they garbage collectors, plumbers, electricians, police or doctors. They begin to appreciate what these jobs entail as they visit the post office, airport, railway station or watch the builders, bulldozer operators and council employees at work.

Excursions provide the best opportunities for language development because the environment of the school and community abounds with new words on signs, as well as sights and experiences. Young children will learn how this new environmental print relates to them. They can look for new signs, match familiar ones and learn new words by using them in context, guessing and discussing what they mean. Teachers and students can assist children by being alert to learning opportunities, listening carefully and responding promptly. On their return to school, stories, reference books, discussion and writing will further the language concept and broaden the knowledge base. After a period of discussion and consolidation, the teacher may record the dictated sentences for nonreaders and assist others to write their own records, stories or poems about some special aspect of the visit. Sometimes, young children will incorporate their experiences into play, art or drama.

Planning the excursion as an academic exercise, many teachers tell the children what to look for on their visits and older children are often given assignments to complete. Adults should bear in mind that children are learning continually but they do not necessarily learn what we expect and want them to learn. Children have a very different perspective to adults, due to the differences in height and life experience. They do not necessarily see the things that adults notice because they view the world from a lower eye-level and note the things that are near to them, active and dramatic. These are the observations and experiences that will be of greatest significance and capture their imaginations, much to the disappointment of eager teachers who expected a different response. Although adults should point out the important items of interest, they should not be surprised to find that the most fascinating feature of a visit to the railway station is the station cat. Real understanding will come if the learning is directed towards extending something that children already know. One of the important reasons for going on excursions is to stimulate children's 'how?...what?...why?...where?' questions.

Organising the excursion

Student teachers may have to organise excursions at comparatively short notice, while they are on teaching practice. Careful planning is necessary for the effectiveness of any excursion. The teacher should be familiar with the proposed destination and ensure that students have a clear plan and purpose.

Preparation of the children is essential for maximum learning. This may take place over a period of weeks: for example, a visit to an airport may culminate in a project on air, transport or jet propulsion. Stories, films or videos, books, visiting experts, models and experiments will help the children to gain maximum benefit from the visit. Role play involving excursions helps young children to feel self-assured in a strange place. They can make tickets for public transport, pretend to be conductors or drivers or pilots of planes and have pretend picnics.

Where the field excursion is not the culmination of a unit of work but an introduction, preparatory discussion can be kept to a minimum because the most important work takes place during and after the visit itself. The teacher will tell the children where they are going and what they might see, hear and feel so that they are mentally prepared. Too much talking can, however, be counterproductive, causing over-excitement or anxiety.

On the day of the visit, a quiet briefing of children and parents is necessary to discuss rules, clarify organisational details and issue name tags. Teachers should ensure that parent-helpers know exactly what is expected in terms of children's behaviour, where they will go, time constraints, dangers, the types of discussion to encourage, etc. Parent participation in excursions is valuable to children and teachers alike. Their presence contributes to children's security and safety, while helping parents to understand how their children can benefit from visits to a wide range of places.

During the excursion, the atmosphere should be relaxed and unrushed. The adult's major role is to respond to and extend children's curiosity and enthusiasm through meaningful questioning. When unexpected learning opportunities arise, adults should seize and develop them.

After the visit, children will review the experience, share it in different contexts, use new knowledge and build upon it. A visit from one of the people who acted as guides will enable children to return the hospitality they experienced and revive memories of the excursion.

Despite careful planning, and meticulous attention to detail and safety, the unexpected can happen on excursions of all kinds. Children may hurt themselves, instructions may be ignored in the excitement of the movement and, eager to see everything at close quarters, someone may overbalance and fall into the duck pond. Teachers should be prepared for all contingencies whenever they take groups of children outside the boundaries of the school. However, the advantages of excursions far outweigh the risk of minor mishaps.

The enthusiastic and well-organised teacher is clearly the key to a successful excursion. The teacher's personality, interest, enthusiasm, creativity, sensitivity, willingness and ability to explore can turn seemingly mundane trips into exciting and rewarding educational experiences (Buschhoff 1971).

Places to visit with children of five to eight years

Adventure playgrounds	Fire stations
Airports	Folk museum
Aquariums	Markets
Art galleries	Model railways
Aviaries	Museums
Bakery	National parks
Beaches	Orchestras rehearsing
BMX tracks	Planetarium
Botanic Gardens	Police stations
Building site	Ports
Bus ride to the bus depot	Post offices
Cemeteries	Railway stations
Central market	Recreation park
Children's library	Royal Show
Churches of special interest	RSPCA shelter
Cinema	Shopping Centres
Circus	Theatre for children
Concerts for children	Town or City Hall or Parliament
Exhibitions	Toy factory
Factories	Train rides
Farms	Tram ride
Fauna and flora reserves	Wholesale market
Festivals	Zoo

The school excursion file should contain all relevant information about places to visit with children, contact telephone numbers, costs, transport arrangements necessary and tips for teachers who may be considering making a visit. Although some details will change from year to year and will be necessary, maps, facilities and advertising literature should be retained for future use.

Checklist for planning excursions

Teacher preparation

1 **Select which planning tasks can be undertaken with or by individuals or groups of children.** For example:
   - plan letters to parents to tell them of the visit;
   - visit tourist offices to obtain advertising literature;
   - buy film for the camera and batteries for cassette recorders;
   - research related topics in the library;
   - examine large maps of the area or street maps;
   - look at train or bus timetables;
   - make tags to be worn showing the child's name and school.

2 **Initial contact.**
   - Contact the person in charge of the centres you would like to visit;
   - indicate the purpose of the visit, what you would like children to see, hear, do and learn and how the staff of the centre can help. This is especially necessary if visiting a centre that does not traditionally cater for the five-to eight-year age group;
   - enquire about the most appropriate time of day to gain maximum benefit from the visit (for example, at what time are zoo animals fed?);
   - enquire whether a guide will be available;
   - enquire about possible charges for visits.

3 **Make a preliminary visit.**
   Prior to the planned excursion, visit the venue to evaluate the possibilities for learning.
   Check whether:
   - children have already been there with their parents;
   - parents could achieve the same objective;
   - the cost is justifiable;
   - learning experiences will be available;
   - suitable toilet facilities are available;
   - snacks and drinks are available;
   - there is a bus stop or parking area nearby;
   - children can eat picnic lunches in safety;
   - handouts and samples are available to help you to prepare children for the visit;
   - there are potential hazards such as difficult road crossings, ponds, frightening noises, sirens etc.

4 **Notify the school administrator.**
Prior to confirming the visit, request official permission to undertake it. Ensure that you are covered by insurance and that you complete all the necessary forms. Clarify the necessary adult:child ratio as laid down by the guidelines of the education authority. Check whether the school has an excursion file containing relevant information.

5 **Invite an expert.**
A parent or community member who has knowledge of the subject should be invited to accompany and contribute to the preparation of the class and follow-up sessions. For example, if the children are visiting a fire or police station, considerable enrichment can be gained by involving a parent who is a police or fire officer.

6 **Notify parents.**
Write to parents outlining the nature and purpose of the visit and the cost. Provide a tear-off slip for reply. Ensure that special arrangements are made for children in government-assisted families. A return form can be on the following lines:

I give permission for my child .... *to join the school excursion to* ....

I understand that the excursion will be under the supervision of a teacher. I also give permission for the teacher in charge to arrange for my child to receive emergency medical or surgical treatment if I am not available to give that permission.

Name & telephone number of doctor ....

Name, address and work/home telephone numbers of parents

....

....

Signed..

Parents should be informed of:
- transport arrangements;
- cost and the final day for payment;
- arrangements to be made for children who cannot attend;
- place to be visited;
- day, date and times of visit and time of return;
- clothing needed;
- food and drink requirements. If a long journey is to be undertaken, ask parents not to give their children confectionery to eat between meals or anything that might contribute to travel sickness;

- spending money requirements (it is sometimes advisable to stipulate limits);
- supervision arrangements;
- whether parent-helpers are needed and who to contact;
- the reasons for the excursion and how it fits into the curriculum.

The adult:child ratio required will depend not only on regulations but on the type of visit to be undertaken. A walk into an adjacent park will clearly require fewer adults than an excursion to the circus where children are in rows and their activities cannot be readily scanned by the teacher. Similarly, an excursion to a large produce market or an agricultural show could necessitate a minimum ratio of one adult to every five children.

7 **Confirm arrangements.**

Confirm transport and all other arrangements in writing as well as by phone on the day before departure. This is necessary whether or not public transport is to be used. Send reminder letters home with the children.

8 **Prepare the children for the visit.**

Carefully planned, related activities should precede the excursion. What do children already know about it? What do they expect of the visit? Teachers should encourage children to find and read relevant library books to widen their knowledge for the visit. Follow-up activities should also be considered. Children need to know what sounds and sights to expect and what questions to ask.

On the day of the excursion

Brief both adults and children relating to:

- safety rules and why they are necessary;
- procedures and group organisation (walking in pairs, holding hands, keeping together, which children with which adults, etc.);
- attach children's nametags;
- who is responsible for first aid equipment, prescribed medicines, food and drink;
- procedures for meals and toileting;

In addition:

- check that children are appropriately dressed;
- make arrangements for the distribution of 'unauthorised' confectionery to ensure that it is not consumed between meals or on buses or trains;
- load the camera with film;
- dispatch all children to toilets under supervision before departure;
- count the children participating;
- take a list of names and contact phone numbers with you;
- leave details of your whereabouts with the school secretary as well as senior staff;

- give consideration to the placement of children and avoid placing mischievous ones together;
- carry spare pairs of junior-sized pants and plastic bags in case of toileting accidents.

When walking, one teacher should lead the group, another adult should walk in the middle and a second teacher should bring up the rear. The most responsible children should be recruited to keep young children safe. Remind children of safety rules when approaching roads to be crossed or busy areas.

If a coach is hired for a long journey, adults should ensure that they have a bucket, a container of water, paper tissues and a cloth or sponge available for mopping up in the case of sickness or accident. The availability of equipment should be checked initially with the coach company and with the driver before departure.

Brief the driver relating to the destination, the most appropriate stopping point for children to alight and the place and time for picking up. Obtain the name of the driver and the number of the bus, especially if visiting a circus or agricultural show where there could be many vehicles of similar appearance. In these circumstances it is useful to write the bus number on children's nametags.

During the excursion, encourage children's astute observation, questions and discussion.

Children's behaviour is always affected by excitement. If teachers keep a fairly 'tight rein' in the initial stages children will gradually settle down to a responsible working attitude. In the early stages, however, they regard excursions in much the same way as Christmas parties.

Provide appropriate opportunities for toileting.

Always count the children before leaving the place visited and count them again as they board the transport.

Most benefit can be gained if the class returns to school before dismissal and children are given the opportunity to evaluate the important findings.

Children should be involved, as far as possible, in the development and printing of film and the creation of a photographic record and big book.

It is worth noting that popular reading material can be made from visits of comparatively insignificant proportions, such as a visit to the local adventure playground or shopping centre, or even the school kitchen.

The 'feeling environment'

The 'feeling environment' refers to the relationships between the people in the classroom: teacher–child relationships, adult relationships and children's relationships with each other. The way that people feel about themselves and each other pervades the entire atmosphere and directly affects behaviours. Teachers have by far the greatest impact on this feeling environment.

Through their verbal and nonverbal communication with children, teachers model interpersonal skills and children imitate their examples. If adults are harsh or teasing, children will be harsh or teasing to each other. If an adult is caring and fair with consistent rules, children are more likely to become caring and co-operative, too. Communication is the basis of human interaction and it may be deliberate or unintentional; messages will be conveyed by posture and body language such as facial expressions as well as tone of voice, silence or the distance that is kept. Children are very perceptive and quickly interpret a teacher's behaviour and its relevance for them.

Developing a child's positive self-concept

The most important influences on effective communication are those of self-concept and self-esteem which affect both sender and receiver of communication. Self-concept refers to the image that people have of themselves; the way they think of themselves with all the characteristics that they acknowledge and deny. Self-esteem involves our judgement and feelings about our own personal worth. These are influenced by perceived achievements and failures and the way in which we interpret the reactions of others. There are other influences too, such as personality traits, attitudes, beliefs, home conditioning, expectations, power and status, degree of familiarity, background and experience, etc. It has been shown, however, that the feelings that you have about yourself colour all other feelings and actions. People who feel good about themselves are confident, enjoy self-respect and have a sense of belonging. People who feel badly about themselves lack self-respect, feel inadequate, foolish, insignificant and lack a sense of belonging.

Children begin to mould their self-images or pictures of themselves at a very young age. Positive and successful experiences enhance the formation of a positive self-concept in these crucial early years. The development of self-image is influenced by children's impressions of their worth which, in turn, are influenced by others such as teachers, parents, peers and families. In the pre-school years it is the parent who is the earliest source of nurture for the child, but as the child grows older, other sources bring their influences to bear. At school, for example, teachers and children are influential in the development of the individual child's self-image. A child who is led to believe that he or she is stupid or inadequate will accept the consensus of opinion, and may cease making efforts. Clearly, the most important task for teachers to accomplish is the development of a positive self-image in every child.

Teachers become significant to individual children when those children feel significant to the adults. The adult's attitudes must invite and nurture positive self-enhancement in the children. As teachers' attitudes are controlled by their own feelings of competency and self-worth, they should have the following qualities:

- a genuine interest and concern for each child irrespective of race, religion, family background or physical appearance;
- the capacity to develop a good rapport with each child;
- a genuine recognition of the positive qualities of the child;
- a willingness to make the effort and take the time to help each child to feel positive.

The teacher, as a significant other, must create an environment which encourages positive self-image building. Such environments could be described as caring, open, nonthreatening, trusting, nonjudgemental, secure, happy, inviting, child-centred, encouraging and accepting. Borba and Borba (1982) described the environments that are most effective in enhancing self-esteem as those in which children:

- perceive a sense of warmth and caring;
- are offered a degree of security which allows them to grow and try new things without an overriding concern about failure;
- are respected as individuals;
- are encouraged to use their own ideas and initiatives;
- are invited to express opinions;
- recognise that there are clear and definite limits within the environment;
- are exposed to reasonable and consistent rules and standards;
- have a chance to succeed at their own levels;
- are encouraged to beat their own best effort rather than compete with others;
- are praised for effort as well as achievement.

Developing positive relationships within the learning environment

There are many strategies that a teacher can use to develop positive relationships within the class environment and so contribute to the feeling of wellbeing. In relation to those characteristics already identified above by Borba and Borba (1982):

Children perceive a sense of warmth and caring when teachers:

- use eye-to-eye contact while talking to children;
- greet each child and say goodbye to each child individually;
- offer a cuddle, smile, hug or wink to each child at appropriate times;
- value children's conversation, explanations and suggestions by encouragement as well as verbal acknowledgment;
- show a sincere interest in each child; and
- encourage positive interactions between children.

Children are offered a degree of security when teachers:

- give simple instructions that are clear and concise;
- assist children to understand acceptable and unacceptable behaviour;
- are consistent in behaviour reinforcement;
- are of equable temperament;
- encourage children to share in the responsibility of taking care of the classroom; and
- involve children in decision-making and rule-making.

Children are respected as individuals when teachers:

- take advantage of opportunities to speak to children in a one-to-one relationship;
- encourage the quiet, shy children to participate;
- provide areas in the environment where children can be alone or with a small group;
- value children's opinions, interests, cultures and gender and assist them to value others;
- ensure that activities and materials are suited to individual needs and interests;
- give positive feedback to children and encourage them to do likewise with others;
- encourage children to express their feelings and fears; and
- ensure that children are aware of their rights and responsibilities in school.

Children's ideas and initiatives are encouraged by teachers:

- involving them in decision-making and offering choices;
- involving them in the creation of their learning environment;
- encouraging improvement and effort as well as accomplishment;
- encouraging children to research and experiment independently; and
- encouraging children to work on contracts of work.

Children learn to express their views when teachers:

- encourage discussion on interpersonal relationships in class;
- actively seek children's ideas and opinions, both on a one-to-one basis and in groups;
- encourage children to participate in curriculum planning, room arrangements, outings, fund-raising activities, cultural experiences, invitations to guest speakers etc., using their ideas when appropriate.

Children realise there are clear and definite limits when teachers:

- involve them in discussion about appropriate class rules;
- state the class rules clearly and display them in written form if necessary;
- remind children of the limits;
- positively reinforce socially acceptable behaviours;
- encourage children to help each other in keeping mutually agreed rules;

- develop awareness in children of the logical consequences of their actions;
- encourage children to assert themselves appropriately and reject unwanted touching, etc.

Rules and standards are reasonably and consistently enforced by teachers who:

- discuss with children the acceptability or otherwise of their behaviour in class;
- positively reinforce good behaviour;
- use consistent conflict resolution procedures for handling behaviour problems.

Children have a chance to succeed at their own level when teachers:

- set achievable tasks to ensure that each child experiences success;
- offer an activity-based programme so that children can work independently;
- offer a flexible timetable to enable children to negotiate for extra time to complete their tasks, as necessary;
- provide an integrated programme so that children have opportunity to reinforce concepts, experiences etc., which leads to success;
- develop a child-centred environment in which children can make choices, take initiatives and pursue their areas of interest while being guided towards learning across all areas of the curriculum.

These strategies are but a few of the many ways in which teachers may develop positive relationships in the classroom. The physical and feeling environments are interdependent and reflect not only the teachers' beliefs relating to children's learning but their attitudes towards children's emotional, social, physical and intellectual needs.

TASKS FOR STUDENTS

1 On your visit to a classroom catering for children from five to eight years, please note examples of the teacher:

- providing positive reinforcement for effort;
- encouraging children to beat their own previous achievements;
- encouraging children to help each other;
- listening carefully to children;
- engaging children in problem-solving activities
- using positive reinforcement for acceptable behaviour rather than criticism of undesirable behaviour.

2 Describe details of games and activities designed to develop the self-esteem of children in the five- to eight-year age group.

3 Sometimes, a parent will tell you (in the child's presence) that his or her child is bad, hopeless or stupid and 'takes after' an unpopular relative. Discuss the likely effects of such comments on the child. How would you respond to such comments without alienating the parent?

Creating a positive learning environment for children with special needs

Introduction

While all children are unique and have special needs that must be met within school programmes, some needs are more urgent than others, requiring uniquely different responses, skills and resources. These 'special needs' children include the gifted, those with learning disabilities, the physically disabled, non-English speaking migrants and maltreated children.

The authors make no apology for the length of this chapter. Children of the 1990s have become the unwilling, unintended victims of overwhelming stress born of rapid social, moral and technological change and economic recession. Today's parents dwell in what Elkind (1981, p. 3) described as a 'pressure-cooker of competing demands, role changes and both professional and personal uncertainties over which they have no control'.

Most education authorities have espoused the philosophy of 'equality of opportunity' in education since the Second World War, but the ideal has not been matched by practice. Equal opportunity does not mean identical programmes for all; it means diversity within programmes to enable each child to reach his or her potential.

Children with special needs provide a challenge to both teachers and educational institutions. In the past, teachers have not been educated for their role with atypical children, despite their substantial numbers in the education system. As a result, teachers have missed children's cues and cries for help, often increasing, albeit unintentionally, the psychological damage that has its origins in disability, disadvantage or maltreatment.

Increasingly, we find that children with disabilities are placed in 'normal', rather than special, schools. Increasingly, teachers are becoming involved in the treatment of abused, neglected and emotionally disturbed children because teachers are the only professionals who work with those children throughout the day, week and year. Furthermore, most teachers now recognise that children who are severely stressed are unable to benefit from the learning experiences provided. To solve the learning problem, they have to identify the causes of stress and take steps to obtain the necessary specialist help.

The child's first three years in school are critical for future child development. Delay in the recognition of and attention to the signs of maltreatment or developmental delay can lead to the deterioration of children's emotional and physical health and reduce their potential for sound adjustment and success in life.

While most children can benefit from attending a normal class in a normal school, some children will require additional equipment, space and an increase in adult:child staffing ratios. There will be some whose condition necessitates frequent parent–school communications. Parents of children with disabilities are often under a great deal of stress, experiencing strong feelings of guilt and inadequacy. They are, rightly, apprehensive about their children joining classes consisting of 30 or more others. They often worry about whether teachers will be able to provide sufficient support and whether peers will be accepting. It is essential that teachers and parents work to form the mutual trust necessary to enable children to develop confidence and feel sufficiently secure to benefit from the school programme.

The teacher cannot ignore the social, moral and health stresses that affect children because these stresses are often responsible for behaviour and learning problems in the classroom. Teachers create the child's learning environment. It is essential that they are acquainted with basic guidelines for the identification and sound handling of the special needs situations they are likely to encounter in school, both on teaching practice and as qualified teachers. There is considerable professional literature on each of the topics discussed and it is hoped that students and teachers will extend their knowledge of specific needs by further reading and in-service education.

Helping children to cope with stress

Children in the 1990s are likely to meet a variety of stressful challenges. Many of these are a natural part of life, such as coping with fear, the death of a loved one or the arrival of a new baby in the family. Some children will experience the trauma of parental separation or divorce, unemployment and impoverishment. Increasing numbers of children suffer maltreatment at the hands of parents under stress. Some children suffer because their parents are ignorant of normal child development and, in particular, their children's emotional needs. Working parents may find it difficult to provide the quality of care and attention that children need daily. In addition, many young children encounter unrealistic pressures to succeed in school and in sport. Due to adult ignorance or irresponsibility, some children are given too much responsibility or they are pushed into independence too quickly. The teacher who believes in affective education and who chooses to develop a positive learning environment, will try to help children to cope with stress.

Helping children to cope with fears

There is a distinct pattern in the developmental sequence of children's fears. Fears begin in infancy when children encounter unfamiliar versions of concrete objects or persons. Imaginary symbolic fears appear in the later pre-school years while in the primary school, children's attention shifts to more realistic concerns (Briggs & Hawkins 1993).

These changes appear to be linked to important changes in the cognitive processes through which children interpret and evaluate the significance of a potentially threatening event, as well as being connected to changes in the social and emotional issues that dominate children's needs (McCracken 1986). Teachers and parents need to understand the range of normal fears to help children overcome them. Common fears include being afraid of monsters, strangers and the dark. Teachers can help when they:

- *Talk about fears with children and their parents.* With the best of intentions, parents assure children that there is nothing to be frightened of when their children are terrified. As a result, children become reluctant to disclose fears in public. Given the opportunity to put them into words, they are often pleasantly surprised to find that other children suffer them too. Sharing often helps to diminish their importance and bringing fears into the open has a therapeutic effect.
- *Provide opportunities for dramatic play.* This gives children the chance to re-create scary feelings in a situation over which they have control. Sometimes there may be role reversals so that the children have an opportunity to act out the situations which causes the fear. It may be that they are afraid of having their hair cut, of going to the dentist or hospital. In dramatic play, they can take on the roles of hairdresser, doctor or dentist. Similarly, shy children often take the part of a fearsome animal or a tyrant, enjoying the power that they lack in real life.
- *Provide experiences for individual children to help them to cope with specific fears.* If a child is afraid of big dogs, a little puppy may be brought into the classroom. Where there is a fear of the swimming pool, the teacher may provide water-play, graduating to paddling pools and swimming lessons.
- *Help children to develop a range of coping skills through posing questions* such as 'Let's suppose that . . .' or 'What would you do if . . .?'. The purpose is not to find a specific answer but to help children to think of a range of solutions to problems.
- *Encourage children to think of ways in which they can make themselves feel safer*: for example, school-aged children can provide their own suggestions for conquering their fear of the dark.

- *Discourage the victim stance to life*: teachers should encourage children to reword their statements to accept responsibility for their own feelings and actions:

  'I forgot to bring my...' (instead of 'Mummy forgot to pack my . . .')
  'I feel cross because...' (instead of 'He made me cross')
  'I did it because...' (instead of 'He made me do it')

- *Provide children with information about places to be visited* to enable them to anticipate and predict the sounds and sights that will be experienced. This helps to allay fears of the unknown.
- *Use relevant children's story books.* Examples of appropriate stories for children aged five to eight years are:

Aliki 1989, *Feelings*, Australian Piper Press.
Aylesworth, J. 1991, *The Bad Dream*, Chicago, Albert Whitman & Co., USA.
Bourgeois, P. 1987, *Franklin in the Dark*, Ashton Scholastic, Sydney.
Simon, N. 1991, *How Do I Feel?*, Albert Whitman & Co., Chicago.
Sonneborn, R.A. 1987, *Friday Night is Papa's Night*, Picture Puffin, New York.
Tomlinson, J. 1968, *The Owl Who Was Afraid of the Dark*, Methuen, London.
Watson, J.W. 1986, *Sometimes I'm Afraid*, Crown Publishers, NY.

Helping children to cope with death

Children can be very disturbed by their first experience of death, irrespective of whether it involves a grandparent, relative, sibling, peer or pet.

As children are growing up, the ideal time to introduce the concept of death is when flowers or plants die and when a dead bird or a dead animal is discovered. At these times, the cycle of life and death can be introduced. Children can also be told about the natural event of death through ageing or accident. It is dangerous to use platitudes such as 'The bird has gone to live with Jesus' or in the case of the death of a grandparent, 'Grandma went to sleep and didn't wake up'. Such statements are likely to increase fears; children who fear dying in their sleep will try to stay awake at night, causing nightmares, night fears and bedtime problems. Jesus may also be viewed as someone to be feared because he snatches away the people they love. Young children must be made to feel safe. Evasive statements can cause additional emotional disturbance.

Children should be taught that it is natural for people to grow up, and, as they become old, their bodies wear out and stop working. In the case of an accidental death, children can readily understand the dangers of living in the world; they are often being reminded to take care while crossing the road, riding their bike or swimming. Children need to acknowledge that accidental death can occur due to misfortune but that it is the exception rather than the natural course of events. Similarly, where death of a usually strong child or adult occurs as a result of sudden illness, children need to understand that sometimes, parts of the body which are faulty cannot always be fixed by doctors and nurses. However, most people remain well, grow old and then die.

When children ask questions about the death of animals and humans, it sometimes reflects their own underlying fears of dying when they are unwell or have been naughty. Their questions might arise from a visit to a cemetery, the passing of a funeral cortege or television news. Answers should be well-considered and truthful. At a time of personal crisis, very young children may attach themselves to a familiar person for comfort. Children need security in a world that is not yet fully understood. It is common for grieving children to throw temper tantrums as a natural but unacceptable way of releasing anger. At such times, a bereaved child should be given the time and place to talk about the anger and feelings of unhappiness which will then help the angry reactions to subside. Some children withdraw into their own world, becoming absent-minded and unable to concentrate. This behaviour will diminish with time as the child adapts to the changed world of family, friends and school.

Teachers of bereaved young children must be prepared to offer as much caring support and security as possible. They should provide therapeutic activities that will provide success and require little concentration, such as water-play, painting, finger-painting, dough, clay and family dolls.

The stages of grief through which bereaved people pass include shock, denial, emotional release, anger, guilt and self-recrimination, an inability to return to the usual life activities, and finally adjustment and healing. Some people pass through these stages sequentially while others experience several stages simultaneously. Problems arise when a person remains in one stage for a prolonged period of time and grieving becomes a fixed state rather than a passing stage. Adults at home find it difficult to talk to young children about a death. They are often embarrassed and want to protect children from hurt. Despite good intentions, the veil of secrecy increases the trauma. Children hear adults whispering and sense that something is seriously wrong. This is especially common when the dead are thought to have contributed to their own deaths in some way. Children may have to bottle up their anxieties while the truth becomes a secret. Problems of mental ill health are then likely to explode in adolescence or later. Teachers should be sensitive to the stage of grief through which the child is passing and be prepared to provide appropriate support. This may entail:

- mentioning the death and expressing sympathy in a way that says 'I know that you are missing [name] and I'm sorry that you are feeling so sad. I am happy to talk about it when you need me'. It is dangerous to build a barrier of silence because young children cannot be expected to contain their feelings, particularly in the early stages of grief.
- talking with the child at appropriate moments about what actually happened, how the loved one died, where he or she was buried, and changes in the family setting;

- sharing stories with the child which may contribute to understanding. Appropriate books include:

Anon. 1985, *Why did Grandpa Die?* A Golden Learn Book, New York
Brown, M.W. 1979, *The Dead Bird*, Dell, NY.
Fine, P.D. 1981, *Let's Remember Corky*, P. D. Fine, Ohio.
Keller, H. 1987, *Goodbye Max*, Julia McRae Books, London.
Mellonie, B. 1983, *Beginnings and Endings with Lifetimes in Between*, Hill of Content, Melbourne.
Padoan, G. 1987a, *Remembering Grandad*, Child's Play International.
Townsend, M. & Stern, R. 1980, *Pop's Secret*, Addison-Wesley, Reading, Mass.
Wilhelm, H. 1985, *I'll Always Love You*, Hodder & Stoughton, Sydney.

Helping children to cope with separation and divorce

Marital breakdown is a crisis which disrupts the family structure. The role of the teacher is particularly important because the child's sense of continuity and stability is likely to depend on the teacher's support. Children react to divorce in many ways; for some it may represent a sense of loss, a sense of failure in interpersonal relationships and the beginnings of a difficult change to a new life. For some, it may be the release from family disharmony, violence and unhappiness. The way children behave will vary according to their unique personalities, the quality of their lost relationship and the support systems available to them.

The first year after divorce is usually characterised by anxiety, depression and anger with feelings of rejection and incompetence. Parents are often in a state of emotional flux and cannot cope with the needs of their children, who are also under stress. Courts and counsellors often focus on the adults' needs, rather than those of children. In reorganised settings, family disorganisation is often a serious problem with irregular meal times, erratic bedtimes and fewer affectionate interactions between parents and child. There is usually less time spent playing games, reading stories or going out together (Cox & Desforges 1987). Parents may show marked inconsistency in discipline, be less nurturing and more selfish. They may withdraw and make either fewer demands or excessive demands for mature behaviour from their children (Hetherington 1976).

Some parents unwittingly cause psychological disturbances by using their children as pawns to spite their former partners. They are often used as 'spies' and are given instructions about what to tell or not tell the other parent on access visits. Some custodial parents deliberately try to spoil children's access visits in the hope that they will cease. Children in turn, feel confused and resentful, becoming more provocative and difficult with their parents, peers and teachers.

Following parental separation, about two-thirds of children will show marked changes in school behaviour. There may be a deterioration in work standards, noticeable restlessness and an inability to concentrate. About one-fifth of these children may show sadness, adversely affecting their social and emotional development. These changes often disrupt friendship patterns. They abandon long-standing friendships or seem to be at war with the world (Cox & Desforges 1987).

The school as a major socialising institution may play an important part in offsetting some of the negative effects of family disruption. Teachers have considerable expertise in the normal range of behaviours which may be expected of children in class. This knowledge enables them to be aware of any behavioural changes which may be reactions to stress. 'Schools are firmly in the front line for dealing with both the practical and emotional difficulties that can occur when a family breaks up' (Rogers 1982). Yet, for reasons of their own, many adults believe that domestic upset is of no concern to schools. Teachers who have children's interests as their priority can ensure that school is a neutral, predictable, secure and caring sanctuary for children under stress. Before their sixteenth birthday, 20 per cent of children experience a parental divorce. An unknown number are affected by parental separation. It is not possible for schools to ignore these events because teachers cannot teach children effectively without paying some attention to what is happening in their lives (Cox & Desforges 1987).

How can teachers help?

If teachers enjoy good relationships with parents, they will be aware of distressing situations that occur in families. Sensitive teachers will offer sensible sympathy, pastoral care and opportunities to express and understand the sense of hurt, hostility or confusion. They will be alert to opportunities to make the child feel useful, needed and a worthwhile person by seeking help with day-to-day tasks, praising effort and giving personal encouragement.

Teachers will take cognisance of the effects of grief on concentration and plan a suitable programme that will facilitate achievement. There are usually many children in any one class who have experienced divorce, separation or life in one-parent families. Handled sensitively and through the use of children's books on the subject, distressed children may gain comfort from the realisation that there are many others in the same position.

Teachers frequently have to put children's needs and viewpoints to parents. An aggrieved parent seeks a sympathetic ear and may recount distressing events repetitiously in an effort to understand and come to terms with them. Such parents rarely refer to their children's problems. They may deny that they exist; first, because few children express their emotions verbally and say 'I miss my father'. Secondly, custodians are often themselves immersed in shock, jealousy, a sense of failure, self-pity or grief and are incapable of handling children's feelings and the sense of guilt that might ensue. As a result, parents often assure teachers that all is well and their children have 'settled down and don't even miss their dad'. When they are at school, however, these children often show signs of serious emotional disturbance for up to two years after separation.

Schools can help parents by lending appropriate publications such as Joy Connolly's *Stepfamilies*, Ailsa Burns' *Breaking Up* or Lynne McNamara and Jennifer Morrison's *Separation, Divorce and After*. They should also have up-to-date information available relating to services for families: legal aid, pensions and benefits and the whereabouts of social agencies.

Schools should ensure that their records are accurate in relation to the custody, care and control of children, access arrangements and the contact addresses and emergency telephone numbers of both parents. Unless estranged parents are deprived of access by court orders, they should continue to receive copies of school reports, PTA correspondence and other school handouts. Teachers should ask to see access orders if parents claim that their former spouses are not allowed to see their children when, for example, child abuse or violence has been involved.

Most schools have sufficient numbers of separated/divorced/single parents to facilitate a self-help social group and to provide accommodation for meetings. This takes some of the pressure away from teachers and provides parents with support from others in similar situations.

Teachers are in the best position to help children retain their all important self-esteem. The child with hostile feelings needs a more controlled environment than hitherto. Teachers help by praising effort (rather than achievement) and desirable behaviour (instead of focusing on misbehaviour). Teachers of young children are also in a good position to encourage peer group relationships.

Schools increasingly recognise children's varied 'family' structures in their curriculum; it can no longer be assumed that children live with both parents or in nuclear families, and the curriculum should reflect a balance. Children should not be asked to produce cards for Mothers' Day or Fathers' Day without first ensuring that there are recipients waiting for them.

Teachers *in loco parentis* must act as responsible parents when children are in school. It may be necessary to emphasise the children's interest and to ask separated or divorced parents to reach an amicable agreement about who visits the school and when. Some schools arrange Fathers' Days, 'Dads and lads' camps and other opportunities for parents to maintain contact with their children. It is appropriate for a school to contact parents if there is reason to believe that the child is suffering from the estrangement. Similarly, the school may seek a change to a court order if a parent is abusing access, causing distress to the child.

The data in American surveys confirms the belief that the best thing for a child's mental health is to have two parents who remain together in a happy marriage. However, divorce does not necessarily lead to psychological problems. To quote Zill (1982 p. 152):

> It depends on what kind of divorce it is: a tranquil arrangement in which the interests of the children are one of the foremost considerations or a rancorous battle in which the children are considered part of the spoils. It depends on the resilience and the personal strengths of the children as well as the parents—the circumstances, age of the child, economic resources of the family, stability of the child's home after divorce, supports which are provided by the departed parent, relatives and friends.

Perhaps we should also add 'schools'.

Some story books have been written specifically to help children in distress. Examples are:

Anon. 1985, *Daddy Doesn't Live Here Anymore—A Book About Divorce*, A Golden Learn Book, New York.

Galloway, P. 1985, *Jennifer Has Two Daddies*, Women's Education Press, Toronto.

Girard, L.W. 1991, *At Daddy's On Saturdays*, Albert Whitman & Co., Chicago.

Hazen, B.S. 1983, *Two Homes to Live In*, Human Services Press, NY.

Padoan, G. 1987b, *Breakup*, Child's Play International.

Vigna, J. 1980, *She's Not My Real Mother*, Albert Whitman & Co., Chicago.

Vigna, J. 1991, *Mommy and Me By Ourselves Again*, Albert Whitman & Co., Chicago.

Students and teachers are urged to read:

Cox, K.M. & Desforges, M. 1987, *Divorce and the School*, Methuen, NY.

Helping children who have suffered or are at risk of maltreatment

The maltreated child

Child maltreatment crosses all social, racial, ethnic, cultural, educational and economic boundaries and damages the psychological, social, physical and intellectual development of its victims.

All abused and neglected children over five to six years of age attend school. Because of this and the fact that teachers are trained to observe and respond to differences in children's behaviour and seek specialist help as necessary, the teaching profession offers the most important link in the protection of children and the prevention of maltreatment. Whether they like it or not, teachers are at the forefront in the child's defence against all forms of abuse and neglect. Some teachers protest that this is social work and they are only there to teach. As research findings show, however, no teacher can teach effectively if a child is suffering from maltreatment.

In his keynote address to the 7th Congress on the Prevention of Child Abuse and Neglect in Rio de Janeiro, 1988, Oates revealed the results of a controlled study in New South Wales which showed that up to nine and a half years after hospital treatment, abused children were below the average in their socio-economic group in self-concept, measurable intelligence and language development. Twice as many abused children were labelled 'abnormal' by their teachers. The children were less confident, less trusting, more subdued and saw themselves as friendless compared to others.

Among neglected children at 12–13 years, there was less emotional stability, less ego strength, lower social maturity and more anti-social behaviour than in peers from the same socio-economic environment. Mothers of these children were less knowledgeable, more anxious, less aware of children's school progress and needed practical help to handle their problems. Oates concluded that the family must have ongoing support for the development of parenting skills to achieve a lasting effect.

The effects of sexual abuse are also evident in school. In Oates' study, teachers reported that school work deteriorated and victims became aggressive and attention-seeking. They exhibited serious behaviour problems in school, played truant, were more sexually aware and sometimes more withdrawn than other children. They were also most likely to repeat a year in the same class because of retardation in all aspects of their work.

Most child victims suffer increased distress when cases of abuse result in prosecutions and trials. Although it could be argued that these cases are likely to be the most serious, the children show more persistent problems and behaviour difficulties and they have a higher incidence than control groups of offending against the law at a later age. Oates also noted that children with the highest level of self-esteem were the ones least likely to be victimised by strangers.

Because maltreated children are in the presence of teachers for up to seven hours a day, five days of the week, teachers encounter the signs of abuse and neglect but, if they lack knowledge, they may label the children as having social, emotional, learning and behaviour problems without identifying the cause. In ignorance, teachers are likely to add to these children's problems; with perception and understanding, the classroom can provide a safe, predictable, caring environment. Please note that children with disabilities are at much greater risk of all forms of child maltreatment than non-disabled children.

The neglected child

Despite the comparative affluence of Western society, the problem of the neglected child persists. The term 'neglect' encompasses a broad range of omissions that endanger the child's wellbeing, including failure to provide the necessary protection, food, clothing, shelter, medical attention, hygiene and parental love. Neglected children tend to have a lower than average weight and height for their age and are more likely to suffer from accidents, chronic ill health and persistent ear, nose and throat problems. Environmental deprivation also results in developmental delay and associated behavioural difficulties. Language delay in itself inhibits the neglected child and lowers self-esteem, contributing to frustration, stress and school failure.

In the first few months at school, neglected children are likely to be completely confused by teachers' expectations. Those who suffer inconsistent home discipline may test the teacher's limits (and patience) persistently. They are sometimes mistakenly labelled as hyperactive when they rush around aimlessly and cannot sit still long enough to concentrate on a short story. When accustomed to parents who shout and scream negative commands, they are unlikely to respond to teacher's polite-requests for courtesy and consideration. Those who lack verbal communication skills may use force to achieve their needs, thus alienating their peers.

The most obviously neglected children are those who arrive at school so dirty and malodorous that they are ostracised in the classroom. They are unable to create friendships and teachers' attempts to include them in groups are often hampered by honest but humiliating rejection. Self-esteem then falls to a very low level and, feeling wretched and unhappy, neglected children cannot concentrate and achieve sound progress.

Child neglect occurs across all social classes but the neglected poor child is the most obvious in school. Neglected middle-class children often receive money and material goods in lieu of attention and affection.

Responsibility of the teacher and school

Laws in most Australian states require the teachers (not their senior staff) to report their suspicions of child maltreatment directly to statutory authorities, usually the departments responsible for family, community and social welfare services. In Western Australia and the ACT, teachers are expected to make reports to senior staff or education authorities. Students and teachers must familiarise themselves with the relevant laws and reporting procedures. It is now recognised, however, that schools have a much wider role to play than the detection and reporting of child abuse and neglect. These roles can be classified as family support, child protection, education for personal safety and the provision of a stable, caring, positive learning environment for maltreated children.

Schools provide a community service and constitute a vital part of the multi-professional team engaged in child protection work. They have regular formal and informal contacts with local health and welfare agencies and are well placed to act as a focal point for these services, ensuring that they reach families in greatest need. They have direct access to negligent parents and 'at risk' families and, especially in priority areas, offer a wide range of supportive functions. They provide programmes to empower parents within their own communities, giving them the knowledge and confidence to assert themselves and gain improvements in public services. They provide opportunities for parent education in child management, nutrition cooking on a budget and other relevant subjects. They involve parents in school and community life and provide inexpensive opportunities for socialisation. In addition, they encourage parents to befriend and offer support to each other at times of crisis. These services are necessary because parents who have multiple problems are usually ignorant of available resources or lack the skills and confidence needed to make approaches. They are unlikely to know about practical home help facilities, telephone support services, behaviour modification programmes, emergency childcare, respite care, emergency housing, legal and social welfare rights. Schools are highly effective in obtaining help for needy families incapable of helping themselves. For example, at Swallowcliffe (Elizabeth) Primary School in South Australia, a community health research project showed that a large number of children arrived at school without breakfast. The remainder consumed sugar-laden confectionery which produced short bursts of energy followed by a rapid decline. The researchers found a relationship between low energy levels and children's negative views of themselves and school in general.

A breakfast programme was introduced and the effects were carefully monitored by the staff at the local hospital. There were rapid improvements in the children's bodily functions, concentration, skill development and learning. These findings led to a search for corporate funding to support a regular programme. The local press provided free advertising of a kind that did not damage the dignity of needy families. Each morning, the children have the choice of 12 different learning centres, one of which provides breakfast. This has resulted in fewer behaviour problems and teachers find that they can present more rewarding challenges for learning. (See also pp. 105–7.)

In 1992–95, school breakfast programmes were provided in other needy schools by Save the Children Fund (SA).

The problem of the dirty, malodorous child is probably the most sensitive. Children never enjoy being so dirty that they are rejected and humiliated by others in school. All children need to be accepted and regarded as having a worthwhile contribution to make. Furthermore, they will only make progress in school if they are socially acceptable.

When teachers ignore dirty children, they defend their inaction by referring to parents' responsibilities. Remember that teachers are expected to behave as responsible parents and no responsible parent would allow children to attend school so dirty and neglected that their presence became unwholesome. The question is not whether children should be given the opportunity to 'clean up' at school, but how this can be achieved with maximum dignity. Teachers in the first three years of school are usually well equipped to clean and change children who have had painting or toileting accidents. Parent helpers and support staff are often willing to wash, bath or shower and shampoo neglected children and launder their clothing as necessary. This has to be done in a way that is least likely to cause offence to depressed, negligent parents.

Many teachers expose neglected children to messy play early in the morning so that the bath directly relates to school activities rather than the negligence of the home. Neglected children like to be clean and when the activity is made enjoyable, they ask, 'Am I dirty enough to go for a bath yet?' or 'When will I be dirty enough?' If there are no showers or deep sinks, young children can be accommodated in a plastic portable bath in the staffroom. They enjoy the smell of shampoo and talcum powder and the luxury of a big, soft towel. They admire their new selves in a mirror and return to the classroom with beaming faces and shining hair to a chorus of envy. In the summer, the problem of the dirty child can sometimes be alleviated by offering waterplay, an inflatable paddling pool and a hosepipe.

Most teachers of young children have stocks of clothing available for emergencies. In general, it is probably better to launder children's own garments at school rather than send them home in school clothing.

If home visits are made to establish the seriousness of the family's problems, school staff must take care that their verbal communications and body language do not register shock or disapproval, irrespective of the state of the home. Children are likely to suffer more if school is viewed by parents as hostile and critical.

It becomes harder to help neglected children as they grow older. Some teachers try to help by introducing the topic of hygiene, hoping that the offensive children will 'take the hint'. It is unrealistic to expect children to change their parents' behaviour and take responsibility for cleanliness at home. This exercise is more likely to draw the attention of others to the victim's deficiencies and increase, rather than reduce, their problems in the classroom.

When teachers recognise the need to report child neglect to statutory authorities, it is best if parents can be brought to accept that help is needed, so that they are involved in the reporting process. Teachers must report all child maltreatment but how the report is made is important. Schools have contact with children and their families long after social workers have closed their files and it is better for everyone if school and parents are not in conflict.

Marginal cases of neglect are the most common and the most responsive to community help. Neglect may be spasmodic, precipitated by intermittent pressures.

If a parent is approached in school, a quiet, private area should be provided. Tea or coffee, tissues and an ashtray should also be accessible.

Teachers worry, often unnecessarily, about how to introduce their concerns. If there has been little previous contact with the parents the first conversation should be at the 'getting to know you' level. Find out whether there are other children at home, whether both parents work, whether there are relatives in the neighbourhood, whether the family has any friends and whether there is support. With a sympathetic listener, family problems are soon revealed, either directly or indirectly.

The next step is: 'What can we do to help you and your child?'.

It may be that the parent has already had dealings with agencies and the experiences were negative. It may be that the parent does not realise that there are helping services available. There may be strong fears that the 'welfare department' will inflict some kind of punishment and take the children away. Reassurances can be given by teachers who are already aware of family support services in the neighbourhood. Schools should not only have an up-to-date list of services and personnel to contact but should encourage occasional informal meetings between workers, teaching staff and parent groups. In disadvantaged areas, schools often arrange monthly meetings with local health and welfare workers, police and general practitioners who are interested in the protection of children and the prevention of abuse. They invite community workers to social events and parent information sessions on child protection. Teachers are often surprised to find that other professionals are concerned about the same families.

When possible, the teacher should telephone the welfare worker in the parent's presence, reporting on the following lines:

Hello. This is [name] at [name] School. I have Mrs [name] with me right now. She is concerned about the safety/welfare of her children who attend this school. Her husband is a chronic invalid and she suffers from poor health (etc.). She is finding it very difficult to look after the children and we are all worried about them. She is in need of urgent help...Would you have a word with her...she's here now.

If the school is seen as concerned, not punitive, staff can maintain contact with the family and return to the social agencies if the necessary assistance is not provided. If children are severely neglected and/or parents deny that there is a problem, or the situation worsens, a report should be made to the statutory authority immediately.

Schools in disadvantaged areas often employ counsellors who take responsibility for helping neglected children and their families. Interestingly, school administrators suggest that the problem of dirty, malodorous children has reduced as a result of early intervention by counsellors.

Risk factors

Neglected children may be:

- consistently dirty, hungry or inadequately dressed for prevailing weather conditions;
- accompanied by a pungent, unpleasant odour;
- consistently passive or withdrawn in class;
- unable to create relationships with other children;

- uncommunicative with the teacher;
- often hungry, stealing or begging food from other children;
- often tired in class and indicate that they are out unsupervised or in the house alone late at night ;
- retarded in language development and speech;
- retarded in fine motor skills;
- unable to play alone or with others;
- underweight and undersized bearing in mind age, health record and family traits;
- often late for school, with poor attendance and unexplained absences;
- seldom accompanied by a parent; parents ignore invitations to school events;
- often sick, especially prone to chronic ear, nose, throat and chest problems;
- dull-eyed and sad in appearance;
- sent to school when school is closed;
- uncontrolled and uncontrollable, shifting from one activity to another with very short spans of concentration;
- incapable of listening to a simple story;
- engaging in glue or adhesive sniffing, alcohol consumption or acts of self-destruction;
- given an inbuilt expectation of failure;
- aggressive, using force to meet needs because of the lack in communication skills;
- unusual in their lack of response to pain and distress;
- lacking medical treatment when needed for abscesses, septic cuts, burns etc.;
- clinging and immature in their behaviour.

The adult assessing these risks will look at the pattern of behaviour, the frequency and variety of signs and the family history to determine the degree of risk present.

Some risk indicators based on the observation of parents may include some of the following:

- the family has a history of poor parenting: for example, the parents lived in negligent homes, lacked sound parenting models or were placed in residential care in childhood;
- the parents are overwhelmed by a variety of problems: personal, financial, housing, unemployment etc.;
- family organisation is known to be chaotic;
- parents are very young and/or immature and life seems to be out of control;
- the home appears to be neglected;
- parents avoid contact with the school;
- parents appear unkempt, depressed, angry or unwell;
- the parent has no partner, frequent changes of partner or a partner who is chronically sick or unemployed;
- there is a history of mental illness in the family;

- the child is given inappropriate responsibilities or freedom at home;
- parents say that they did not want the child, an abortion was desired but the mothers were 'talked out of it' by the other parent or extended family members;
- parents say that they can't cope with their children;
- parents greet their children indifferently or impatiently;
- parents grab their children and tug when movement is desired;
- adult–child communications tend to be restricted to commands or complaints;
- parents complain of children's eating or toilet habits: 'he still wets the bed', 'she won't eat the food I give her', 'he's a finicky eater';
- parents show no concern for their children's wellbeing when one could reasonably expect concern;
- parents work shifts or nights or go away for weekends leaving children unsupervised;
- the family has become isolated from other families in the community;
- parents do not know how to talk to their children or play with them; in the classroom, they tend to play alone, as a child, indicating a lack of play in childhood.

The physically abused child

Physical abuse commonly includes non-accidental injury by beating with fists, hands, belts, electrical cords or hard objects, by burning, scalding, banging children or throwing them against a hard surface, or biting them. Children are often injured in a fit of temper when the adult is frustrated, has low tolerance and unrealistic expectations. When injury is inflicted, the perpetrator often explains that the punishment was intended to stop the children crying or punish misbehaviour. Abusers have faulty notions about normal and abnormal behaviour and how to discipline children. Sinister motives are often attributed to quite normal childish reactions.

Children at greatest risk are those whose parents were also abused in childhood and those who have seemingly insurmountable problems and lack family support. Most abusive families can be helped by the provision of practical help, support networks, daycare, health care and the opportunities to learn and develop positive child management techniques and improve child–parent relationships.

Approaching the parent suspected of physical abuse

When physical abuse is suspected, it is helpful if teachers know the parents sufficiently well to assess their expectations. Parents often reveal that their children are unmanageable and that one parent or the other punishes excessively.

It is useful if teachers are sufficiently at ease with parents to receive information relating to domestic and financial problems, unemployment or separation. Pre-school staff find it relatively easy to maintain this kind of contact because most parents accompany their pre-school children and are encouraged to linger and become involved in activities. Open communications are also comparatively easy to maintain in the early years of school when an 'open door' policy is practised and parent–teacher contact is not limited to before and after school. Schools can often prevent abuse and neglect from becoming serious if home visits are made routinely and problems are identified in the early stages.

When suspicions are first aroused, the teacher must consider the signs of abuse in relation to other factors. Have there been earlier warning signals? Is the child making good progress? Is the child happy and well-adjusted?

Have there been signs of problems at home? Are there other family members in school? How are they?

If the suspicion of maltreatment involves a recently enrolled child, is the family new to the neighbourhood? Were problems noted by teachers or social workers in the previous school?

Is the child Vietnamese? Traditional Vietnamese medicine involves digital pressure on specific areas, sometimes resulting in bruises. If in doubt, contact Vietnamese welfare agencies for information and guidance.

If teachers ask abused children how they received their injuries, they typically recite what the perpetrators instructed them to say, often threatened by further violence if the truth is revealed. Sometimes a child will inadvertently disclose what happened if the question is worded unexpectedly, such as: 'Why was Mummy cross with you last night?' However, there is a moral dilemma about questioning children, and it is far better if the facts can be obtained from the parent in a non-threatening way.

Many teachers make the mistake of confronting parents directly with statements such as 'I'm concerned about your child's bruises. How did they happen?'. This approach is unproductive because the perpetrators become defensive, fearful and feel obliged to concoct accident stories that teachers are then obliged to accept. When injuries are caused by genuine accidents, parents usually inform teachers with a sense of guilt or embarrassment. Abusive parents make no such confession, appearing indifferent to their children's suffering and lacking remorse. If explanations are made, they are often bizarre: cigarette burns, for example, may be explained away with 'He walks into my cigarettes'.

Contact with parents should be made when the first indicators are noticed. Contact must, of necessity, be personal (not by letter), noncritical and nonthreatening. The art of developing a useful relationship with parents depends less on the ability to talk to them than the ability to listen and make them feel comfortable. If parents can talk about the stresses that engulf the family, the teacher will be in a better position to help their children.

If teachers have a comfortable relationship with parents, confrontation is unnecessary. They make it clear that they are concerned about the parents, (not their children). They confirm that the parents are under a lot of strain. Parents are often relieved to find that someone is genuinely concerned about them.

Child abuse and neglect are signals that a family needs help. We are all capable of hurting our children if and when they and our circumstances press us beyond the point of endurance. When parents care for their children, they can be persuaded to accept help simply because they care. This should he put forward as a positive step, not a sign of weakness. Mothers are more likely to admit the need for help than fathers because of their social conditioning: males often see themselves as failures if they cannot solve their problems alone.

As with child neglect, schools that maintain contact with helping agencies can assist parents in a practical way on the lines of 'I can see that you need help...I know just the person who can help you...Let's give him/her a call now'. The conversation is likely to be on the same lines as that given for helping the negligent parent (pp. 167–8).

Even when we are obliged by law to report suspicions of abuse to statutory authorities, this is by far the most effective way of reporting. The teacher who tells the parent at the outset that: 'I think your child is being abused and I am required to report it' runs several risks. First, the relationship between parent and school may be damaged. Second, the parents may remove the child and leave the neighbourhood, putting the child at greater risk. Third, the child is likely to be blamed and re-abused.

By first adopting a helping approach, the teacher–parent relationship is not damaged, the teacher is more likely to receive the confidences of parents when further problems occur and the school is better able to help the child and family.

Some indicators of physical abuse

The signs of physical abuse are numerous and include:

- bruises of varying ages and colours: thumb or handprints where the child has been firmly grasped or limbs have been twisted;
- cigarette burns: circular red marks of varying hues (according to age) where cigarettes have been stubbed on the skin;
- rope marks on wrists, neck, or ankles where the child has been tied up;
- human bite marks on the child's face or body;
- long, slim abrasions inflicted by whipping with an electric cord;
- scalds inflicted by either pouring hot liquid over the child or by standing or sitting a child in a bowl or bath of hot water. The latter involves neat sock-like marks where the child has been held still. No child who accidentally places one foot in a hot bath would leave it there, add another, or sit down in scalding hot water;
- burns indicating the shape of the object used, such as the pointed end of an electric iron, the mark of a hot poker, the bar of an electric fire etc.;

- abrasions resulting from the use of a belt;
- black eyes. Children do not usually injure their eyes when they accidentally fall. The cut tends to be on the protruding bony area in the vicinity of the eyebrow and the chin. A black eye might occur if the child was hit by a cricket ball, but this could not account for two black eyes;
- bald patches on the child's head where hair has been pulled out;
- fractures;
- injuries inside the mouth;
- serious abuse may be indicated if the child is suffering from concussion or there is blood inside the ear;
- implausible explanations for injuries or discrepancies between explanations given.

Risk indicators: parents' behaviour

Some of the risk indicators may be similar to those of negligent parents, with the following additions:

- the parent avoids seeking medical help when it is needed;
- the parent has a low tolerance threshold;
- the parent shows no concern for the child's discomfort and volunteers no explanation for the injury, or injuries are explained in a vague or bizarre way;
- the parent is unsupported, socially isolated and/or suffers from high levels of stress;
- there is a history of child abuse in the family;
- there is a history of mental ill health in the family;
- the parent complains that the child is bad, different, stupid, unmanageable, difficult to rear and a nuisance;
- the child was premature or separated from the mother soon after birth;
- the parent thinks that the child is abnormal, irrespective of evidence to the contrary;
- the child is physically or mentally handicapped or different in some way;
- the parent takes the child to different hospital casualty departments for treatment;
- the parent avoids contact with school;
- the parents think that the child is being deliberately difficult when behaviour is normal;
- the parent is immature and looks to the child for care, attention and satisfaction of emotional needs;
- the parent shows unrealistically high expectations for the child's behaviour, school, athletic or other performance.

Although mothers are responsible for most acts of physical abuse, serious injury is often inflicted by immature male partners who have no blood ties with their victims. Mothers often protect and defend male abusers when they are economically and emotionally dependent upon them or they have been conditioned to protect adult males rather than children. In most cases, however, abusers are ordinary people who love their children but are not coping with life, suffer tremendous pressures and problems, lack skills in child management and can be helped within their own communities (O'Neill 1994).

When children are injured by parents, they usually give implausible explanations for injuries and deny that they have problems or need help. Teachers must report their findings as a matter of urgency. If the abuse is repeated, social services should always be informed. Detailed records of dates, injuries, parents' explanations and reports should be maintained by the school. Injured children must always be examined by paediatricians, at local or children's hospitals.

The emotionally abused child

All forms of child maltreatment involve emotional abuse but this can also occur without other forms of maltreatment being present. Emotional abuse is difficult to define and just as difficult to prove. Definitions include a 'chronic attitude or act' that is detrimental to or prevents the development of a positive self-image in the child. Consideration of parents' attitudes or actions should not be limited to isolated instances which probably occur in all families. Emotional abuse involves a persistent chronic pattern of behaviour which then becomes the dominant characteristic in the child's life. 'Scapegoating, belittling, denigrating or other overly hostile treatment including threats of sexual or physical assault, overworking, close confinement or the withholding of food, sleep or shelter as a form of punishment' was added to the definition by the US Department of Health and Human Services in 1980.

In 1983, Mayhall and Norgaard considered in addition, punishing the child for normal behaviour, preventing or inhibiting the child from bonding with the primary care giver and punishing the use of accepted social skills normally used outside the family setting.

More recently, Garbarino, Guttman and Seeley (1986) identified five other areas of abuse: rejecting, isolating, terrorising, ignoring and corrupting.

- *Rejecting*: refusing to acknowledge the child's worth and the legitimacy of needs.
- *Isolating*: the child is cut off from normal social relationships, preventing the formation of friendships and making the child feel alone in the world.
- *Terrorising*: by verbal assault, fear, bullying, frightening and making the child feel that the world is hostile.
- *Ignoring*: by depriving the child of essential stimulation and responsiveness, stifling emotional growth and intellectual development.

- *Corrupting*: stimulating the child to engage in destructive anti-social behaviour, reinforcing deviance and making the child unfit for normal social experience.

In 1987, Brassard, Germain and Hart added:

- *Degrading*: persistently calling a child stupid; humiliating, deprecating and labelling as inferior.
- *Exploiting*: for the adult's advantage or profit.
- *Denying emotional responsiveness*: failure to provide the sensitive response necessary for healthy social and emotional development. This includes detachment, ignoring children's attempts to interact and mechanistic child handling which is devoid of cuddles and talk.

Possible consequences of psychological maltreatment include:

- habit disorders
- conduct disorders
- anxiety traits (thumb sucking, twitching, poor bladder and bowel control)
- psychoneurotic reactions (illnesses that cannot be readily diagnosed)
- behaviour extremes
- overly adaptive behaviours
- lags in emotional, social and intellectual development
- self-destructive behaviour
- lying and stealing
- involuntary defecation and urination
- low self-esteem or negative self-concept
- emotional instability or maladjustment
- reduced emotional responsiveness
- inability to become independent
- lack of confidence and inability to risk failure, resulting in under achievement
- inability to trust others
- insatiable search for affection and approval
- depression
- failure to thrive
- withdrawal
- aggression
- a tendency to abuse their own or other children in later years.

These consequences can persist into adulthood (Klugman 1988).

One of the difficult decisions that a teacher has to make is at what stage to report the emotionally abusive behaviour of a fellow teacher. Weak teachers sometimes use emotional abuse to gain and retain control of a class, belittling, deriding and scapegoating vulnerable children. These methods were often learned in childhood and are practised when positive child management skills were not taught in pre-service teacher education.

The sexually abused child

All children are vulnerable to sexual abuse, irrespective of their age, sex, nationality, race, social class or religion. The greatest risk is to children with disabilities but comparatively few cases are reported. The most common age of victims involved in cases reported to authorities in Australia and the USA is four to five years. Most offenders are known and trusted by their victims. They achieve their objectives by the betrayal of trust, the misuse of authority, the use of attractive inducements and the imposition of secrecy on children who are told repeatedly that they will suffer horrendous consequences if they reveal what is happening.

The common characteristics of offenders are those of gender and experience: most abusers are male and most were sexually molested by multiple abusers in childhood. (Briggs 1994; Briggs, Hawkins & Williams 1994). Molestation can cause severe trauma, damaging the victims' sexual development. Therapists and researchers confirm that offences are seldom 'one-off' incidents. A single molester can damage hundreds of children before being apprehended. Victims often repeat the offences with other children. Very young victims may behave sexually in the preschool, classroom or toilets, showing an obsession with genitals and sexual matters. Offences committed by adolescents and young children should be treated with the same care and concern as offences committed by adults. If these child perpetrators are not reported and helped, they are likely to continue abusing children and become adult offenders.

People who sexually abuse children often give the appearance of being 'normal' heterosexual family men. Incestuous fathers are sometimes perceived by teachers as caring, overprotective, overattentive, strict and even religious parents.

Adults suspected of sexual abuse should never be confronted directly by teachers. Child sexual abuse is the most universally denied crime. Denial is understandable. The abuser has much at stake, for if the child is believed, his or her professional and community status, employment, marriage, freedom and family life will all be in jeopardy. Many abusers convince themselves that they have done no harm. When charged with offences, they call upon local clergy, psychiatrists and friends to provide evidence of good character. Sadly, because sexual abuse is such an abhorrent crime, some judges and juries have been all too willing to apportion blame to victims. Children have been trained to obey and please adults and they should never be blamed for what adults do to them.

Reporting suspicions of child sexual abuse

The method of handling suspicions of child sexual abuse is somewhat different to that of reporting neglect or physical abuse. The teacher must make the report to the local agency responsible for investigations, immediately after suspicions have been aroused. If the offender is not a member of the child's family and if there is a possibility that he or she will escape, police must be notified. If a child has been molested by a stranger on the way to school, for example, it is important that a search is commenced immediately to apprehend the perpetrator.

Parents and offenders are then interviewed by social workers and police from child protection units. Social workers from statutory departments of social services or community welfare are responsible for investigating reports involving family members.

When teachers have reason to suspect that children have been abused by family friends, relatives or caregivers, they must report directly to the appropriate department, NOT to the victim's parents. There are several reasons for this. The victim's parents may:

- be aware of the offences;
- be directly involved in the abuse;
- warn the offenders of the impending investigation;
- press victims to withdraw allegations or make different statements;
- either refuse to report the offender or, at the opposite extreme, take the law into their own hands;
- handle the information inappropriately at a time when there is no-one present to protect the child's interests (see Briggs 1993).

A medical examination may be necessary to provide evidence of assault and to ensure the child's physical wellbeing. Such an examination is usually the province of specialist paediatricians in child sexual assault units attached to children's hospitals. Arrangements will be made by police or social workers. Examinations should not be undertaken by family doctors.

So far as teachers are concerned, the priorities are:

- to handle disclosures and suspicions of abuse with the utmost sensitivity to protect child victims;
- to provide maximum support for those victims;
- to ensure children's safety; and
- to report suspicions of abuse to the appropriate authorities

How do teachers know that children have been sexually abused?

Sexually abused children come to the notice of teachers when they:

- act out the sexual abuse with dolls or other children;
- behave in a sexually promiscuous way, for example with male teachers or with older children;
- expose sexual knowledge inappropriate for the age group;
- show an obsession with sexual matters, genitals, sexual play, masturbation etc.;

- tell other children about what happened and those others tell their teacher;
- withdraw from friendships or groups previously enjoyed;
- show an unexplained change of personality, different emotional responses and anxiety traits: an outgoing child may become sad and withdrawn, a happy child may become angry;
- cling excessively to the teacher to the extent that the adult feels uncomfortable;
- engage in acts of self-mutilation or self-destruction such as jabbing themselves with sharp instruments, taking harmful substances or petrol/adhesive sniffing;
- draw pictures that reveal emotional disturbance;
- draw sexually explicit pictures;
- display emotionally disturbed behaviours that cannot be explained;
- reveal offences inadvertently, for example when a child was reprimanded for masturbating in class, he responded with 'My daddy does it to me';
- give vague verbal clues, such as 'My Uncle Jack wears funny underpants', 'I don't like Uncle Jack any more', 'I don't like the games we play at Uncle Jack's. He makes me take my clothes off', and 'I've got a secret I can't tell' etc.;
- complain of physical discomfort in the anal/genital area.

Sometimes the mother of an abused child confides in the teacher that she is concerned about the behaviour of a lodger, babysitter or family member. Such parents are usually seeking assurance that their child is safe when their intuition tells them otherwise. A parent may also complain that a child is fretful, refuses to go to bed, won't eat, clings, has nightmares and there is no known cause. **Teachers must consider all indicators in relation to the child as a whole**. Quite often, teachers have been concerned about a child for several weeks before suspicions of abuse are aroused. We must strike a balance between overreacting to vague indications of sexual abuse and ignoring them. If children are giving signals that they need help, talk to them gently, privately and reassuringly. Give children the assurance that it is safe for them to talk about it when someone is upsetting them and that you are there to help.

Children's drawings give clues that they are unsafe

Young children express their emotions through their artwork. As a result, drawings can be especially useful in revealing their anxieties and feelings about themselves and others.

Sexually abused children often produce drawings that seem immature or even bizarre. Some have a nightmarish quality and the teacher intuitively recognises that 'something is wrong'. Special interest should be taken in the artist if the colours used are predominantly black, purple and red when there is a choice of colours (Lewis & Green 1983), or if the artists draw themselves without arms or without a mouth or other facial features when they are technically capable of drawing these features and incorporate them in drawings of other people. These are classic signs of helplessness commonly exhibited by child victims of sexual abuse (Yates, Beutler & Crago 1985). Abusers are often depicted with huge arms, hands and long fingernails. Young children add belly-buttons to drawings of people but they do not normally draw genitals unless they are worried about sexual matters. Victims of male abusers often add an outsize, erect penis to their drawings of humans and animals. Victims of oral sex often depict humans with large, open, round mouths and prominent teeth (Briggs 1989, 1991).

When drawings suggest emotional disturbances, the teacher should find an opportunity for private conversation and indicate concern on the lines of:

'I'm really worried about you.'

'I know that something is troubling you.'

'I want to help you.'

'It may be hard for you to talk about it but if you can tell me why you are so sad, I can help you to feel better.'

If a child indicates an inability to talk about something unpleasant, enquire whether it is a 'nice secret or a yukky secret'. Ask 'What will happen if you tell me about this?', 'Who said so', and 'Who else knows the secret?' This may reveal the name of the abuser and the nature of the threat, clarifying the size of the problem and providing the teacher with an opportunity to reassure the child. Offenders often tell children that they are to blame for the abuse and if this behaviour is disclosed 'The police will come and take you away'. This is why threats need to be investigated and explained at the outset. Adults want victims to keep their behaviour secret because they know they are doing wrong things and they are frightened of getting into trouble.

Drawings can also be useful for helping children to expose what is happening to them in difficult circumstances. Sometimes a child will agree that he or she is troubled but will remain silent about the cause and the identity of the person involved. 'Let's see if we can find out who is making you sad,' says the teacher. 'Let's draw pictures of all the people in your family.' The teacher remains with the child while the drawings are made and the child is encouraged to talk about each individual in turn. The question is then put. 'Is it x who is upsetting you?' Eventually it may be necessary to say, 'OK, you've told me that you're upset. You say that it isn't Mummy who is upsetting you. It isn't Daddy. It isn't your brother. It isn't your grandad. How about drawing me a picture of the person who is upsetting you?' and later, 'What is his/her name?'. The teacher may find that the child's problem is quite trivial, based on a misunderstanding that can easily be remedied. On the other hand, it may be serious.

Sometimes drawings are vague but verbal descriptions are significant. The

Figure 8.1: After one incident of sexual touching by a stranger, this child drew her self-portraits armless and rooted to the ground. This continued until she underwent therapy six months after the offence. Drawings then returned to being free-standing with arms

statement that 'This is a picture of a man with his pants down and that's his big wee-wee up to his chin', left the teacher in no doubt that the child was unsafe. The information needed from the child is:

'Who is the man in your picture?'

'What is he doing?'

'Where does this happen?'

'What do you do?'

'Who else was with you when this happened?'

Questions should be designed to provide the teacher with sufficient information to decide:

- whether suspicions of abuse are sufficient to warrant making a report; and
- whether the child is safe to return home at the end of the afternoon.

When children draw pictures of figures engaged in sexual activity, teachers should enquire, as casually as possible, who the people are in the picture, what they are doing and where this happens. It should never be assumed that sexually explicit pictures or children's sexual behaviour is the result of accidental exposure to pornography, or 'blue' movies. If young children reveal that they are exposed to pornography, the matter should be reported because those children are at risk of abuse. Some adults and adolescents involve young children in acting out pornographic video scenes.

Normal sexual development and abuse

Teachers and parents are often confused about what is normal and what is abnormal in children's sexual development. Adults often dismiss children's disclosures of molestation on the grounds that 'children have good imaginations—it couldn't possibly be true'. Children are imaginative but imagination is based on experience; their ideas do not evolve out of the blue. Furthermore, young children are incapable of imagining the details of adult sexual behaviour and the things that abusers typically say to their victims.

Researchers show that 'normal' children are mildly curious about their bodies but, when presented with anatomically correct dolls, interest in the body parts is very brief and no attempt is made to engage the dolls in sexual activity (Sivan et al. 1988). In other experiments, 90 per cent of sexually abused children used dolls for acting out sexual behaviours. In their free play, they demonstrated oral sex and intercourse between the dolls and also between the dolls and themselves (Jampole & Weber 1987).

Teachers often encounter reports of sexual activity in and around school toilets. The question then is whether the behaviour amounts to normal sexual curiosity or child abuse. Normal curiosity involves equality between participants and behaviour is on the lines of 'You show me yours and I'll show you mine'. Behaviour initiated by victims who have already become juvenile abusers is likely to include the use of power, force, tricks, bribes, threats, secrecy and, sometimes, the involvement of groups against a smaller or weaker child. The victim is forced to participate in masturbation or oral sex and abusers may engage in the insertion of objects into openings. These activities are learned from sexual abuse and do not constitute normal sexual curiosity. All too often, schools merely punish offenders without enquiring who showed them how to behave in this way. The behaviour continues but participants take greater care to ensure that they don't get caught. Boys tend to regard peer group sexual activity as 'normal' or as a game. If peer group sex becomes habitual, children become more vulnerable to adult offenders.

It is important that incidents are investigated calmly, sensitively and without blame so that all victims of sexual abuse can be referred for therapy.

Handling disclosures of sexual abuse

When teachers realise that a child has been sexually abused, they invariably experience powerful emotions of shock, horror and fear. In these circumstances, we must remind ourselves that we are not the victims; it is the child who has been abused. It is vital that we put our own personal feelings aside and concentrate on helping the child who trusts us and needs our protection. If our feelings of revulsion are revealed, the victim will suffer increased feelings of low self-worth, and withdraw.

It is important to tell the child that he or she is very sensible and has done the right thing. By disclosing what has happened, the child has helped to protect other children from being upset and hurt by the offender. Abuse victims must be told very clearly that children are never to blame when adults behave in this way. Victims must also be told that this has happened to lots of other children in the same school. They must be made to realise that they are not unusual and this did not occur because they are weak, naughty or different. It is also important to explain that bigger children or adults know that they are not allowed to do these things to children and that it will be necessary to tell someone else about what happened. 'There are special people employed to help children. They are called child protection (or social) workers. When adults do things that upset children; they must be told to stop.' The child should know that this special person will see the offender and tell him/her that he/she is not allowed to do this to children.

Supporting parents of sexually abused children

School staff often find themselves giving support to shocked and bewildered mothers whose trusted partners are their children's abusers. Teachers sometimes have to persuade parents of the need for personal counselling so that they can provide better and informed support for their children. At times, teachers may also need to persuade parents of the need for therapy for children who have been traumatised by their experiences. Parents often deny that treatment is necessary. They assume, wrongly, that if the offences are ignored, children will forget. To be effective, teachers and school personnel should be aware of the specialist services available for children and their families (Briggs 1993).

Providing a positive environment for victims of maltreatment

All forms of child maltreatment contain a strong emotional component and have the potential for inflicting psychological damage on victims. There are many variables that determine how children are affected. These include the personality of the child and the level of self-esteem before the abuse began, the relationship between the abused and the offender, the type, duration and degree of maltreatment and the context in which it occurred. After incidents of maltreatment, the important factors are the way in which others react to their disclosure, what is done to protect the child, and what support is available after the revelation.

Schools and teachers have an important role to play in providing a positive, supportive and stable environment in which abuse victims can learn to trust others and feel safe. They need special programmes designed to develop self-esteem, assertiveness, confidence and personal safety skills. They need opportunities for success, praise for effort and achievement. Abused children need to know that they are worthwhile human beings, that others care for them and that they are not helpless and powerless.

Teachers who report suspicions of abuse should always ask to be involved in case conferences. When teachers are in close daily contact with victims, they have an important contribution to make to professional knowledge and it is important that they are informed of the steps that welfare authorities take, especially in the closing of files. Unfortunately, inexperienced social workers tend to undervalue their role and teachers may need to be assertive to obtain information. Teachers who are dissatisfied with the actions or responses of social welfare workers should contact regional managers and, if necessary, call their own case conference of relevant parties. Teachers are working with child victims long after the social workers have closed their files.

Most education authorities now accept responsibility for teaching children the skills necessary for safety with people alongside road safety, health and social skills. New Zealand has its own school curriculum 'Keeping Ourselves Safe', while the USA has a wide range of video programmes and kits. Michele Elliott introduced a protective education kit to British schools and Peg West's Wisconsin Protective Behaviours Programme and the Canadian CARE kit have been adopted by Australian schools, supplemented by Freda Briggs' books, *Keep Children Safe* (1988b) and *Teaching Personal Safety Skills to Chil-*

dren with Disabilities (1995a). The most effective programmes teach problem-solving and assertiveness skills, how to identify, reject escape from and report sexual misbehaviour, how to differentiate between good surprises and bad secrets and develop skills needed to stay safe with strangers. Although programmes are most effective when parents reinforce them (Briggs & Hawkins 1994), education cannot be left entirely to the home, since some children are sexually abused by trusted parents and family members. It is absolutely essential that schools provide child protection programmes for children with disabilities.

There are now many inexpensive publications available for parents and teachers on child protection, developing self-esteem and helping children who have been abused. These are available from educational booksellers, feminist bookshops and counselling services. Some suggested titles are as follows:

Useful reading for teachers:
Bornemann, K, 1992, *Everything You Need to Know About Incest*, Rosen Publishing Group, New York.
Goldman, R. & Goldman, J. 1988, *Show Me Yours*, Penguin Books, Melbourne.
Saphira, M. 1985, *The Sexual Abuse of Children*, Mental Health Foundation, Auckland.
Stark, E. 1991, *Everything You Need To Know About Sexual Abuse*, Rosen Publishing Group, New York.

Books for adults to use with children:
Appelbe, A., Sippel, J.E. & Smailes, C., 1984, *Trust Your Feelings* (included in the CARE Kit), CARE Productions Associations, British Columbia.
Briggs, F. 1988b, *Keep Children Safe*, Longman Chesire, Melbourne.
Christensen, C. et al., 1991, *Feeling Safe* (booklet & audio tape), Essence Publications, Adelaide, SA (Distributors).
Elliott, M. 1986, *The Willow Street Kids—It's Your Right to be Safe*, Andre Deutsch, London.
Freeman, L. 1984, *It's My Body*, Parenting Press Seattle, Washington.
Girard, L.W. 1984, *My Body is Private*, Albert Whitman & Co., Chicago.
Hart-Rossi, J. 1984, *Protect Your Child From Sexual Abuse*, Parenting Press Seattle, Wash.
Hessel, J. 1987, *What's Wrong With Bottoms?*, Century Hutchinson, London.
Lippett, I. 1990, *Trust Your Feelings: A Protective Behaviours Resource Manual for Primary School Teachers*, Essence Publications, Burnside, SA.
Pithers, D. & Greene, S. 1986, *We Can Say No*, Beaver Books, in association with National Children's Home, London.
Wachter, O. 1985, *No More Secrets for Me*, Penguin Harmondsworth, Middlesex.

The depressed and suicidal child

Recent Australian and international research has drawn attention to the prevalence of depression and self-destructive behaviour in very young children. Statistics hide this phenomenon because authorities keep no records of suicides involving children under ten years. However, psychiatrists are treating an increasing number of six-, seven- and eight-year-olds whose suicidal thoughts and actions have been identified by teachers. For example, a six-year-old boy who had suffered sexual abuse, told his teacher repeatedly that he wanted to join the armed forces so that someone would kill him. His drawings and writing showed an obsession with morbidity. Dr George Halasz (1988) of Monash University, Melbourne, explains that suicidal children are rushed to hospital and everyone focuses on saving life, not enquiring how and why 'the accident' happened. Myths about happy childhood have prevented professionals from recognising that childhood is often distressing. Suicidal children are often thought to be hyperactive or accident-prone. Fortunately, young children will tell caring adults why they swallowed mum's pills, threw themselves from high places, stepped into busy traffic or walked along the railway lines. We only have to ask and ensure that they get help from the appropriate services.

Identifying and helping children with low self-esteem

The child who suffers from low self-esteem can be identified when he or she:

- consistently expresses feelings of inadequacy when given a new challenge;
- is self-derogatory: 'Nobody likes me. Nobody wants to play with me', 'I'm no good at…', 'I can't do that', or 'I can't think of anything';
- fears failure and feels the need to copy the work of others to stay safe;
- will not tackle new words when reading;
- chooses the activities repetitively, to be certain of success;
- is always a follower, never a leader;
- has bad posture, looks at the ground and avoids eye contact;
- is fearful and timid;
- is unable to make decisions when choices are available or makes the same choice repeatedly;
- seems depressed — sad appearance, especially sad-eyed;
- lacks goals and motivation;
- is defensive;
- conforms with others and blames them for misbehaviour: 'They made me do it'.
- sees actual achievements as insignificant;

- lacks inner resources to tolerate or reduce anxiety aroused by day-to-day events;
- is unwilling to contribute to discussion or express an opinion;
- exaggerates mistakes;
- bullies, brags and reports on others to cover up personal inadequacies;
- has no sense of belonging to the group.

Ways in which school may positively influence children's self-esteem:

- By a careful reappraisal of the effects of school climate, school policies, school curriculum, and parent–teacher relations on children's self-esteem.
- By individual teachers reappraising the effects of their own self-esteem and consequent attitudes, and the atmosphere of the classroom.
- By using curricula specifically designed to develop self-esteem, relating programmes to the needs of individuals and using activities sensitively. For ideas, see:

Borba M. & Borba, C. 1982, *Self-Esteem: A Classroom Affair*, Dove Communications, Melbourne.

Farnette, C., Forte, I. & Loss, B. 1989, *I've Got Me and I'm Glad: A Self Awareness Activity Book*, rev. edn, Incentive Publications, Nashville, Tenn.

McInnes, L. 1988, *I'm a Walking Talking Miracle*, Cassette Learning Systems Pty Ltd, Melbourne.

Purkey, W. 1970, *Self Concept and School Achievement*, Prentice Hall, Englewood Cliffs, NJ.

Reasoner, R.W. 1982, 'Building Self-Esteem', in *A Teacher's Guide and Classroom Materials*, Consulting Psychologists Press, Palo Alto, Calif.

Equity for children in the classroom

The notion of equity within the class is an implicit part of the teacher's response to children as individuals, understanding their needs and interests and providing appropriate learning experiences which enable the children to realise their full potential. In recent years educators have identified four groups of children who do not enjoy equal opportunities for learning:

- girls as opposed to boys;
- disabled children and children with special needs;
- children for whom English is a second language or who are from minority cultures;
- gifted children.

These children are sometimes deprived of school opportunities necessary for them to reach their full potential.

The gender issue

Concerns have been expressed about sex-role stereotyping and the consequent narrowing of options for both boys and girls. In schools and in society alike, there has been an overlay of expectations based on gender. This has been particularly damaging to girls. In schools, sex-related experiences have restricted the options available, and as a result there has been marked inequality of educational outcomes. Girls have traditionally left school with fewer career choices, lower self-esteem and inferior physical fitness.

Several factors can be identified in this process, but the most significant one is the dynamics of class interaction. It has been shown that boys use more classroom space and demand more talk time and attention than girls (Schofield 1986). Teachers tolerate these activities in boys but girls who emulate these behaviours are often criticised, covertly discouraging their participation in behaviours crucial to active, positive learning. Teachers have a responsibility to provide equal opportunities for all children so that they can develop skills and abilities for effective functioning in society. When potential attainments are inadvertently constrained by roles and labels ascribed because of background, ability and sex, children are channelled in certain directions to pursue particular interests, activities, sports etc. which relate to gender.

What can teachers do to provide equal opportunities for learning?
They can:

- encourage children to respect each other and consider the feelings of others irrespective of their sex;
- teach children about their rights and the rights of others;
- encourage high self-esteem in both girls and boys;
- encourage appropriately assertive behaviour and discourage the stereotyped non-assertiveness of girls and aggressiveness in boys;
- help children of both sexes to develop values of gentleness, helpfulness, assertiveness and tolerance;
- encourage girls to be active, to take more initiative, to be more self-reliant and develop leadership skills;
- develop a critical awareness of our own conditioning, cultural prejudices and pressures to conform to stereotyped sex roles;
- actively encourage children to expand their aspirations and participate in as many experiences within the curriculum as possible;
- help all children to enjoy maths, science, cooking, woodwork, drama, dance, sewing, block play, music, reading etc.;
- involve girls and boys in all areas of sport and physical fitness;

- use non-sexist curriculum materials, textbooks, picture books and other written materials;
- ensure that all children have equal access to play materials in the learning environment;
- encourage children to engage in activities in the classroom irrespective of sex;
- monitor own reactions and interactions with girls and boys;
- do not seat or line-up children according to their sex;
- do not make threats that boys will 'have to sit with the girls' if their unacceptable behaviour continues;
- do not make stereotyped comments indicating that boys must not show their emotions: for example, 'Be a brave boy and stop crying', or 'Come on, get up. It doesn't hurt';
- do not use the opposite sex for derogatory comparisons: for example, comments such as 'Peter, don't tell tales. You're worse than the girls' and 'Stop fussing Marco...you're worse than an old woman' are unacceptable;
- ensure that displays of work represent boys and girls equally;
- discourage competition between the sexes: do not present the behaviour or achievements of boys or girls as examples for the opposite sex to emulate;
- do not present stereotyped expectations relating to children's abilities: for example, 'Can I have two strong boys to help me move this table, please?';
- ensure that boys are involved and are seen to be involved in caring roles and domestic responsibilities;
- ensure that both boys and girls are depicted as involved in positive behaviours, problem-solving and decision-making;
- provide a variety of dressing-up materials for both sexes;
- encourage boys to engage in domestic play and language activities and girls to participate in construction, woodwork and activities that lead to the development of numeracy and science;
- use books and pictures that show both males and females in caring and professional roles;
- inform parents of what the school is doing and why.

The work of Dr Anne Smith (1985) shows that, to attract girls to maths-related activities, female early childhood educators must make a conscious effort to become involved in the maths and construction areas. Girls will follow female teachers to these work areas but they are reluctant to go there alone. Unfortunately, due to the shortage of men in early childhood education, there is a dearth of information to show how children respond to male teachers.

The development of non-sexist attitudes depends heavily on the attitudes and levels of awareness of class teachers and parents. When the focus is on individuals and all children are encouraged to respect themselves and each other, problems are less likely to arise. When teachers model the sex-role reinforcing behaviours that they were taught provide sexist curriculum materials or indicate expectations based on gender, children will emulate them and develop sexist attitudes and behaviours.

Children with disabilities

The term 'disability' reflects the consequences of an impairment, which is an abnormality or lack of ability to perform an activity in a manner that is considered to be normal. A handicap is concerned with the cultural, social, economic or environmental consequences that may be experienced by an individual as a result of a disabling condition (Bochner 1987). In a nutshell, all handicapped people are disabled but not all disabled people feel handicapped.

In many places, the integration or mainstreaming of disabled children into the regular school system is expressed government policy and reflects a changing philosophy in the provision of services for the disabled as a whole. There is a growing awareness that the disabled have a right to participate in the mainstream life of the community, enjoying the same benefits and assuming the same responsibilities as the others. The integration of children with disabilities into the mainstream of the school system is a logical extension of that philosophy to education (Jenkinson 1984).

In principle, the concept of integration is laudable. It means that there should be provision for special education for children with disabilities in regular schools, organised in such a way that both the disabled and the non-disabled can participate together in a significant proportion of activities. In practice, it has been one of the most challenging issues facing teachers. Lacking special training, many class teachers feel ill-equipped to understand and to cope with the special needs of these children. Some also feel that the increased demands placed upon them threaten the standards of teaching for the non-disabled members of the class. Many parents worry that their disabled children will experience great difficulty and frustration in meeting the demands of the regular school in terms of the physical, social, emotional and academic challenges. Parents of able children are often apprehensive about the amount of time that teachers have to devote to disabled members, and the resulting potential for disruption. Special education teachers fear that their role in education will disappear and the quality of education will diminish without the specialist facility.

The concept of integration is often discussed by educators. Some see it in terms of a complex of additional services additional to the ordinary class teacher. Others equate integration with the placement of disabled children in regular classrooms because this is less expensive than the provision of special schools. Some accept integration as children spending part of the time in ordinary classrooms and part of the time either at special schools or attending special sessions. A single definition of integration has never been determined. It is believed, however, that disabled children should spend at least 75 per cent of their time in an ordinary classroom for integration to be effective (Thomas 1986).

Types of disability

> Mainstreamed children are those children whose needs are so great that they present a challenge which is over and above the normal challenge of teaching and cannot be met without additional support or pro-gramme changes (Taranaki Education Centre 1987).

Although all children have special education needs at one point or another in their lives, some children require specialised support more consistently. This group includes those who have physical disabilities, those who have emotional disturbance and those who are experiencing developmental delays. More specifically the range may include:

- *High severity–low prevalence disabilities*. This includes children whose diffi-culties are severe to profound in nature and, organically based, are usually identified at an early age as their failure to master developmental mile-stones becomes evident. They include severe sensory (deaf/blind), physi-cal, psychiatric, intellectual and biological (epileptic, diabetic) impairments. If appropriate treatment (drugs etc.) and/or prostheses (hear-ing aids, wheelchairs) are provided, the impact of the disability on some of these children's schooling may be minimal. However, not all severe impairments can be treated like this and the children will therefore require highly specialised education and care.
- *Low severity–high prevalence disabilities*. This includes children whose diffi-culties are relatively mild and often hard to quantify. They are frequently not identified until they fail to achieve at the level of their normal peers. Many are classified as mildly mentally retarded, learning-disabled and emotionally-disturbed and the disabilities can usually be remedied at school. Also included in this group are children with speech and language difficulties. These problems usually disappear as the children mature, although some children continue to have problems throughout their school life (Bochner 1987).

What can teachers do to assist integration and offer equal learning opportuni-ties?

1 Co-opt the support of the principal/head teacher who should attend to the following (Taranaki Education Centre 1987):
   - the collection of information to enable children's needs to be met;
   - meetings with parents/guardians to discuss the children's physical needs, social requirements, relationship with others and the reason for enrolment;

- identification of the appropriate community support systems available and making contact with them;
- identification of school and classroom requirements and rectification of deficiencies, such as the building of a ramp, appropriate toilet facilities, special equipment, for example physiotherapy equipment;
- discussions with the teacher and the rest of the staff relating to the child's placement, the nature of the disability, the classroom layout and the availability of resources;
- organising meetings between teacher and parents/guardians to discuss class programmes, school activities and organisation relating to mobility, medication, feeding, toileting, communication and behaviour management;
- continuing to organise support and provide relief time for staff.

2 Identify the resources and equipment needed in the classroom, and the class layout with reference to accessibility to resources and easy mobility.

3 Consider class trips, class helpers, swimming time, sports day, physical education, etc.

4 Continue discussions with people who have previously worked with the child.

5 Create a positive learning environment. Before the 'special needs' child arrives:
- encourage class discussion on the theme that everyone has needs and problems;
- share similarities and differences in an informal way;
- discuss the fact that everyone has special talents and that everyone is good at something and needs help with something else;
- discuss feelings, particularly if children are feeling unsure and embarrassed;
- identify the new child's needs and the ways in which the children may help;
- discuss the specific ways of dealing with relevant matters such as deafness, slow speech, impaired vision, wheelchairs, callipers or other necessary equipment.

After the child arrives:
- give the child every opportunity to do things independently and to take part in everyday class and school activities;
- assist other children to cope with the child's basic needs;
- build positive relationships between all the children in the class, helping them to feel secure, successful and at home;
- model and reinforce in children's behaviour a caring, supporting role;
- facilitate (using systematic strategies) positive interactions and co-operative learning within the classroom context;
- use children's literature to foster understanding between the children.

Placing children with special needs into the regular classroom is the beginning of an opportunity. However, like all opportunities, it carries the risk of making things worse as well as the possibility of making things better. If integration goes badly, children with special needs will be stigmatised, stereotyped, rejected or ignored. If integration is effective, true friendships and positive relations will develop between these children and their non-handicapped peers. Effective integration depends as much upon the receptivity and contribution of children and parents as upon the skills and accommodative capacities of teachers and the personnel who support them (Barry 1986 p. 24).

Some useful children's books to share are:

Althea 1991a, *I Have Epilepsy*, Dinosaur, London.
Althea 1991b, *I Use a Wheelchair*, Dinosaur, London.
Brindze, R. 1978, *Look How Many People Wear Glasses—The Magic of Lenses*, Atheneum, NY.
Cleaver, V. 1977, *The Mimosa Tree*, Oxford University Press, London (blindness, epilepsy).
Fanshawe, E. 1975, *Rachel*, Bodley Head, London (child confined to a wheelchair).
Hawker, F. 1979a, *With a Little Help from My Friends*, Jacaranda, Milton, UK (spina bifida).
Hawker, F. 1979b, *I Can Read in the Dark*, Jacaranda, Milton (blindness).
Hawker, F. 1979c, *Donna Finds Another Way*, Jacaranda, Milton (cerebral palsy).
Jessel, C. 1975, *Mark's Wheelchair Adventure*, Methuen, London.
Kamien, J. 1979, *What if You Couldn't...?*, Scribner, NY.
Keats, E. J.K. 1972, *Apt 3*, Hamilton, London (blindness).
Levine, E. 1974, *Lin and Her Soundless World*, Human Sciences, NY (deafness).
Litchfield, A.B. 1976, *A Button in Her Ear*, George J. McLeod, Toronto (deafness).
Petersen, P. 1976, *Sally Can't See*, Black, London (blindness).
Sanders, P. 1991, *Let's Talk About Disabled People*, Franklin Watts, UK.
Smith, S. 1978, *Happy Birthday, Antoinette*, Open Leaves Press, Windsor, Vic (blindness).
Southall, I. 1968, *Let the Balloon Go*, Methuen, London (cerebral palsy).
Wilson, P. 1978, *Mummy Why Can't I Breathe?*, Nelson, Melbourne (asthma).
Winch, G. 1990, *Samantha Seagull's Sandals*, Childerset, Melbourne.

Helping children with learning disabilities

Leeper, Skipper and Witherspoon (1979, p. 528) defined the learning disabled child as having the following characteristics:

Does not benefit from classroom instruction that aids most children. Possesses an average or better than average level of intelligence. There are no evident physical, emotional or cultural handicaps.

This means that the child with a learning disability is not intellectually retarded, emotionally disturbed or culturally disadvantaged. It says that the child is unable to learn by the methods used by the teacher in the classroom. When the appropriate type of teaching strategy is found and used, the problem disappears (Ross 1977). Children who have such learning problems have often been labelled dyslexic, minimally brain-damaged, underachievers and other deprecatory terms. The teacher who suspects that a child has a learning disability should be prepared to experiment with different teaching methods, especially, for example in the teaching of reading and mathematics.

Some degree of learning disability should be suspected in children who exhibit any combination of the following:

- poor visual discrimination, such as difficulty in distinguishing between vastly different letters and numbers;
- poor visual memory, forgetting what has been seen, written or read;
- poor auditory discrimination, as shown by the inability to distinguish between different sounds and words;
- poor hand-eye co-ordination, resulting in problems with making the hands do what the eyes see and the brain tells them to do (often labelled as clumsy children);
- inability to make choices;
- poor self-image;
- inability to concentrate on an activity (often labelled as hyperactive).

When new teachers encounter children with learning disabilities who fail to respond to a wide range of teaching methods, they should seek specialist support and help from their education authority.

Helping children with developmental disabilities

In working with children who have developmental disabilities, the teacher needs sensitivity and insight into possibilities for developing their potential strengths and self-esteem. It is important that children's problems are identified quickly, that specialist support is sought and that plans are made to provide an integrated education programme to cater for children's individual needs.

When children with developmental disabilities are mainstreamed in a 'normal' class, then progress is likely to be slower than that of their peers. They may need more adult attention and encouragement to complete small tasks, attention that can often be provided very successfully by sensitive parent helpers supported by strong teacher-guidance. It is customary, however, for the adult:child ratio to be increased to cater for the needs of the seriously disabled child in the mainstream class.

When working with these children, more positive reinforcement and repetition may be necessary. Challenges may have to be less complex, requiring less concentration and initiative, ensuring that there is always scope for the child to succeed. All children should be encouraged to beat their own previous best efforts to achieve educational gains. Positive attitudes are needed on the lines of, 'I know you can do it' as opposed to, 'That's much too difficult for you'. If a child accepts a challenge that is too difficult, the adult should quietly assist the child to complete it without loss of dignity.

In choosing activities for children with developmental disabilities it is likely that more and possibly different concrete materials and experiences will be needed and teachers sometimes have to be satisfied with very slow progress.

Above all, it is important that children with developmental problems are respected and accepted by peers and adults alike. Self-confidence, emotional stability and the motivation to learn will depend on the attitudes and behaviours of classroom inhabitants and the provision of a positive learning environment.

Starting school is a time for major adjustment for all children but, for those with disabilities, the process is especially demanding and confusing. New safety factors are introduced along with new routines and new people. There are new expectations and demands to both conform and use initiative. It is usually helpful if the child has already attended a pre-school. Some special early childhood centres teach basic social skills, literacy and numeracy skills to Down syndrome children at the very early age of two to three years. This is achieved by regular attendance from the age of eighteen months, with the parent acting as teacher. The purpose of these programmes is to ensure that, at the age of five, the children will possess the skills that make them acceptable to non-specialist teachers in mainstreamed schools. It is often suggested that educable developmentally delayed children should be placed in special pre-school classes at the earliest possible age.

Because it is difficult to predict how well a child with disabilities will fit into a mainstream class, schools usually accept such children on a trial basis. Teachers and parents then need expert guidance relating to each child's specific needs and how they can be met. Most countries have specialist state provision for children who are not capable of gaining benefit from attendance at a 'normal' school. Parents will need counselling when teachers decide that their children cannot be accommodated in a mainstream class.

Teachers should be alert to behavioural cues associated with developmental disability. They should observe the child carefully when the following characteristics are in evidence:

- inability to follow simple or multi-step instructions;
- lacks self-direction in selecting activities;
- regularly copies other children's work or imitates rather than creates;
- lacks ability in abstract reasoning;
- lacks concentration;
- poor memory and inability to recall recent experiences or events;
- lacks ability to apply learned material to new but related situations;
- unable to identify similarities and differences in objects and situations;
- unable to anticipate the consequences of actions;
- delays to motor co-ordination;

- delays in social development: toilet training, talking, dressing, feeding;
- poor hand and eye co-ordination (adapted from Leeper, Skipper & Witherspoon 1979, pp. 527–8).

Care must be taken not to confuse developmental delay with maladjustment caused by severe emotional problems relating to child abuse.

Children for whom English is a second language

Multi-culturalism and multi-lingualism exist throughout the world and multi-cultural education is neither a unique phenomenon nor a recent innovation. One of the many goals of early childhood education has been the socialisation of young children, which means that teachers have accepted the responsibility for helping children to learn ways of behaving and interacting which may be different from those at home. Children need to learn to meet certain behavioural expectations, to use other language styles, to develop independence and interactional skills, and satisfaction in a variety of ways. While this learning does not present problems to many children because the differences between home and school are not dramatic, for others the move from home to school represents a major break.

> Language patterns, social interactions, and the manifestations of values and culture may be unfamiliar to these children…they may be forced to use a language that is foreign to them, and the social patterns and interactions expected of them may be equally foreign (Saracho & Spodek 1983, p. viii).

Teachers, however, are learning to value cultures other than the dominant one in the class, recognising their uniqueness and their contribution. Socialisation is taking on a new meaning, where children are being encouraged to celebrate their similarities as well as their differences. Nevertheless, multi-cultural education is not relevant only to those classes where minority cultural groups are represented. It is relevant to all children who grow up in culturally mixed settings and who are exposed to other cultures through television and books as well as community and school experiences. Children need to expand their realm of awareness, concern and understanding beyond their immediate experience, and this may be achieved in the classroom by providing opportunities for children to see life from different viewpoints.

How can teachers help?

Teachers must take care not to offer children a tourist curriculum, where the study of other countries reads like a holiday brochure. Instead, relevant everyday experiences can be explored across cultures so that the children begin to understand about cultural backgrounds and attitudes. Stories, art activities, discussions, pictures, films, and research projects about families, homes, children's games, special events, food, music, dress and other related topics are approaches which can show how children's lives are similar yet different; they enhance the identification with one's own culture as well as awareness of other cultures (Ramsey 1984). For children who have had little opportunity to mix with people from other cultural backgrounds, the idea that people who look different have similar needs is comparatively easy to grasp. This supports their own development of cultural identity and their awareness of diversity, while diluting the traditional stereotypes. Furthermore, children are more likely to integrate the new information when they can relate it to their own experiences (Forman & Kuschner 1977).

In a culturally diverse classroom, teachers can incorporate a wide cultural content in the curriculum by including experiences and resources that reflect the children's cultural groups. Collaboration with parents and community groups is basic to the success of a programme where the teacher is wanting the children to see, discuss and play with different musical instruments, art materials, cooking equipment, clothes, food, ways of carrying things, ways of eating, dancing and children's games, songs, rhymes, language and favourite stories. Holidays provide high-interest occasions for incorporating cultural experiences into the classroom; there are many similar celebrations across cultures, such as carnivals for the new year, commemorations of independence, national birthdays, Easter and Christmas (Flemming, Hamilton & Hicks 1977). Young children can experience the rich variety of human experience in many concrete and meaningful ways. Children's literature is a powerful medium for extending children's horizons and valuing the culturally specific activities of others. Teachers who offer an inclusive curriculum can be guided by the following when choosing children's books.

Look for:

- books which are not solely relevant to the dominant ethnic group in the class;
- books which do not contain any derogatory references or patronising attitudes to specific ethnic characters;
- books which contain accurate information about other cultures;
- books which reflect present situations and people relevant to the experiences of the children.

Beware of:

- books which show stereotypes in the illustrations;
- books which have the token inclusion of a minority character when it is incidental to the story;
- books which have the dominant culture in positions of power, making important decisions for minority groups;
- books which lack sensitivity to other cultures either in the story or illustrations.

Figure 8.2: Shared experiences can be included in all aspects of a multi-cultural curriculum

Consider:

- the credibility of the author, their experiential background;
- the date of the publication;
- value laden language, e.g. primitive, savage or lazy.

The new arrival to the country

If there are children in the class who have recently arrived in the country, studying their homeland can assist their entry to school. This approach makes the adjustment and learning process a reciprocal one instead of it being the sole responsibility of the recent arrival (Ramsey 1984). Some sense of the political and social realities should be incorporated into the curriculum, but the depth and complexity of the information will depend very much on the age and experiences of the children involved.

New migrants may, understandably, appear bewildered and timid. They may speak little or no English but make quick progress with 'hello' and 'good-bye'. The teacher points at objects and speaks carefully. These children are often insecure and dependent on parents who are unable to help in the learning of English. When children have a restricted linguistic ability in their own language, there must be a focus on developing oral ability before any written aspects of language are expected. Children's language develops through concrete experiences and it is necessary for teachers to provide a wide variety of opportunities for using language. Young children appear to learn a second language in much the same way as they learn their first but they are able and willing to keep the two languages apart (Padilla & Leibman 1975). Children acquiring a second language go through a silent period in the classroom during which time they are building up a competence in the second language. They may not wish to speak but respond with gesture as well as their first language to indicate understanding. It is counterproductive to insist that children speak in English during this time (Huang & Hatch 1979).

Children learn most from each other, and where English is a second language, peer support and tutoring is highly successful both in the classroom and in the playground. In some schools, new arrivals are able to attend language classes where they gain additional experience and confidence with English in a more formalised way.

Research indicates that parents play a major role in helping or hindering the new arrival's progress (Education Department of South Australia 1975). It is important for the teacher to meet the new parents and, using an interpreter as necessary, discuss the child's welfare. Sometimes, migrant parents become concerned because they feel that their children are learning very little. The teacher should explain the system of education and how parents can help. While encouraging parents to co-operate in the speaking of English at home, the continued use of the first language should also be emphasised. This indicates the value of and respect for the language and culture of the new arrivals. It is important too, that any notices, announcements, labels or written communication be written in the parents' first language to ensure understanding and to offer a warmth and welcome.

The concept of shared human experience can be woven into all aspects of the curriculum. The primary objective of multi-cultural education is to affirm cultural diversity by correcting stereotypes, myths and omissions and to assist in the genuine understanding of and concern for all people. Each person has the right to be respected as an individual. Each person has the duty to respect the individuality of others while developing awareness of the common themes. This is quite compatible with the notion of affective education within a positive learning environment which offers an inclusive curriculum based on equal opportunity.

Gifted children

Virtually all early childhood teachers have gifted children in their classrooms. Unfortunately, contrary to popular opinion, these children do not succeed without special help. Several authors (Fox 1971; Whitmore 1979, 1980) pointed to lack of support in the early years as one source for the devastatingly wasteful under-achievement of many gifted adolescents (Kitano 1982).

Several reports highlight the importance of meeting the special needs of young gifted children within the normal classroom setting:

Gifted children comprise 3–5 per cent of the school-age population and can be found in every age, ethnic and socio-economic group (Sisk 1979). Fox (1971) reported a four year spread in development among five-year-olds tested at the beginning of the school year. There is a notable sparsity of special services, private or public for gifted children (Kitano 1982). Gifted young children must receive the opportunities and challenges that they need in an environment that is conducive to sound emotional and social development. Most teachers feel a moral obligation to help the disadvantaged but may feel less obligated to those who are already advantaged (Hallahan & Kauffman 1986).

Identifying gifted children

Gifted children may be identified by their high achievement or potential in any one of five areas: intellectual, creative, specific academic, leadership, or in the performing and visual arts (Kitano 1982). It is worth noting that intellectual giftedness is but one of many categories of giftedness. It is also extremely difficult to identify gifted young children. As Roeper (1977) points out, such children do not necessarily exhibit outstanding talents. Some are withdrawn, while others are troublesome and aggressive in class. These traits are most likely to be the result of home, peer or teacher expectations and discrepancies between children's intellectual abilities and their social and emotional development. In addition, those who have the potential for high achievement in science, mathematics or the arts, may lack the opportunities to gain the necessary experience for their talents to develop. Kitano (1982, p. 16) provides the following checklist to help teachers recognise signs of giftedness in young children:

Intellectual and academic:

- is attentive, alert;
- possesses advanced vocabulary for age;
- shows early interest in books and reading;
- learns rapidly and completes tasks rapidly;
- has high level of curiosity;
- enjoys being with older children;
- pursues interests, collects things;
- has long attention span;
- possesses high standards;
- shows mature sense of humour for age;
- prefers new and challenging experiences;
- retains information;
- displays high level of planning, problem-solving, and abstract thinking compared to peers.

Creative:

- asks many questions;
- does things in own way (independent);
- may prefer to work alone;
- experiments with whatever is at hand;
- is highly imaginative;
- thinks up many ways to accomplish a goal;
- may respond with unexpected ('smart-alec') answers;
- produces original ideas.

Musical:

- makes up original tunes;
- shows degree of tonal memory;
- enjoys musical activities;
- responds sensitively to music;
- easily repeats rhythm patterns;
- easily discriminates tones, melodies, rhythm patterns.

Artistic:

- fills extra time by drawing, painting, etc.;
- draws a variety of things, not just people, horses, flowers;
- remembers things in detail;
- takes art activities seriously and derives satisfaction from them;
- has long attention span for art activities;
- shows planning in composing the artwork.

A leader:

- is frequently sought out by peers;
- interacts easily with other children and adults;
- adapts easily to new situations;
- can influence others to work toward goals, desirable or undesirable;
- others rely on him/her for ideas and decisions;
- is chosen first by peers.

Catering for the needs of gifted children

It is often argued that gifted children should be segregated from other children and accelerated through the school to maximise their giftedness. When this occurs, their achievements may be spectacular in special areas but there is no real evidence to show that they gain materially over what they would have acquired in a heterogenous group working in a rich environment under the guidance of a competent teacher (Leeper, Skipper & Witherspoon 1979). Any good early childhood education programme allows and provides for individual differences and the curriculum is developed to meet the needs of exceptional, as well as average and slower children. The needs of individuals are identified and planned for in such a way that each child becomes an accepted, contributing member of the group.

All children have gifts. Some excel in some aspect of creative activity. Some read more proficiently than their peers. Some are particularly agile and adept in physical activity. The teacher's task is to identify these talents and provide a suitable climate for optimum growth. As abilities are observed, they are recorded and referred to for guidance in curriculum planning. When children appear to have exceptional talents, the teacher should seek confirmation, counselling and assistance from specialist professional sources.

Gifted children have needs common to all children, including the development of basic concepts across all areas. It is vitally important that teachers plan a programme that will provide a balance in their experience. The child who is advanced in language arts may avoid mathematical, creative or scientific activities if there is less chance of success in those fields. It then becomes necessary for the teacher to actively encourage such children to participate in these less popular pursuits. Children who know that they excel in one particular skill and restrict their efforts to that skill are likely to become isolated within the classroom. They often avoid group activities which, in turn, impairs their social and emotional development.

Parents sometimes think that their children are gifted because they have a particular aptitude in a specific but limited area. When such children are coached at home, parents often emphasise the importance of formal work and devalue learning through activity. Given a free choice in the classroom, the children tend to select work involving writing and numbers, work that their parents would consider to be important. If this continues, the children miss a wide range of beneficial social and creative experiences, such as drama, games, group collages, etc. This can be resolved, first, by inviting the parents into the classroom and explaining what children are learning, how they learn and how the parents can help. Second, it can be resolved by providing integrated activities and challenges that involve concrete experiences and recording, reading back, creative writing, etc.

Gifted children should be provided with challenges that take account of their social and emotional needs. Those who are accelerated into classes with older children are often disadvantaged; while the seven-year-old may operate at the ten-year-old's intellectual level, the seven-year-old is unlikely to have the necessary physical and social skills or the necessary emotional development and life experience to facilitate good social relationships with children who are much older.

What are the long-term advantages of segregation and acceleration? There have been reported cases of twelve-year-olds gaining access to universities, but to what end? Can a twelve-year-old really benefit from the breadth and richness of university life? Is there any real advantage in possessing a university degree at the age of fifteen? There is a real danger that these super-brain children will develop in a lopsided way with interests and expertise confined to a single, very limited area. Such children are at risk of becoming 'mental giants' and 'social dwarfs' who, as adults, are capable of making very little contribution to society (Leeper, Skipper & Witherspoon 1979, p. 524).

Gifted children need provision for many stimulating and varied opportunities to develop initiative, increase the range and scope of their ability and knowledge, have the acceptance of peers and overcome emotional stress, especially the stress associated with the risk of failure. Teachers should place an emphasis on independent thinking and action, and provide activities to build relationships and concepts as distinct from learning multiple facts. Teachers can unwittingly contribute to antisocial attitudes, not realising that gifted children lose the respect of peers when they are repeatedly encouraged to display their attributes, are recipients of constant praise and are held up as examples to be emulated. Some gifted children avoid appearing different to others and deliberately conceal their talents. Bored, they are likely to use their creativity in a variety of misbehaviours to entertain their peers and test the teacher's limits.

Gifted children should be provided with challenging situations to develop critical thinking and the skills of evaluation, synthesis, analysis, and application as well as comprehension and knowledge (Bloom 1972). Children's thought processes can be challenged by providing activities that:

1 *enhance creativity in situations where there is no single correct response.* These activities should foster problem-solving skills, for example, by challenging children to suggest and experiment with alternative ways of achieving an end result. It is important that teachers plan pertinent questions that will encourage children to estimate and test answers for themselves (see chapter 10 for further information on questioning techniques). Probing questions should be asked to encourage the elaboration of children's answers and challenge their ability to view things from a different perspective;

2 *enhance higher cognitive processes,* such as activities that require children to find out how things work, either by close observation or taking them apart. Such items are old clocks, vacuum cleaners, bicycles, telephone switchboards, television sets, etc. Learning how to break down a familiar item into component parts and reassemble it, children can begin to understand the complexity of both structure and process and evaluate worth;

3 *foster decision-making, planning and communication.* The children should be involved in predicting cause and effect relationships and take responsibility for planning and implementing their own projects to integrate curriculum;

4 *foster learning by discovery.* 'Even young children can acquire the fundamentals of the scientific process of observing, hypothesising, experimenting and evaluating' (Kitano 1982, pp. 20–1). Discovery is followed by the children's explanations which, in turn, are followed by experimentation to test their conclusions;

5 *help gifted children's moral development and ethical judgement,* providing opportunities to evaluate social issues that are relevant to them;

6 *arise from an integrated unit of work that facilitates application, analysis, synthesis and evaluation*, such as a visit to the zoo, questioning on the lines of:

'What do you think would happen if...' (application).

'How are these animals alike...how are they different...how did nature prepare them for their natural environment...could they live in hot/cold climates...why not?' (analysis).

'Create and draw a new zoo animal. Describe its native habitat and characteristics' (synthesis).

'Should there be zoos? Is it cruel to keep animals in cages? What would it be like if you were kept in a cage? Do you think we could do anything to change the situation for the animals in very small cages? Does it make any difference if you were born in a cage and have never seen the natural environment?' (evaluation);

7 *develop additional language skills*, for example, by encouraging the interested child to find out more about zoo animals from library books and from the zoo itself, extending their vocabulary as well as their awareness of how to find information for themselves. Gifted children may enjoy more sophisticated stories than their peers and they are often able to write their own complicated adventure stories with detailed and advanced language. Discussion should be employed at every opportunity to help children to put their ideas into words, think of alternatives and test them out.

Gifted children may be found in any classroom. Their early school experiences contribute substantially to their emotional stability, social relationships, attitudes to learning and, as a consequence, to whether or not they will achieve their full potential in life.

TASKS FOR STUDENTS

READING TASK

1 Read and note the main points of any journal article relating to creating learning environments for children.
2 Discuss how children are different and how they are the same.
3 Discuss how you would cater for children with learning disabilities in a vertically grouped class of twenty-eight pupils.
4 Consider the implications for teachers and class members when a child starts school who:

- is already a competent reader;
- speaks no English;
- has deficient eyesight but avoids wearing his thick-lensed spectacles because he is teased by other children;

- is partially deaf;
- is from a minority culture;
- is living in her fifth foster home in two years;
- has a minor speech problem;
- knows more about computers than you.

CASE STUDIES

Case study 1. Lisa's mother recently gave birth to a baby. The child was premature and the mother was obliged to spend a great deal of time at the Special Care Unit until the baby was permitted to go home. Lisa, aged five, often complains of stomach aches and headaches. She is fretful in class. Her work and behaviour have regressed. She often sucks her thumb and is antagonistic to her former friends.

Discuss the possible reasons for Lisa's changed behaviour. Discuss what you, as a teacher, could do to help the child. Note your conclusions.

Case study 2. You have a well-established class with strong group cohesion. Rashid, aged six, joins the class in the middle of term. Rashid has a bad squint. His mother explains that he recently underwent surgery but the operation failed to provide any improvement. He is the only darkskinned child in the class. He has just moved into the locality and has no friends. He is thoroughly unhappy and spends most of the time clinging to you and crying. Other class members are totally unsympathetic and clearly resent his presence.

Discuss the various stresses on the new pupil. Discuss the possible viewpoints of the other class members. What steps would you take to change this situation?

Case study 3. Maria, aged seven, transfers from a neighbouring school when her parents separate. Her mother informs you that she is expecting a child to a man who is not Maria's father. She, Maria and her three-year-old son are temporarily living with her retired parents on a nearby housing estate. The father of the expected child is married but is contemplating divorce. Following the marriage breakup, Maria's father sold the family home and joined the navy.

Maria is a very sad, isolated child who, when given a free choice of activities, invariably selects water-play or painting. After several weeks in school, Maria appears to be making no progress. She is content to fill and empty receptacles with water and, every day, she paints a picture. Whatever her choice of subjects, she includes four people, her father, mother and brother and she writes her former address across the top of the paper.

Discuss the various stresses on the child, the stresses on the mother, and the stresses on the grandparents who are providing temporary housing. What can the school do to help this child? Could you suggest to the mother that the child might benefit from contact with her father?

Assuming that there is no court order depriving the father of access to his daughter, has the school the right to contact him? Give your reasons.

If the mother has no objections to Maria making contact with her father through school, how could this contact be incorporated in your learning programme for the child, bearing in mind that he is in the navy?

Case study 4. The teacher had long been concerned about Nasser, aged almost 6 years. He often seemed sad and showed signs of marginal neglect. He lacked confidence and made slow progress in class. He wore the same clothing repeatedly and, on hot days, there was an unpleasant smell. Sometimes, he had small bruises on his arms, legs and face but they were always of a minor nature. When questioned, he always responded, 'I fell'.

A parent-helper was the one who spotted the cigarette burns on Nasser's arms. When his mother came to collect him, the teacher said that she was concerned about the child's bruises and burns and asked for an explanation. The mother became defensive and said that Nasser was a clumsy, stupid child who gave her more trouble than 'all the others put together'. She said, 'I left a cigarette in an ashtray while I went to clean up the flood he had made in the toilet block. While I was gone, he walked into the cigarette'. The next day, this single parent left the caravan site with her family, and left no forwarding address. The child did not return to school.

- The teacher made at least two big mistakes in handling this situation. What were they? What were the consequences of those mistakes?
- How would the mother feel when she was being interviewed by the teacher? Was her explanation acceptable? Give your reasons.
- How could the teacher have approached this mother differently? How could the teacher have reported her suspicions of abuse while keeping the parent 'on-side'?
- Plan step by step what you would do and say if you found yourself in these circumstances. To whom would you report your suspicions? What services are available to help 'at risk' families in your area?
- Should the teacher have ignored the fact that the child was unclean and malodorous? How would the other children respond to an unpleasant smell in the classroom? How would the child have felt? How would this have affected his social development and learning?
- What could the teacher have done to resolve this problem without offending and alienating the parent or damaging the child's self-esteem?

Case study 5. Daniel, aged eight, is about to be transferred to a special unit for children with developmental delays. You are new to the school but you quickly note that his drawing and writing skills are at about the four-five-year level, his social skills are poor and he lacks concentration. One day, Daniel presents you with the drawing shown overleaf and says, 'This is a man with his trousers down and that's his big wee-wee up to his chin'.

- Consider carefully what information you need from this child to find out a) whether he is a victim or at risk of sexual abuse, and b) whether it is safe for him to return home at the end of the day.
  Plan and record (word by word) the questions that you would ask Daniel to obtain this information. Consider the implications of these questions very carefully.
- What steps will you take to ensure that the whole class does not become aware of your conversation?
- Daniel tells you that the man in the picture is Uncle Joe and that they play games and wrestle together. What would your next question be?
- Daniel confirms that Uncle Joe is not only a child molester but he lives with Daniel's mother in the family home. Record word for word what you will say to the child following his disclosure.
- When you report this to senior staff, you are told that Daniel was punished for sexually abusing younger boys in the school toilet at the beginning of term but the incident was attributed to his retardation. The senior teacher tells you that he won't report the matter at this stage because 'it isn't worth bothering about...he'll be leaving this school in a couple of weeks' time...and what's the use...the police won't do anything when the victim has an intellectual disability'. What would you say? What would you do? To whom should this matter be reported?
- Discuss what should be done if the disclosure takes place half an hour before school closes and the child is normally collected by his mother or the alleged offender. Could you detain the child at school after school hours? Given that the abuse has been going on for some time, would it be better to allow Daniel to return home as if nothing had happened, requesting social services or police to interview him at school early the next day? Present arguments for and against postponement.

The next day, Daniel's mother tells you that her son has revealed Uncle Joe's behaviour and that she has 'kicked him (the perpetrator) out of the house'.
The head teacher says that he is prepared to postpone Daniel's transfer to the special unit if you are willing to accept responsibility for handling

Figure 8.3: Daniel's drawing

his special needs. Discuss some of these needs and how you might cater for them. Which services are available in your area to help you? Which services are available to help the mother to deal with her feelings about the abuse? Which service would help the victim?

USEFUL REFERENCES

Allen, K.E. 1992, *The Exceptional Child: Mainstreaming in Early Childhood Education*, 2nd edn, Delmar Publishers Inc., USA.

Butler, S. 1990, *The Exceptional Child*, Harcourt Brace Jovanovich, Sydney.

Pettman, J. 1992, *Living in the Margins: Racism, Sexism and Feminism in Australia*, Allen & Unwin, Sydney

Rule, S. *et al.* 1990, 'Preparation for Transition to Mainstreamed Post-Preschool Environments: Development of a Survival Skills Curriculum', *Topics in Early Childhood Special Education*, vol. 9, no. 4, Winter.

York, S. 1991, *Roots and Wings: Affirming Culture in Early Childhood Programmes*, Toys 'n' Things, Minnesota.

Curriculum planning and evaluation

The concept of curriculum

The word 'curriculum' is a term that is often used but rarely understood. Some people imagine that it refers to the list of subjects, while others confuse curriculum with the topics that combine to form a specific syllabus or course.

A curriculum is much broader than subject matter and syllabus. It concerns interactions and transactions between people as well as everything that takes place in schools and classrooms. As Jenkins and Shipman (1981, p. 5) explain:

> This takes us beyond a narrow concentration on pre-specified content and the related issues of resources, text books and time-tabling, towards a realisation that a curriculum is a trading post on the cultural boundary between generations, between sexes and between cultures, to which ideas and artefacts are brought, exchanged and taken away.

Schools are expected to provide a sound, general education for all children, assisting them to develop intellectually, creatively, socially, physically, emotionally and morally. Teachers face the challenge of matching the political, social and economic demands of society with those for development of the individual child, helping each child to gain the many kinds of skills, attitudes, and knowledge necessary for social growth. The school cannot teach its children all that there is to know about the world; teachers have to take responsibility for deciding what is important for children to learn and how this can be organised to provide a continuous and cohesive education. The decisions must be based upon a sound philosophy of learning and a statement of beliefs relating to what children should learn, how they should learn it and why it is necessary. Curriculum, therefore, can be seen to be derived from several sources: the child, the context and the society.

Influences on school curriculum

The Education Department of South Australia (1983a) indicated that effective school curriculum development and management depend upon the following assumptions. Schools have a responsibility to establish and develop their own curriculum which accommodates:

- Departmental requirements (including departmental responses to government's education policies);
- the needs of the children in school;
- the expectations of the community.

Development of the curriculum is a continuous process which involves

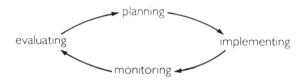

Staff and parent participation in decision-making is an important part of effective curriculum development and is supported by clear definitions of roles and responsibilities. Documentation of the school's philosophy, policy and programme is necessary to provide continuity, accountability and the means to evaluate and improve the curriculum. Staff development is an integral part of curriculum development.

School curriculum is influenced by external factors which impinge directly on its development and management:

- The state or federal government in power has a minister responsible for the funding of education, the structure of the managing department/authority, policies relating to teachers, the staffing of schools, syllabus content, social direction and perceived educational needs for society as a whole.
- The Department or Authority for Education designs policies outlining the aims and purposes of schools and schooling with guidelines for the development of school curriculum. They create the educational framework within which schools must operate.
- The Department or Authority may publish curriculum guidelines for all areas of the curriculum, providing the basic framework for curriculum development and specific subject content.
- The Department or Authority may publish expected learning outcomes or attainment levels which provide the framework for monitoring and evaluating children's progress. As a result, teachers may be required to develop profiles of their students which indicate attainment.
- The Department or Authority outlines requirements which must be

adhered to by school personnel. These requirements are published in their regulations and administrative guidelines and other policy documents.

- The local community in which a school operates will have various characteristics which must be considered in any curriculum development, such as:
  — unique geographical or socio-economic factors which could limit or enhance activities within the school;
  — resources of a specific nature which may or may not be available;
  — expectations of the parents (who should always be consulted about the school's aims and curriculum);
  — employment patterns.

Within the school itself there are very important, influential factors which impinge upon the curriculum. For example, individual staff members have widely different experiences, interests and expertise affecting the nature, variety and efficiency of curriculum. Also the needs of children vary considerably depending upon their home experiences, abilities and aspirations.

Finally, it must be emphasised that the style and content of curriculum is vulnerable to rapid change, for good or ill, in the wider social, political, technological, economic and legal environments. As the purpose of school curriculum is to assist children to take their place in these environments, it follows that curriculum must also be dynamic. There are many examples of recent curriculum responses to changed circumstances. Some very obvious ones are the introduction of Protective Education programmes to develop personal safety skills, AIDS education and the use of computers in pre-school and primary schools. Electronics in the classroom have necessitated changes in the grouping of children, the use of self-paced learning techniques and a wide variety of new and different instructional methods.

The many factors which influence school curriculum development must be considered before priorities are identified. These priorities affect the choice and availability of resources, and appropriate teaching strategies as well as administrative and organisational matters. Underpinning all planning and decisions, must be a sound educational philosophy and an understanding of current theories relating to child development. However, it must be remembered that research is continuous, theoretical knowledge increases, philosophies change and curricula must respond accordingly.

Once the school curriculum is defined, the teacher has a framework within which to plan the class curriculum.

Influences on the class curriculum

School policies are obviously very important influences on the class curriculum but so are teachers' perceptions of their own role and their consequent behaviour in the classroom.

Good teaching is recognised as the successful matching of individual learners of varied abilities with experiences most likely to create the desired changes in thinking and behaviour. Learning has replaced teaching as the centre of instructional planning. Planning and directing learning experiences are now central to the teaching role (Branscombe & Newson 1977).

Gage (1963, p. 96) defines teaching as 'any interpersonal influence aimed at changing the ways other persons can or will behave'. He claims that any theory of teaching should consider how teachers behave, why they behave as they do and with what effect. The way in which teachers behave is influenced by the enormous amount of information that they must have. This is best summarised by the diagram adapted from Brady (1985, p. 3).

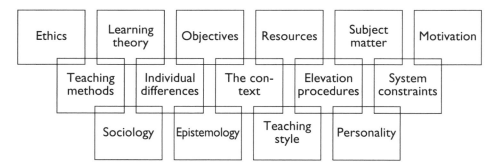

Figure 9.1: Factors affecting teaching behaviour

This diagram shows the number of variables which impinge on teaching and the decisions which teachers make about their own curriculum. It highlights too, the unlikelihood that any two teachers will behave in exactly the same way. It also answers such questions as 'What particular teaching procedure should I use?' or 'Should I find a comfortable style and stick to it?' There is no one way to teach nor is it possible for a well-informed teacher to teach in the same way continuously. The decisions which teachers make about their teaching style and their learning environment reflect their valuation of the different components in Brady's diagram. It is important to note, however, that:

> The behaviour of teachers is only one factor in children's learning. A great deal of learning occurs without teachers. Learning is a more all-embracing experience than teaching and a theory of learning is therefore broader than a theory of teaching (Brady 1985, p. 7).

Several researchers have suggested models of teaching which range on a continuum from being teacher-centred to child-centred (Stallings 1977; Lapp, Bender, Ellenwood & John 1975; Joyce & Weil 1980). Brady (1985) identifies five models which he says are guides only and are not rigidly separated one from the other. He comments that a knowledge of several models is desirable for quality teaching. His models, which he says are representative of teaching practice over the full range of teacher direction, have differing emphases on both the cognitive and affective domains. These are the:

- *exposition model*, a teacher-centred model which is typical of the traditional education where focus is on the subjects, basic skills, whole-group teaching and teacher direction;
- *behavioural model*, also teacher-directed, which is based on tightly sequenced steps of learning;
- *cognitive developmental model*, which focuses on the nature of children's reasoning and developmental stages. Emphasis is placed on planning small instructional steps;
- *interaction model*, emphasising personal interaction with learning resulting from children's interactions with other people and society;
- *transaction model*, a pupil-centred approach, where the teacher structures the learning environment so that self-directed learners can interact with each other and with physical and human resources, changing as a result of their experiences. This model allows for varying degrees of teacher direction and pupil discovery.

The classroom curriculum is then a reflection of both the model of teaching chosen by the individual teacher and the policy and organisation of the school. The school timetable, for example, can assist or constrain the classroom curriculum, especially where there are shared facilities and specialist teachers. However, the classroom timetable should be designed to give teachers maximum flexibility and control to allow for spontaneity, innovation, evaluation and modification.

Organising the class curriculum: preparing the programme

What is a programme?

A teacher's programme includes the documentation of plans for individual and group learning experiences within and outside the classroom. The programme shows future directions, children's needs and the activities and resources needed to satisfy them. Of necessity, the programme must reflect current educational theory and practice as well as the policy and organisation of the school. The programme also acts as a record of class activities and individual progress and is an integral part of the evaluation of the curriculum which should include:

- aims — what the teacher wants to achieve in general terms (the broad intention);
- rationale — why the teacher wants to achieve these aims;

- objectives — what the teacher expects children to learn; that is, the skills, concepts and knowledge;
- content — the learning experiences to be offered;
- strategies — the ways in which the aims and objectives will be achieved, that is, the processes used to ensure that children acquire skills and knowledge through problem solving, play, learning centres etc.;
- resources — the materials and personnel that will be used to assist children's learning;
- evaluation — the ongoing assessment of how far the aims and objectives were achieved, including the effectiveness of the teaching strategies, resources and classroom management.

The teacher's programme therefore acts as the scaffolding around which the class curriculum will develop.

Preparation for writing the programme

Before writing up a teaching programme, some preparatory work is necessary (Education Department of South Australia 1983b). The recently appointed teacher must find out about:

- the school policies, daily routines, administrative structures, use of department or local authority curriculum guidelines, and timetabling across the school;
- the expectations of the head teacher/principal, with regard to programming;
- the school priorities for the year;
- the calendar of events for the year;
- the year level to be taught;
- classroom facilities and budget;
- parent participation and expectations.

The newly appointed teacher must arrange to meet other classroom and specialist teachers and find out about regional support personnel, resources and facilities.

The new teacher must become acquainted with:

- school resources and facilities and how they are booked or acquired;
- school routines;
- school expectations relating to discipline;
- school programme formats, timetable formats;
- the distribution of books.

All teachers should plan their classrooms taking into account:

- traffic ways;
- children with special needs;
- grouping of tables;

- provision for display;
- amount and use of furniture;
- use of outside areas;
- balance and location of learning dimensions.

All teachers should locate materials and consider:

- their storage, suitability, accessibility and labelling;
- the provision and storage of scrap paper, pencils, paste, scissors, crayons, paints, textas.

All teachers should learn about the children who will be in their class by checking:

- relevant details with their previous teachers;
- previous teachers' records;
- medical information;
- family information;
- whether there are any special learning difficulties and abilities;
- assessment records and profiles;
- with previous teachers about topics, themes and units of work previously covered.

Planning the programme

For effective teaching to occur, time should be spent on careful and detailed planning. When the teacher has completed the necessary background data collection already described, it is time to think about what is to be achieved by, and with, the children. This involves:

- writing belief statements about how children learn;
- identifying curriculum area aims and objectives;
- reviewing curriculum area content as written in the relevant curriculum guidelines;
- deciding on teaching strategies;
- checking resources and references;
- determining class organisation;
- selecting evaluation procedures.

Cole and Chan (1987) have expressed this procedure as a model for instructional planning (figure 9.2). Such a model not only forms the basis of yearly planning but may also be translated into a term, a month, a theme, or a unit programme. This programme in turn offers the framework within which weekly, daily and single lesson planning can occur. Thus, the short-term planning reflects the long-term planning, while being more closely attuned to the needs and interests of the children in the class. Such comprehensive planning ensures that the teacher is well organised and knows the direction

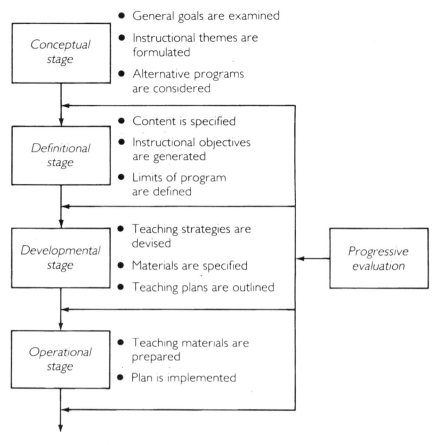

Figure 9.2: A model of instructional planning and preparation

in which the children's learning should go. It should not be prescriptive or stop the teacher from having the flexibility to respond to the children's individual requirements.

The programme format

There is no one way of writing up a programme but the end result must be easily understood by the teacher and any others who are involved in the classroom management. It may be written up in any of the following formats:

- a commercially produced programme book for teachers;
- a flow chart;
- a wall chart;
- a manilla folder;

- a concertina file;
- a ring folder with loose-leafed pages;
- a programme book produced by the school or education authority;
- a scrap book, lined book or project book;
- any other format designed by the individual teacher.

For easy access to information, it is suggested that the programme be divided into several sections (Education Department of South Australia 1983b).

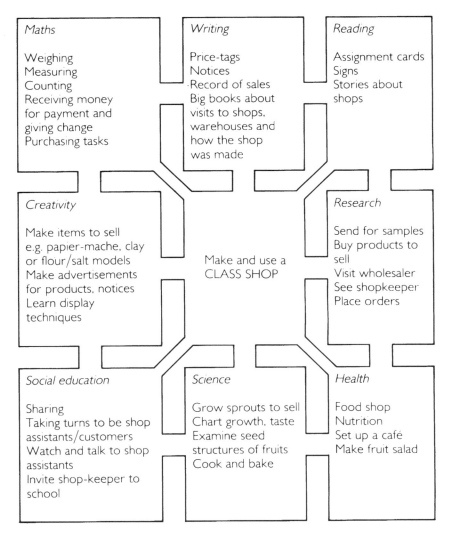

Maths

Weighing
Measuring
Counting
Receiving money
for payment and
giving change
Purchasing tasks

Writing

Price-tags
Notices
Record of sales
Big books about
visits to shops,
warehouses and
how the shop
was made

Reading

Assignment cards
Signs
Stories about
shops

Creativity

Make items to sell
e.g. papier-mache, clay
or flour/salt models
Make advertisements
for products, notices
Learn display
techniques

Make and use a
CLASS SHOP

Research

Send for samples
Buy products to
sell
Visit wholesaler
See shopkeeper
Place orders

Social education

Sharing
Taking turns to be shop
assistants/customers
Watch and talk to shop
assistants
Invite shop-keeper to
school

Science

Grow sprouts to sell
Chart growth, taste
Examine seed
structures of fruits
Cook and bake

Health

Food shop
Nutrition
Set up a café
Make fruit salad

Figure 9.3: Sample of an integrated plan of flow chart, 'A Class Shop'
Source: O'Brien, S. & O'Brien, T. 1988, *Teacher's Day: Diary and Program Planner*, Horwitz Graham, Sydney.

Figure 9.4: Daily planner: suggested format I

	Monday	Tuesday	Wednesday	Thursday	Friday	Reminders/Notes Resources needed
Recess						
Lunch						
Evaluation						

Figure 9.5: Suggested format 2

Daily Planner
Week commencing _____

Monday	Tuesday	Wednesday	Thursday	Friday

Lunchtime

Observations/evaluations

Figure 9.6: Weekly planner: condensed example

Language Word study Handwriting	Written	Stories	Oral	Art	Music	Science	Social Edn	Maths	Health	PE	Evaluation for the week
Week's objectives											
Monday	Tuesday	Wednesday	Thursday	Friday				Reminders/Notes Resources needed			
Recess											
Lunch											
Evaluation											

Figure 9.7: Weekly planner: expanded example

Language				Art	Music	Science	Social Edn	Maths	Health	PE	Evaluation for the week
Word study	Written	Stories	Oral								
Handwriting											
Week's objectives											

Figure 9.8: A weekly planner

Week beginning _____

Language arts	Maths	Social Education	Science	Exp. Arts	Physical Education
Objectives	Objectives	Objectives	Objectives	Objectives	Objectives
1					
2					
3					
4					
5					
Resources needed					
Evaluation					

Information and resources: timetable; year–term planner; calendar; holidays, special days (school, community, national festivals and celebrations); resource people and places; staff meeting notes.

Policy and curriculum: school policy and philosophy; school curriculum area policies; teacher's beliefs statements; curriculum aims.

Working section: curriculum objectives; theme or curriculum area development; resources; teaching strategies; content (weekly/daily lesson plans and task lists); evaluation; jottings/notes.

Record keeping: student lists with curriculum area records; parent contact (notes to parents, summary of parent interview); record of money received, consent forms etc; budget (income and itemised expenditure).

At this stage, let us assume that a year-long plan has been drawn up and divided approximately into the three or four terms as appropriate. It is the teacher's task now to plan a unit of work. The task is best achieved by referring to the model for instructional planning, then documenting ideas on a wall chart or the double page of a programme book showing:

- the theme title;
- aims and objectives in all curriculum areas which relate to the theme;
- content for all curriculum areas;
- teaching strategies in all curriculum areas;
- required resources/materials in all curriculum areas;
- evaluation techniques.

Some teachers prefer to draw up a flow chart or diagram to clearly demonstrate their programme (see on p. 217). Some teachers use a more elaborate daily planner which offers more detail on what will take place, when, how, and the materials required, as shown in the previous examples on pp. 218–22.

Students on teaching practice

When students commence their teaching practice, they need to acquaint themselves with the teacher's long-term and short-term plans so that they can see how their own lessons or learning experiences fit into the total curriculum. Students' lessons must be carefully planned and prepared so that:

- they know what, when, how and why the children will learn;
- they have confidence in what they are doing;
- potential problems can be identified and prevention plans made in advance.

Lesson plans may take one of several forms, but it is important to note that there are basic components for planning.

Aims and objectives

Derived from children's developmental levels, observed needs and curriculum content, these should contribute to the ongoing programme for the group or class. Aims and objectives may relate to concepts, skills and attitudes. Aims are general, long-term expressions of general intent. Objectives are specified and short-term, indicating how the aims will be achieved.

Aims: These should be written in terms of what the teacher is doing, although teacher-directed aims should be expressed from the children's point of view, for example

> To lead the children to see...
> To give the children practice in...
> To teach the children...
> To develop in children...
> To introduce to children...
> To increase the children's appreciation of...
> To give the children the opportunity of self-expression in...
> To lead the children to discover...
> To revise...

Objectives: These aims (often referred to as the anticipated learning outcomes) should be written in terms of what the children are expected to gain from the lesson, that is, the skills, concept and knowledge. They should directly relate to the aim, for example

> That the children will understand...
> That the children will gain practice in...
> That the children develop an appreciation of...
> That the children can...
> That the children will know...
> That the children will learn to...
> For the children to make...
> For the children to complete...
> For the children to create...

Aims and objectives should relate clearly to children's needs. Objectives (anticipated learning outcomes) are evaluated in terms of the completed task. **Activities should be planned to meet the aims and objectives, not vice versa.**

Implementation of content

There are many different ways of providing learning experiences. Developing judgement in the selection of the best materials and activities to be used at a particular time for a particular child or group of children is basic to good teaching. Organisation of time, space, children and resources must be identified. The implementation should indicate the progression from the preparation of the classroom, the introduction of the session, questions to be used and method of conclusion.

Evaluation and extension

This section directs attention to children's individual responses and achievements in a session. It also acts as a running record of which children were included in the various groupings, who lost interest, finished quickly, lacked concentration, experienced certain difficulties, etc. Ongoing planning (extensions) develops from this participant observation, that is, which children need more practice and which children can move on to new challenges.

Planning at all levels, long-term and short-term, needs to be thoughtful, perceptive and well-researched. It comprises:

- identifying appropriate curriculum content;
- planning teaching/learning strategies;
- identifying the necessary experiences and resources to facilitate learning;
- getting organised.

Having done this, the student or newly qualified teacher will develop the confidence to respond to the observed needs and interests of the children, secure within this general framework. See two suggested lesson formats on pp. 228–9.

Preparation for teaching

The successful implementation of any planned programme will depend heavily on the level of preparation undertaken by the teacher or student teacher. Cole and Chan (1987) suggest four basic principles for effective teacher organisation:

1 **Organise a workable timetable of class activities** so that children can move from one activity to another with minimal disruption to learning time. The more time that the children spend actively engaged in learning experiences, the greater will be their achievements.

2 **Ensure that all necessary teaching materials and equipment are prepared in advance,** so that children's learning time is not wasted.

3 **Plan effective classroom routines** which respond to the children's need for varied, interesting and challenging learning experiences. Children must understand work requirements, organisational procedures for the distribution and collection of materials, and behaviour codes and rules associated with moving around the classroom. When effective routines are adopted children's learning time is not wasted and frustration is avoided.

4 **Organise the efficient use of instructional space for learning** so that chil-

Planning format
(suggestions for student teachers)

Overall aims
1
2

Specific objectives (what you are aiming to teach/wanting children to learn, that is, specific skills, concepts and knowledge. You are going to evaluate them so please ensure that they are relevant and realistic)
1
2

Brief details of the activity to be offered, that is, curriculum area and nature/style of activity

Relevant information relating to the children to be taught (name individuals in a small group, indicating their developmental levels/learning needs. When teaching the whole class, it is sometimes useful to list the quiet children individually. Teachers who do not, are apt to note the same extrovert and difficult children repetitively and forget the withdrawn and compliant members of the class)

Preparation (room, equipment and materials needed; things to do in the organisation of the area, hygiene etc.)

Introduction (details of how you intend to capture the children's interest and motivate them, for example, how a story or activity will be introduced)

Procedure (the stages involved in the lesson/activity)

Conclusion (show how you will conclude the session. Detail the questions you will ask to clarify what children have learned. Note how you will involve children in clearing away, etc.)

Evaluation (look at your specific objectives and show how far you achieved them, using the evidence presented by individual children—verbal, behavioural, written, etc.) Answer the following questions:

Which children learned what you planned to teach?

Which children found the material was easy or too difficult? How do you know?

What incidental learning took place?

How could this learning be extended?

How do you know?

Who needs more practice? (Note individual levels of concentration and competence and the problems that individuals experienced. Did anyone find it too easy or much too difficult? If you were to repeat the activity, what would you do differently?)

Opportunities for extension (if you were in charge of the class tomorrow, how would you extend this session? For whom?)

dren have different areas for different activities, separated appropriately by traffic ways. Activity areas, seating arrangements, grouping and children's movement around the classroom must be thoughtfully planned and organised to maximise participant learning.

Evaluation of the curriculum

Evaluation is a time for reflecting on the effectiveness of the curriculum and making informed decisions about future planning. The teacher and student must take time to evaluate the appropriateness of the identified aims and objectives, the teaching strategies, resources used and the suitability of the learning experiences that were offered. More specifically, these evaluations should focus on whether or not children were able to extend their knowledge and skills through the learning experiences provided, what exactly was achieved and not achieved, and why this occurred.

Teachers evaluate from two distinct perspectives, first, their own performance and, secondly, the children's responses.

Self-evaluation

Self-evaluation is a crucial part of the curriculum process, but it is often omitted in day-to-day practice. Teacher behaviour markedly affects children's learning and poor results do not necessarily indicate pupil inadequacy. Teachers' attitudes, demeanour, choice of subject matter, teaching method, organisation, failure to take account of inclement weather conditions and problems associated with classroom environment, all contribute to learning failure.

Self-evaluation is crucial to the personal and professional development of a teacher. The student should use the following checklist for this purpose and discuss his or her self-evaluation with the teacher week by week.

Sample of student teacher's own checklist of teaching competencies

---

(Please tick competencies gained)

Working with children   During week 1 2 3 4 etc.

1   I gained competence in relating to:
   a) individual children
   b) individual children with specific needs
   c) children in a whole class situation
   d) understanding and helping children with
      specific problems
   e) managing the behaviour of 'difficult' children
2   I gained competence in:

Activity: Date: Group of Children

Aims: 1

       2

Objectives	Organisation	Implementation/procedure	Evaluation and extension
	Time:	Intro:	
	Children:	Procedural Steps:	
1	Materials:	Conclusion:	
2			

Figure 9.9: Lesson planning: suggested format 1. This plan should act as a means of organising thoughts and enabling students to see the interrelationship between each section, when they are preparing lessons and activities

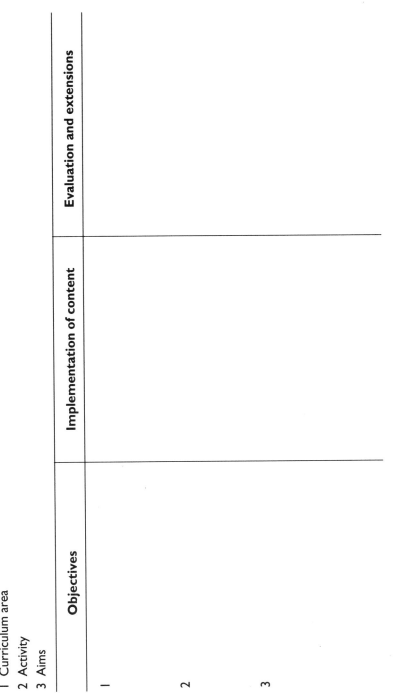

Figure 9.10: Lesson planning: suggested format 2. For more experienced and competent students, this abbreviated plan may be appropriate

a) responding to and extending a child's interest'
b) planning for excursions which relate to children's learning
c) fostering independence and self-reliance in children
d) sequencing the presentation of curriculum content
e) integrating aspects of the total curriculum
f) planning and catering for individual differences
g) developing children's self-esteem

Interaction skills

1 *Questioning skills*
   I gained competence in:
   a) asking enabling (open-ended) questions which promote discussion
   b) developing techniques for asking specific questions
   c) encouraging children to contribute to conversation
   d) listening to children and identifying those who do/do not participate in conversations/discussions
   e) using problem-solving methods
2 *Working with others*
   I gained competence in:
   a) relating to other teachers and staff members
   b) relating to parents
   c) team teaching

Curriculum issues

1 I ensured that
   a) I used a multi-cultural approach across the curriculum
   b) I offered an inclusive curriculum
   c) quiet children received equal attention with more verbal children
   d) I noted and responded to individual differences

Specific curriculum areas

1 *Language arts*
   I gained competence in:
   a) recognising and teaching reading skills
   b) presenting a range of literature to children (verse, stories, etc.), both told and read
   c) developing children's oral language
   d) developing children's listening skills
   e) recognising and teaching writing skills

    f) developing a variety of approaches to
       teaching the structure of language

2 *Mathematical/social studies/science*
   I gained competence in:
    a) recognising when children have understood
       new concepts
    b) teaching numeracy/space/measurement skills
    c) recognising and extending children's
       knowledge in all areas
    d) planning for environmental extensions
    e) introducing information to individual children
    f) presenting information of interest to small
       groups
    g) organising activity/learning centres

3 *Music/movement/drama/physical education*
   I gained competence in:
    a) encouraging children's spontaneous singing,
       movement, etc.
    b) singing with, and teaching songs to children
    c) sharing music with children—own music;
       recorded music; other
    d) encouraging children to explore sound and
       make their own
    e) sharing movement with children—child
       initiated; teacher introduced presenting
       opportunities for drama to children
    g) using puppets with children
    h) planning and implementing physical education
    i) initiating listening activities using verse, stories,
       etc. for drama, music, movement

4 *Art*
    a) I provided frequent experiences with a
       variety of art media

Management and administration

1 I gained knowledge of:
    a) enrolment and admission procedures
    b) pre-entry arrangements
    c) the responsibilities of each staff member
    d) the community role of the school
    e) the role of parents
    f) accident procedures
    g) petty cash procedures
    h) the staff handbook/Policy statement/Parents'
       handbook

2 *Skills related to teaching*

I gained an understanding of:
a) the physical set-up of the indoor play area/unit classroom
b) the physical set-up of the outdoor play area
c) team-teaching arrangements
d) how to keep children's records
e) the integrated curriculum
f) planning the curriculum
g) implementing all curriculum areas
h) the value of each activity offered, as part of the total curriculum
i) timetabling—the use of, and flexibility of time
j) the importance of presenting materials well
k) how to create effective displays—teacher initiated; child initiated

3 I gained experience in:
a) planning and implementing short-term objectives
b) the daily evaluation of my teaching, including children's responses
c) further planning from (b)
d) planning and teaching and integrated curriculum
e) developing children's comprehension skills

Evaluating children's progress

Assessing and evaluating children's progress is necessary to enable teachers to make sound decisions about instruction and curriculum development. Teachers may collect information about children in several ways. The method chosen will be determined by the purpose for the collection. Each procedure yields a different kind of information and for this reason, data collected should only be used as a guide for future planning and action. Over-generalisations should be avoided because each data collection technique has its limitations.

Observation (see also chapter 4).

a) Controlled observations involve systematic formal data collection about a pre-specified type of behaviour for a pre-determined period of time on a carefully designed recording schedule.

b) Anecdotal records provide a less formal way of noting an observation which was ostensibly unplanned.

c) Checklists or rating scales are useful for organising or summarising observations.

Questioning. Teachers can gain relevant educational information by asking appropriate questions. Questions should be designed specifically to appraise comprehension, attitudes, experiences etc. and may be asked in interviews through questionnaires, self-reporting checklists and rating scales. Results should be recorded and compared for progress.

Collection of children's work. Samples of children's work, when collected on a regular basis, provide useful information about the quality of their learning. Careful analysis of samples of children's writing, for example, will disclose the nature of their errors and provide important diagnostic information relating to their thinking. Similarly, where specific written tasks or work sheets are completed the results can be collated and examined collectively.

Tests. Non-standardised tests are sometimes used by teachers to gain specific information relating to a curriculum area. Such tests are usually devised by the teacher because they need to be relevant to the purpose.

Teachers should use several different assessment techniques to facilitate the collection of comprehensive information about the progress of every child in the class. The information gained is crucial to future curriculum planning. It indicates whether the objectives were appropriate, how far they were achieved, whether to continue on the same lines, provide extensions or adopt a completely different approach.

Curriculum assessment and evaluation must be systematic and continuous for maximum efficiency in the teaching and learning process.

Record keeping

In a learning environment where children are engaged in different levels of activity, not only does the teacher's planning and organisation need to be meticulous but the monitoring and recording of children's progress must be well organised. One of the teacher's first concerns should be knowing what each child is doing and with what degree of success. Record keeping in an open classroom is far more complex than in a traditional classroom where all children are doing similar things at the same time and teachers' records are related primarily to grades. Even where children are working in small groups teachers must know how each child is progressing, their interests, needs, strengths, talents and problems! Teachers must be able to gauge whether the child's work is consistent with his/her ability and whether the learning experiences that have been offered are challenging or unstimulating and frustrating. Teachers must evaluate not only academic progress but a child's emotional, social and physical development also. The child is not graded according to a class standard but in the context of his/her own pattern of growth.

Several kinds of records may be used but they will be valuable only if they are maintained consistently. Teachers must decide what records are essential for the efficient and effective functioning of the class, using the clearest and simplest forms available so that valuable time is not diverted from working with children. Similarly, where children are expected to record completed activities and assignments, the system of recording must be simple. Teachers usually experiment with various systems of record-keeping to find the best for their specific purposes. The following suggestions are worthy of consideration:

1   In a traditional classroom, teachers may have a chronicle, describing precisely the work to be covered by all the children in all the curriculum areas for the week. At the end of the week, the teacher will check off the children's work samples, tests, work sheets etc. against the chronicle entry, and note progress.

2   In an open classroom, a teacher may use a loose-leaf file to summarise the overall work of the class. There are separate pages for subjects, projects and various activities, as well as weekly summary sheets. On the subject pages, the teacher lists highlights of the week's work, group assignments and general plans. The notebook is used both for planning work and for chronicling events. Its purpose is to help the teacher to focus on each subject, project and activity, weekly, to evaluate each in relation to the overall work of the class and to assess whether or not certain experiences should be planned, additional materials provided for a centre, some activities abandoned or others introduced (Stephens 1974).

3   Where teachers have children working at learning centres on projects, contracts or other forms of individualised learning, the children will need to take more responsibility for recording work completed:
    a) A bulletin board indicating all the children's names down the left-hand side with colour-coded curriculum areas, extending from left to right across the chart, may be used. When the children finish work in a curriculum area they put a coloured pin or peg in the appropriate box. The teacher can then see at a glance at the end of the day what work has been completed by whom.
    b) A bar graph can be used in exactly the same way. Children will colour a curriculum area in the correct coded colour on the completion of their work.
    c) Accompanying the above two suggestions must be a deposit box for the children to place completed work when it is not possible to have an immediate conference with the teacher. All children can use the same deposit box or each child may have a personal file for completed work. The teacher must check the box or files daily so that the children can receive feedback on their work as soon as possible. The files form the record of the child's work and progress.

4   Index cards kept in a filing box form a common but effective way of keeping records. For each child, there is a clearly identified section which contains a colour-coded card for all curriculum areas. On the completion of a unit of work (a contract, an assignment or a test), evaluative comments and results should be entered. These cumulative records offer a detailed profile of the child's progress over time.

5   Anecdotal records are often preferred by teachers as they may comprise expansive comments on all areas of the child's development, not simply

academic progress. This enables the teacher to reflect on the child's interests, independence, social interactions, use of resources, initiative, etc. Care must be taken, however, that comments do not become stereotyped, general and lacking in detail. These records may he kept on index cards, in a notebook or in a larger scrapbook with split pages and careful indexing.

6 Most teachers, including those in traditional classrooms, compile folders or files of children's work. By carefully dating each piece of work that is inserted in the folder, teachers, children and parents have a developmental picture of both academic and expressive arts work completed over time. The work to be filed should represent all areas of the curriculum and include paintings, drawings, pieces of writing, mathematics recordings, photographs of projects, activity/assignment cards and any other work which the child or teacher wishes to keep.

7 Checklists form one of the easiest systems of record-keeping, but not necessarily the most accurate. Teachers may keep a checklist for each child relating to work completed and one relating to skill/concept development. Often, the children themselves can date the checklist indicating when work is complete, but the teacher checks off the second form of record after a test, a conference or a period of observation.

The disadvantages of checklists are that they offer no indication of the quality of the child's work or the level of attainment. They assume a segmental development of skills/concepts for all children and they do not allow learning to remain an integrated phenomenon. Rather, they divide curriculum areas into specific skills, concepts, content, etc.

8 Where there is a whole-school approach to monitoring, assessing and reporting on children's progress, teachers may be required to use a specific style of collecting and recording information. This may be in response to the Education Authority's requirement to respond to attainment levels and to develop profiles of children's development.

9 Specific curriculum area records are sometimes kept in addition to the more general ones. Teachers who focus on the process of children's learning as opposed to the product alone, need to keep regular, relevant well-organised and carefully analysed data on each child, because future planning derives immediately from the information.

a) **Language arts**. A range of data collection techniques and records is necessary to ensure a balance of information (Parry & Hornsby 1985):
   - *weekly record*: comprises general impressions and observations of individual and small group behaviour, a journal or diary of evaluative comments of the language arts activities records;
   - *conference/small teaching group*: comments may be made on small cards during individual writing/reading conferences with individual or small groups indicating literacy development;
   - *pupil writing folder*: includes a list of possible topics for writing or books to read, a list of writing or books completed and a list of skills demonstrated in reading or writing;

- *writing record*: indicates participation in individual and group conferences, publishing or book review conferences and how often the folder has been checked;
- *class collections*: represent a selection of completed writings or book reviews from the children;
- *word banks*: consist of class combined lists of often-used words and topics;
- *reading cards*: index cards may be used for a running record of the child's reading in a conference, including the date of the conference, the book title, pages read and reading proficiency, with diagnostic comments and future activities. Such information may also be kept in a notebook which has a page for each child for the term;

b) **Mathematics**
- A folder, similar to that for language arts, may be kept to include samples of written work over time as well as work to be attempted and concepts/skills acquired;
- The teacher may wish to keep a maths card or notebook to record diagnostic comments and future directions.

During the term, samples of work from the specific curriculum areas may be transferred to the general file where it contributes to the overall profile of the child.

The maintenance of accurate and helpful records is imperative, not only to assist the teacher in identifying curriculum content and direction but to enable information-sharing with parents, other relevant teaching staff, the principal or head teacher, and the children themselves.

TASKS FOR STUDENTS

1 Describe the range of external political, economical and social influences that currently affect school curriculum.
2 Discuss the many ways in which the teachers' perceptions of their own role affects classroom curriculum.
3 Obtain copies of curriculum guidelines published by the education authorities.
4 Students visiting schools prior to teaching practice must:
- request access to the teacher's immediate and long-term curriculum plans;
- ask the teacher for access to samples of record-keeping.
5 Students on teaching practice must always ask to be included in planning meetings.

USEFUL REFERENCES

Arthur, L., Beecher, B., Dockett, S., Farmer, S. & Richards, E. 1993, *Programming and Planning in Early Childhood Settings*, Delmar Publishers Inc., USA.

Essa, E. & Rogers, P. 1992, *Introduction to Early Childhood Education*, Delmar Publishers Inc. USA

Classroom management and control

Few teachers would describe themselves as managers, although classroom management and leadership are vital components of the teaching role. It is interesting to note that the word 'leader' derives from the same root as 'teacher'. Furthermore, most managers accept that they have a teaching and leadership function, providing leadership by example as well as developing the potential of others in the organisation.

This chapter is devoted to the role of the teacher as classroom manager and will examine some of the factors involved in classroom control. Control itself has been defined as 'that phase of the managerial system which maintains an organisation's activity within allowable limits as measured from expectations which may be implicit or explicit in terms of stated objectives, plans, procedures or rules and regulations' (Kast & Rosenzweig 1973, p. 490).

In the case of the teacher, the expectations referred to include those of others involved in the 'open system' of the school, such as the education authority, parents, school management and professional associations as well as the expectations of the children in the class.

The word 'control' has several different meanings, including:

- to check and verify;
- to regulate;
- to compare with given standards;
- to exercise authority over; and
- to curb or restrain (Kast & Rosenzweig 1973, p. 466).

In early childhood education, authority is exercised by motivating children, and curbs and restraints are subtle. The elements of control can be divided into five interacting components.

In the case of classroom control, the operating system is the classroom itself and the characteristic numbered (1) involves the expectations of those who influence the 'open system' of the school. The sensor (2) and the com-

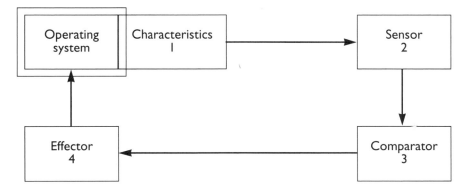

parator (3) include teachers who are expected to identify the characteristics or expectations and assess the extent to which they are being achieved. The effector (4) recognises the deviations from requirements and manipulates the system to effect the necessary changes.

In operating a control system, teachers take four basic steps. They:

- analyse and define the expectations of those in the open system so as to gain a clear picture of the learning environment required;
- note dysfunctional behaviours that interfere with the creation of that environment;
- compare the actual learning environment with that expected;
- adjust the dysfunction by changing either the learning environment itself or the expectations of others (colleagues, parents, management, etc.) in the system.

Prevention is better than cure

When student teachers are asked what worries them most about their teaching practice, they invariably respond with one word, 'discipline'. They make the mistake of thinking that the control of children is a separate skill, unrelated to lesson plans, classroom organisation, motivation and the quality of the learning environment. This narrow view of discipline implies that the effective teacher is one who gives commands that children instantly obey. A few minutes in a classroom is sufficient to demonstrate otherwise.

Although classroom management is often discussed in terms of handling the effects of dysfunction, this approach is undesirable because it puts the cart before the horse (Bandura 1969; Kounin 1970, quoted in Good & Brophy 1978, p. 165). An emphasis on behaviour problems and punishment in the classroom is invariably ineffective and may even worsen the situation. In general, it is better to stress and reward desirable behaviour and use management techniques that prevent problems arising. The old adage 'prevention is better than cure', is supported by research findings. Effective teachers have fewer control problems than ineffective teachers.

> This is because their preparation, relationships, teaching skill and management behaviours prevent or minimise control problems. They are able to anticipate problems or, should they arise, act quickly to prevent them spreading or becoming more serious (Barry & King 1988, p. 146).

Until student teachers accept that dysfunction is the product of many different influences and until they can identify these influences and make the necessary adjustments, behaviour problems will continue and prevent the realisation of educational aims and objectives.

Good classroom management: good teaching

There is not a clear distinction between good classroom management and good teaching; they are inextricably linked. **Classroom management** concerns the creation of an effective learning environment, the establishment of conditions in which learning can occur with ease and enjoyment. It ensures that there are high levels of quality student activity and that instructional time is well used. To achieve these circumstances, classroom management should minimise disruptive behaviour and facilitate maximum on-task application.

Good teaching is directly concerned with ensuring effective learning by all children in the context of a well managed classroom.

The importance of planning and preparation

Although students often resent the necessity of recording their teaching plans in detail, the key to success in classroom management lies in the planning that is undertaken specifically to avoid potential difficulties. When new teachers experience behaviour problems, they have usually omitted to take very basic, common-sense measures in their organisation. Without careful thought and preparation, teachers and students can unwittingly cause confusion, frustration, boredom and subsequent misbehaviours. In the early stages, students and new teachers must make a deliberate effort to think ahead and predict the potential for disruptive behaviour in their plans for the day. Only then can they take the necessary practical steps to prevent those problems from arising. Planning and preparation were discussed more fully in chapter 9.

Choosing the optimum group size

Students and teachers often make the mistake of trying to teach a group that is far too large for the subject or activity involved. Before making plans for the day, the optimum group size should be carefully considered, taking account of:

- children's different levels of development and abilities to listen or concentrate for varying periods of time. For example, should recently-enrolled children be included with six- and seven-year-olds? Is the material appropriate for all age-groups and developmental levels? Is there a possibility that some of the younger children might not be ready for the content or that the older children might not be sufficiently challenged? Immature children sit quietly, irrespective of the appropriateness of what is happening, merely because they lack the confidence to protest. Children of six to eight years show their boredom by chatting to or teasing others, fidgeting and causing disruption in the hope that the teacher will terminate the activity;
- the fact that children need activity and dislike having to sit still, take turns, watch, wait and listen for more than a few minutes at a time. Most discipline problems arise when students or teachers try to involve large groups or the whole class in activities in which there is only one participant at a time, and the waiting children lose interest. Children do not misbehave when they are absorbed in purposeful activity. They do, however, misbehave when students and teachers ignore their stages of development and proceed with unsuitable plans;
- the nature of the activity to be offered. Woodwork and cooking, for example, should involve no more than four to six children with one competent adult. Consideration must be given to the size of the workbench, safety factors, the need to share tools and take turns, the need for space to move around the table and the fact that teachers can only effectively challenge children's thinking and problem-solving in small groups. An effective strategy for limiting group size is to provide only four to six smocks or aprons and restrict participation to wearers. Kite construction and tie-dying require considerable space to prevent the risk of string entanglement and distress. It is wise to offer several well-managed, small groups on consecutive days rather than suffer a whole-class disaster.

The supervision of a high-risk group is comparatively easy when there are parents participating in the classroom. A teacher working alone resolves the problem by providing safe activities for other groups (activities that do not necessitate close adult attention and regular feedback) by scanning the room and circulating from time to time.

Students and new teachers are taking foolish risks when they impose sharing activities on the whole class or large groups. News time, times for reading personal writing or other situations where only one child performs and others are expected to sit still and listen are often counterproductive. Most young children want to contribute and receive approval. Young children often read in slow, hesitant, monotonous tones and others quickly lose interest. Teachers remind them about 'good manners' and criticise the miscreants. Trying to be fair, some teachers extend the sessions to enable all children to contribute. Time could be spent more profitably in small, informal group-sessions to which children could contribute without prolonged waiting periods.

Providing appropriate challenges for children

Given the ages and developmental levels of the proposed group, students and teachers must consider whether the planned activities are worthwhile, relevant and sufficiently challenging for all the children concerned. Students and teachers must constantly ask themselves, 'What can this child learn from this experience? Is my goal appropriate for this particular child at this particular time?'.

Behaviour problems arise when students and teachers provide 'busy-work' to keep children occupied. Students often mistake this for learning. This confusion occurs when an activity is considered to be a 'good idea' and is provided without first clarifying aims and objectives based on the educational needs of individual children.

Materials and activities must be sufficiently stimulating to motivate learning. Boredom occurs when the same stories, puzzles, games and tasks are provided repeatedly. Boredom occurs when children are required to sit still while students and teachers talk **at** them for more than a few minutes at a time. Boredom is inevitable when there are no appropriate challenges to provide success and a sense of achievement. Young, recently-enrolled children may escape into quiet daydreaming. They learn nothing, but they present few problems to adults. Bright, confident, older children will devise ingenious ways to counteract the monotony, providing entertainment for themselves and their companions. As a result, these children are often mistakenly labelled as having low concentration and even low intelligence.

Dysfunction also occurs when children are presented with challenges that require knowledge and experience beyond their level of understanding. In 1988, the Australian bicentenary year, many teachers were forced to abandon lessons relating to the settlement of their country. Information about Captain Cook was insufficient to stimulate young city children to draw pictures about 'what Australia was like when the first Europeans landed'.

Timing and pacing activities to meet children's needs

Given the ages and developmental levels of the proposed group, students and teachers must ensure that the allocated time for activities is realistic.

The pacing and timing of activities is a crucial element in the maintenance of children's attention and interest. Adults can provoke misbehaviour if they overstimulate or provide one exhausting activity after another with no quiet time for recovery. Problems are just as inevitable if a session requiring listening is prolonged and followed by another that necessitates waiting and taking turns. Teachers must be sensitive to individual responses. Some children are slow and painstaking while others work very quickly. Plans should include challenging extensions for those children who finish quickly. It is inadvisable to direct early-finishers to the reading corner, first because this strategy denigrates the importance of reading to a time-filling exercise and secondly, because few teachers allow children to remain in the book corner to finish their chosen story when others have finished their work. This is, of course, discourteous to readers and the disruption is likely to cause irritation.

Similarly, it is annoying to be told to 'clear away' when fully absorbed in the creation of a model or writing a story. It is especially annoying if the disturbance is for nothing more important than the mid-morning break. 'Do I have to go outside?' the enthusiast wails. 'Can I stay here and finish this?' To the five-, six- and seven-year-old, now attuned to the joys of creativity, there seems to be a lack of consistency and logic in the teacher's priorities.

Flexibility is the keynote to successful teaching. When students and teachers sense that children have lost interest in what they are doing or what the adult is saying, it is counterproductive to persist. Different strategies must be adopted immediately to avoid a battle of wills, and discipline problems. The successful teacher is not the one who sticks to plans regardless of negative responses, but the one who is sufficiently flexible to change plans to cater for children's interests, concentration and energy levels.

Planning the use of physical space

In planning activities, students and teachers must take account of where children will be placed in relation to the adult and the equipment to be used. When children are to sit on the floor, care must be taken to ensure that:

- the adult sits in a position where eye-to-eye contact can be maintained with all group members. When students and teachers are writing on the blackboard, working with individuals or a small group, they should develop the habit of pausing to scan the room at regular intervals;
- children known to have short concentration spans are placed within touching distance of the adult;
- all children are sitting comfortably with room to stretch their limbs without trespassing on the personal space of others;
- teaching materials such as big books, pictures, felt-boards or puppets must be clearly visible to all children. If this is not possible, the size of the group must be reduced or the teaching strategy changed. Small books and pictures are not appropriate for working with the whole class. Children at the

back of the group will either lose interest or push forward to get a better view of the picture, disturbing those sitting in front of them;

- furniture must be moved if there is any risk of visual obstruction between the child and the adult;
- children do not sit with their backs to the blackboard when they are copying from it;
- the room can be scanned with ease so that potentially disruptive situations can be defused.

Students must be sensitive to possible problems and make the necessary changes to avoid them, irrespective of current classroom practices. Seating or grouping must be considered carefully in relation to all planned activities.

The establishment of rules

The effective teacher has very few rules but the ones that are chosen are simple, clearly understood and democratically created. Some aspects of classroom and school life recur regularly and rules are found necessary for the care of property, for movement around the building and for behavioural expectations. Long lists of school regulations are likely to result in more frustration than order, first because they are imposed rather than mutually agreed and secondly, because they are too numerous to be remembered.

Class and individual discussion should take place about the need for rules, as and when problems arise. Children should be invited to discuss the consequences of aggravating situations and to examine a variety of possible solutions. Children who perceive the need for rules are most likely to keep them and help others to do so.

By positively reinforcing behaviour that meets rules, teachers assist children to maintain a safe, orderly environment. For example, 'Thank you for closing the door quietly', 'Thank you for walking carefully' and 'Thank you for clearing away' are much more effective than, 'Don't slam the door', 'Don't run' and 'You know you're supposed to clear everything away when you've finished'. Praise for keeping rules creates a more positive atmosphere than reprimanding those who break rules.

Rules may be necessary for using pencil sharpeners, woodwork tools and scissors, and what to do when a task is finished. New rules will be necessary to establish codes of conduct in new situations such as excursions, the use of new learning centres or listening posts.

The establishment of conflict resolution procedures

All classroom management strategies should have the long-term aim and effect of helping children to develop self-discipline and trust, and feel more competent and in control of themselves. Adults show respect for children when they help them to see the possible consequences of their actions and give them the option of controlling their behaviour. This should be on the lines of, 'This is what you are doing. What do you think will happen if you continue? Is that what you really want? What can you do instead?'. This kind of approach indicates that we regard children as sufficiently sensible and reasonable to control themselves. Most will respond to this approach most of the time. Teachers who use shame and humiliation to control behaviour communicate to children that they are bad, worthless, unlovable and inadequate. This increases the potential for sadness, withdrawal, frustration and aggression in the classroom.

> It is important to keep in mind the fit between what you do and what you value…Your decision about the success of management techniques should focus on whether the outcome was consistent with your goals for children's development rather than whether the technique was effective at a particular moment (Feeney, Christensen & Moravcike 1983, p. 178).

Minimising disruptions and delays

If children are kept waiting for an anticipated event, they invariably become restless and irritated and find other things to do. Dysfunction can be expected if children have been highly motivated prior to the delay. Students and teachers often create problems by not preparing the room or equipping work areas before sessions begin.

Teaching plans must list the materials and equipment needed for the completion of the tasks. The adults must also anticipate the range of equipment that children might request. If children are expected to examine the structures of seeds or fruits, the adults should predict that some will request magnifying glasses. If these are not immediately available, the adult faces the choice of leaving the class unattended to collect them from the science store or refusing the request. If the latter, children are likely to become dissatisfied and frustrated. To avoid delays and disruptions, adults should ensure that:

- cookery, science, woodwork and art materials are in the work areas before sessions commence;
- instructions are clear, enabling children to start work when they arrive at their work area;
- matches are readily available if gas cookers are to be used;
- scissors are available for all participants in activities involving cutting-out;
- challenging extension-work is readily available for those who finish early;
- children know how and when to seek help;
- children are not interrupted unnecessarily when they are absorbed in activity;
- children are given plenty of warning to terminate activity and tidy up;
- children are not expected to queue at the teacher's desk for work to be marked;

- equipment for games and outdoor activities will be available for the required period of time;
- television sets, projectors and videos are in place and functioning before the lesson commences.

Children are disappointed and become impatient when adults are only half-prepared or a promised activity fails to eventuate because the equipment is either unavailable or malfunctioning.

The need for credibility

Classroom management is so complex that there are no recipes that guarantee success. There are general principles that apply and certain strategies that reduce risks but other dimensions come into play, such as the personality and frame of mind of the adult in control, the consistency with which rules are maintained, and the general atmosphere of the classroom. If all the necessary precautions are taken, problems will not be eliminated entirely but the student or teacher will be in the best possible position for handling those that occur. It follows that, for sound classroom management, teachers must enjoy being with the children they teach. They must respect their rights and individuality. When teachers are kind and courteous, children are kind and courteous to each other. When teachers are warm and accepting, there is an atmosphere of warmth and acceptance in the classroom. Children who have disinterested or critical families and chaotic home lives are most likely to present negative or attention-seeking behaviours but it is interesting to note that, in schools where the majority of children are disadvantaged, there are marked differences in behaviours from one classroom to another. These differences can only relate to the different personalities, attitudes and management styles of the teachers.

Teachers who circulate well and get down to the children's level are more likely to be respected than those who remain cold, critical and aloof. Those who show concern when children are sad or unwell, who encourage with a pat on the shoulder and share the joys of success, are least likely to find themselves engaged in battles of will.

Students and new teachers are closely observed and children spot their weaknesses. They recognise the teacher who says 'No' to an activity one moment and permits it the next. They will test the teacher's limits repeatedly if those limits are not consistent. They also recognise and ignore teachers who make foolish threats that are never kept.

Students and teachers must decide what they want from the class, then monitor their own behaviour so that it is consistent with their expectations of children.

When children like, respect and trust their teachers, they want to please them. Children will then imitate the adults' behaviours, adopting their values while they are in school, giving support when support is appropriate. If teachers are dependable, classrooms are predictable and the rules are fair, there is little reason to test out limits with misbehaviour.

Complex methods of social control and coercion in the classroom

To cater for the developmental needs of five to eight year olds, the learning environment must be consistent yet varied, stimulating and rewarding. Teachers must encourage individual effort because children of this age are now likely to experience stress relating to their intellectual competence. They worry about their ability to perform the necessary tasks. Parents' questions such as 'What did you do at school today?' and 'Have you brought your reader home?' can, unwittingly, cause anxiety for insecure children. Furthermore, self-evaluation is no longer solely dependent on the views of parents and siblings; the children are forced to evaluate their own performance in comparison with others in the class. Peers are highly critical; teachers often encourage conformity and competition in achievement (King 1978). Children's learning experiences involve making frequent approaches to teachers for comments, approval and instructions for what to do next. Control over behaviour and learning are often exercised together in the same situation. When visitors ask five to eight year olds why they are doing something, their common reply is that their teacher told them to do it. (Student teachers often make the same response!) However, children don't just have to give the right answer; they have to give it in an approved way. All too often, children who give correct answers to questions are disqualified because they didn't put up their hands or they called out the answer uninvited.

King (1978) found that children of five to eight have to interpret teachers' wishes transmitted in a myriad of different and oblique ways, often in a fashion that exposes individuals as negative or positive models. When a child drops something, the teacher scans the room to see what is happening. This scan implies omniscience over classroom events, giving children the impression that teachers see and know everything. When the object falls, children look up to gauge the teacher's reaction. Those children who sense that they are not conforming to teacher expectations look guilty and uncomfortable. Others are complacent because they are not likely to be in the firing line on this particular occasion. Some report their peers for misbehaviour, drawing attention to their own goodness and conformity to adult rules.

King also noted that new children learn from others that it is necessary to look at the teacher looking at the class and interpret the meaning of the 'looks'. They learn to interpret the adults' facial expressions and body language. They learn how to react to a smile with a smile, to an enquiring look with an explanation and to an 'I am disappointed with you' look with downcast eyes.

Teachers often use individuals to create what Kounin (1970) described as a 'ripple effect'. The teacher says 'I can see one little girl who is sitting up beautifully'. Most members of the class then copy the recipient of the praise in anticipation of the same approval.

Many school teachers maintain control by recruiting the support of other class members in opposition to the miscreants. Statements such as, 'Someone is trying to spoil OUR nice story' succeed in changing the offender's behaviour by making him or her feel isolated, guilty and anti-social. Teachers commonly blame individual children for their own decisions to punish others. For instance, we hear statements along the lines of, 'We can't go out to play until everyone has tidied up. Oh dear! I don't think Luey wants us to go out. If she doesn't hurry, we won't get a playtime at all today'. What is happening here is that the teacher makes the decision to punish all the children because one child has failed to conform to expectations; the teacher unjustly transfers the responsibility for this decision to the culprit. Any ill-feeling about the decision is then directed at the unco-operative child rather than the teacher. This is achieved very subtly by using the word 'we' instead of the direct 'I', thereby depriving the victim of any sense of group support.

The oblique method of control is commonly used when teachers address children. Instead of asking or instructing an individual child to do something that he or she is not doing, teachers sometimes address the whole class as if the offender is not present. For example, the teacher may ask, 'Is Dale ever going to get his book out?' In addition, teachers sometimes maintain control by talking about miscreants in such a way that the eavesdropper might be forgiven for thinking that they were talking to themselves, for example, 'I don't think that Dale intends to take his book out today.'

Sometimes teachers utilise external authorities to help them maintain order, such as 'Tony, do put on an apron. What will your mummy say if you go home covered in paint?'

Teachers sometimes use jokes to change children's behaviour. These can achieve their objective by directing the laughter of others towards the individuals, causing humiliation. The victims smile or laugh along with everyone else but the laughter often conceals their hurt.

King (1978) found that infant teachers use five distinct variations to their voices, each with accompanying facial expressions and meanings beyond those of the phrases spoken. There is the slightly aggrieved, sad voice that indicates disappointment in the individual or the group and says, 'How could you let me down by behaving thus? I would never have expected it of YOU'. There is the 'I am being very patient with you but my patience won't last much longer' voice. There is also the impatient, 'Don't fuss' voice as well as the 'Now we're going to do something really exciting' voice. Children learn to respond to all of these voices in appropriate, recognised, desirable, approved ways. However, learning the rules can be extremely stressful, because most children learn by experience.

Children also recognise the hidden meanings in the use of their names.

The tone of voice used when a child's name is called out indicates one of many things:

'Stop doing that immediately.'

'Oh dear, how could you be so stupid.'

'Get on with what you're supposed to be doing.' or

'Leave the others alone.'

Similarly, when teachers use the adult prefix of Mr or Miss before children's surnames, they soon realise that it represents disapproval.

King (1978) found that social control involves implicit as well as explicit classroom rules. Children's actions or children themselves are often labelled in dichotomous ways. Approved behaviour is termed sensible; undesirable behaviour is branded as silly or naughty. Approved behaviour is good, nice and worthy of emulation; unwanted behaviour is naughty and disruptive to the whole class. Being busy is associated with being sensible. Conformists are judged to be nice, sensible and helpful children who are rewarded. Quietness is often praised while noisiness is designated as silly and naughty.

These methods of control have been widely used for many years. They are effective in persuading children to conform and, on the surface, they may seem to be quite harmless. When examined closely, however, many of these methods are insidious in their reliance on the humiliation and social isolation of individual children and the manipulation of group solidarity. Children seeking approval gain a perverse sense of satisfaction from someone else's humiliation and happily respond to teachers' invitations to denigrate their peers.

Responsible teachers should avoid situations that lead to insecurity, unkindness and an unhappy classroom environment. Many exploit these situations without realising that they are doing so. This is because these methods of control are learned from other teacher models, in childhood, on teaching practice and in team teaching situations. They are passed on from one generation of teachers to the next, often subconsciously and without thought for how and why they are effective. It is particularly important that student teachers and class teachers examine their management techniques very carefully to ensure that they do not rely on subtle humiliation, social isolation and damage to self-esteem to maintain order in the classroom.

Gaining children's attention

Most student teachers find it difficult to attract children's attention when attention is needed. Behaviour problems arise when students launch into a story or give instructions for activities without first gaining everyone's attention.

Some teachers try to make themselves heard by raising their voices. This is inconsistent with the behaviour that they are trying to promote in the classroom and it has the opposite effect to that desired. Shouting and screaming denote disrespect to the point of rudeness. The message that noisy teachers give is that it is acceptable to interrupt other people's conversations by yelling at them.

Shouting may cause a temporary lull in the conversation but, a few seconds later, the noise level becomes even higher than before because the teacher has set a new limit. In the long term, children get accustomed to the noise and disregard it. Furthermore, a noisy teacher creates a noisy class and a quiet but firm teacher creates a quiet and calm class. A quiet, calm student can have a positive impact on a noisy environment. Children thrive best in calm, safe, predictable surroundings and it is neither necessary nor desirable for students to emulate noisy teachers and shout at children to gain their attention. Instead of raising their voices, students and teachers should experiment with alternative and more effective attention-seeking strategies. Examples of these include:

- lowering the tone of voice so that children stop what they are doing to listen attentively;
- remaining silent until children are listening;
- speaking more slowly, deliberately and clearly, changing the tone of voice to attract attention (this is especially effective when the teacher wishes to attract the attention of a single child who is not listening to the story);
- use of eye-to-eye contact with miscreants, in conjunction with the above;
- interrupting activities politely with requests such as, 'Excuse me everyone, can I have your attention for a moment please';
- using a tiny bell which, because of its high frequency, is easily heard above the sound of voices without increasing the volume of noise;
- placing inattentive children within touching distance of the adult.

When teachers wish to maintain the attention of a group while other members continue to join in, the use of poetry, songs, finger-plays, raps and action rhymes are strongly recommended. Students should have a collection of these readily available for use in the classroom.

When children are too noisy for the teacher to start a session, some teachers ask children to 'freeze', or become statues. Others use games that encourage quietness and only start the main activity when everyone is settled.

When children have been involved in exhausting play, it is sometimes wise to introduce restful music and teach children to relax on the floor for several minutes before introducing more activity. If children become overexcited or out of control, strategies should be used to restore order. Students often experience difficulties when they invite children to pretend to be circus or zoo animals. Some will opt to be lions and tigers that rush around bumping into others. Control can be restored by inviting children either to be lions prowling slowly and quietly or change to become turtles, tortoises, lizards and other slow-moving animals. Similarly, children can be invited to 'walk' very slowly, then 'slower still' and 'even slower' until they are virtually balancing on one foot. This requires a great deal of concentration and has a calming effect.

Students and teachers should avoid the use of punitive methods of control, such as 'hands on heads' and 'fingers on lips'. All too frequently, these commands become a habit and are given in inappropriate situations in moments of panic. Children who are absorbed in purposeful activity are unlikely to comply with the order, leaving the adult with the dilemma of whether to proceed without the full attention of the class or battle with the individuals to enforce the instruction. Neither of these lines of action is likely to be productive. Similarly, when children are sent out of the classroom as a punishment, their negative behaviour is merely reinforced. Miscreants often continue their attention-seeking strategies from the safety of the school corridor, providing entertainment for their classmates in the room. This places the teacher in a very difficult situation because, by sending the child out of the room, the teacher used the last available strategy and is no longer in control of the situation. Teachers not only have to be in control, they have to be seen to be in control to be effective.

Students and teachers who adopt the habit of saying 'shush-shush' fail to achieve their objective because 'shush' becomes repetitive and irritating to listeners. The 'shush' may be aimed at a particular child but it has a ripple effect, distracting those who were concentrating. Furthermore, when it becomes a habit, it is completely ignored by the class.

Students and teachers should practise and prepare for story-telling without using books. Eye-to-eye contact can then be maintained and children's responses monitored. It is important that students and teachers have a range of stories readily available to capture and maintain children's attention. When stories are told, it is helpful if puppets, large pictures, large felt-board figures or other good-quality visual aids are used.

Most students avoid telling stories because they worry about memorising the words. This is neither desirable nor necessary. If the brief outline of the story is written on a postcard for reference, the student can be flexible, extending the story or contracting it, depending on the children's level of interest. The student who tells stories without books has a much greater level of control over the group with better opportunities for eye contact and dramatisation.

When reading stories to large groups, attention is best maintained by the use of big books with enlarged print and illustrations. Stories must always be well-structured and made interesting through expressive use of the face, voice and hands.

Students and teachers must maintain children's attention once they have gained it. This can only be achieved by constantly scanning the class, varying the tone of voice, presenting appropriate challenges, moving around the classroom quietly and efficiently and providing positive reinforcement for desired behaviours.

Misbehaviour

Handling minor misbehaviours

Whatever precautions are taken, behaviour problems will occur from time to time. The adult should aim to eliminate the problem as quickly and inconspicuously as possible, keeping disruption to a minimum. If, in repressing the misbehaviour of one child, we disturb the concentration of three others, the problems increase.

Many potential problems can be spotted early and 'nipped in the bud'. By looking around the room, teachers can spot children who are not concentrating on the task in hand. They can help those who are inactive for want of ideas. They can encourage those who protest that they 'can't draw' the things that they want to draw. By giving children confidence in themselves and encouraging effort, the potential for mischief diminishes.

Minor misbehaviours can often be quelled with a stern glance or a change of voice, by moving close and providing a gentle touch. Drawing attention to minor incidents is often undesirable in its reinforcement of negative behaviour. If children are whispering, giggling or talking about unrelated matters, it is best to bring their attention back to the task in hand without mentioning the unacceptable behaviour. Similarly, some daydreaming can be ignored because we all daydream at times and children, like adults, need time to think. Close observation is necessary, however, if the behaviour is persistent and becomes detrimental to learning.

In a large group, a child's attention can be recovered by asking a relevant question without mentioning the misbehaviour. The question must be one that the child is capable of answering, not designed to humiliate the child by showing that he or she was not listening. Teachers who challenge inattentive children with questions such as, 'Daniel, what did I just say?' merely advertise the misbehaviour and create resentment. It is usually best to avoid drawing attention to inattentive children in the middle of a story or discussion because of the risk of disruption to the concentration of others in the group.

Handling persistent or serious misbehaviours

To help students and new teachers judge the seriousness of behaviour and the level of intervention required, it is suggested that the following questions should be posed:

- Is the behaviour likely to cause physical or psychological harm to the perpetrator or other children?
- Is the behaviour preventing other children from learning?
- Is the behaviour the result of inadequate classroom management as indicated on pp. 240–6.
- Does the behaviour constitute a serious breach of rules?

- Can the behaviour be linked to an insecure or unsupportive home?
- Can the behaviour be linked to lack of academic achievement or poor social relationships in school?

In other words, is the behaviour creating dysfunction in the class as a whole and are there mitigating factors? If the answers to the first three questions are in the affirmative but there are no known mitigating circumstances, the teacher should have a quiet talk to the culprit to ensure that he or she is aware of the results, understands the consequences of behaviour and is given the opportunity to talk about why he or she is feeling so unhappy as to wish to hurt others. The child is then involved in working out an acceptable solution and is given positive feedback when efforts are made in that direction.

Summary

There are no perfect teachers because teaching involves human relationships, which are complex and unpredictable. Some students have the good fortune to be placed with teachers who possess sound management skills which they can model with confidence. Others have to learn and model more selectively, noting the things that they will and will not adopt. It is very difficult for these students to avoid learning and repeating some of the less desirable behaviours.

Even the best of teachers have bad days as well as good days. A highly successful lesson may be disastrous when repeated with a different group on a different day when different external forces are at work.

Students must realise the importance of developing their own teaching styles and their own class-management skills. Teachers develop bad habits and 'get away' with poor teaching because children recognise their power and bow to their authority. The children may not learn much from the lessons but they will sit quietly and obediently for long periods of time in large groups. Students lack the status and authority of teachers and children are aware of this. Students feel inadequate when, indiscriminately, they try the methods that the teacher uses and the methods prove ineffective. Supervising teachers must also be prepared to examine their own methods in a critical way and they must realise that students have to be more interesting, more careful and more challenging to gain and retain the interest of the class. Supervising teachers should also re-examine the physical layout of the classroom and encourage students to make whatever changes are needed to improve safety, visibility and the use of space.

Students should question their supervising teachers, asking 'Why did you…? What do you expect children to learn? How could that situation have been handled differently and more effectively?'.

Students should discuss their teaching plans in advance so that teachers can advise them of the potential for dysfunction. 'Have you checked that the…will be available at that time? How many children do you propose to have in that group? Who do you suggest is ready for that kind of activity? What do you expect them to learn? Why do you think that it is appropriate?' Good students are often judged by the quality of the questions they ask as well as their ability to relate to children.

Checklist for identifying the causes of minor misbehaviours

 1 Did I have the full attention of the group before I started the session?
 2 Were my instructions clear?
 3 Did I talk for too long?
 4 Were the children sitting comfortably?
 5 Did I stimulate their interest?
 6 Did I bury my head in a book to read a story?
 7 Could all the children clearly see the illustrations, pictures, puppets, etc.?
 8 Did I use my voice effectively to make the story interesting?
 9 Did the children understand the concepts in the story?
10 Was the disruptive child bored? If so, why?
11 Was there adequate space for stretching legs and changing position?
12 Was I using eye-to-eye contact and scanning effectively?
13 Did I cause disruption or delay?
14 Was the activity sufficiently challenging?
15 Was the activity too difficult?
16 Had the children been inactive for too long?
17 Did I have all the materials and equipment ready for the children?
18 Were the children over-stimulated?
19 Did the children have to wait to take turns?
20 Could only one child perform at a time?
21 Did I check all safety aspects of the activity?
22 Were children reminded of the rules?
23 Was I irritable and negative at the time?

Suggestions for handling repetitive misbehaviours

Situation

Child 1 throws sand into the air while playing in the sand-tray. Child 2 splashes water over other children while working on capacity and volume at the water trough. Child 3 splashes paint so energetically that it splashes other children and their paintings. Other children protest but the offenders continue their activities.

Stage 1

Approach the children to establish whether they have lost interest in their activities and are in need of redirection or another related challenge.

Does Child 1 or 2 need a change of equipment?

Have the same play materials been available in those trays for several days? What changes can be made?

Ask Child 1 what he would do with the sand if water were added to it.

Are there small wheeled vehicles available for making roads and mountains?

What materials are available in the water-tray?

Is Child 2 playing aimlessly in the water? If so, either provide different equipment and new challenges or redirect the child to another activity.

Is Child 3 painting a serious, experimental, 'splashing' picture or merely exhibiting the signs of frustration or boredom? If Child 3 is seriously interested in creating an energetic painting, the location should be changed. The artist should be suitably clad and the easel placed in a more appropriate place, preferably out of doors.

If the children do not respond to new challenges, they should always be encouraged to participate in other activities of interest. If they express a wish to remain in the sand, water or painting areas, they should be given the opportunity to discuss the rules: 'We have a rule that children don't throw sand when we play in the sand-tray. Do you know why? What might happen if someone threw sand in your face?'.

Children should be told calmly and clearly that if they decide to throw sand (or water or paint) again, they will not be allowed to work in that area for the rest of the morning. Conclude with, 'Now let's clean up this mess together'.

Stage 2
If children persist in repeating the misbehaviour after showing that they understand the consequences, the adult must act swiftly and calmly.

'You have decided to throw sand/water/paint once again. You realise that you have now lost your right to play here.' Hold the culprit's hand and take him or her to a quiet corner, saying, 'Come and sit with me until you are prepared to behave sensibly. What might happen if I let you throw sand/paint/water on other people? Then what might they do? Would you want that to happen?'.

It is better for the child to remain with the teacher than to move elsewhere to create more mischief. It is also better for the child to remain physically close to the teacher than to be isolated. Isolation can cause resentment and draw undesirable attention to misbehaviour.

Situation
The offending child claims that the behaviour witnessed by the teacher was in retaliation for a similar act of provocation perpetrated by Child 4. 'He did it to me first', wails the offender.

Stage 1
Provide time for the actor to describe how he felt when Child 4 threw the

sand, water or paint over him. Did the sand get in his eyes? Was his picture spoilt by the splashing water or paint? Did paint splash on his clothing? Are his clothes damp and uncomfortable? 'What would have happened if the sand had gone in your eyes? Would it have hurt? How do you think we could get sand out of your eyes? Do you think that you would be able to see properly if you had sand in your eyes? Why not?'

When the perpetrator has been given the opportunity to express his grievances, conclude with: 'I can see that you were cross with Child 4 and wanted to get even with him. It's all right for you to feel angry but it isn't all right for you to hurt Child 4 or spoil his work or clothes. Furthermore, Child 4 has no right to hurt you or spoil your things. Everyone in this class has a right to be safe. You have that right. Child 4 has that right. I have the right to be safe, too. What could you have said to Child 4 when you were cross with him?'

Ideally, the offender will be encouraged to apologise to Child 4 for what happened, explaining that he felt angry because of the earlier occurrence. Without delving further into who did what and when, children are usually willing to apologise for upsetting each other and they will hug and feel happier than before.

When these methods are practised routinely, children will learn to sort out their own disputes without involving the teacher.

Situation
The teacher allows the debarred child to return to the forbidden activity.

Stage 1
After a predetermined time, the child should be given the opportunity to decide when he or she is ready to return to the activity. 'Tell me when you think that you are ready to use the sand/water/paint safely and we'll talk about what you would like to do.'

Stage 2
Return with the child to the banned play area and help him or her to substitute positive experiences for negative ones. 'Show me how to pat the sand down safely. Good! Now, what equipment would you like to use in the sand-tray?'

If the child has no ideas, offer suggestions as to how the materials can be used. Provide challenges, such as, 'How many of these small containers do you think you would need to fill this bucket full of sand? Do you know what a bucket looks like when it is full? Show me what level sand comes to when you think that it is full. Right, now let me write this down. "X thinks that the bucket will hold six full jugs of sand." Now, how about checking that out and we'll write down what you discovered'.

Provide positive reinforcement on the lines of, 'I can see that you are going to work safely today. Well done!'

Situation

Sometimes the offending child continues to misbehave and resists moving from the play area with pleas of, 'Let me stay here. I'll be good. I promise to be good'. Some teachers capitulate with 'All right, I'll let you stay this time but don't let me catch you misbehaving again'.

If the child is allowed to remain, all the children in the class realise that the teacher is inconsistent and they will test the teacher's limits, knowing that the rules are capable of being changed. Furthermore, if the teacher capitulates to the wishes of one child, others will be resentful if they do not receive the same treatment.

Stage 1

Intervene firmly and swiftly but gently to remove the child. 'I can see that you have decided that you are not going to play safely. Come and sit with me until you are feeling better. You cannot play in the sand/water/paint area any longer. Do you know why?' When the offender is calm and decides that it is time to be active again, the teacher should accompany the child and comment favourably upon the renewed interest and self-control.

Summary

The most effective ways of handling misbehaviour of this kind involve:

- redirection by offering different opportunities for success;
- reminding the child of the rules, why they are needed and the consequences of violating them;
- discussing the feelings of offenders and victims;
- giving the child the opportunity to decide when he or she is ready to return to the forbidden activity;
- helping the child to succeed in the desired ways after returning;
- taking firmer action if the child does not respond.

Teachers can help children to restore self-control by explaining, 'I care about you and it's because I care about you that I cannot let you hurt yourself or other people...I understand that you are cross/angry/unhappy but there are better ways of telling me that you are upset'.

It is important that children are given the chance to decide that they are ready to return to the activities because this puts responsibility for self-control back in their own hands.

When misbehaviour is repeated

Some minor misbehaviours occur frequently; the same child disrupts the story, the same child becomes aggressive at the woodwork bench, the same child strikes others. When problem behaviours persist, teachers should consider how the situation can be changed rather than nag the offenders. For example, is it essential for the child to sit with the story group if he or she lacks sufficient concentration to benefit from it? Story-time should be enjoyable; would it be better for everyone if the reluctant participant were given an alternative activity away from the group? If two children constantly disagree, isn't it better to separate them and ensure that they do not work in the same activity area? When does the misbehaviour occur? Is it at the end of the day when children are tired? Is it mid-morning when children who have not eaten are showing fatigue from hunger? Is it possible to change the order of the day so that children can retain their self-control? Are there facilities for children to take a rest on a sunbed or beanbag? What did the culprits eat for breakfast and lunch?

Investigate and take account of contributing factors

As we have already noted, children become fractious, seek attention, lose control, feel angry and insecure for many different reasons. Behaviour deteriorates at the onset of illness such as mumps or chickenpox. Fatigue can relate to sickness or lack of sleep as well as poor nutrition. Inadequate sleep may be the result of overcrowding, fears, discomfort or neglect. Attention-seeking or negative behaviour may also be the result of insecurity and that, in turn, may relate to disruptions at home, such as separation, divorce, parental arguments, the arrival of a step-parent or step-sibling, etc. The behavioural effects of physical, emotional and sexual abuse and neglect were discussed in detail in chapter 8.

When the behaviour continues and can be attributed to home factors, it may be necessary to talk to the parents. Care must be taken that this is along the lines of, 'Do you have concerns about your child? Something seems to be troubling him/her. Can we talk about what's happening at home? We would appreciate your help'.

Routines for resolving fights and arguments between children

1 Stop the action.
2 Tell the children in dispute that they will all be heard.
3 Encourage each child to explain what happened in terms of, 'I was angry because', 'I was frightened that', 'I was upset because'.
4 Each child will be asked, in turn, to indicate how he or she would like the situation to be handled 'next time'.
5 In serious cases, it may be necessary to verify what happened by questioning other witnesses.
6 The teacher then questions the participants' knowledge of the rules and how the situation should have been handled.
7 The teacher asks the primary aggressor to indicate more appropriate ways of achieving his/her needs.

Figure 10.1: This is an example of a five-year-old child's efforts to resolve conflict without the help of the teacher: 'Nadine was offending me. I said "No" but it didn't stop so I said "Go" but that didn't work so I dobbed her (reported her)'

8 The other children involved are asked how they would feel about this; are there better ways of doing it?
9 The teacher gains agreement on how these kinds of situations should be handled and states the agreement.
10 The teacher asks the children to describe the agreement for themselves.

In the initial stages this takes time, but it is time well spent because children soon learn the routine and learn to resolve disputes for themselves.

Some parents will already be aware that their children are experiencing problems but they may not know how to handle behaviours effectively. Some well-meaning parents make matters worse by responding punitively. Teachers must take care not to give the impression that they are blaming the family or the child for causing trouble in school. Blaming can result in the parent reprimanding the child and increasing the parent–child alienation which may be at the root of the problem. For example, a boy persistently kicked girls in the playground. When the matter was discussed, he revealed that his father did it to his mother and his sister. The teacher merely reported the boy's behaviour in a letter to the parents, hoping that they would 'take the hint' and obtain counselling to remedy their own problems. The teacher did not provide any opportunity for the mother to discuss the matter and it was assumed that she knew where to seek professional help. The following day, the teacher received a note to the effect that 'it will not happen again. We've told him never to kick anyone again and, just to make sure, his dad gave him a good hiding last night'.

Step in at the right time

In high-risk activities, it is important that adults learn to step in at the right moment, not so soon as to cause frustration yet not so late as to allow an accident to occur.

In woodwork, every child must have a vice, hammer, pincers and saw so that it is unnecessary for children to move into the personal workspace of other participants to borrow tools. Problems invariably arise when children have to share and one tool proves to be more popular than the rest.

Before children commence work in a high-risk area involving heat or sharp tools, they should be asked questions to ensure that they are aware and conscious of safety rules. When instructions are given, they should always be worded positively, such as, 'Keep your hand away from the saw', rather than, 'Don't put your hand in front of the saw', and 'Please use your own workspace' rather than, 'Don't ...' When children take steps towards maintaining a safe environment, positive reinforcement should be used: 'It's good to see that you have remembered to use your clamp. We need safe workers at the woodwork bench'.

Handling serious aggression

Aggression often starts when one child accidentally knocks another, fails to apologise and is then accused of deliberate provocation. Sometimes, children behave so outrageously that the adults have to force them apart. However bad the behaviour, it is important that the teacher remains calm and in control.

When a child has committed a serious act of aggression, it is best to take the culprit to a quiet place and say, 'Sit with me for a moment. What you have just done is quite unacceptable and I am very angry. We need time to calm down and think about it'. This not only gives the adult the opportunity to recover composure and think more coherently, it presents a positive model for handling angry feelings.

When children resort to aggression, it is often because they lack the skills to achieve their aims by acceptable methods. This is why teachers must suggest and practise alternative strategies. Most acts of aggression start with one party using force to grab something that he or she wants immediately. The child who loses the coveted item may respond with further violence. This is a good opportunity to discuss alternative behaviours rather than become involved in arguments about who started what. Discuss what happens when one person snatches something without making a polite request. 'How do you feel when this happens? Yes, you are frightened that it might not be returned…that you will lose it forever…that it will not be there when you need it. How does this make you feel?…People will usually lend you things if you ask politely and return them as soon as you've used them but you can't expect someone to give you a rubber or a piece of equipment if they are just about to use it themselves. Do you still wish to borrow the [item] from [name]? Let's try asking him/her politely.' If the child responds in an acceptable way, commend the desired behaviour with, 'Good. If you do that whenever you need to borrow something, there will be no need for anyone to get cross'.

Needless to say, there will be occasions when a child makes courteous requests and the owner refuses to part with the desired object. Teachers should be sensitive to these situations and help the borrower to think of alternative strategies. 'Who else do you think might have a rubber that is not in use? Do you think that I might have one?' If the desired object is a piece of equipment, enquire why it is needed and ask the child to suggest other ways of achieving the same objective.

Children feel more secure and there are likely to be fewer behaviour problems when they know that they have rights as well as responsibilities and, furthermore, their rights will be upheld by adults. Children are more likely to share if they sense that their property will be respected and returned. However, teachers should never force children to share unwillingly. If the disputed item is personal property, it is often best for the teacher to take it into safe-keeping until home-time.

Authoritarian teachers who rely heavily on punishment succeed in a very temporary sense. They may achieve a grudging compliance, but at the cost of a high level of tension, frustration and conflict. Fear may bring obedience while the teacher is in full control but the children are apt to go wild when the teacher's attention is distracted by a visitor or other member of staff.

Punishment is the last resort. It indicates that the adult cannot cope with the child and that the offender is bad and unworthy of group membership. This can harm the child's self-esteem and prevent the adult from discussing and resolving the problem.

If the punishment fails to achieve the desired behaviour, the teacher has no more effective strategies available and can only increase the punishment. The relationship becomes entirely negative. Children do not learn the required behaviours from demonstrations of power. Punishment is usually inflicted unwisely, in haste and in response to the teacher's own frustration rather than because it will benefit the child. It tells the children, 'I'm going to show you who is the boss around here', usually in emotional outbursts that create a vindictive, insecure environment for all children.

Some teachers punish children by giving them additional work of a tedious nature. This happens more frequently in the upper primary school but, at any level, it merely relates education to drudgery and that is undesirable. In some circumstances, it might be possible to invite older miscreants to write about why there is a need for the rules that they have broken but they will need helpful questioning from the teacher to make the exercise worthwhile.

Personal criticism is never appropriate. Children often lash out at the world because their self-esteem is low. Those who behave defiantly usually come from homes where verbal abuse and physical punishment are meted out regularly and indiscriminately, with damaging results.

Punishments that are used as a last resort include the removal of privileges, exclusion from specific group activities and restrictions on behaviour. Such punishments are given calmly and decisively when children have already been made aware that they are responsible for their own behaviour, that they have a choice and that they chose the behaviour that is not acceptable. It is unacceptable because it disrupts and upsets others, endangers safety, causes hurt or damage to property. The adult's tone of voice should suggest bewilderment, disappointment and sadness, not anger or revenge. The punishment must relate directly to the offence, not to the personality of the child. Offenders must be told precisely how they can redeem themselves. This leaves them in no doubt that they have only themselves to blame for the punishment but they have the opportunity to change their behaviour. This is in contrast to the fixed punishment approach which bans children from activities for a week or sends them to the withdrawal room for the rest of the morning. The traditional punitive methods make no demands for improving behaviour and makes it easy for offenders to think in terms of 'It's not fair...I'm always picked on...I hate this place...I'll just have to take care that I don't get caught next time'.

Some classrooms now have children who suffer from severe emotional problems. Their behaviour requires individualised specialist treatment of a kind that is beyond the scope of the responses previously mentioned. For example:

- a six-year-old child stabbed several children with a sharp household knife while they were playing in the school playground. The child had brought the knife from home, which suggested that the acts were premeditated as well as unprovoked;
- a seven-year-old repeatedly slashed another child's jacket which had been placed on the back of his chair.

In both cases, the children had histories of disruptive behaviours and unsupportive families.

Children who behave in undesirable sexual ways were discussed in chapter 8.

Repetitive, serious problems can be viewed as cries for help from children suffering severe emotional distress. The behaviour is a symptom of a problem and the child needs specialist help. In the meantime, however, the teacher has to handle the behaviours.

Interactions with the child should be as private as possible to reduce the need for face-saving strategies within the group. In some circumstances, it can be helpful to call a case conference involving social worker, parents, other interested parties and the child, demonstrating that there are many people who are concerned and wish to help.

Praising and encouraging children

As we have already noted, the teacher has to be credible and respected by children to be effective. Most early childhood teachers realise that positive comments are better than negative ones. There is often an assumption that any positive comment is helpful to motivation and learning. This is not necessarily the case. The purpose of this section is to help students and teachers have better insights into how to make their praise more consistent and effective.

Hitz and Driscoll (1988) show that there are three motivations for using praise in the classroom: teachers want to help children to feel good about themselves, they want to reinforce or encourage learning and, finally, they use praise as a classroom management strategy. Unless careful consideration is given to the use of praise, none of these aims will be achieved and the teacher's credibility is undermined.

If praise is given too liberally, it becomes a meaningless habit and, ultimately, an irritant. Children are quick to realise the insincerity behind praise for a 'beautiful picture' which they know is second-rate and effortless. Similarly, there is nothing to be achieved by praising a child for using a skill that was developed a year or more ago. Such indiscriminate use of praise may, in fact, work negatively if it takes no account of the challenge involved. Praise for low effort conditions children to avoid more difficult tasks. Accustomed to praise, they may avoid taking chances that risk failure and may deprive them of assurances that they are 'clever', 'smart' or 'good'.

Kamii (1984) found that the indiscriminate, common use of praise has the same effect as other rewards, preventing children from making accurate assessments of themselves. It can even lead to dependence on the teacher, to indicate what is right and wrong. Ineffective praise creates anxiety defensiveness and causes the antithesis of self-reliance, self-direction and self-control. When teachers make judgements about children's work, be they good or bad, they remove the children's powers and diminish their capacities to judge their own work. Anxiety was exhibited and created when a five-year-old gave his artistic effort to the student teacher for comment. Without asking any questions about the picture, she described it as 'beautiful' and offered to display it on the wall. The child was clearly not convinced that his work merited display and took it to the class teacher for a second opinion. Not early childhood trained and unaware of what had just transpired, the teacher admonished the child for producing work that was only fit for the garbage heap and she threw it into the waste-bin, upsetting the child and destroying the student's credibility as a judge.

Good and Brophy (1978) and Cooper and Baron (1977) found that teachers give most praise to children from whom they consistently expect high achievement. They ignore those whom they have labelled as low achievers, even when there is scope for praise. If teachers are interested in promoting feelings of success, it would seem more profitable to encourage those who have fewer opportunities to feel good about themselves.

More alarming is Brophy's finding that when teachers try to give praise to low achievers who need it, they adopt different techniques and a disparaging manner. The high achiever is praised with warmth, smiles and eye-to-eye contact of the 'I knew you wouldn't let me down...I can depend on you to succeed and set the example' variety. For low achievers, praise was given grudgingly, without warmth or sincerity and teachers looked elsewhere while delivering the praise. In other words, the verbal praise was accompanied by negative body language.

Brophy found that children who receive praise regularly have learned how to extract it from their teachers. They produce work specifically designed to please the adult. They beam proudly when they present it and even communicate their expectation of praise, prompting the teacher to respond as required. This may be on the lines of 'I have worked really hard today haven't I...I have made this especially for you...aren't I a good girl/boy'.

If we are not careful in how and when we praise children, we condition them to focus on external rewards rather than the challenge of the task in hand (Brophy 1981). This is particularly evident in classrooms that distribute stamps and stars for achievement. Children bring out their work to enquire whether their effort merits the allocation of a reward at this particular stage. 'Have I done good work to get a star?' enquires the star collector. If the teacher responds negatively, the child will go away and add a bit more and a bit more until the star is granted.

When positive feedback and rewards become ends in themselves, children may never have the opportunity to experience the joy that comes from learning something new, the satisfaction of a challenge and a job well done. The use of stamps and stars and similar rewards results in children making comparisons and becoming dissatisfied. 'It isn't fair...my picture is better than hers and she's been given a star and I haven't.' Rewards of this kind leave the teacher inclined to stamp all work 'excellent', depriving children of the challenge to beat their own best previous efforts. Green and Lepper (1974) found that when teachers praise children who are already highly motivated, praise has a deadening effect and children lose interest.

What emerges is that praise can be ineffective and even harmful if it is misused. As an effective teaching tool, praise has to be credible, timed appropriately for encouraging responses. As with most aspects of teaching, this requires considerable skill.

The harmful use of praise in classroom management

We have already discussed the disadvantages of praising one child for behaviours desired of the rest of the class. Teachers often praise a child for sitting up straight, resulting in other reward-seeking, compliant children following the example. As Hitz and Driscoll (1988) point out, these methods 'reek of manipulation' and even the youngest class members know what is happening and resent it. They cannot articulate their irritation but resentment is expressed in a stubborn refusal to comply. Conformists suddenly become non-conformists and those favoured by the teacher may suffer taunts from their peers. 'That's not like you', says the despairing teacher, addressing her formerly favoured pupil: 'I can usually depend on you'. Gordon (1974) found that teachers use this technique because it appears to work in the short term. 'But eventually, most children come to resent this type of control.'

Bad praise versus good encouragement

Research by Dinkmeyer, McKay and Dinkmeyer (1980), Good and Brophy (1984) and others confirms that there are effective and ineffective ways of using praise. Effective praise is referred to as 'encouragement' because its effectiveness depends on encouragement.

Encouragement focuses positively on children's efforts and specific aspects of their work. Praise, on the other hand, is general approval and, by its very nature, is judgemental; specific behaviours are not referred to. Praise incorporates descriptive words denoting above average results such as, 'Good work, Rick', 'What a great picture, Kim', 'Well done, Lee', giving the child a notion of position within the group on a continuum of excellent to very bad. Encouragement involves specific feedback about behaviours; no judgements are made about the quality of the product and no admiration is involved. No work is set up as an example to emulate. Encouragement is given, for example, by discussing how a picture was created. 'Tell me about your picture' is more effective than merely admiring it.

Conversation opens up ideas for extension and improvement—in other words, for creating a challenge. This can be at odds with the philosophies and practices of some preschool teachers who view children's creativity as experimental and not to be questioned.

Encouragement is personal and private. Its content will vary from child to child. It should be private to avoid the potential for embarrassment, unhealthy comparisons and competition. The teacher who circulates can do this discreetly and children will not sense that they are being used to manipulate others.

Encouragement focuses on effort rather than judgement of the end product. If a child has just read a whole sentence for the first time, the teacher should respond honestly and enthusiastically. Praising the child's reading ability will be ineffective because the child realises that she is not proficient and has a long way to go to achieve proficiency. Encouragement should be on the lines of, 'I'm sure you must be pleased that you read all that by yourself. You read a whole sentence without help for the very first time'.

Encouragement is factual, realistic, warm and sincere. When teachers over exaggerate and produce a special kind of voice to praise children, recipients recognise the insincerity but play the game. 'This is so exciting', says the teacher and children agree while secretly thinking, 'I must be odd, I don't find this exciting at all. But if everyone says it is, I suppose it must be.' By using specific encouragement, teachers are less likely to send conflicting messages with their body language.

Children know that they cannot always be good, great or excellent but when these superlatives are used, there is a high risk of failure. Over-lavish compliments can create feelings of guilt and anxiety. For instance, if we praise a child for kindness in helping another, the recipient of praise is likely to feel uncomfortable if the help was given reluctantly. It is sufficient to say, 'I noticed that you helped (name) today. Thank you very much', leaving the child to decide whether he was being kind or merely acting under pressure.

Acknowledgment of behaviour is a form of reinforcement but it does not remove either the intrinsic rewards of the behaviour itself or the child's own ability to assess its value. Using this method, children are less likely to become dependent on rewards for their own sake.

Early childhood classrooms abound with teachers who say, 'I like...', 'I'm pleased with you', statements which condition children to seek the adults' approval for all things and discourage independence and self-evaluation. Instead of heaping praise on the achiever, the competent teacher makes comments such as, 'You should feel proud of the improvement you've made. Let's take a look at the work you did last week and you'll see how much you've learned'.

Prior accomplishments are referred to so that recent achievements can be viewed in context and there is encouragement to do even better. This is helped with comments such as, 'The work you did today was much more difficult than the work you did yesterday', 'You read your book much faster than the last one and you understood all the words. Let's see if you can tackle another'.

Examples of encouragement

Situation	**Encouragement**
Child who avoids cleaning up and putting things away.	*Watch for an opportunity to say:* 'Thank you for helping to tidy up. It made the job so much easier for everyone.'
Child who lacks concentration, cannot sit still for stories, and disrupts others.	'I noticed that you listened to the story this morning. I hope you enjoyed it.'
Child who dislikes sharing and taking turns.	'I saw that you helped X this morning. I'm sure that he was pleased to have your help. It would have been harder without you.'

Child produces a painting and says 'Look at my picture. Isn't it beautiful? Aren't I clever? Do you like it?' Little effort was made but the child expects praise.	*Respond on the the lines of:* 'You mixed your colours to make interesting shades. Can you tell me their names? Could you make these colours again? Which paints would you use?' *or* 'I see that you've painted a house. Do you know someone who lives in a house like this? Is this the front or the back of the house? Does the owner have a car? Should there be a carport or a garage? Is there a dog? What is growing in the garden? Would you like to add more to your picture?' *or* 'I see that you've drawn a car. Is it moving or is it parked? if it is moving, where is the driver? Are there any other vehicles on this road? What about houses? Shops?'

Discussion on these lines encourages the imagination and children will make an attempt to add petrol stations, people, tow-trucks etc., providing greater scope for developing vocabulary, writing and reading.

Child who has shown no interest in writing produces scribble and seeks approval.	'You must be very pleased that you've managed to write that all by yourself. Can you read it to me?'
First attempts at writing words	'That's the best work you've done yet. Look, you've never written so much before. I expect that you will do even more tomorrow.'

Young children thrive in an environment where they are valued equally, are not held up for comparison with others, where they are given help to better their own best efforts and help to learn from their shortcomings and mistakes. Children should not feel that they have to strive to compete with someone else's standards of excellence, least of all in a mixed-age class. Such standards are subjective, biased and can be destructive.

Questioning techniques and the management of discussion groups

Questioning is one of the most commonly used teaching and learning strategies. Children ask questions when they want to find things out for themselves. Teachers ask questions to check what children know. Questioning is also used as an effective teaching strategy to draw out relevant information and help children to sense important relationships. Questioning challenges children's thinking and helps them to reason, participate and expose their knowledge.

For questioning to be effective, the student teacher must plan questions carefully. The categories of questions can be identified as follows:

Questions to motivate: arousing curiosity before a new challenge is presented. They stimulate discussion and are open-ended.

Questions to present new learning concepts, drawing out existing knowledge to relate to new experiences.

Questions to clarify knowledge, for example, asking children to predict what might happen or to explain what is happening.

Questions to evaluate whether children have learned what the adult expected them to learn. Such questions will start with 'How...? Why...? What if...? Let's suppose that...'.

Application questions, such as 'Can you show me what this will do? How does it work? How did you make it?'

Questions to facilitate communication, such as 'getting to know you' questions to develop relationships.

Questions focusing on a specific subject, for example, children playing in water are unlikely to develop concepts of full and empty without this type of question.

Questions for social control, focusing on desired behaviour, for example 'Should you have taken someone else's...without asking? What should you have said?'

Questions to stimulate or challenge particular kinds of thinking, requiring the recollection of facts, the application of knowledge or the labelling and classification of objects.

Closed questions require specific answers. Yes/No questions encourage children to guess at the answers, as they have a 50 per cent chance of being right even if they do not know. Children responding to closed questions watch the adult's body language and, at the slightest hint of a puckered brow, change their answer: 'Yes...I mean no'. Because of the guesswork factor, answers to Yes/No questions do not provide a reliable guide as to whether children have been listening and understand what has been said.

Open questions, on the other hand, may involve divergent or creative thinking and allow for a range of possible answers. These may begin with 'Just suppose that...', 'What do you think might happen if...', 'What else could he have done?', 'What do you think happened next?'.

Memory questions test the capacity to recall information.

Search questions necessitate the availability and use of reference materials and libraries. In daily life, we are not expected to know the answers to everything, but much depends on our ability to find information for ourselves, use it and analyse it. Memory questions in a classroom tend to be explicit, requiring answers that relate to information given in the lesson. Implicit questions investigate the possible meanings or inferences, requiring children to judge the motives of the characters in the story and suggest alternative solutions to problems.

Background questions require a knowledge of information beyond that presented by the teacher. Children from disadvantaged homes are least able to answer such questions that depend on global knowledge acquired by travel, reading books or watching television documentaries.

Guessing questions are useful if they are followed by accurate checking. We spend most of our lives assessing and predicting without checking but accuracy is essential for safety, especially when we are assessing such things as the speed of oncoming cars and their distance from us. Too many guessing questions can result in undesirable habits in which children guess randomly, without checking their answers.

Questions to avoid misunderstandings and resultant behaviour problems. Students/teachers should:

- start out with questions that children are likely to answer competently to provide success and increase their confidence;
- plan questions that are constructed unambiguously using short, clear, simple sentences, avoiding either/or situations;
- ask questions one at a time;
- sequence questions in order of difficulty;
- use open-ended questions whenever possible;
- ask questions in logical sequence;
- present the question then invite a named child to answer; wait calmly if the child does not respond, then provide clues;
- encourage children who fail to respond correctly by thanking them for trying hard;
- acknowledge a partial response and provide encouragement with, 'That was a good effort. Have you thought about…';
- repeat the question if necessary, stressing key words to highlight meaning;
- rephrase the question if the child seems confused, 'Let's see if we can put that question differently';
- use supplementary questions to extend children's thinking and clarify their thoughts;
- encourage children to make predictions when they are unsure of their answers, such as 'What do you think could have happened if…';
- ensure that all children are given opportunities to answer questions;
- ask questions that relate to children's experiences; young children find it difficult to respond to questions about abstract subjects, history, outer

space, planets and other countries on the strength of information given in a lesson;

- avoid favouritism; when teachers consistently select the same high achievers to give the desired answers, others will stop trying.

Children's responses to questions

When teachers put questions to a large group they often point to those with their hands raised and the pointing acts as an invitation to speak. They then ignore those who give incorrect answers and move on to the next respondents in rapid succession until someone eventually says what the teachers want to hear. They never pause to say, 'Sorry, that's not quite right'. There is no second chance and no 'thank you for trying'. This is a habit adopted by some lecturers, secondary and primary teachers. It is both discourteous and discouraging to participants who offer a response to the question and find their contribution is ignored. The teacher often points to another child, then another, without a word being said.

Children are often nervous about how they will be judged by adults and peers when they answer questions in class. Nervousness affects their willingness to contribute and causes panic and hesitation when questions are directed to them. Children worry that others will laugh at them if they do not give the expected responses. If anxiety is high, they may choose to give no answers at all, preferring to accept criticism for inattention. They watch teachers carefully and know their idiosyncrasies. If teachers ask questions of those who fail to raise their hands, shy children will join the handraisers, hoping to escape notice among the majority. They withdraw in embarrassment and confusion when their names are called.

Children only enjoy questions when they have a reasonable chance of answering them well, when they receive encouraging responses and when teachers are perceived as fair and reasonable people.

Some teachers have low expectations of children identified as disadvantaged or slow learners. Low expectations result in the children being overlooked at question times. Knowing that they are unlikely to be able to contribute, such children are apt to daydream or look for alternative amusement, distracting others in the group. Some cast their eyes to the ground, hoping that the teacher will not notice their presence and they will escape the questions. Teachers' low expectations are transferred to the children, thus creating a self-fulfilling prophecy. The likely result is that disadvantaged children become more disadvantaged because they do not develop the confidence to either ask or answer questions, thereby jeopardising their curiosity and learning.

If teachers ask questions individually as they move around the room, children become less fearful of questions addressed to groups. When teachers encourage children to accept challenges and 'have a go' and when they use more open-ended questions than closed ones, there are fewer risks involved in participation.

Class discussions are the most difficult for the student and new teacher to stimulate and control. In discussion groups, children are invited to share information and opinions about a diverse range of subjects. If the stimulation is successful, however, all the children will wish to contribute their news and views simultaneously. The teacher then has to decide how to prevent 25 or more children from all speaking at the same time, how to choose the speakers and how to persuade the remainder to listen quietly when they are only interested in their own contribution. The adult adopts an organising role, guiding and facilitating rather than dominating the discussion, but the potential for pandemonium is always there.

How do teachers select children to speak? Some insist that children may only address the group if they first raise their hand. Enthusiasts will persist in calling out the answers and are usually reprimanded for disobeying the rule. Attention to the rule then distracts attention from the topic discussed and some lose interest. Others try to attract attention by raising their hands higher and higher to ensure that they are seen. Those at the back of the group will kneel, push themselves forward or even stand, imagining that greater visibility will give them a better chance of selection. In this situation, teachers often find themselves spending more time resolving problems of control than listening to children. Who has a hand raised becomes more important than the quality of the contributions. This may be avoided if the adult addresses questions to individuals rather than to the whole class. The disadvantage is that the discussion then loses much of its vigour and spontaneity.

Class discussion has to be steered along the lines of the central theme so that objectives are achieved. From time to time the adult is likely to interrupt to link statements together, clarify view points and emphasise key issues. The pace has to be lively to maintain the interests of listeners but not so lively that children do not have time to think.

Because children's answers are often inaudible and inadequately expressed, some teachers develop the habit of repeating these answers for the whole class to hear. If this happens on a regular basis, children do not listen to their peers, knowing that the teacher will not only repeat what is said but do it more succinctly. When working with young children, it is often necessary to repeat their responses in whole sentence form using correct grammar to present a sound language model. Repetition is also useful when a closed question is asked requiring the recall of rote learning. The teacher then says, 'Yes, you are right. Ten is four more than six'.

Questioning is a skill that requires careful planning and practice and yet most teacher education courses mention it only briefly. Before attempting to take a discussion involving the whole class, students should develop their questioning skills with individual children and small groups. Appropriate questioning contributes to the evaluation of curriculum and teaching strategies. Supervising teachers must realise, however, that to place a new student in charge of whole-class discussion is a recipe for disaster.

Readers who wish to know more about questioning techniques are urged to read chapter 5 of Cole and Chan (1987) and pages 360–71 of Good and Brophy (1978). For other management issues, we also recommend Roberts (1983) and chapter 11 of Hendricks (1986).

Conclusion

There are teachers and schools who make it appear that they have no children with social, emotional and behavioural problems in their classes. Such teachers are presented with reputedly difficult children and transform them into an enthusiastic, cohesive group.

As we have seen however, some management methods contribute to maladjustment. Some teachers handle children in provocative ways, causing frustration and resentment. Particularly damaging are those who are inflexible and unwilling to spend the time necessary to develop the self-esteem and interest of difficult children.

Outlandish behaviour causes the unhappy child to suffer further unhappiness. If disturbed children cannot live comfortably with others, their chances of success in life are poor. Children need a kindly environment in which to grow, an environment that is kind, predictable and fair.

There is often much to be gained by talking openly about unacceptable behaviour and discussing it with the difficult child as a problem to which a mutually acceptable solution must be found. In the same way, progress towards the solution may be examined at regular intervals (Roberts 1983, chapter 8). Unless the relationship between child and teacher is right, little progress will be made.

It is crucial that the problem child experiences the satisfaction from achievement in school activities. Tasks must be graded to provide success for the child accustomed to failure, yet sufficiently taxing for the child who finds challenges contemptibly easy. Matched to the appropriate ability level, the tasks should also be designed to engage the child's interest.

One of the most important requirements for dealing with difficult children is to retain a good sense of humour. This is especially necessary when the teacher might otherwise be overwhelmed by the personal tragedies that surround difficult children. Sometimes, children can be brought to see the funny side of a situation and take the first step in gaining an objective view of themselves.

Once working conditions are conducive to helping children, it is necessary to construct policies for helping individuals within the context of the peer group. Account must be taken of the need for specialist help and parental support.

As Roberts (1983) points out, many problem children have problem parents, but it is worth making the effort to involve them and remove the rebellious child's classic weapon against teachers, 'I'll tell my dad about you and he'll come and bash you up'.

While problems and children vary, the principles of problem avoidance and problem handling are clear.

TASKS FOR STUDENTS

When observing teachers in schools, please note the following:

1 A situation in which a teacher resolves a dispute in such a way that both parties emerge with a sense of dignity.
2 A child who frequently 'tells tales' about other children in the hope of gaining the teacher's approval. Find out more about the child's personality, social skills, success in school, popularity with peers. Why does this child need to gain attention in this way?
3 Occasions when the teacher uses positive reinforcement for desirable behaviour.
4 Occasions when the teacher encourages effort (rather than achievement).
5 Occasions when a teacher encourages a child to beat his or her previous best effort.
6 The teachers' different methods of control and in what circumstances these were used: eye to eye contact, room scanning, facial expression (sad, disappointed, frowns, surprise), variation in tone of voice, touching a child gently to gain attention, others (please specify).
7 The different ways in which teachers attract childrens' attention. In particular, note the games, songs, rhymes etc. that are used.

USEFUL REFERENCE

Turney, C. *et al.* 1982, *Supervisor Development Programmes: Role Handbook*, Sydney University Press, Sydney.

Parent participation in classrooms

Historical factors

Parents, education and social equality

Parent involvement has always been an important aspect of pre-school education, especially in centres funded by governments, charities and religious denominations. The rationale for parental involvement in the early twentieth century kindergarten and nursery school was to teach the poor working classes how to raise their children in a healthier and more genteel manner. Through involvement with families, teachers taught social niceties, basic cleanliness, nutrition and Christian morality. The relationship depicted in early childhood education literature was one of the teacher dispensing advice to ignorant but eternally grateful, poor families. It was particularly patronising in that the teachers were generally middle class, unmarried and childless.

Private schools involved parents but only as raisers of funds for new projects and new buildings. Their presence in school was restricted to open days and formal occasions. Classroom participation was deemed unnecessary because it was assumed that parents chose independent schools with values that coincided with their own. State schools could make no such assumption because parents of state school pupils lacked choice. State schools usually catered for specific regions and the only sure way to escape the local school was to move house. In these circumstances, the demand for admission to a reputable school can have an inflationary effect on house prices in its catchment zone.

Apart from having no choice of school, the parent in the state sector of education was often deprived of common courtesies. Into the mid 1970s, it was not unusual to see signs at school gates to the effect that 'Parents may not proceed beyond this point without permission from the principal/head teacher'. It was never explained how a parent could obtain management permission to enter the building without proceeding beyond that point. The message was sufficient to deter parents from attempting to see their children's teachers. School heads only contacted parents when their children misbehaved.

Open evenings were entirely open. Queues of parents waited in classrooms for teachers' ten-minute oral report on their children's progress. There were often no appointments and no opportunities for privacy. Individual achievement, or lack of it, became common knowledge in the community. At these meetings, many parents learned, much too late, that their children had been unhappy throughout the year, or that they had not progressed in certain subjects. Not surprisingly the parents of unsuccessful children began to avoid the annual ordeal. Teachers complained that the parents they needed to see most of all were those who did not attend. Supportive parents were also dissatisfied with the ten-minute, once-a-year, ill-timed interview. Because the teachers distanced themselves from parents, they did not always receive the co-operation that they expected and needed for success. Children suffered as a result.

Until the mid 1960s, the long-held belief enshrined in educational practice was that intelligence was inherited and unchangeable. This was best demonstrated by the third verse of Mrs Alexander's famous hymn, 'All things bright and beautiful' in which children sang:

> The rich man in his castle,
> The poor man at his gate,
> He made them high and lowly,
> And ordered their estate.

Post-war society refuted the inevitability of disadvantage. There were unprecedented demands for social equality and that, in turn, necessitated equal opportunity in education.

American and British researchers looked more closely at the relationship between intelligence and environment and found a strong relationship between fathers' occupations and their children's performance in school. They also discovered that the gap between working and middle-class children's academic performance increased as they progressed through the primary school into high school. Douglas (1964) found that working-class children with high intellectual potential were more likely to drop out of the education system than their less able, middle-class peers and, furthermore, that the crucial determinant of the child's success was the parents' ability to provide appropriate support.

Jencks and his American colleagues:

> found that family background had much more influence than IQ genotype on an individual's educational attainment. The family's influence depended partly on its socio-economic status and partly on cultural and psychological characteristics that were independent of socio-economic level. The effect of cognitive skill on educational attainment proved difficult to estimate but it was clearly significant. We found no evidence

that the role of family background was declining or that the role of cognitive skill was increasing. Qualitative differences between schools played a very minor role in determining how much schooling people eventually got (1972, p. 254).

Jencks concluded that schools had failed to gain social equality for children because they could not make parents equal and because children are influenced more by what happens at home than by what happens at school. The post-war school reforms had no effect on children's home lives.

Another American researcher, George Mayeske (1973), confirmed that:

family background plays a profound role in children's achievement not only through the social and economic well-being of the family but through the values its members hold with regard to education and the activities that parents and parental surrogates engage in with their children to make these values operational.

Burton L. White and Jean Carew Watts (1973) looked at child-rearing practices and concluded that the informal education that families provide for their children makes more of an impact on a child's total development than the formal education system. If a family does well, the professional can provide effective training. If not, there is little the professional can do to save the child from mediocrity.

A number of British surveys quickly disposed of the teachers' long-held myth that parents in disadvantaged areas were unconcerned and careless about their offspring. Most parents were found to be profoundly concerned about their children's education and their opportunities in life. Most wanted children to have more comfortable and satisfying lives than their parents (Midwinter 1972). The problem was that poor parents didn't know how to help their children to acquire the necessary study skills.

By definition, parents in low socio-economic areas are likely to have failed in school. Those who failed are likely to have negative feelings about the education system. It was realised that, unless those negative feelings could be replaced by positive ones, parents would feel uncomfortable whenever they entered school buildings. Looking in classrooms can bring back sharp reminders of humiliation, inadequacy, the cruelty of other children, sarcastic teachers and failure. These are feelings that most of us would prefer to avoid.

The British researchers found that parents in low socio-economic areas were painfully conscious of their inability to support their children because of their own lack of education. They were totally confused by the jargon used by educationalists. Yet, despite their lack of understanding, parents had a high regard for schools and thought that teachers did a good and difficult job. They did not know how to emulate them, however, when relating to their children at home.

Disadvantaged parents have strong reasons for wanting academic success for their children. They know that school success is helpful for upward social mobility, career choice and a rewarding life. Unfortunately, they tend to put all their faith in the teacher's skill, not realising that they, the parents, are the child's most important teachers. They face disappointment when their children do not make the same progress as other children in the class. They note that others are more articulate, more confident and more creative. They see that other children are able to read and write while their own are often still struggling to hold pencils. As the gap widens, some disadvantaged parents lose interest in school and education, avoiding the uncomfortable feelings that come with contact. They become apathetic because they feel helpless and hopeless.

Revolution in the classroom

The 1960s brought a revolution in educational thinking and this, in turn, affected primary school teaching methods and organisation, especially in the first three years of school. By 1968, large numbers of schools gave young children a free choice in activities with opportunities to learn through play. A pioneering minority went ahead with even greater flexibility in the timetable, known as the 'integrated day'.

Dorothy Gardner's evaluations of formal and informal infant schools helped to establish confidence in the child-centred classroom. In several studies conducted over two decades, she found that children from 'informal' classrooms were superior to those from old-fashioned, formal classrooms when tested for listening and remembering, ingenuity, English (including composition and poetry), free drawing and painting (Gardner 1962).

There were major changes to primary school curriculum and organisation. The 'new activity-based' maths replaced sums, problems and mental arithmetic. Infant classes dispensed with rows of desks and lessons extended into corridors, floor space and out of doors. New school buildings were designed with large open areas challenging classroom organisation and teaching methods. For the first time in educational history, teachers aimed to make learning enjoyable. Sociometric grouping, learning by discovery, open education, free play, the integrated day, family grouping, vertical grouping and destreaming were introduced in quick succession, carrying along many new devotees. With a paucity of in-service training, many teachers did not understand the theory behind the change and there were many contradictions in practice. Some teachers became confused and insecure and clung defiantly to their rigid, 'old-fashioned' methods. Many sought and gained the support of the equally confused parents who may have hated their own schooling but were highly suspicious of the notion that learning could and should be enjoyable. As a result, old-fashioned, formal schools existed alongside modern, open education and the need for communication between teachers and parents became more important than ever.

Researchers Jackson and Marsden (1962) found that middle-class parents had the facility to investigate and help their children's transition through educational change, and working-class parents did not. School was now so different from their own educational experience that working-class parents did not even know how to question what was happening. Parent participation in school life was recommended by educationalists to equalise parents' knowledge and ability to provide support for children.

Education for social equity had to be relevant to children's lives and teachers began experimenting with a variety of new and innovative strategies. Research findings supported those teachers who strove to meet individual needs. Nonetheless, the changes tended to be restricted to separate infant and junior primary schools in areas served by specialist early childhood teacher training courses. Other classrooms retained their traditional methods and parents who attempted to become involved in them found that they had no role to play.

It was no coincidence that the innovations in Australian education came from South Australia, where separate junior primary schools, a specialist Director of Early Childhood Education in the Education Department and specialist teacher training courses ensured that the needs of young children and their families superseded the needs of bureaucracies. South Australia adopted the British ideas of community education in disadvantaged areas, made them work and extended them in a variety of ways.

Introducing parents to classrooms to create social equality

The introduction of parents as participants in the classroom took account of the wider context of the child's experiences and the relationship to home. Following the recommendations published in the British Plowden Report (1967), the aim of the primary school changed to become a partnership between home and school. The British government conceived the concept of the Educational Priority Area and initiated an action research project (1968–71) to find the best ways of raising educational standards in primary schools in disadvantaged areas.

The British exponents, Professor A.H. Halsey and Eric Midwinter, argued that the most important factors contributing to the failure of lower working-class children were the differences in values, language and life experiences between parents and teachers. Schools used middle-class language and had middle-class expectations wherever they were situated. Teachers had the same expectations of pupils; they were taught and measured by the same yardstick whatever their background. Halsey and Midwinter saw the solution to the problem as changing the nature of education to equip children with the knowledge and skills necessary to cope with, gain power over and, in the end, improve the living conditions of their own community (Halsey 1972). This aim necessitated the transformation of primary schools into community schools to act as focal points for the neighbourhood, offering activities and experiences that would change the attitudes of parents to education and the attitudes of teachers to the communities in which they worked. The school in the disadvantaged area began to use the community as a focus for curriculum, drawing on local resources for geography, history and social studies to involve local people as well as children. The new primary schools, as perceived by Halsey and Midwinter, were not just concerned with raising educational standards of disadvantaged children. They were intended to develop self-esteem and give members a degree of power over their lives that they had not previously experienced. To achieve this, they obliterated the boundary between school and community, turning the school into a community and the community into a school (Tizard *et al.* 1981).

Parent participation was first introduced to classrooms in disadvantaged areas to complement and extend children's home experiences rather than compensate for the deficiencies of their homes. Parent participation was seen as crucial, not so much as a method of enabling parents to learn from teachers but to establish better links between home, school and community, enabling parents to make a unique contribution to the school and to their children's education. Gradually, it was realised that all children benefit when their parents are interested and involved in their education (Woodhead 1976).

In the late 1960s and early 1970s, schools in low socio-economic areas were conspicuous by their run-down buildings and rapid changes of staff. As families improved their financial positions, they moved out to more salubrious areas, leaving a core of seriously disadvantaged families behind. In England and Australia this problem was tackled by the creation of a system of educational priority. Schools in areas with substantial unemployment rates, high migrant levels, large families and poverty were given a facelift, additional funds for community ventures, better teacher: pupil ratios, welfare officers and financial inducements for teachers in the hope of providing better quality staff and stability through continuity of employment.

Primary teachers had no training in parental involvement and, at best, were mildly apprehensive of letting parents step over the traditional boundaries of the teacher's area of responsibility. In the late 1960s teachers' unions were also hostile to the presence of parents in classrooms. They objected to non-professionals listening to children read and jealously guarded the areas of teaching that were perceived as areas requiring professional training. Unions feared that teacher:child ratios might be reduced to make way for unpaid, untrained parent auxiliaries. They also argued that, in low socio-economic areas, teachers had enough problems to handle without having to organise parents.

By this time, middle-class parents were already involved in schools through Parent–Teacher Associations and school councils. These were too formal, too committee-minded and too middle-class to attract disadvantaged parents. They appealed to those who were already confident and successful in handling professionals. They also concentrated on social aspects of school life, fund-raising events and school maintenance, all of which were useful but did nothing to resolve the problems of educating disadvantaged children.

The major factor to be faced was the sheer weight of material and psychological oppression that single parents, the chronically sick and the unemployed faced in large outer-suburban housing estates and inner-city slums. Low-rental, outer-suburban housing estates lacked inexpensive social facilities, especially facilities for housebound parents and children. Bus services were often infrequent and unreliable and shopping facilities were sparse, concentrating on alcohol and gambling rather than laundrettes, pharmaceuticals and baby clothes. Parents expended all their resources on survival from day to day, many confined to four walls, living a life of prolonged loneliness. They tended to watch television 'soapies' to escape from the drabness of reality and the temptation to spend money.

Schools in run-down areas often had empty, unused classrooms available and, with additional funding and enthusiastic and imaginative staff, the educational priority concept of parent involvement as a social equaliser quickly became a successful reality.

Parent involvement versus parent participation

Many agencies, especially pre-school services, have a long history of working with parents. What is 'new' is that primary school programmes now focus on the education of the parent and child for mutual benefit, especially in the area of school achievement and enhanced self-image (Morrison 1978). Some of the effort that goes into home/school programmes is to make families aware of and help them to use existing social, welfare and health services. Potential clients often need help to locate services and make contact.

In many schools, there is a very narrow definition of parent involvement. This involves the parent as an unpaid, untrained teacher aide performing custodial or routine tasks relating to the preparation of materials, hygiene and safety. This view of parent involvement is concerned solely with what parents can do for teachers rather than what schools can do for parents. Loyal parents make very effective domestic workers in and around the classroom. The view of the parent as voluntary worker has gained popularity in schools where there are few or no paid teacher-aides.

Another concept of parent involvement is that of the school as a source for the provision of services for, rather than with, parents. Students who visited a multi-cultural primary school that proclaimed the effectiveness of its parental involvement, were puzzled by the fact that at the end of the day, not a single parent had entered a classroom. When they enquired about the programme, they learned that 'all the parents are in the drop-in centre', which was located at considerable distance from the main school building.

Suggestions for providing services for parents should be discouraged if those parents are not regarded as equal partners. Doing things 'for' people merely reinforces the powerlessness and low self-concept of already disadvantaged families. The central question must be 'How can parents help us and we help them?'. There must be reciprocity. To keep this in mind, we may need to delete the words 'parent involvement' from our vocabulary and replace them with 'parent participation'.

Parent involvement is often shallow, ineffectual, unrewarding and even frustrating to those parents involved. Bruner (1980, p. 79) describes parent involvement as a 'dustbin term' which means all things to all people. Teachers need to go beyond involvement to give recognition to the vital role parents play as co-educators of their children. Simultaneously, they must accept that there will be varying degrees of participation, depending on varying degrees of reluctance or enthusiasm which, in turn, depend on the quality of individual teacher/parent relationships, early school experiences and home stresses.

Preparation for parent participation

Different kinds of participation

Teachers of children in the five- to eight-year age group have the best opportunities to involve parents in the classroom and the school programme, first because parental interest in children's development is at its highest in the first three years of school and, secondly, because it is comparatively easy to involve parents in activity-based programmes. Most education authorities recognise this and have adopted parent participation in their policies and aims.

Parents may participate in the life of the school in a variety of ways, either on an organised basis in the classroom or informally elsewhere on school premises. The participation of parents in the education programme can only occur if both teachers and parents feel comfortable and confident in their roles. Schools have to prepare both parties for involvement.

Some teachers complain that parents are not interested in school and do not respond to invitations. Others complain that parents lose interest after their children have left the reception class. Many more teachers and school principals assure enquirers that there is a high level of parental participation in their school but, on many visits, not a parent is seen. There may be parents on the premises but they do not venture into their children's classrooms. Parents may be invited to join school excursions or participate in weekend working parties of various kinds. Different teachers have different ideas about what parent participation really is.

Parents are interested in the education of their children when they realise how important they are in the education process. If they do not take advantage of invitations to visit school, it is usually because their interest has not been encouraged or that no provision has been made for parents in full-time employment. When parents attend only once and do not reappear, it is often a sign that they felt neither welcome nor useful. Parents feel unwanted and their self-esteem is damaged if teachers do not provide them with opportunities to make worthwhile contributions. When school involvement reinforces the domestic, non-educator role, requiring parents to clean up work areas or cut up paper in the isolation of the staffroom, few are likely to volunteer their services.

The essential components of parent participation are communication and recognition of the parents' educative role. Participation can only begin at a point where both parents and teachers feel comfortable.

Within the climate of open communication, the dimensions of parent participation may be extended until they have encompassed most of the following:

- observing classroom activities;
- working with children, teachers and other parents in and around the classroom;
- contributing audio-visual aids for children's use;
- contributing ideas and practical assistance in organising, implementing and administering the programme;
- participating in some aspect of parent education;
- befriending other parents and helping them to contribute to the programme;
- evaluating their participation in the programme;
- participating in planning and policy-making; and
- participating in social activities on school premises.

In planning parental participation, school staff must explore their reasons for wanting parents involved. Aims must be examined honestly.

- Are parents needed in the school library? Can they contribute to making teaching aids, preparing materials, raising funds and participating in working bees? Can parents help to supervise children on school excursions?
- Will parents provide greater scope for personal teaching with groups of children in the classroom while teachers work with individuals?
- Are parents being involved to improve home/school relationships?
- Are parents to be involved in ways that will increase their self-confidence and self-esteem?
- Will participation help them to understand child development, children's needs and how to cater for those needs? Will participation in the school programme help them to gain more pleasure from parenting?
- Are parents being involved to link the school more effectively with the community so that teachers may seek opinions, establish community needs and respond to them?
- Do teachers wish to involve parents in decision-making, to offer community services on school premises, or to use the community for curriculum purposes?

The teachers' aims will determine the level to which parents and community members will have advisory roles on school councils, parent clubs etc. They will determine the extent to which parents may use school facilities for parent and community groups that are not part of the education programme. Teachers' aims will also define the limits of parental participation in the education programme and how far the school goes towards the creation of an open, non-threatening school environment in which parents feel welcome, and gain understanding and satisfaction.

The first communication has to take place between teachers and school management to ascertain whether teachers are aware of the advantages and disadvantages of parents in the classroom. Teachers should be encouraged to discuss their fears and anxieties as well as the positive aspects of having parents in school. Staff also need to discuss what space is available for parent meetings and whether parents may use the staffroom for coffee, tea and lunch breaks or afternoon meetings.

Paradoxically, it is often the desire to preserve the sanctity of the staffroom that negates planning for open school/parent relationships. It should be borne in mind, however, that not all parents feel comfortable about joining large numbers of teachers in the staffroom. If they sense that teachers feel uncomfortable, they prefer to take their morning break separately, either with other parents or in their own classroom with their own class teacher. The latter has the advantage of providing that teacher with the opportunity to evaluate the previous session, discuss forthcoming activities and how the parents might help.

Many schools have an open staffroom that provides an excellent venue for communication between parent participants, teachers, students and visitors. Some schools welcome local social and health workers who drop in at lunchtime or recess to provide support and advice for parents and school staff.

Sometimes, a small number of teachers decide to involve parents in their own classrooms without the approval of their less secure and less confident peers. Although this is better than no involvement at all, the school cannot offer an 'open door policy' in terms of parents and community members coming into school, nor can the school population go out and make the best use of the community. When parents are welcome and sense that they are welcome, foundations are laid for constructive, effective information exchange.

The lack of a staff consensus should not deter individual teachers from making a start on a limited programme because, when the value of parent participation has been demonstrated, others are likely to join in. In the early stages, however, it may be necessary to protect parents and unco-operative teachers from each other. This means that the limits of school participation have to be identified and stated openly. No teacher should be pressured into having parents in the classroom. If parents sense that they are unwelcome, they will stay away and the scheme will collapse. In any parent/school programme, it is important that the school takes the first initiative in establishing communications and trust.

When should parents be consulted?

Consultation means seeking an opinion. Parents may be consulted to help decision-making. The people to be consulted may not be responsible for making the decision, but their support may be necessary for the success of the project. Before consulting, teachers need to be clear about why they are consulting, who they need to consult and how they can obtain the breadth of relevant opinion that they need. They should ask themselves:

- What will we do when we receive the information?
- How will we inform the respondents about the results of the consultation?
- Do the parents we are consulting have sufficient information to give an informed opinion?
- Do they realise that we are only seeking a viewpoint and are not asking them to make a decision?
- What will we do if the parent opinion is not what we want to hear?

Parents should be consulted about a range of issues at an individual level. All adults need to have some control over their lives. If schools merely use parents as labourers and control all aspects of management, they reinforce parents' powerlessness and low self-esteem. To gain satisfaction, parents must feel that they have some influence over what they do and, as in any learning process, there must be scope for those who are able to contribute to more demanding levels of involvement.

When parents need to participate in decision-making

- *Fundraising* issues necessitate joint decision-making. How can the money be raised? How will it be used? Who in the community can be approached for help?
- *School canteen*: what is to be sold, by whom and at what price?
- *Writing submissions* when special funds are needed for school innovations or community projects, to government departments for improvements to community services, or to politicians to lobby for the support of projects.
- *Curriculum issues*: the School Council should be advised of the availability of new curricula and materials and presented with sufficient information to understand the advantages and any disadvantages associated with their adoption. Parents should be introduced to new curricula at both day and evening sessions when they can take on the learner role. Parents may also be capable of contributing their many untapped resources to programme planning.
- *School/class excursions and plans for camps, sleep-ins etc.*

For joint decision-making to be successful, the situation to be decided must be made clear. Decision-makers must be in possession of all necessary information before and at the meeting. Parents need to know why and how they are involved in the decision. Will they be expected to carry it out? Will their children's lives or education be affected by it? Who else is involved? Does everyone concerned have the necessary information needed to make the decision? If not, what can be done to make the information available? An example of this is the school's desire to introduce a child protection programme to protect children from the risk of sexual abuse:

1 the teachers explore the range of curriculum materials and persons from whom they can get additional help;
2 the school invites parents to attend an evening meeting to learn how they can provide better protection for their children;
3 the school invites speakers who have knowledge about the risks to children and curricula for child protection;
4 school staff tell the audience about how they propose to help parents provide better protection for children and how they can contribute.

Unless parents are given information, they are likely to reject new curricula because of misunderstandings and fears.

Parents who are apprehensive of teachers

Some teachers oppose parental participation on the basis that parents 'won't want to come'. International surveys have left no doubt that parents are strongly interested in learning, even in homes where teachers have labelled parents as apathetic and children as retarded. Griffiths and Hamilton (1985, p. 14) quoted a British survey which covered the social and ethnic spectrum of inner-city society, including the most disadvantaged homes. Parents repeatedly told researchers of their attempts to play a useful part in their children's learning; For example, they:

• tried to teach their children the alphabet, or simple writing and wanted assurance that they were 'doing it right';
• felt shut out because they didn't understand what was happening at school;
• were unhappy and confused because, when they tried to help, their children told them 'No, that's not right. My teacher doesn't do it like that'.
• were worried about many things and wanted to talk to the teacher but felt 'too shy to go up to the school';
• felt that teachers disapproved of them because they worked (including some who worked as teachers);
• hated going to school because everyone else knew where to go and what to do and they felt lost;

- would like to be involved but felt uncomfortable with bossy teachers who 'talk to us as if we're children', etc.

In addition, fathers who wanted to help children to read, were told to stop (by their wives) because 'I think they do it differently now';

The researchers found that the teachers were largely unaware of the parents' fears and feelings and their efforts to help at home. The high level of interest was consistent across the social spectrum and included families so disadvantaged that 'it was difficult to imagine where parents found the necessary energy and enthusiasm' (Griffiths & Hamilton 1985, p. 15).

Often, teachers were saying, 'They're apathetic, they never come to school', 'They only want to criticise', 'We hold meetings and no-one comes'. Meanwhile the parents were saying, 'The teachers are too busy to bother with us', 'They don't listen to what we have to say about our kids', 'I always feel she's blaming me for something'.

There is still a bogeyman image of the teacher as an authoritative, punitive figure who gives parents black marks and has favourites. Parents sometimes feel that teachers are still assessing and criticising them. They feel uncomfortable. What we often forget is that many teachers are parents too. They can experience the same sense of unease or foreboding when they encounter their own children's teachers, especially at meetings set aside for oral reports.

Making a start

Publicising the school in the neighbourhood

With a long history of distancing themselves from families, teachers now face the problem of trying to convince parents that they are welcome in school and have a valuable contribution to make to education as well as a lot to gain from participation.

To attract parents in depressed areas, it may be necessary for schools to proclaim the energetic and imaginative work that they are doing in the community. This publicity can be achieved by:

- involving the local press whenever possible;
- involving the free press that reaches every home;
- producing a glossy publication describing the school's aims and methods (written in non-jargon language) with photographs of staff, children and parent involvement. (Art schools are often pleased to be involved in design and production);
- regular, attractive, multi-lingual newsletters that are clearly printed and easy to read (most newsletters are drab, poorly printed and many are patronising);

- the use of community facilities for displays of children's work, for example the health centre or doctor's waiting room, a sea project for the fish shop or a local project in the social security office, baby clinic, factory, super-market or place where people gather. Complex displays are appropriate for places where people wait for prolonged periods of time;
- the production of an attractive calendar using photographs of school activ-ities and children's artwork, giving important dates, school events and hol-idays, etc.;
- the use of community facilities for curriculum purposes, first seeking the support of the appropriate members with explanations of how they can help and what children will learn, for example maths in the vegetable market or butchers' shops.

Meeting parents

Given the willingness of teachers to work with parents, there has to be a pre-liminary meeting of teachers and parents to discuss the school's proposal and set up the basis of the partnership.

The first contacts between school and home must be carefully planned because of their potential impact on the community. If the first communica-tion emphasises the importance of parents to their children's development and education, most parents will be interested in becoming involved. If, on the other hand, the letter emphasises the role of the parent as a teacher's helper and asks for parents to complete a questionnaire relating to what com-mitment they are prepared to make, we can expect negative responses. Most schools launch parent participation schemes with mass-produced letters and mass meetings that are least satisfactory for parents who lack the confidence to speak up and ask questions about the things that worry them. They are afraid to reveal their ignorance and may return home, not only disappointed that the meeting did not answer their queries but angry with themselves for not having the courage to ask. Negative feelings are likely to reduce the par-ents' capacity for later involvement.

The main tasks of the first meeting are to stimulate and increase parents' interest in children's learning and to encourage active participation in that learning. It is helpful to adopt a logo with a bold slogan such as,

PARENTS ARE THE MOST IMPORTANT TEACHERS

with sub-slogans that are changed from time to time, such as:

LET'S WORK TOGETHER TO HELP YOUR CHILD
SHARE A GOOD BOOK WITH YOUR CHILD TODAY
YOUR CHILD WANTS YOU TO SHARE A LESSON

Children are good advocates and should be kept well-informed about what is happening, the reasons for what is happening, and what part they will play.

Talking to parents

In the course of conversation, teachers should ask parents about how their children learn and what their children like to do at home. The responses could supply useful insights and help to identify appropriate approaches in the classroom.

Parents should be asked what they would like their children to achieve in the forthcoming year; what do they think is important in their children's education? Parents should also be asked how they think they can help their children's learning at home and at school.

Responses may identify topics for parent education programmes. For example, parents may reveal that they do not regard activity methods as 'work' and that they would like their child to spend more time behind a desk doing sums. Parents may also reveal that they underrate their own importance in the educational process.

Good communication between parents and teacher are essential if progress is to be made with slow learners. Teachers need to know about the children's medical history, whether there have been any major traumas in their lives, what methods have already been tried and how far they were successful. Parents can be asked to give insights into reasons for the lack of development, where there are deficiencies, and to offer their views of their children's personalities, likes and dislikes.

Parent education

Parent education is defined by the Education Department of South Australia as the 'sharing of knowledge between teachers, children, parents and the community' (1984, p. 5). This sharing takes place in both formal and informal ways.

The role of the school in parent education is to help parents to recognise their own value and worth as children's first and most important teachers. This worth is increased by the development of effective parenting skills through an increased understanding of child development, an awareness of children's needs and the use of positive reinforcement in child management techniques. This assumes that teachers are already cognisant of children's developmental needs and practise appropriate management techniques. Through appropriate modelling, the school aims to foster parenting skills that are conducive to the child's healthy growth and emotional, social and intellectual development. Teachers are expected to provide examples of nonsexist, nonracist, mutually caring environments.

Teachers have a duty to ensure that all parents understand the contents of the education programme so that they can help their children at home. Term by term, parents should be informed about what their children are expected to learn, how and why. The best way to demonstrate learning is, of course, to invite parents into the classroom as participants. All too frequently, teachers discourage parents from helping in the classroom because they 'do things the wrong way'. Parents only make mistakes when teachers fail to provide the necessary guidance.

If all parents are to be involved effectively in their children's learning, teachers will need to acquaint them with basic principles of good teaching. It will be necessary to create a set of very simple guidelines for use by parents, especially for the teaching of reading. Guidelines that have proven helpful in practice are along these lines:

- Hear your child read regularly, if possible three times a week.
- Keep reading sessions short, say from 10 to 15 minutes. Five minutes of enjoyable reading is more valuable than hours of boring struggle.
- Praise your child for reading difficult words, tackling new ones, self-correcting wrong words and reading sentences well. Praise for effort irrespective of success.
- Talk about the book, the pictures and the story. Reading is not just 'getting words right', it is about understanding and enjoyment.
- Make sure the session are comfortable and enjoyable. You should both be relaxed. This is a good time for a cuddle. If you find yourself getting irritated, impatient or tempted to scold, put the book away.
- If your child makes a mistake, ask him/her to guess what the word might be. If he/she can't guess, give the word and ask again later.

In disadvantaged areas, there is a special need to encourage the development of parents' self-esteem and their capacity to participate effectively in community life. Through school involvement, parents can develop group-work and decision-making skills. They may learn how to utilise and extend the community's facilities; they may gain specific skills to fulfil a specific support role, either in mutual support or in the care and protection of other people's children. They may benefit from opportunities for personal development, such as by participating in creative activities or developing study skills. In some British primary schools, teachers provide study space and practical support for parents enrolled in Open University courses relating to child development and child-minding. Most of these students are early school leavers with no previous history of academic success. Children gain when their previously depressed parents acquire new skills and self-confidence, especially when the encouragement and facility to learn comes from school.

In providing opportunities for parent participation, schools acknowledge that parents have a right to be involved in their children's education, because education does not start at 9 a.m. and end at 3.30 p.m. when the bell rings. Parent participation makes all the difference between education and mere 'schooling'. Education is not just about the development of literacy and numeracy but about the growth of the whole person and that person's capacity to operate in the world.

To put the position of school in perspective, teachers have to realise that school is just another community resource. It is not special or separate from the community and there is nothing mystical about the education process.

Traditional schools have been mainly concerned with learning that takes place from books in the confines of the classroom. Today, it is recognised that the quality of children's total learning environment must be considered in order to make schools more effective teaching units within the larger community. With home and school in unison, teaching and learning become easier, more enjoyable and therefore more effective (Education Department of South Australia 1984).

Making it easy for parents to come to school

The key to parent participation in school is to make all parents feel welcome. With imperfect communications, there are often misunderstandings between school and parents about the purpose of involvement, particularly in disadvantaged areas where parents are unlikely to realise their own importance in education. It is the school's responsibility to transmit that information. Transmission requires more than a duplicated note or a class coffee morning to offset years of negative feelings and low self-esteem.

The way a school attracts parents will depend on the area it serves. There is a need, especially in the early stages, for organised activities where parents and staff can meet informally. Some schools organise a class barbecue at the beginning of the year to enable parents and children to meet the teachers of the classes they are about to join. It is important for teachers to foster attitude changes, helping parents to feel confident as partners in their children's education.

Home visits can be made routinely before or shortly after the commencement of the new school year. They are especially useful to meet parents who have not attended social functions. Parents are not likely to respond negatively to home visits if they are common practice. They only become defensive when they suspect that the visit relates to their children's behaviour or their perceived negligence.

Letters from teachers to parents may be effective as a means of communication in middle-class areas but they are less useful in high migrant populations where many parents have English as a second language. Some parents may have reading problems. Severely depressed parents may not even read school communications. When parents do not respond to letters, the class teacher or school welfare worker should make a personal telephone call or arrange to visit the family.

There are many ways in which teachers can make parents feel more comfortable in school:

- Some schools are so large that parents get lost in them. The first task is to ensure that the school is clearly signposted with labels, arrows and even painted footprints on the floor for maximum effect. Highlight the whereabouts of the drop-in centre, the reception desk and the principal/head teacher's office.

- Display plans of the school building with 'You're Here' marked. Label classroom doors with class and teachers' names.
- Publicise the fact that the principal/head teacher or deputy will be available to speak to parents during the last hour of the day or at specific times.
- Enlist the help of established, friendly parents or members of the council to visit and invite new residents, those who are in full-time employment and those who do not come to school with their children.
- Have a 'getting to know each other' informal evening, with light refreshments in the week before the programme starts and, thereafter, during the first week of term. Some of last year's parents can be invited to meet and talk to new parents.
- Make up home kits of educational games with simple instructions and details of possible learning that may take place.
- Introduce new staff members to parents as well as children.
- Display photographs and names of all members of staff (including caretakers, cleaners and secretaries) on a conspicuous noticeboard in the foyer. Indicate what they do in the school.
- Initiate a befriending scheme to ensure that shy, reluctant visitors are collected and made welcome by established parents.
- Create an open-door policy for part, if not all, of the day and advertise the times that parents may drop in to talk to head teachers or join their children in class.
- Encourage children to invite their parents, by letter, to share books with them in the classroom or library.
- Compile and distribute a class booklet giving school telephone numbers, names of staff and a photograph of the teacher. Add a little personal information, such as interests, school holidays, planned excursions and details of local support services for families.
- Include parents in an occasional 'happy hour' in the staffroom.
- Organise a 'thank you' lunch once a year for parents who have been actively involved in school life.
- Visit the local daycare and early childhood centres, with and without children from your class. Arrange to meet the parents whose children will be joining you in the following term. It is often easier to talk to new parents away from school premises.
- Help children to send letters of invitation to parents to attend small group or class coffee mornings that will conclude in the classroom.
- Be a good listener. Encourage parents to talk about themselves, their own school experiences and their concerns about their children.
- Give positive feedback to parents who have helped in the classroom. Praise effort and seek their advice: 'How do you think it went?', 'What would you do next time?', 'Have you any ideas how we could make it more interesting?' etc.
- Involve parents in making books for sharing with other parents and children on overnight loans. For example, the most popular book was made

with parent help after a road accident outside the school. A child ran out of school, into the path of a car and was seriously injured. This worried the class so much that they dramatised the accident. The teacher used the opportunity to photograph the dramatisation. Parents developed and printed the film. They made a big book which was in great demand for overnight loan.

- Most parents dislike the ten-minute oral reports on Open Day. Give parents options to: meet you at their home, out of school hours, lunchtime, before or after school or on school premises. Ask them for other suggestions.
- Provide daytime and evening workshops of different kinds for parents with children involving teachers and specialists, for example introducing children to music or maths.
- Send personal thank you notes to parents who help.
- Make personal contact with parents when children are absent, to show that you care. Give parents details of television programmes that the children would have seen at school. Explain what you expect children to learn. Suggest suitable activities for those recovering from sickness, with simple explanations on how it will help the children's learning.
- Provide a playgroup facility on school premises if required.
- Provide the facility for a baby and toddler group, young parents group, dads at home group or any other group that parents need.
- Provide a welfare club with parents on hand to help others.
- Provide a drop-in centre with tea and coffee facilities. Such a centre could offer both recreational and educational facilities, inviting speakers to run workshops on child-rearing, child and adolescent issues, health, family planning and other sessions of interest to parents. Drop-in centres can also facilitate the acquisition of new skills while raising money for school use. Starting with a small loan from school funds, parents learn to print T-shirts, paint fabrics and sew clothing which are then sold to other parents. Profits are donated to the school after supplies are replenished.

In addition, the following have been particularly successful in attracting parents to schools in disadvantaged areas:

- Invitations to special treats of various kinds involving their children, for example six or eight children make cakes, sandwiches, jellies etc. and invite their parents for afternoon tea at school, or teachers organise a class barbecue or multi-cultural lunch etc.
- Family outings outside the school. A large department store allowed small groups of children and parents to visit the restaurant for coffee and biscuits and watch a fashion display on Monday mornings when the store was not very busy. Most of the children who attended had no experience of sitting down to meals, least of all at tables set with cutlery, flowers and table-cloths.
- Parents are invited to join class outings, including visits to other schools,

Figure 11.1: Classroom participation need not be limited to parents. Grandparents, aunts, uncles and community members should be invited too

firestations, markets etc. with involvement in the related learning, recording, making books, developing and printing photographs, etc.

- Cheap or free lunches funded by school, PTA or shared low cost, attract disadvantaged parents who might not attend other more formal activities. Schools can involve parents in the preparation of the food and incorporate Asian, Italian or Greek food etc. according to the nationalities of the children enrolled. Parents should also be invited to talk to children about their different cultural backgrounds.

- Leisure activities for parents can be provided. A school that failed to attract parents by other means, succeeded by offering lunchtime fund-raising bingo sessions once a week using the caretaker as the caller. This attracted parents who would not normally visit the school, enabling teachers to communicate with them. Barbecues and dinner-dances are also regular features of some schools. Parents and teachers work together to make these events successful.

- Invitations to social activities should extend to joining the children in the classroom. Most parents prefer the informality of the class to the formal ceremony of school occasions.

With many parents working, it is inevitable that some children will not be able to invite their parents into their classroom. When this occurs, children should be encouraged, after consultation with their parents, to invite other adults as their representatives, such as grandparents, aunts and uncles, family

Figure 11.2 (above and below): These children invited a parachutist to school. He brought and demonstrated his equipment, and helped children to make mini-parachutes

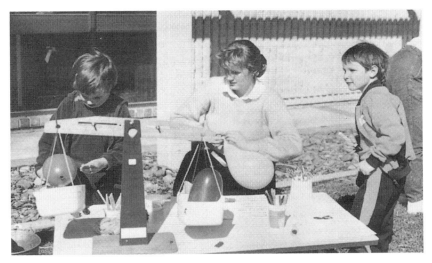

Figure 11.3: This led to a science project revolving around air and gravity

friends or kind neighbours. Some activities should be arranged at weekends or in the evenings, with childminding provided by secondary students, parents and staff who are not involved in the proceedings.

What children's relatives can offer to teachers

Children's relatives provide schools with a wide range of skills, abilities, life experiences and interests that go far beyond those of the most outstanding individual teacher. These interests can be tapped for the benefit of parents, children and school. Family members bring experiences of different ethnic and cultural groups, or different music and lifestyles, from which all children can benefit. They can provide visual aids, such as national costumes, books, artefacts and family treasures that provide scope for conversation, themes and exploration. They can bring their own national songs as well as share culinary delights in cooking sessions.

A grandfather took an old telephone switchboard to a primary school and let the children dismantle it, explaining how it functioned. They reassembled it and created an internal telephone system throughout the school, making plans and diagrams and recording the process. A father took his motorcycle to school, taught the children the names of parts and how they functioned, adding a large number of new words to their vocabularies.

Parents who work in the school neighbourhood can often be persuaded to participate in school life by utilising the workplace for exhibitions of children's work or direct involvement in the curriculum. A grocer was somewhat cynical about the value of covering his walls with school artwork until he realised that people were coming in to the shop to look at the children's work and made purchases before they left. When his takings increased, he offered his services for further involvement. He took a group of children to the wholesale warehouse to show them where he purchased the groceries on his shelves. He showed them how to order and pay for stock and ensured that they were there when deliveries were made. With the help of the teacher, the visits became lessons in maths and social studies, integrating writing, reading and creative activities.

Every school has access to parents who can be invited into classrooms to talk about their jobs. Children always enjoy the opportunity to use radio receivers and hear sirens (on police cars, ambulances and fire engines). The parent who is a postal worker can be asked to arrange a visit to the post office. Children write letters, sometimes to themselves, and are invited to watch them being processed. An imaginative teacher can extend the children's interest and stimulate a tremendous amount of integrated learning with the help of parents.

Many of the children's mothers, fathers and grandparents have skills that teachers lack. They can teach tatting, weaving, crochet, knitting, lacework and sewing to boys and girls. They can supervise woodwork, claywork and engineering activities that require the close attention of one adult with a very small group. Being labour-intensive, they are the kinds of activities that teachers rarely offer when they have to supervise classes of 30 or more children.

Parents can provide practical assistance for teachers by working with small groups or individuals in the classroom, releasing the teacher for more formal work. They can supervise number games to ensure that children don't cheat. They can read stories to small groups and listen to children read to each other. By increasing the number of adult models in the classroom, we have more adult language available. With teacher guidance, this can be directed towards the children's acquisition of vocabulary and learning. Some schools involve parents as regular quasi-teachers working with individual children who have speech or language problems. Their services are invaluable when speech therapists or TESL teachers make infrequent visits but are prepared to work with parents as assistants. In addition, parents can give support to each other, helping new arrivals to feel comfortable and welcome.

Parents are in a position to present useful insights to teachers about their children, ensuring that the school curriculum and methods used are relevant to the children's interests and levels of development. When teachers have an open, honest relationship with parents, they learn about the problems within the family. If communications are sound, parents will tell teachers when children are distressed because of family arguments, when a separation or divorce is imminent, when another adult has moved into the family home, etc. Insights into family life are essential if teachers are to understand and respond to children's needs appropriately. It is much easier to handle attention-seeking behaviour or a temper tantrum if we know and understand the cause. This kind of knowledge only comes with an open classroom, sincerity and confidentiality in communications and a genuine welcome to parents who need to talk.

Parents who participate in school programmes have a much better opportunity of providing their children with a secure, stable and enjoyable learning environment. They are less likely to put unrealistic academic pressures on their children at home. They are less likely to use inappropriate methods of child management. They are more likely to consider the importance of encouragement and self-esteem if they are given good teacher models to emulate. In other words, parents who participate in school life are better equipped to provide continuity of learning from school to home and this, in turn, makes teaching more rewarding for the teacher.

Occasionally, a child may show off and exhibit silly behaviour. Sometimes, a child appears to be embarrassed and shy. These reactions change when they become accustomed to having parents around them. Children like to have their relatives in school as it gives them a sense of security and provides a visible bridge between school and home. Most are on their best behaviour when parents are present.

There are many other contributions that parents make to schools. They are often involved in making teaching aids, contributing their own ideas. Parents should be involved in discussion about what is needed, how materials can be made and used and what children can learn from their use, for example:

- maths modules, counting games, charts and equipment;
- big books, wall stories, class books (in company with children);
- games to develop literacy, numeracy, safety skills, etc.;
- reading materials such as large recipe cards for cookery;
- collecting and making materials with the children, to set up a learning centre or shop, for example heavy and light, large and small parcels for weighing purposes, pretend bank books, shop signs and notices, papier-mâché print and vegetables for a grocer's shop, flour and salt, cakes and pastries for a baker's shop etc.

Parents learn very quickly and soon contribute their own valuable ideas to the teachers.

They see how children learn when they supervise small group activities that are labour-intensive, such as:

- *cooking*: providing guidance on safety, hygiene, taking turns, learning weighing, measuring, counting sharing, etc.
- *creative activities*, sculptures using chicken wire, papier-mache, cartons, boxes or block salt; spinning and weaving (if parents are interested); collage (ask parents to contribute ideas and materials); puppet making and puppetry (supply books for ideas); knitting, sewing, crochet, tatting, embroidering; music of all kinds; woodwork; teaching children how to feed and care for pets in the classroom.

- *listening to their own children* and to those who need one-to-one help for their special needs.

In addition, many parents enjoy and contribute valuable and varied expertise in recreational activities. Teachers may use parents to coach or organise groups during or out of school hours, such as football coaching, swimming, camping, drama for school plays, kite making, photography. A parent at Gawler in South Australia taught children how to assemble a hang glider, helped them to make model gliders and took them to a gliding club to investigate real gliding. Teachers also seek parents' help on Gala Sports Days—staff, children and parents can work together as a team to raise funds.

If the school has a bus, teachers should enquire whether parents have a bus driver's licence and are willing to help. Interested drivers should be encouraged to take the test. School heads should contact their Road Transport Industry Training authorities for information about the availability of training courses.

Teachers can organise combined staff/parent working bees, helping to produce school booklets and news sheets for parents as well as maintaining school equipment and grounds.

Margery Renwick, researching parent involvement in New Zealand (1977), found that parent participation in school had long-term advantages for teaching staff, producing marked improvements in home support and children's attitudes. There was evidence that parents who gained familiarity with school activities and methods used their knowledge in the home.

The authors questioned a school head-teacher about the problems of working in a Sheffield (Yorkshire) educational priority school with such a successful open-door policy that, on average, 40 parents were present at any one time. 'Problems?', she repeated with an air of surprise. 'The only problems we have are with the parents who never come to school. They sit alone in their high-rise flats and look down at us, misinterpreting what they see. They telephone us frequently to complain. Those who join us are soon on our side. They are appreciative of all that we do. After a couple of hours in an open-plan school, they say, "I don't know how you cope with all those children, their noise and activity. It would drive me mad!" But they come back for more and are helpful, sympathetic and supportive. They cook with children, look after the school pets, teach children to knit, grow vegetables in window-boxes, do carpentry, crochet, make tapestry, cook and sew. Our parents have lots of talents and we depend on them for the variety of activities that we can offer.'

The role of the parent in the classroom

Parents who accept invitations to participate in the classroom should be given clear instructions, in a friendly, non-authoritarian way, about their role, its limitations, responsibilities and how they can help children. For instance, if a parent is to supervise four children playing Snakes and Ladders or similar games, that parent needs to be aware of the importance of accurate counting for learning maths. A parent working in the woodwork corner needs to know how children learn from woodwork, how children can be stretched by questioning and how they can be challenged to extend their learning. The parent must be told about safety and control. Teachers can make it easier by making clear rules, such as the fact that only children can work at the woodwork bench at any one time and membership of the group is limited by the wearing of a joiner's apron. Rules must be simple and clear. Parents need to know how and when to help children, how to talk to children to develop concepts of size, space, density, etc. and what children learn from 'playing' with different materials.

Most parents are pleased to be able to help in the classroom but they are fearful of making mistakes. Praise for effort and success are vital for the development of the parent-helper's self-esteem. Parents can work with their own children in a variety of projects. They can help to make family books using family photographs or picture postcards. They can act as scribes for young children making their own big books. They can be involved in a group mural, collage or sculpture. Again, the teacher must acquaint the parent with the importance of letting the child paint his or her own picture in the colours of his or her choice. Parents with strong memories of secondary school art may, with the best of intentions, pick up the paintbrush and demonstrate how they think it should be done.

Ideally, before a session commences, the teacher and parents are involved in brief discussion during which the teacher indicates clearly and concisely what activities will be available, how parents can help and why they are important. When parents become accustomed to the classroom and can anticipate what is required of them, seminars become shorter and evaluations more meaningful.

If the children clean up the room as part of their social learning, the parents need to know the procedures. If certain activities are banned, the parents should be informed. Parents learn quickly and become a tremendous asset in the activity-based classroom where several activities are taking place simultaneously.

Some schools have times available for parents to come into libraries to listen to their children read library books or to read them together. Parent involvement in reading should be pleasurable and not involve the use of school readers. Parents should be made aware of their own importance in promoting the written word to develop children's vocabulary, an interest in books for pleasure, and as a source of information. They should be warned of children's difficulties in reading seemingly simple words, such as 'this', 'that', 'there', 'their' 'but' etc. because of their lack of pictorial connection. Most parents do not realise that words such as 'helicopter' and 'ice-cream' are comparatively easy to read because of their interesting appearance and meaning.

The school as a community centre

Schools should be used as community centres for community-based activities. The whole school must become community-oriented; with a complete reappraisal of the curriculum to ensure that it is community-focused.

In disadvantaged areas, it is especially important that work is relevant to the children's social reality so that parents understand the substance and are able to help. If curriculum embraces the values and knowledge systems familiar to parents, one of the major issues is resolved. As Midwinter (1972) points out, deprivation is relative. There is a rich subculture in low socio-economic areas that makes life in middle-class suburban schools seem shallow and boring. Teachers regale visitors with anecdotes of goodwill, affection and endurance. They talk of children's survival skills and business acumen, potential that can be encouraged and tapped. In other words, the cultural climate does not have to be as drab as the neighbourhood surroundings.

Schools are now active in providing social and support services for parents with problems. A school was concerned about the low self-esteem of parents, a large proportion of whom were unemployed. A school welfare worker researched the learning needs of people in the local community and found that there was a lack of knowledge about car repairs and car maintenance. Most families had an old broken-down car in their driveways but could not afford the cost of repairs. Other parents longed to make their own and their children's clothes. Some wanted to learn how to cook economical but tasty meals on a budget. The school researched parents' needs and paid the fees of those willing to go to Further Education courses on condition that they returned to teach other parents what they had learned, week by week. Shortly afterwards, informal classes were taking place in unused classrooms with the parents as teachers of other parents. The growth in personal development was rapid and long-lasting. As one 'tutor' said to the authors, 'I'd never succeeded in anything in my life. If you'd told me six months ago that I was capable of teaching anybody anything, I wouldn't have believed it. The fact that I'm teaching people in a school is just incredible. If only my old teachers could see me now!'.

In poor areas, depressed and harassed parents are often driven to eating fast, high-carbohydrate foods that cause weight problems. Overweight people tend to suffer low self-esteem and poor health. Some schools offer weight watchers clubs for parents and others in the community. Parents provide school-based childminding facilities for babies and toddlers while their parents consult hospital nutritionists.

Because of the enormous pressures on parents in disadvantaged areas, some schools offer emergency daycare and family daycare facilities with approved parents acting as caregivers, for which they receive a small remuneration. Emergency childcare is essential for parents visiting other sick children in distant hospitals, especially when they are dependent on public transport. Daycare facilities are always supervised by statutory community welfare/social services departments. A Tasmanian school near Hobart went one stage further and opened a daycare centre on its premises. As schools are state-funded and the daycare project was federally funded, this involved the precedent of selling a school building to the federal government.

Old school buildings with diminishing enrolments are ideal for providing space for drop-in centres. Some parents spend their entire day in and around school because there is 'nothing better to do'. Coffee-making, food preparation facilities and comfortable seating are necessary. Parents often initiate their own school-based wholesale food store and used-clothes boutique on school premises.

Some schools have initiated clubs and mutual help groups for unemployed parents who, not surprisingly, have developed employment skills through involvement in community tasks, such as painting community buildings, repairing roofs etc.

An additional activity has been to develop community awareness and provide parents with the power to make changes. Most parents in disadvantaged areas do not know how to pressurise housing authorities to make repairs. They do not know how to lobby politicians or government departments for necessary services. They tend to respond to bureaucracy with frustration and anger and fail to achieve their objectives. Parents in deprived areas often suffer from a sense that their lives are out of control. This results in depression and affects the children in school. Community involvement can teach parents how to help themselves, who to contact when things go wrong and how to write letters to appropriate people. Schools can help to return power to the people and when parents gain self-esteem, children benefit.

Schools can invite the professionals to talk to parents in school in their familiar environment. The housing manager may come to school to explain why better housing cannot be provided. The social security officer may come in to tell parents about their rights and answer their questions. Politicians may come to school to meet members of their electorates. Parents are often afraid of contacting authorities in government offices but feel more confident when meeting officials on their own home ground. This helps to restore the balance of power and, over time, changes the outlook of residents in the community.

Parent education takes many forms. Parents want to know how to gain more pleasure from parenthood and how to give their children a better start in the education system. Schools can provide facilities for health services, playgroups, toy libraries, and parent and toddler clubs. They can arrange for specialist nurses to call on club days and talk to parents about their child rearing problems. Young parents' clubs attract the very young, single parents who are at greatest risk of neglecting and abusing their children. Where there are a lot of separated parents, the school can provide a single parents' club for mutual support. Even when schools are overcrowded, they can offer the use of the staffroom for most of the day.

Whenever a school becomes part of the community, the activities offered must be the ones that parents want, not those that teachers think they want. Teachers should make the opportunity to canvass the views of those who do not spend much time at school as well as those who are present and articulate. Much will depend on the availability or lack of necessary services in the community. Parents on distant, low-rental housing estates are often so far away from community welfare offices and feel so threatened by public servants that they do not enquire about their rights to welfare benefits. In some schools, this has led to small groups of parents getting together to act as school-based advice bureaux for welfare rights. The parents offering the service gain knowledge and confidence from their research and their contacts with authorities and users of the service, while others find them readily available, approachable and helpful.

School questionnaires can be a nightmare to parents in low socio-economic areas. Forms represent authority, bureaucracy and feelings of discomfort. Some schools send questionnaires to parents to try to identify what activities are needed. They are often disappointed by the response. Teachers are accustomed to form-filling. Most parents are not. Forms are associated with government departments, authority and their own powerlessness. Only the most highly motivated and middle-class parents are likely to fill in non-compulsory questionnaires asking them what they expect to gain from a community school. To be successful, enquiries about parents' needs have to include personal contact.

School-based child–parent resource centres

Some South Australian schools have child–parent resource centres adjacent to the main school buildings. These provide excellent community support facilities in disadvantaged areas but they should not be confused with, or regarded as replacements for, parent participation in the school programme. Resource centres cater for pre-school education and family needs, providing a range of referral and support services for individuals, community groups, organisations and institutions within the locality, including daycare centres and kindergartens. Centres offer toy libraries and other parent resources. They provide materials for playgroups and offer health care for parents and children. They communicate with and provide for parents and children. They communicate with and provide for the needs of ethnic minority groups. Centres are staffed by health department nursing sisters, social and ethnic community workers from community welfare departments, teachers and school assistants provided by the Education Department. A number of different types of playgroups are offered at these centres. A group of Vietnamese parents provided classes for learning English as a second language as well as opportunities for parents and children to meet their countryfolk and their native community workers.

Some school-based playgroups cater for parents referred by social workers and health workers because they are considered to be at risk of abusing or neglecting their children. The centres occupy unused classrooms or temporary units in school yards. They are jointly funded by Social Service Departments and charities. Referred parents, and children and ethnic minority groups are conveyed to and from the centre by taxi or department transport. Parents attend educational groups and have opportunities for socialising while their children are cared for by staff. Such children are usually retarded in language development, social development and the ability to play. As some 'at risk' parents have been deprived of opportunities for play in early childhood, it may be necessary to let parents play with clay, water and paint etc., before they can learn to play with their children. Most have experienced negative child management techniques from their own parents when they were young and tend to reproduce these models when they try to discipline their children at home and in school. Many parents think that the good child is the one who sits quietly in front of the television set and does not talk.

Workers teach new parenting skills with a view to gaining greater pleasure from children. They use positive reinforcement, praising parents for their children's achievements. They create situations to develop the parents' self-esteem. It is important that staff do not rely on direct teaching and modelling because inadequate parents are apt to despair and say 'He'll do it for you because you're a teacher but he won't do it for me'. That response confirms the parent's sense of hopelessness and poor self-image. Some teachers have found video cameras useful for showing parents the detail of their own interactions with their children. Parents are encouraged to work out how they could have handled the situation differently. They assess what skills they need and discuss how they can achieve them.

Sometimes, whole families are referred to centres. Staff visit their homes routinely in their non-contact time and after school-hours. They give practical help on cooking matters, budgeting, family planning etc. and contact other support services for used clothing, basic furniture, home-maker help and so on. Nursing sisters are involved in screening the children, providing emergency treatment and advising on parents' health care. They also liaise with other health agencies. Weekly clinics are held on the premises for parents and babies.

The resource centre has two aspects: first, the centre itself provides a base for a more comprehensive service to children and their parents. Secondly, through the co-operation of individuals in the team and by coordinating with other agencies, existing health, education and welfare services in the neighbourhood can be used more effectively.

Parent participation in language programmes

The acquisition of children's language presents a major task for teachers, and depends on the help of parents and other adults. The constant stimulation of new words leads children to develop new concepts, and this basic learning leads to later academic achievements.

Most schools teach reading and writing through language experience. Language is considered to be central to all learning and, as such, forms a basis for all curriculum and current methodology. Parent participation in language development should be a feature throughout the early years at school. Parents can then continue the language development approach with their own children, narrowing the gap between home and school.

Parents are involved in a variety of ways, some of which have already been mentioned. They can:

- read stories to children and be helped to question the listener to find out whether they have understood the concepts involved;
- read stories to introduce new words and question children appropriately for comprehension;
- play reading games and word games with small groups of children;
- help children to make their own reading books and read back what they have written;
- participate in conference writing: spelling conferences, typing, talking, exchanging ideas;
- accompany children to the library and help them to choose appropriate books or seek information;
- record children's ideas and statements when the children are not able to write;
- supervise children who are reading to each other;
- listen to children reading stories for enjoyment;
- learn to talk to children and ask questions that promote investigation, learning, problem solving and reflection;
- talk to children who need 1:1 conversation, such as children undergoing speech therapy or learning English as a second language;
- talk with children and listen so that they can have a wide variety of adult models and a large number of people who have the time and interest to give to them.

An example of the latter is the parent who brings a new baby to school, baths it, changes it and feeds it in the classroom, answering children's questions and stimulating interest that results in reading and writing about babies, aspects of hygiene and the acquisition of new vocabulary for body parts.

Open, friendly, non-threatening relationships with teachers reveal that some parents are print- or language-deficient and need help for themselves so that they can help their children. As a result, some schools provide both formal and informal tuition for parents. Families involved in language programmes with their own children find that child/parent relationships become more productive and enjoyable.

The Haringey Reading Project confirmed that reading standards can be raised substantially with parent participation in school. Six schools took part in the project in the same multi-ethnic, inner-city London area where reading standards were well below the national average (Hewison 1981). The project involved children of six to eight years over a two-year period. In two schools, one class established parent participation with all the parents involved. One class was given extra teacher help and two schools had no help at all. The children whose parents helped them (with teacher guidance) made rapid progress while the others retained their previous poor performance. It became clear that well-organised parent help can lead to striking improvements in children's reading performance and, furthermore, with appropriate encouragement from school, most parents are willing and able to help their children effectively.

Further confirmation came from the British Belfield Primary Experiment (Wilby 1982, pp. 5, 8) involving parents who had been labelled as 'feckless, apathetic, ignorant and disinterested in their children'. In a three-year project, every parent participated. Teachers visited each family and explained how members could help. They provided a simple list of 'do's and don'ts' such as 'talk about the picture first—read the page first—point to new words and emphasise them—repeat the whole sentence' etc. 'Don'ts' included: 'don't threaten to tell the teacher—don't make reading unpleasant—don't let the child think he/she is in competition with others'. Every night the child took home a carefully selected book and the next day the parent sent written comments back to school. Teachers checked the passages and helped with difficulties. The children made rapid strides and their success led to success in other fields.

Professor Jack Tizard achieved the same results with a group of working-class seven-year-olds in Barking, Essex. Tests after two years showed that children who had not taken books home had reading scores below the national average while 50 per cent of those with parent-helpers had reached levels well above average (Wilby 1982).

Teachers usually discourage pushy, competitive parents from helping in the classroom. Researchers found that this kind of competition usually relates to children's progress through graded reading schemes. Experience now suggests that parents lose this competitiveness when they acquire knowledge about the reading process and when schools use a wide variety of reading materials. Timid, anxious parents are more difficult to help. Negative parents are usually negative because they experienced negative parent models in early childhood. Again, experience shows that parents' attitudes are changeable. If parents have clear guidelines about child management and positive reinforcement, they will follow the guidelines in school, developing a more enjoyable relationship with their children.

Some parents say they cannot help because they cannot read, or cannot read English. Poor adult readers can listen to children read, drawing attention to errors with 'Try that again please. I don't think it makes sense'. Teachers can point out that there is a good chance of parents improving their reading if they listen to children regularly using easy-to-read books.

Children gain pleasure from 'learning together'. Some parents are not made welcome because they are accompanied by babies and young children. A few well-placed questions may suggest useful strategies. If there are sufficient parents with young children, the parents may be able to create their own creche or childminding service. Sometimes, it may be possible to accommodate young children in the classroom. Alternatively, there may be an older sibling or grandparent who can come to school to help a child.

Children in residential care in children's homes or foster homes should be treated in the same way as other children, with caregivers acting as parent participants.

Why some teachers don't want parents in classrooms

The most common reason for a teacher's unwillingness to become involved with parents is the teacher's own lack of professional confidence. Unlike early childhood educators, primary teachers are given few opportunities to practise relating to parents before they graduate. Although parent involvement has been a significant feature of Australian, British and New Zealand education for almost two decades, skills in human relations are given low priority in most teacher training courses. In addition, young, recently-graduated teachers are at a tremendous disadvantage in that they are often still working through their own problems relating to gaining independence from their families and, at that stage, may find it difficult to sympathise with parents' problems. Married teachers who are also parents have a big advantage over their young, single peers, but all teachers involved in parental participation programmes need mutual support and management support in what they are trying to achieve.

In looking at parent involvement in schools in New Zealand, Renwick (1977) collected the teachers' reasons for not having parents in their classrooms. These were typical responses that could be heard in any non-participating classroom:

- Parents might compare their children with others if they stayed for any length of time in the classroom. This was viewed as an undesirable activity.
- Parents are not restricted by professional confidentiality. They may repeat what they hear in school or misunderstand what is happening and alarm other parents unnecessarily, causing more problems for teachers.
- Parents are unreliable. Teachers may plan an activity with parents in mind and they don't turn up. As volunteers, they have no obligation to the school.
- Parents need training in ways of doing things in the classroom. Teachers don't have time to train them.
- 'I don't like sharing my classroom with anyone.'

- 'I'm not going to risk having parents telling me what to do in my classroom.'
- 'Our parents aren't interested in school. They wouldn't come if we invited them. Their attitude is that the teacher is paid to teach so we can get on with it.'
- 'Most of my parents work full-time.'
- 'They came once and didn't come back.'

Few teachers involved in parent participation experience any difficulty in relating to parents. When teachers complain of parental disinterest, it is usually an indication that the visitors have either not been made welcome, or, if welcome, the experience has not convinced them that they are important to their children's education.

Some parents are not invited into the classroom because they are deemed to be 'unsuitable' by virtue of their personalities, aggressiveness, competitiveness, their use of unacceptable language or perceived negative attitudes to their own children.

Problems that can arise

Disadvantaged parents can be disadvantaged in school

In her study of New Zealand reception class teachers, Margery Renwick (1977) expressed fears that disadvantaged parents were also disadvantaged in parent participation in the classroom. Unless schools have policies that welcome all parents, there is a strong tendency for teachers to encourage only the competent parents that they like—that is, professionals like themselves. Renwick commented in her paper that:

> There isn't much evidence in New Zealand of schemes being viewed as opportunities either to help less well-educated parents to understand more about school or to help children with particular problems by having their parents in the classroom. Either the school is not approaching this groups of parents or they are not availing themselves of the opportunity to come. One wonders if, like so many educational innovations, parental involvement may serve to widen the gap between the privileged and less privileged. If it's the parents of well adjusted, high achieving children who tend to be involved, these are the children who are going to gain the most from the experience of having their parent present in the classroom.

Individual teachers play a very large part in making parents feel welcome. It is the teacher's responsibility to find ways of communicating with parents about teaching methods, curriculum and what parents can do to help their children. Without that advice, some parents may place undue pressure on their children to learn. Others will leave education to teachers. Parents are then disappointed when their efforts are in vain and their children do not progress or they display anxiety traits. Parents need to know how they can help their children. They need to know that maths can be taught by playing dominoes, card games and handling money. They need to know that reading can be taught informally in supermarkets and bus stops. All parents must be welcomed and invited into the classroom to see what their children are doing.

Care must be taken that shy and inhibited parents receive special attention. Unless deliberate efforts are made to include all parents, there is always a tendency for the same successful, confident parents to monopolise schools. They are on the PTA and are highly visible on all public occasions. Their children tend to be the successful ones who win trophies on sports days and take major roles in nativity plays and school concerts. The less successful are behind the scenes as stage-hands or appear briefly as sheep. Other parents become disillusioned and disgruntled through hours of entertainment, limited to the same few children. Informal class efforts are more appropriate for the majority of children's parents. Few school concerts or plays have the facility to turn every child into a star. Shy parents will avoid schools and school functions that are dominated repeatedly by the same families.

Some schools avoid opportunities for parent domination by creating small committees of two parents and a seconded staff member to organise each activity. No parent is allowed to be on more than one committee, ensuring that responsibilities and learning opportunities are shared. In a Bristol (England) school, two parents negotiated with Woolworth's public relations officer to provide party fare and Christmas gifts for the children in a disadvantaged area, while others organised a used-clothing boutique and a wholesale food store. All parents have talents that should be investigated and encouraged.

Befriending can be organised by establishing parents to help new arrivals to the school or district. New parents are visited, invited, accompanied and introduced to teachers and other parents. When they feel confident in school, they too are encouraged to befriend and introduce others.

Some teachers complain that parents never respond to letters or notes. There are many problems with written communications. Children lose notes, forget to take them home or forget to hand them over. The only way of checking this is to incorporate reply slips and make phone calls to parents who don't reply.

Teachers should make sure that the children of 'reluctant' parent attenders are participating to encourage attendance at school sports days, plays, concerts etc. Select these parents for children's invitations to lunches or tea parties. Invite parents personally or by telephone and make home visits if they do not attend. Teachers complain that some parents are 'too busy' to attend. They should find out when the parents are available and plan to meet them at convenient times. Sometimes parents refuse to attend because they don't like other parents. Teachers should consider providing opportunities to meet shy parents when others are not present.

Home visiting is an integral part of school programmes in disadvantaged areas. Some teachers feel uncomfortable about visiting and prefer to leave it to welfare workers. Others visit every family at least once a term in non-contact time, lunch time, after school or when another member of staff is available to free them from the classroom. It is clearly advantageous if parents regard home visits as routine, friendly and normal.

Home visiting cannot be forced on teachers or parents. Teachers have to be convinced of the mutual benefits. Parents have to feel comfortable about teachers coming into their homes. Some teachers accept invitations home for meals and attend children's birthday parties. Although these invitations are accepted with the best of intentions, they can cause ill-feelings among other parents and children and lead to charges of favouritism. Young children want to please their teachers and have their approval. Not all children can have birthday parties and the child who produces a birthday gift from the teacher is likely to cause a great deal of envy and distress among the less fortunate.

Teachers complain that some parents don't read newsletters. Such parents are identified when they send children to school and school is closed. Teachers should look carefully at the format of the newsletter and ensure that it is presented and written appropriately for the school community.

One common difficulty for teachers arranging parent participation is that a large number of mothers and fathers are in full-time employment. Those at home may be busy with their pre-school children. Working parents need opportunities for evening contact and the housebound parent needs childminding facilities to enable him or her to come to school during the day.

Another commonly experienced difficulty is that of welcoming new parent helpers to groups that are already well established. Drop-in centres are useful but some intervention may be necessary to ensure that they are not dominated by a few 'regulars' who regard the centre as their own territory. Sometimes, regular users are insensitive to new arrivals and fail to make them feel welcome. It can take up to six months for a shy parent to feel comfortable on school premises. The school principal should invite new families to drop in together on a particular day and offer time for an informal chat. Some schools ask the well-established parents or befrienders to visit or collect the new arrivals so that they get to know someone before they arrive.

Schools with a high number of multi-cultural families may find it particularly difficult to involve parents in school activities. This may also relate to the different cultural view of the teacher's role. Sometimes both parents are working. New migrant parents often work long hours to provide for all the family members, but they also live in extended families that should be tapped to provide support for children in school. Language presents a barrier to involvement, especially for non-English speaking parents. Staff find it beneficial to contact ethnic support services when there is poor parent representation in school

Parent participation is no longer the prerogative of schools in low socio-economic areas. Parents of young children in independent schools are now given the opportunity to participate in the classroom. To teachers who have no experience of working alongside professional, middle-class parents who are paying fees for their children's education and teachers' salaries, there are sometimes unexpected pitfalls. Some teachers find that well-educated parents have very high, often unrealistic expectations of what should go on in the classroom and that a little knowledge can be a dangerous thing. As a result, some teachers feel pressured to conform to parents' expectations even when they differ from what they believe is educationally desirable. Some staff complain of parents invading their privacy and personal space. With hindsight, they realise that they did not lay down appropriate guidelines and limits at the outset and had allowed parents to encroach on their professional role.

In conclusion, it is accepted that all parents and children can benefit from joint involvement in the education process, that all parents need to know about child development and how they can become effective co-educators of their children. Parent participation makes all the difference between education and 'schooling'. It helps parents to think about the whole development of the child, including emotional development, and causes them to rethink some of their earlier assumptions about the value of competition and intellectual prowess.

To prevent problems arising, teachers should have regular low-key meetings or workshops with parent participants. In the early stages, it may be necessary to discuss such matters as the need for reliability, punctuality, confidentiality and responsibility in a non-authoritarian way.

Teachers will need to emphasise the parents' value to school and their importance to their own children's education, especially as models. In addition, parents may need help to introduce positive child management techniques and cope with children's behaviour problems.

Orientation sessions for parent-helpers

It is helpful if schools initiate orientation programmes for small groups of parents who are willing to participate in classrooms. These sessions are additional to beginning of the year information evenings and may consist of six to eight half-days of intensive training for which recipients receive a certificate of attendance. When these sessions are successful, parents often proceed to further study, sometimes with a view to teacher training or work in child care. Tutors may be class teachers or parent helpers who have been trained for teaching or childcare. In some priority schools, there are school assistants employed to take responsibility for co-ordinating home–school programmes.

Orientation sessions usually include the following:

1 School orientation:
  - welcome by senior staff;
  - refreshments with other parents and the staff member responsible for the group;

- a tour of the school;
- the distribution of school plans to show the whereabouts of different classrooms and teachers, science, art or book stores, libraries and other facilities.

2 An overview of the school's aims and philosophies, presented in everyday, jargon-free language, including:
   - what staff are trying to do and why in relation to building children's self esteem and self confidence;
   - how staff handle behavioural problems and why;
   - the importance of parents in children's education, both in the home and in the classroom.

3 Hands-on experience with the different types of concrete materials used in classrooms, simulating the child's learning experience. Tutors will encourage parents to experiment with materials and describe their tactile experiences. A useful exercise for the introductory session is to invite parents to make illustrated name tags using a variety of collage materials on card that has been pre-cut to the size of a saucer. Most adults create something personal and meaningful; for instance, the father who arrived late made an apologetic picture, the parent who had seven children drew her family and the mother who had smashed crockery at breakfast made a collage of pictures advertising Royal Doulton and Wedgwood porcelain. Parents are invited to tell each other about their pictures. This gives tutors the opportunity to demonstrate how human beings are personally involved in their creative work and that children put their emotional selves into their creations. This helps parents to understand why they must not interfere with or devalue children's creative efforts.

4 Discussion of specific curriculum areas that parents will encounter in classrooms, including some basic theory about how children learn maths, acquire language and how parents can help in the literacy programme.

5 The use of audio-visual aids and technical equipment. Parents who have no previous experience should be taught how to:
   - use a computer and printer;
   - use an overhead projector;
   - load and unload a movie projector;
   - load and unload a slide projector;
   - use a tape recorder with children;
   - use a sewing machine;
   - use the school cooking equipment;
   - use a video recorder;
   - use a large-script typewriter for making children's own books;
   - use a camera and, if equipment is available, print and develop black/white film.

6 Role play can be used to help parents to learn how to handle minor misbe-

haviours and disputes using positive management techniques. Parents need to know when to refer a behaviour problem to the teacher and when to deal with it on the spot. They need to know what children are allowed or not allowed to do in and outside classrooms.

7 How to help individual children with special needs. Parents should also be given information about how to identify the signs of maltreatment and handle disclosures sensitively. Parents often pick up children's cries for help when they are working together in a 1:1 situation.

Discipline: when and how parents should intervene

Some teachers expect parents to take action when they see unacceptable behaviour. Some expect to retain sole responsibility for classroom management. Others assume that parents will act sensibly and use reasonable discretion when children misbehave. These are matters for discussion and teacher agreement prior to the orientation programme, because parents and teachers are unlikely to have identical interpretations of what is reasonable and sensible. Parents should not be left to find out the rules for themselves, by trial and error, especially those parents who offer their skills throughout the school. 'Discipline' becomes a problem only when staff-parent communications are inadequate and parents are not regarded as partners in the teaching process. It is important, then, that teachers and parents are clear about who does what, when, how and why.

Parents benefit enormously from learning positive reinforcement and child management techniques. Tutors act as models and use role-play to demonstrate commonly experienced situations. Teachers should ensure that the methods taught in orientation programmes are practised in the classrooms.

Parents working with their own children

In the early stages, parents are always anxious about the behaviours of their own children when they are working in school. As a result, they often make extraordinary demands on their behaviour and become highly critical, stern or unnecessarily harsh. Parents are afraid of being 'shown-up' in the presence of other parents or staff. They need reassurance from teachers when their children become overexcited and silly. Parents can be encouraged with assurances that they help all members of the class and their own children will benefit from their involvement in the curriculum. Furthermore, when children become accustomed to their parents' presence and learn the rules for these occasions, problems tend to disappear.

Teachers may also feel inhibited about a parent being present when they are teaching or need to reprimand that parent's child. These uncomfortable feelings should be shared with other teachers and parent helpers to find mutually helpful solutions.

Professional parents

Nothing inhibits teachers more than being questioned by highly articulate parents of superior education and professional status. Teachers often feel threatened and inadequate when they try to relate to parents who are doctors, lawyers or members of the teaching profession, especially those in lecturing or administrative positions. Some of the most critical parents are those who have been trained as secondary school teachers. Although expert in their areas of specialisation, few have a knowledge of child development or early childhood education. They are often unwilling to be convinced of the value of activity methods for young children and demand formal, abstract work before the necessary basic concepts have been acquired. Some convey the impression that they know more about education than their children's teachers.

When teachers realise that they are not meeting parents' expectations, they often react negatively and defensively. Educated parents make the greatest demands on our professionalism and when they sense that we are uncomfortable, they become suspicious. Inexperienced teachers who do not have a strong theoretical base to their work, who find it difficult to explain their educational philosophies and justify their teaching methods, are most likely to be subjected to parental questioning triggered by distrust. Weak teachers sometimes accede to the pressures of educated parents and use methods that are totally inappropriate for the age-group, excusing themselves with, 'It's what the parents want'.

Great sensitivity is needed on the part of parents and teachers to develop trusting relationships. All parents have the right to a coherent explanation for what goes on in the classroom, why certain methods are used, what children are expected to learn, how they learn and why. Parents' questions and suggestions must be considered respectfully but as suggestions, not instructions. When teachers change their professional philosophies and teaching strategies to satisfy forceful parents, they lose their professional credibility, the respect of their colleagues and their own self-respect.

These problems can be avoided and resolved by the provision of information sessions at the beginning of each term, by discussion at orientation sessions and by regular teacher–parent contact.

Parents who lack confidence

Many parents avoid school involvement because they find the challenge of the classroom a daunting one. They worry about their lack of knowledge, experience and skill and are afraid of making mistakes that will result in reprimand.

Teachers also feel insecure and uncomfortable when they first have parents in their classrooms. If previous teaching experience has been limited to working with children in an enclosed space, parent participation may be viewed as the opening up of their private domain to the scrutiny of harsh critics who have a vested interest in what is happening.

It is important that teachers are aware of their own feelings and of the feelings of parents. It is also important that parents are given the opportunity to discuss their feelings in orientation sessions. Parents may need practice and support to develop the confidence to express their own needs, such as making requests to help with tasks that they enjoy or asking a teacher to repeat instructions.

Worrying about other parents

Sometimes, parents become alarmed when they hear that their children are being taught by an unqualified neighbour or someone else's parent. The worried parent may complain to the teacher or even to the parent helper. This is a sensitive situation in which it is important to stress that teachers are in control and classroom helpers work under their direction. Misunderstandings can be sorted out by inviting all parents into school for evening sessions, providing creches to facilitate attendance. Home visits should be made when parents remain distant. All should be encouraged to participate in school life.

Confidentiality

A basic condition of working in classrooms must be an undertaking never to discuss individual children or other parents with people other than the class teacher. No parents want others to discuss their own or their child's behaviour, strengths and weaknesses and most will understand and respect this fundamental courtesy.

Assured confidentiality is a tremendous asset in developing mutual support. Parents in a priority school claimed that their mutual trust had developed to the extent that they could talk freely to each other about personal problems with the certain knowledge that information would not 'go beyond the four walls of the parents' room'. They shared experiences of how they had handled their own difficulties, suggested support services and strategies on a 'we all have problems and can help each other' basis.

Resolving home–school conflict

In a society consisting of people with different backgrounds, values and authority positions, conflict in home–school relations is inevitable and should be used to advantage. As Andrews (1982) points out however, most people have a psychological block about conflict and, instead of regarding it as a challenge and an opportunity to re-think priorities, they view conflict as dangerous, threatening their status and, therefore, to be avoided at all costs.

Andrews suggested that one of the most characteristic things about schools-and-parent relationships is the suppression of conflict. From day to day, teachers go on pretending that parents are basically in complete consensus and harmony over what the teacher and school should be doing. Usually this illusion is created by never giving parents the opportunity to voice dissenting views. This myth of consensus is dangerous because it not only suggests that there are no legitimate differences of opinion but it makes people feel guilty about standing up for their differences (Andrews 1982).

The avoidance of conflict is often revealed in the responses of teachers and administrators to parents' complaints and suggestions for improvements.

They blame someone else
- 'Yes, I know that it's a problem but I can't do anything about it because...'
- 'The department is to blame.'
- 'You can blame the Teachers' Union for that.'
- 'It's the policy of the regional office, I'm afraid.'
- 'We can't get other parents interested. They don't care as much as you.'
- 'With those kinds of families, we really can't make much impact.'

We're the experts and we know best
- 'As the professionals, we have to make the decisions about...'
- 'I'm responsible for this school. I can't have parents telling me what to do.'
- 'Yes, but I'm afraid that parents don't understand the complexities of the situation. It isn't as straightforward as you might think.'
- 'Are you questioning my expertise?'

We're OK really
- 'You could be right but it would be much worse if you sent your child to [another] school. Would you really want your child to go there?'
- 'That may be so but lots of people would give their back teeth to get their children into this school.'
- 'No one has ever complained about that before.'
- 'If you're dissatisfied, you can always take your children somewhere else.'

I hear you but your problem is insignificant
- 'Yes, I know, but it's a question of priorities.'
- 'Just leave it with me, I'll look into it.'
- 'I can't ask the staff to take on any more. They have enough to do as it is.'
- 'If you sat in my office for a day, you'd realise just how unimportant this is.'

Denial
- 'I'm sorry but you're wrong.'
- 'It's just not practical.'
- 'It's not really necessary.'
- 'You're mistaken.'

- 'It's not a problem in this school.'

Teachers are not noted for making significant changes without pressures being placed upon them either by education authorities, new school administrators or parent pressure groups. Some teachers approach retirement without having made any significant changes to their programme or their teaching style. Giving parents the avenue to express their viewpoints can be productive in initiating change for the better.

When parents are given a voice for the very first time, they sometimes say that they are afraid to approach teachers or that teachers do not listen when suggestions are made. Parents also fear that their children will be victimised if they appear critical. Non-professional parents often feel that teachers 'talk down' to them, dismiss their concerns lightly and make them feel uncomfortable.

Teachers are often accused of using educational jargon and 'they never give a straight answer to a question' with the result that parents 'don't really understand what is going on' (Education Department of South Australia 1982).

Inexperienced teachers are often on the defensive when parents approach them. They feel ill-informed and less skilled than they would like to be. Parents who feel uncomfortable are often aggressive when they approach teachers. These mutual feelings of distrust disappear when parents are involved in classrooms and feelings are discussed openly.

When conflict arises, teachers and parents should work together to create new levels of communication. Conflict should be used productively to make people look at situations differently, considering a range of new options and their possible advantages. Only when we do not understand the positive value of conflict does it become disruptive.

In a negative situation, power games arise in which teachers become defensive and locked into their own methods and viewpoints. They are then more likely to resist change. Personal attacks on parents may replace the sharing of ideas and, of course, children will be the losers.

Parent–parent conflict

It is inevitable that, when parents of different nationalities and backgrounds get together, their different values and life experiences will result in some conflict that may seem to risk the success of the project. Conflict may arise between individuals or between faction groups. If the conflict is not discussed openly and resolved, it saps the energy of members, creates an unpleasant atmosphere in school and can damage parent-school relationships through no fault of the staff.

If disagreements are not discussed rationally in the early stages, they are likely to develop to unmanageable proportions. Some school administrators rely on the notion that 'if you leave it for a few days, the problem will go away'. Playing down the importance of differences does not make parents forget them nor does it make them disappear. Compromise often results in a weak solution that satisfies no one. Parents must be encouraged to recognise and respect the rights of others to disagree, while working together to find solutions to problems. Settling differences by using the power of the school administration or the president of the parents' association is rarely satisfactory because it usually results in winners and losers, with the losers losing interest in school and education.

Giving and receiving criticism

Critical analysis, including self-evaluation and parents' evaluations, can be used to improve the quality of all aspects of school life. Constructive criticism can make us re-examine our values, aims and methodology and reassess whether our energies are being used wisely.

Orientation programmes should help parents to relate to teachers and each other in positive ways. Parents and school staff need to examine their own motives before they make negative criticisms of each other. We should ask ourselves whether the intention is to punish or 'put down' to gain power or to protect, help and educate.

In criticising others, it is important to avoid inference and concentrate on direct observation. This calls for precision in description and accepting responsibility for helping without apportioning blame.

It is acceptable to refer to personal feelings about a situation after it has been described simply and accurately. People who have been powerless sometimes exaggerate situations because they think that this is the only way in which they will receive attention. By encouraging members of the school team to expose their feelings early, feelings are less likely to become destructive. It is desirable to express them on the lines of:

'I feel uncomfortable when...'
'I find myself getting angry when...'
'I find it frustrating when...'
'I don't know what to do when...'
'I would rather do..., than...'
'I get worried because...', concluding with,
'Let's see what we can do about it together'.

All members of the school team are likely to find it difficult to express their own needs if they have not been accustomed to working in a home-school programme where openness has been encouraged. Female adults have often been conditioned to reject unwanted situations unconvincingly, by indirect means rather than a firm, assertive 'No, thank you'. Parents should have the freedom and encouragement to state their preferences when working in classrooms. Teachers also need to make their expectations clear to avoid confusion and misunderstandings. It is always best to stress what is needed in a positive way, such as 'We do it like this because...' rather than use negative instructions of the 'Don't do that' variety.

When we receive criticism, it is useful to check to ensure that we have heard and understood the criticism correctly. When we sense that we are about to be criticised, we become tense and are likely to pick up the wrong emphasis. Parents find it especially difficult to pluck up courage to complain to teachers and some plan their speeches several days ahead of their arrival. Some parents with very low self-esteem resort to alcohol to give them the courage to venture into school. The prepared speech then pours forth at a rapid pace and the parent is likely to feel very foolish and inadequate at the end of it. It is useful to let the parent finish without interruption and then paraphrase what has been said: 'I'm so glad that you decided to tell me about this. I've also been concerned about...Now, correct me if I'm wrong but what I think you are telling me is this...Am I right?'

It is very difficult for recipients of criticism to empathise with their critics but empathy is essential. Parents often expect teachers to spring to their own defence or even attack them and they quickly relax when they realise that teachers are equally concerned about their children's wellbeing. The most effective kind of response is on the lines of: 'Yes, I've been concerned, too. I'm so glad that you decided to tell me. Let's see what we can work out.'

When good, open relationships exist between home and school, criticism can be given and taken in a constructive, accepting, impersonal way that benefits everyone. If teachers offer courtesy, consideration and kindness to parents, these will be returned in good measure. If time is given to listening to parents' suggestions and if parents are helped to consider and discuss the practical implications for themselves, it leads to a far healthier environment than when parents are merely told that their ideas are unacceptable or won't work.

Attributes checklists

These points will help you to focus on particular aspects of school that are important when parents visit for the first time. They are only intended to serve as 'starting points' and readers will be able to make their own additions to use as a basis for discussion and change. Some of the following checklist has been adapted from Andrews (1982).

Students and new teachers should bear in mind that when they visit schools for the first time, they will gain impressions similar to those of parents.

School attributes   **Yes   No**
                                                         (Please tick)

1   The route to the office is clearly signposted at all points of entry to the school.
2   There are multi-lingual signs welcoming parents

in languages representing the nationalities of enrolled children.

3   There are easy-to-read posters advertising future social activities, parent meetings and school events.
4   There are signs indicating when senior staff will be accessible without appointment.
5   There are photographs of all school personnel displayed in a prominent place at the main entrance.
6   Bulletin boards are neat and up-to-date.
7   Children's work is well in evidence.
8   Displays are seasonally relevant and carefully mounted.
9   There is an acceptable working noise level throughout the school.
10   The material displayed appears interesting and relevant to children's lives and experiences.
11   You sense a caring atmosphere when you enter the school.
12   There is a room designated for parent use.
13   There are parents in classrooms.
14   Attempts have been made to make school homely and attractive.
15   Children may enter the school building when they arrive.
16   There is an attractive, well-stocked library.
17   There is a library for parents.
18   Parents are welcome in the staffroom.
19   Other (please specify).

Teacher attributes checklist

Yes   No
(Please tick)

1   Makes all parents feel welcome.
2   Introduces visitors to the children.
3   Talks to children respectfully.
4   Listens carefully to parents.
5   Listens carefully to children.
6   Is relaxed with parents and makes them feel at ease.
7   Involves a variety of community members in the programme.
8   Encourages parent helpers to offer evaluations and suggestions.

9   Takes care to thank parents for their help.
10   Shares coffee or lunch-breaks with parent-helpers.
11   Controls the class by acceptance and approval rather than reprimand.
12   When the teacher talks to an adult, the children continue working.
13   Treats boys and girls equally.
14   Encourages kindness and consideration.
15   Does not discuss parents disparagingly.
16   Other (please detail).

School administrator

Yes   No
(Please tick)

1   Welcomes parents personally and sincerely.
2   Children are recognised and referred to by name.
3   Talks to parents in a homely, private place.
4   Accepts complaints graciously and listens.
5   Thanks complainants for expressing their concerns.
6   Treats staff fairly.
7   Relieves class teachers from time to time to 'keep a hand in'.
8   Is knowledgable about current educational methods and provides leadership in curriculum development and theory.
9   Has an infectious enthusiasm and sound practical ideas.
10   Makes a regular daily time available to see parents.
11   Is respected by all school personnel.
12   Is respected by parents.
13   Makes a regular time to observe and counsel students on teaching practice.
14   Is accessible to staff.
15   Uses the staffroom.
16   Socialises with parent groups from time to time.

The classroom

Yes   No
(Please tick)

1   Children are involved, interested and concentrating on their activities.
2   Children are doing diverse things.

3   There are books in the classroom.
4   There is a quiet, cosy corner for readers.
5   Books are attractively displayed.
6   The room is homely and pleasant.
7   There are plants, pets and flowers.
8   There is a place for a tired or sick child to have a rest.
9   There is an area for messy activities.
10 There is a busy hum of activity.
11 Children spill into corridors to work.
12 Children can take work out of doors if they wish.
13 Children know what to do and get on with it.
14 Displayed work is individual, not mass produced.

Curriculum checklist   **Yes   No**
                                                           (Please tick)

Content

1   The teacher's programme helps children to develop:
    • problem solving skills;
    • critical thinking;
    • self discipline;
    • appropriate consideration for the needs of others;
    • self confidence;
    • social and personal responsibility;
    • a positive self concept;
    • research skills;
    • nonsexist attitudes;
    • nonracist attitudes;
    • personal safety skills.
2   The curriculum content caters for:
    • different stages of development and ability levels;
    • fast workers;
    • slow workers;
    • immature children;
    • those with physical disabilities;
    • those with emotional problems,
    • those for whom English is a second language;
    • children with poor concentration;
    • gifted children;
    • children with learning disabilities.
3   The curriculum is:
    • evaluated regularly and changed as necessary;

- planned in advance with specific aims in mind;
- looking to children's needs for the future rather than the past;
- up-to-date and in line with current educational thinking;
- sometimes just 'busy work' to keep children occupied;
- easily explained to parents;
- easily explained to student teachers;
- providing plenty of scope for parents to work with children.

School and community relations checklist

Yes   No
(Please tick)

1 The school issues a multi-lingual handbook to parents in a multi-racial community.
2 Attitudes to parents are not patronising.
3 There is no evidence to suggest that parents are 'just a nuisance' to staff.
4 Teachers are approachable.
5 Parents are afraid to approach teachers.
6 Parents and teachers communicate before problems become large.
7 Home visits are made routinely to families enrolling children.
8 Home visits are made routinely when parents do not have regular contact with school.
9 Home visits are only made when children are having problems.
10 No home visits are made at all.
11 Parents are involved in all major policy decisions.
12 Parents are represented on all school committees.
13 Parents represent the school at important meetings.
14 The community uses school premises for social gatherings.
15 Educational programmes are available for parents.
16 Volunteers are given adequate orientation for the work they do.
17 Parents in low socio-economic areas are supported

in social and welfare matters.

18 Creches are made available to help all parents to attend meetings.

19 Parents are involved in fund-raising and decisions relating to how funds are used.

20 The school assists parents to understand their own importance in their children's development and education.

21 The school empowers parents to have a positive effect on the community as a whole.

22 The school helps parents to create home environments in which education is valued.

23 The school encourages 'no strings attached' parental involvement.

24 Teachers and parents socialise in the staffroom.

25 Teachers and parents socialise in after-school activities.

26 The school provides before and after-school care for children whose parents are in full-time work outside the home.

27 Established parents are always available to help parents of newly-enrolled children.

28 The school has a home–school co-ordinator.

29 Parents are involved in visiting and welcoming the parents of newly enrolled children.

30 Parents publish their own newsletters.

31 Parents are encouraged to use their individual talents for the benefit of all children in school.

32 Parents sometimes attend in-service courses with staff.

33 Each class teacher has an information night to tell parents about the curriculum for the forthcoming term.

34 Efforts are made to maintain contact with working parents who do not visit school.

35 Parents are involved in school excursions.

36 Teachers are made aware of the various skills that parents are willing to make available.

37 Teachers take advantage of parents' offers to make skills available.

38 Senior staff and teachers make time to join parents for coffee and social exchanges.

TASKS FOR STUDENTS

Visit a school for the day and note the following:

1 What is the school's policy relating to parent participation in the education programme?
2 How does this compare with the policy of your education authority?
3 How many parents are working in the classroom on the day of your visit?
4 Do these parents come infrequently or regularly?
5 What proportion of the parents is involved in school activities?
6 What does the school do to involve parents in their children's education?
7 How is the community involved in school curriculum? What community resources are used in and outside school?
8 Are home visits made by members of the school staff? By whom are they made?
9 Are home visits made routinely? If so, how frequently are they made?
10 What preparation are parents given for working in classrooms and by whom?
11 Are parents given any choice in the activities that they will supervise?
12 What kind of activities do parents enjoy most?
13 What does the teacher prefer parents to do in school?
14 Was there any parent–teacher evaluation process at the end of the morning or day?
15 If parents are not involved in classrooms, what reasons are given for this?
16 Ask the school head teacher/principal about the school's plans for community developments and parent involvement.
17 How is the school used (if at all) by community groups?
18 In what circumstances are parents consulted? How are they consulted?

Discuss the following:

19 What specific effects could geographical isolation have on children, their families and schools—for example, when children travel substantial distances by school bus? How can parents and teachers bridge the gap?
20 What are the likely effects when parents transmit very negative views of schools and teachers to their young children? Do you think that the school has any responsibility to try to change these views? Why? How might they have arisen? How might the school or teacher attempt to create such changes?

21 Conduct a mini-survey of parents in your neighbourhood to find out:
- how often they participate in school life;
- their reasons for doing/not doing so;
- how they spend their time in school;
- what they would like to do that they have never been invited to do;
- what kind of social or education groups they would like to have on school premises.

22 Plan a ten-minute talk to persuade reluctant parents to become involved in your classroom.

Teaching practice

For the many participants in teacher education, whether students or education lecturers, teaching practice is deemed to be the focal point of the entire teacher training programme. It has been described as 'the indisputable essential element in professional education' (Conant 1963, p. 210). Student teachers consistently rate teaching practice as the most significant and worthwhile aspect of their pre-service education (Tinning 1984). It enables them to make some sense of theory and they gain satisfaction from their new-found skills and relationships with children. However, while participants recognise the importance of the field experience component, politicians and administrators do not. The practical component has been substantially reduced in most English-speaking countries.

Students in the specialist field of early childhood education (0–8 years) are particularly disadvantaged by this trend because of the requirement that they show competence in working with three contiguous age groups, necessitating proficiency in a range of very different skills.

The reasons for the reductions are entirely monetary. The supervision of teaching practice by lecturers is labour intensive, necessitating considerable time and expenditure on travel, often with students in widely scattered placements. Observation, evaluation and discussion must be on a one-to-one basis, which is very time consuming. Time must also be spent in discussion with the supervising teacher and the senior member of staff responsible for student teachers. Some lecturing staff are highly conscientious, dashing from school to school between presenting lectures, attending the inevitable meetings and marking assignments.

In Australia, in accordance with the award rates handed down by Justice Ludeke, tertiary education authorities bear the burden of having to pay individual class teachers for supervising students in their classrooms. While the sum paid to individuals is comparatively small, the annual bill for university education faculties amounts to multi-millions of dollars.

When the payment to teachers was increased in the 1980s, it was envisaged that they would take much greater responsibility for implementing programmes. In practice, there has been no significant change. Briggs (1984b) found that supervising teachers need and expect high levels of support from training institutions to ensure that the experience they provide meets expectations. Furthermore, there is no obligation and sometimes no facility for supervising teachers to attend inservice seminars or workshops relating to their supervisory responsibilities. Although the payment system appears to be unique to Australia, most English-speaking countries have suffered cuts in teaching practice in recent years. Practising teachers are seriously concerned about the long term consequences of these cuts; with an ever changing and enlarging curriculum, student teachers now have to learn more and more in less and less time. The teaching community fears that this process will inevitably damage teaching standards and, ultimately, the status of teachers. Paradoxically, the teachers' professional associations are largely responsible for the Australian situation; they insisted that teachers should be paid for this work and took the matter to the industrial court. Administrators and governments now argue that, as teachers are paid for supervising students, it is no longer necessary or economically viable for lecturers to duplicate their efforts.

As Katz (1988) comments, the teaching profession is not currently in favour with government authorities in any of the English-speaking countries. Despite huge financial investments in education, many students still emerge illiterate and unemployable. Colleges and universities have also been accused of inefficiency and subjected to massive reductions in government funds. Ironically, the same government authorities advocate that these denigrated schools and teachers should undertake full responsibility for practicum in teacher education, seemingly without the benefit of training for the task.

The selection of schools for practicum

Most tertiary institutions cannot be discriminating in selections for practicum placements. There are invariably many more students requiring places than there are places available. Teacher education competes with secondary school work-experience programmes, childcare training, psychology courses and other institutions for access to classrooms. Such is the demand that we can sympathise with the person who suggested that there should be laws to protect the young and the aged from the student population.

Course clerical staff invariably negotiate directly with school administrators relating to the number of student places available in the school. Teachers are often asked on a whole-school basis, 'Who would like to have a student this year?' Few teachers are selected for their competence with children and student teachers. As a result, students find themselves with teachers who offer their services for a range of reasons. It is inevitable that many students will see practices that are discrepant with those taught and recommended in their college and university courses. Katz (1988) found that the extent to which these practices were discrepant with those taught in the Early Childhood Education Programme at the University of Illinois, Urbana, Champaign, was 'easily 70%'. These discrepancies were in methods of discipline, uses of punishment and the nature of activities provided for children. Katz wrote, 'I will spare the painful details but painful they were! Yes, practice makes perfect; but perhaps bad practice makes perfectly bad'.

Tinning (1984) emphasised the importance of the student's own school experience as the major socialising influence for teaching. Locke (1982) referred to this experience as 'an invisible apprenticeship lasting from 12 to 15 years'. Some mature age students who experienced very rigid schooling excel in college and university studies, but cling to the methods used in their own school years when they take responsibility for a class. With the powerful influence of the first years of school, it is obviously helpful if students have acquired positive attitudes to learning and to children before they face their first practicum.

Negative learning

Tinning (1984, p. 56) commented that student development during teaching practice usually includes 'a shift from idealism to pragmatism'. He shows that student teachers change many of their previous values relating to appropriate teacher behaviour. For example, there is a strong tendency not only to accept previously deplored teacher behaviours, such as pushing stubborn children, but to explain these actions as benefiting those children. In other words, the theoretical component in relation to individual differences, positive classroom management methods and the development of children's self-esteem can be wiped out by the influence of a single teaching practice when students are exposed to unsatisfactory teaching models and methods that are said to 'work'. For students with limited knowledge and no experience, the dangers are numerous. Tinning found that students abandoned the child-centred activity oriented approach taught in their college and university courses and became 'teacher dominated' in both thought and practice. 'Getting through the lesson' became their first priority and, in that state of mind, they are likely to grasp at any method of maintaining an obedient and 'disciplined' class. 'Will it work to solve my current problem?' became the central criterion of the students' curriculum, regardless of the value of what they were trying to teach. Tinning concluded that, although lecturers espouse the need for individualised learning programmes for children, 'the reality is that, for student teachers, the image of teaching competence is whole class oriented', especially when their teacher models operate on 'whole class' lines. Similarly, while lecturers refer to children's learning as a measure of success, students 'kept children busy and doing things that would ensure that children moved through the lesson on time and in a quiet and orderly manner.'

Several researchers have shown that students judge the quality of their lessons by very trivial criteria. Friebus (1977) found that students evaluated their lessons as successful when children were quiet and appeared to be paying attention and when they showed enthusiasm. Kieslar (1981) found that students claimed the credit when they thought that their lessons were successful, but blamed the children when lessons did not go as well as they would have liked. Tinning (1984, p. 56) concluded that, for many student teachers, effective teaching is characterised by 'many things except the amount that children learn'.

Clearly, supervising teachers have tremendous influence, for good or ill, on the kinds of teachers we produce for future generations of children. Briggs (1984b) found that only half of the supervising teachers surveyed regarded teaching practice as the single most important component of teacher education and only 28 per cent realised that new graduates emulate former supervising teachers when they take up their first appointments. Seventy-eight per cent did not think that the models they presented were influential in the long term.

Copeland (1977, 1979, 1980) found that children responded most readily to the student teachers' behaviours that most resembled those of their class teacher. For that reason, most students model themselves on the class teacher, consciously or subconsciously. This is an asset if the teacher is imaginative, enjoys good, caring relationships with children and uses sound teaching strategies based on current learning and curriculum theory. It is disastrous, however, if the teacher model is poor.

Ethical issues

Katz (1988) confirms that university and college lecturers are confronted with 'sticky ethical and pedagogical conflicts' when students are placed with poor teaching models. Should a lecturer undermine the professionalism of the teacher in the eyes of the student? Should lecturers knowingly, intentionally but reluctantly alienate students from the teaching model to which they may be exposed for up to seven hours a day for several weeks at a time? 'Which is the least worst error' asks Katz, 'to disavow the placement sites, practices and practitioners or not?' (p. 14).

Students often face conflicting ideologies and receive contradictory messages from different lecturers and teachers. Immature students tend to respond by dismissing all lecturing staff and their seminars as irrelevant (Katz 1988, p. 14). 'There is certainly reason to believe that cooperating teachers are ready to help the practicum students to dismiss the instructors in this way.' They 'form a united front to keep college staff and their conflicting pedagogies at bay'. This is extremely damaging for students because the weakest teacher models are likely to be those who have least in common with the aims and methods of the training institutions. Weak teachers often protect weak students on the pretext that course expectations are excessive or inappropriate. The student is the sole sufferer in this scenario.

Should students be given the opportunity to learn about competing pedagogical models so that they can select their own? Apart from the fact that
there is insufficient time for students to be exposed to such a selection, inexperienced students are unlikely to be able to make sound choices. To suggest
that free choice is even possible is 'tantamount to abdication of professional
judgment of the knowledge basis' (Katz 1988, p. 14). It is akin to suggesting
that medical students should be exposed to the variety of surgical methods
and treatments used throughout history and given a free choice while they
work in hospitals. Medical students of limited experience might conclude
that chloroform on cotton-wool provides the best form of anaesthetic because
'it works', but they would contribute nothing to medical efficiency by turning
the clock back half a century in medical practice. Katz asserts, however, that
lecturers cannot undermine the professional judgement of teacher-colleagues
by discounting their methods or their views however inappropriate they may
be.

What is the solution? Students who are aware of the discrepancies feel that
they have to satisfy two distinct, uncomplementary examining authorities
and are likely to be disadvantaged in their total assessment. This fear leads to
stress which, in turn, adversely affects teaching capabilities. When lecturers
suggest strategies, they may be markedly different from those used by the class
teacher and, as a result, may not seem to 'work' in the short term.

The importance of good communications

The presence of university and college lecturers may seem insignificant when
students are developing well in the hands of committed and effective teachers, but their assistance is essential when there is conflict between course
expectations and the pedagogy used in the classroom.

The organisers of teaching practice have a responsibility to communicate
with teaching staff to ensure that everyone involved in the programme
understands the philosophies of and strategies used in early childhood education. Such communication is particularly important when the class teachers
were trained to teach older children or children in developing countries
where class sizes, methods and values are very different.

If teachers are not prepared to allow students to practise internationally-
recognised methods of early childhood education, the students should be
given alternative placements. Some teachers accept a compromise, saying,
'I've been using a teacher-centred approach throughout my career. It's what I
am comfortable with. I can't change now. However, I am prepared to let the
student fulfil the requirements of the programme.' Such situations are not
ideal but, given goodwill, opportunities and encouragement, many students
will develop their own teaching styles. Nevertheless, lecturers should ensure
that those students are exposed to sound models in future field experience.

Whatever the situation, students must develop a sound capacity for self-criticism in their own teaching practice. It is not sufficient to manage a class; while management skills are necessary, they do not, by themselves, indicate effective teaching. The student and new teacher must reflect on what is to be learned, by whom, how and why. This incorporates a further question: 'How can I do better?' It is the lecturers' and teachers' task to foster this kind of critical self-analysis. Students must be sensitive to what is happening in the classroom and ask appropriate questions. If a whole class approach is being used, what is happening to the highly competent children and the slow learners? Why is this approach used and what are the children expected to learn from it? If children are very obedient, why is this so? Are they clinging, too eager to please, reward-dependent or fearful? Are they interested, independent and well-organised at a personal level? Effective student teachers are observant and questioning.

Students have responsibilities too

The reduction in the teaching practice component increases the students' own responsibility to learn as much as possible from practicum. With the best of intentions, some teachers try to help students by providing lesson plans and materials for the lessons that lecturers will observe. This can have embarrassing consequences if the lecturers are critical of those lessons and the students protest, 'But it wasn't my idea...the teacher told me to do it'. It is frustrating for students who sense that they have been evaluated unfairly and could have fared better if left to their own devices. Their confidence in the teacher is likely to be undermined.

Students need, should be given and should expect opportunities to use initiative in planning and providing materials for classroom activities. The role of the teacher is to advise, predict possible problems, observe, evaluate and discuss. Similarly, students have a responsibility to ensure that they gain experience across the breadth of the curriculum, including before and after-school programmes, meetings and social activities. Briggs (1984b) found that only 4 per cent of teachers saw this part of their role as important and, as a result, they may need reminders from time to time.

Time in school is much too short and students must ensure that they obtain the maximum benefit from their teaching experience. Some students make unscheduled visits to their school placements before the commencement of the official teaching period. The writers have noted that this makes a significant difference to progress. Students who have already been accepted by the children in the class and know them by name, develop teaching skills very quickly when their teaching practice commences in earnest. This can make all the difference between success and failure in a short, three- or four-week school experience.

Teaching practice organisation

Teaching practice arrangements vary from one institution to another. Organisers are restrained by factors that are unrelated to the needs of student teachers and schools. In Australia and New Zealand, for example, vacancies for newly-qualified teachers are often in remote country schools but most practicum is restricted to metropolitan areas. The selection of placements is a matter of financial expedience and bears no relationship to the needs of the professionals in training. Similarly, in multi-purpose institutions, little consideration is given to the appropriate placement of teaching practice in relation to the academic calendar. Teacher education is just one of many courses in the tertiary sector and it has to fit in with the needs of administrators and other disciplines and courses.

There is no ideal time for teaching practice. While it is useful for students to be in school at the beginning of the school year to see how teachers organise classrooms, welcome new pupils and plan the term's work, some schools feel that the presence of students is the last straw at this busy time of the year (Briggs 1984b). Teachers had very strong feelings about the placement of students at the end of school terms. They were 'too tired' or 'under too much pressure' to do justice to students at the end of term and, as a result, the end-of-term experience was viewed as having limited value (Briggs 1984b).

Although school life may be enjoyable in the months approaching Christmas and in the swimming and sports-day season, related activities can substantially diminish the amount of time that students spend in developing and implementing the whole curriculum with children. It is also unfair to arrange teaching practice in the students' vacation period when they and their teachers are fatigued.

The value of group visits to schools depends on the interest level and preparedness of students, their willingness to ask questions, to be observant and discuss their observations. From the school point of view, the presence of large numbers of strangers is invariably disruptive to both children and teachers. At the same time, it is necessary for students to see a wide variety of schools and programmes and not depend on a few teaching practice placements for their experience.

Given the importance of the practicum and the difficulties of placing students in schools, some institutions are also incorporating the use of simulated classrooms on campuses in their field experience programmes. New Zealand maintained its demonstration schools despite their closure elsewhere. This can be attributed to the fact that New Zealand teacher education has remained the responsibility of the Education Department which is also responsible for schools. Demonstration settings were criticised in the past for offering an atypical learning environment but at a time when practical experience is in short supply, they provide a useful preparation for and adjunct to the main teaching practice block. Demonstration settings on campus also have the additional advantage of providing students with the opportunity to see current methods being used effectively with children, an experience that may not be available in all school placements. In these settings, students can learn to plan and implement learning activities for small groups, taking turn to observe children and evaluate themselves and their peers in action. When children use the simulated classroom on a regular basis accompanied by their own class teacher, there are opportunities to observe different teaching strategies and management skills during demonstration sessions. The writers have noted considerable differences between the performance on teaching practice of students who spent six mornings working in a simulated classroom and those who had not. The students who had this brief experience with children were advantaged, especially in relation to planning curriculum, observation of young children and questioning techniques.

In conclusion, tertiary institutions must accept the reality that, although there are some exemplary teachers in the field, not many teaching practice placements are ideal. Student teachers have to be very aware of this and work to develop their individual teaching style, looking at the broad context of learning rather than what seems to work here and now. Students must strive to practise modern, approved methods. At the same time, all educators must recognise that what is acceptable today may be changed tomorrow as research broadens our knowledge base.

Supervision of teaching practice

Field experience should do more for students than enhance competencies. It provides opportunities for students to think about themselves as individuals and as members of a caring profession in which the development of children is the major concern. Lecturers and supervising teachers have a responsibility to support students in this reflection and to ensure that they are offered opportunities for professional development.

The supervision of student teachers in the practicum is an understudied subject. Stones (1984) found that the majority of teacher supervisors have received no training for their role; their knowledge is developed from the basis of their own limited exposure to supervision when they were student teachers. The lack of induction programmes for supervisors demonstrates the lack of awareness in institution management of the complexities of human learning, helping others to learn and teaching others how to teach.

The skills involved in student supervision are numerous: Stones refers to:

- the need for an expert eye to see what is happening in the classroom;
- the need for insight to understand the significance of what is seen;
- foresight to see what could be happening that isn't happening; and
- 'second sight' to know how to make what didn't happen (and should have happened) happen next time.

Turney *et al.* (1982) reaffirm the crucial and complex nature of student supervision, commenting that if teaching practice is the single most powerful intervention in a teacher's professional development, as research suggests, then supervision is the single most powerful process in such intervention.

The findings of Turney and his associates suggest that supervision in the practicum involves a series of interactions within a cycle. These interactions take place between the supervising teacher, the student, the lecturer and significant others in the school. They should be regular, friendly, sharply focused in purpose and based on observational information.

The process of supervision in general should be concerned with achieving the objectives that the teacher education programme has specified. In particular, it is concerned with the learning and development of student teachers so that they become more effective in influencing the learning and development of children. An important aim of supervision should be to promote the acquisition of skills in self-supervision, which involves autonomy in planning, analysing and improving their own performance.

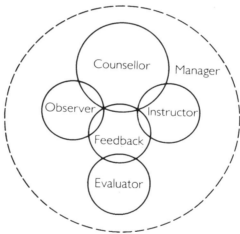

Figure 12.1: Role relationships
Source: Turney *et al.* 1982, *Supervisor Development Programmes: Role Handbook*, Sydney University Press, Sydney, p. 5.

Turney *et al.* (1982) cite six stages in the cycle of the supervising process:

Stage 1: Pre-observation conference
Stage 2: Observation
Stage 3: Analysis
Stage 4: Post-observation conference
Stage 5: Training
Stage 6: Evaluation and closure.

In this process, stages one to four form the basic supervision cycle. They focus on a pre-teaching discussion of what the student might do, followed by the observation of the student implementing the planned activity. This is followed by analysis of what has been observed and the selection of points to be discussed at the end of the session. Finally, there should be a feedback session in which the supervisor seeks a self-evaluation from the student, poses questions to constructive thinking and offers advice as necessary. Stages five and six take place later in the practicum when training to meet a special need is required and where decisions are made about how successful the student has been in meeting the criteria established by the teacher education programme and which aspects of teaching require particular attention.

Linked with these stages of the supervision process, Turney sees the supervisors as having six major roles in their relationships with students during their practicum. Each role has its own distinct objectives and involves a number of skills.

The supervising teacher as counsellor

The counsellor role is based on sensitivity and concern for the student as a person. This role underpins the operation of most other roles since it deals with the affective and interpersonal aspects of the student teacher's work. It is crucial to the resolution of issues and problems that affect teaching, such as matters concerning the student's health, self-concept and conflicting or competing responsibilities outside school. The supervising teacher has to work with students who are confronted by many ideas and demands. There may be conflict between the student's expectations, the course expectations and the reality of the teaching situation.

The aims of the counsellor role include:

- establishing a positive relationship with the student so that there is open communication about strengths and weaknesses;
- providing opportunities for co-operative planning and evaluation;
- assisting students to develop effective ways of coping with stress associated with teaching practice;
- assisting students to develop positive attitudes about themselves.

The supervising teacher as manager

The manager role is concerned with the purposeful and smooth operation of the practicum. It includes those supervisory behaviours that contribute both to successful planning and organising of the practicum and to the development of common understanding, cooperation and morale of all participants. This role builds the setting which facilitates the pursuit of all other roles.

The aims of the manager role include:

- offering experiences to allow all concerned to determine the student's suitability for teaching the particular age group as a vocation;

- offering experiences with a view to increasing the student's interest in teaching;
- introducing students to important aspects of the teaching process, such as planning, preparation, organisation, recording, consolidation, evaluation;
- relating current theory to practical situations;
- giving students opportunities to plan for and implement programmes that cater for children's individual differences;
- encouraging students to use their initiative, testing out their own ideas and materials with teacher guidance;
- enabling students to experience different teaching methods, for example small group work, whole class, team teaching, integrated programmes, individual diagnosis and remedial work;
- providing close liaison with the supervising lecturer;
- ensuring that students are acquainted with the variety of school resources.

The supervising teacher as instructor

This role involves assisting students to explore and improve their teaching performance through the acquisition of information, the development of concepts and understanding, the building and refining of teaching skills and the use of problem solving strategies. The role includes such skills as questioning students, presenting ideas and guiding problem solving which will be commonly applied to the pre-teaching and post-observation teacher–student conferences. The teacher–instructor takes account of students' anxiety levels, confidence, competence and experience as well as appropriate timing.

The aims of the instructor role include:

- communicating verbally and, by example, information, ideas and practices, such as the provision of high quality resources for children's use;
- facilitating the student's critical analysis of ideas, plans and performance by question and discussion;
- encouraging the development of self reliance;
- making regular time available for counselling students on what they have learned, areas of confusion and areas requiring improvement.

The supervising teacher as observer

The observer role is concerned with the systematic and purposeful viewing of students' teaching and the accurate recording of data. The teacher–supervisor then interprets the record to decide which information should be transmitted to students and how it should be transmitted, as part of the feedback process.

Feedback

The feedback role involves conveying to the student teacher selected information arising from the observation of teaching. The main objective of providing feedback is to help students to improve their performance as teachers by gauging progress and planning ways of surmounting difficulties.

The aims of the observation and feedback roles include:

- discussing teaching plans, pointing to potential weaknesses and encouraging students to identify them and suggest alternative strategies;
- discreet observation of the student;
- collecting data about the students' abilities to:
  - — gain children's attention in acceptable ways;
  - — motivate children;
  - — give clear directions;
  - — relate to children, parents and other staff;
  - — use positive reinforcement;
  - —plan activities to cater for children's interests;
  - — produce worthwhile ideas:
  - — question children effectively;
  - — provide accurate feedback;
  - — use flexibility and opportunities for informal teaching;
  - — show warmth and approachability to children and parents;
  - — show awareness of and respond to individual differences;
  - —manage groups of different sizes;
  - — use clarity of speech;
  - — use the voice expressively;
  - — use a varied vocabulary;
  - — arouse, sustain and control effective discussion;
  - — engage in routine management;
  - — use initiative appropriately;
  - — behave in a professional manner;
  - — exhibit a thorough understanding of curriculum for the children etc.

The supervising teacher as evaluator

The evaluator role is concerned with making sound judgements about the level of the students' development as teachers in relation to the aims of the practicum. These judgements are made largely on the basis of evidence accumulated from successive feedback sessions with the student and lecturer. The evaluator role, if not sensitively and supportively played, can conflict with the counsellor role since the making of judgements about teaching progress almost invariably poses something of a threat to student teachers.

Evaluation of the practicum

There are two parts to evaluation: formative and summative. Formative evaluation is consistent and continuous throughout the entire practicum. It forms the basis of all the feedback sessions shared with the student and is based on the supervising teacher's observations and notes made during the teaching experience.

Some teachers use a carbon-copy book in which they write observation notes, providing a copy for the student. If students file the copies with their plans for that session, it provides the visiting lecturer with additional insights into the students' experiences and the level of teacher support received. Such records are valuable for feedback sessions and for building up a profile of the students' professional development. They are especially useful for writing the final report.

Most teacher training courses supply teachers with assessment criteria which can be used as checklists for interim discussion and final evaluation. When teachers and students identify strengths and weaknesses together, there is an excellent basis for support and improvement. The final report then presents few problems because there has already been agreement on the level of progress.

Some teachers write comments on students' curriculum plans, before and after the session has taken place. This is useful for students and lecturers but the teachers then lack copies of their ongoing comments. Making a summative evaluation at the end of the practice is more difficult without this organised data.

Formative evaluation is thus concerned with giving the students feedback. It acts as a base for modification and future planning and is, in form, a continuous monitoring of both goals and procedures. It attempts to assess the extent of the students' achievement and to discover and analyse barriers to progress.

Summative evaluation evolves from the formative and is concerned with the approval of the student's work. It applies when the teaching practice is completed and assesses the students' overall effectiveness in achieving the goals of the practicum. Tertiary institutions vary in the way that they require the summative evaluation to be recorded: some provide lists of competencies which must be checked and rating scales with space for comment, while others require a comprehensive report based on guidelines for students' personal qualities, professional development, curriculum knowledge and implementation. Important aspects of students' development are identified for discussion.

Summary

Teaching practice is regarded by all those involved directly in teacher education as the most powerful influence in students' professional preparation. The supervision of teaching practice by both lecturers and class teachers must be of high quality. Ideally, supervisors should be carefully selected and prepared for these demanding roles. There is widespread and growing recognition of the need for trained supervision from within the profession but considerably more pressure will be necessary before government education authorities and tertiary institutions invest their lessening funds on comprehensive and carefully constructed training programmes. Turney *et al.* (1982) attempt to meet this need for supervisor training in their book, *Supervisor Development Programmes: Role Handbook*, which is strongly recommended to lecturers, school staff and their regional advisers.

Epilogue

The need for continuous professional development

Once established in their careers, some teachers continue to study, take an interest in professional conferences and participate in school and regional in-service programmes. Others, who regard the completion of pre-service training as the end of reading and learning, may settle into safe routines, repeating similar curricula and teaching strategies with the same age group year after year. The rationale for this is that 'it seemed to work last year so I may as well do it again'. This attitude is unacceptable because no two groups of children are ever identical and the abilities and needs of individual children in those groups will vary from year to year. Unless new teachers accept that they have chosen a challenging career that necessitates continuous learning, they will become bored and boring. Although they may not realise it, colleagues, children and their parents realise what is happening.

To maintain their professionalism, motivation and interest, it is important that teachers continue to develop their teaching skills and knowledge. This can be achieved by:

- membership of and participation in professional associations, such as O.M.E.P, the World Education Fellowship, associations of early childhood educators, national reading, mathematics and science associations and regional curriculum development groups;
- reading the publications of professional organisations and professional journals to which the school subscribes: a wider range of journals will be found in libraries of tertiary institutions;
- participating in workshops and seminars organised by the school and outside agencies;
- attending in-service programmes offered by teachers' centres, education authorities and institutions;

- continuing professional study;
- attending regional, national and international conferences relating to education and aspects of the curriculum (for example, Maths, Reading and Early Childhood Education);
- contributing to staff development in their own school or education region;
- participating in curriculum review committees, book selection panels, children's television review committees and contributing to the selection of materials and resources for school;
- speaking at professional and parent meetings;
- writing for professional publications;
- contributing to the school community by acting as an ambassador for education, or helping to shape community attitudes to education by keeping community members informed of events of interest, such as science fairs, book fairs, computer-assisted instructional programmes, music festivals, etc.;
- accepting students for teaching practice;
- adopting a process of regular evaluation and self-evaluation and taking steps to rectify weaknesses.

Evaluation and self-evaluation

Whether by formal procedure or informal conversation, teachers are evaluated by staff, colleagues, management and others. Evaluation is essentially a judgement of staff quality and accomplishment or a comparison between different programmes or individual performances.

Every teacher evaluates his or her performance in some way to obtain job satisfaction. To evaluate effectively, teachers need to be aware of the areas in which they should be competent. These can be divided into four discrete groups:

1 curriculum design;
2 curriculum implementation;
3 personal capabilities;
4 interpersonal capabilities.

It is useful for teachers to make their own personal checklists to measure their progress from term to term and year to year and examine the areas in which they are least competent. On the following pages, we offer guidelines for each of the four areas.

Change takes place only when teachers believe that improvement is both necessary and possible and when they are willing to seek help from books, in-service programmes and further study. Checklists are useful to help individuals to know how well they are progressing and what changes are necessary. The following have been adapted from publications for teachers published by Alberta Education Department (Canada) where evaluations of school pro-

grammes and specific aspects of programmes involve local advisory committees, parents, community resources and service people as well as teachers.

Sample checklist for evaluating curriculum design

The aim of evaluating the programme design is to gauge my ability to organise and use time, space, materials and personnel effectively to achieve the
aims and objectives of the curriculum.

	Always	Circle one only Sometimes	Seldom
I make time to			
• allow a constant flow of individual and/or small group learning	1	2	3
• respond to children's spontaneous interests and events	1	2	3
• provide variety in the types of activities and lessons I offer	1	2	3
I encourage the children's independence by			
• helping them to accept responsibility for developing their own projects and activities	1	2	3
• offering choices and guiding decision-making where necessary	1	2	3
• rewarding each child for completing a planned activity contract, assignment or project	1	2	3
• providing a range of activities requiring varied times for completion	1	2	3
I maximise the use of learning time by			
• discussing and establishing daily routines with the children	1	2	3
• allowing time for children to help in preparation and cleaning up	1	2	3
• ensuring the appropriate and varied supply of materials for activities	1	2	3
• avoiding queues and waiting when children need materials or attention	1	2	3
• constantly moving around the classroom, assisting, questioning and extending children's thinking	1	2	3

	Always	Circle one only Sometimes	Seldom

I organise resources so that
- children are independent
  when working — 1, 2, 3
- resources and activities are
  well displayed — 1, 2, 3
- children are motivated to
  participate and learn — 1, 2, 3
- children are curious and ready to
  learn through discovery and
  appropriate questioning — 1, 2, 3
- children are given wide
  opportunities for problem-solving — 1, 2, 3
- they are accessible to children — 1, 2, 3
- they cater for the different
  developmental levels in the class — 1, 2, 3
- they are appropriate for the
  planned curriculum — 1, 2, 3

I utilise the available space carefully to
- facilitate easy access to necessary
  materials — 1, 2, 3
- facilitate easy movement around
  the room — 1, 2, 3
- provide safe areas for creative
  activities and constructions — 1, 2, 3
- foster social learning, peer tutoring
  and group-work — 1, 2, 3

I encourage parent participation by
- giving them personal, verbal
  invitations to spend time in the classroom — 1, 2, 3
- making home visits to meet parents
  who do not participate in school life — 1, 2, 3
- creating opportunities for parents
  to work with children in and
  around the classroom — 1, 2, 3
- sharing curriculum plans with them
  at regular information sessions — 1, 2, 3
- sharing my knowledge and insights
  about their children with them — 1, 2, 3
- listening to and encouraging the
  expression of their thoughts
  and concerns — 1, 2, 3

	Always	Circle one only Sometimes	Seldom
• offering practical suggestions about how they can help their children to learn	1	2	3
• providing time to tell parents how they can help in the classroom	1	2	3
• providing the time and encouragement for parents to evaluate the activities in which they participated	1	2	3

Sample checklist for the evaluation of curriculum implementation

The aim of evaluating curriculum is to ensure that the curriculum design is appropriate to the children's developmental levels, learning abilities and individual characteristics.

	Always	Circle one only Sometimes	Seldom
I observe children carefully and use these observations as a basis for planning lessons by			
• keeping anecdotal records on children's behaviour, evidence of their understanding of concepts, their attitudes and interests	1	2	3
• using checklists to gauge children's concept development	1	2	3
• using graphs or charts to note activities, assignments and contracts completed	1	2	3
• carefully noting areas for extension as well as for extra assistance and more experience	1	2	3
• noting social interactions, independence	1	2	3
I assist children's social development by			
• facilitating development of positive self-esteem	1	2	3
• modelling sincere and respectful behaviour	1	2	3
• providing opportunities for peer tutoring	1	2	3
• providing opportunities for cross-age tutoring	1	2	3

| | | Circle one only | |
	Always	**Sometimes**	**Seldom**
• providing opportunities for individual and small-group work	1	2	3

I assist intellectual development by

	Always	**Sometimes**	**Seldom**
• questioning and observing children closely to assess their understanding	1	2	3
• offering concrete experiences and opportunities for discovery, supported by dialogue	1	2	3
• using problem-solving techniques	1	2	3
• exposing children to all curriculum areas	1	2	3
• ensuring that activities are challenging to all children	1	2	3
• integrating curriculum to reinforce concepts from different perspectives	1	2	3
• encouraging children to talk about their work, feelings and experiences	1	2	3
• helping children to find information for themselves	1	2	3
• encouraging children to beat their own previous best efforts	1	2	3

I assist children's physical development by

	Always	**Sometimes**	**Seldom**
• teaching regular physical education lessons	1	2	3
• offering experiences for children to develop large muscle control through climbing, balancing, etc.	1	2	3
• encouraging the development of fine motor control through indoor and outdoor activity	1	2	3
• teaching games skills, including ball skills	1	2	3
• offering daily fitness sessions	1	2	3
• providing a safe and healthy physical environment	1	2	3
• by teaching personal safety skills	1	2	3

I foster children's emotional development by

	Always	**Sometimes**	**Seldom**
• providing a safe, secure learning environment	1	2	3
• planning rules and routines with children	1	2	3
• developing each child's self-esteem and confidence	1	2	3

	Always	Circle one only Sometimes	Seldom
• encouraging caring relationships between children by positive reinforcement	1	2	3
• helping children to express their feelings in acceptable ways	1	2	3
• helping children to like themselves and others	1	2	3
• identifying and responding to the special needs of individuals	1	2	3
• ensuring that all children have opportunities for success	1	2	3
• using conflict resolution methods	1	2	3

Checklist for the identification of personal issues or problems relating to your programme

Factors	Size of problem				Detail
	Tick one column				
	Major	**Minor**	**Not a problem**	**Don't know**	
1 Obtaining suitable facilities for teaching the programme effectively					
2 Lack of equipment or materials					
3 Staff conflicts					
4 Obtaining support from senior staff					
5 Obtaining support from parent groups					
6 Obtaining support from the parents of children in the class					
7 Obtaining community support					
8 Children's behaviour and management problems					
9 Providing for the special needs of individual children					
10 Planning, organising and controlling children working on several different activities simultaneously					
11 Catering for the whole class					
12 Personal problems					
13 Poor health					
14 Stress					
15 Parent programmes					
16 School policies					
17 Department policies					
18 List others:					

Checklist of services provided by support personnel

Service	Level of contact			Level of effectiveness
	Size of problem			
	High	Medium	Low	None

1. Early childhood/infant adviser
2. School council
3. School head teacher/principal
4. Deputy head
5. School or local social worker
6. School nurse
7. Speech pathologist
8. Local police
9. Consultants for handicapped children
10. School psychologists or guidance officers
11. Dental service staff
12. School doctor
13. Regional manager
14. Parent resource co-ordinator
15. Teaching practice field experience co-ordinator
16. College or university lecturers
17. In-service programme co-ordinators
18. Parent-helpers
19. Volunteer helpers from the community
20. Non-teaching staff
21. Specialists in migrant education or TESL
22. Others—please specify

Evaluate your wider community involvement

Factors	Indicate level of awareness of available resources				Comment
	High	Medium	Low	None	
1 Contact with other teachers teaching the same age group					
2 Contact with parents through home visits					
3 Contact with parents in the classroom					
4 Contact with parents elsewhere in school					
5 Knowledge of community resources that are available for your programme					
6 Knowledge of the full range of services that welcome children for educational visits					
7 Knowledge of people with special skills, experiences and interests willing to help in your classroom					
8 Contact with resources and services catering for children with special needs					
9 Contact with representatives of child protection services					
10 Contact with local school health workers					
11 Knowledge of the problems and concerns of teachers working with this age-group throughout your region					
12 Awareness of in-service programmes available					
13 Promoting the school in the community					
14 Others please specify					

Checklist for evaluating school–parent relationship

Factors	Available	Not available
Printed material		
Information packages about the school		
Regular newsletters published by parents		
Regular newsletters published by staff		
Regular newsletters published by children		
Gatherings		
General meetings using school facilities		
Family outings		
Regular social events on school premises		
Weekend barbeques		
Working groups to maintain the school in good condition		
Working groups to raise money		
Parent involvement in school camps		
Parent involvement on school excursions		
Parent education		
Regular meetings to acquaint parents with aspects of the curriculum		
Parent information sessions relating to:		
• improving parenting skills		
• child development		
• child protection and safety		
• child health		
• nutrition		
• creative activities		
• household management		
• assisting children's learning		
Parent orientation seminars for helping children in the classroom		
Education classes for the personal development of parents		

Services available for parents at school

Factors	Available	Not available
Toy lending library		
Book lending library		
Community health facilities		

Factors	Available	Not available

Emergency child care facilities
Pre-school facilities (playgroup, nursery,
  kindergarten)
Family counselling services
Parents' mutual help group
Social worker
Clergy

Parent participation in programme
All parents are encouraged to participate
  in the classroom
Parents can participate as resource persons
Parents and teachers meet to share information
Parents work with children
Special provision is made for parents who
  are in employment
Others—please state

School administration
Parents can attend PTA meetings
Parents are on the school council
Parents are on community committees
Parents raise funds
Parents have a say in how funds are spent

Personal objectives for teachers

Following the self-evaluation process, teachers develop personal objectives
for the improvement of their performance. These objectives may focus on:

- aspects of curriculum design;
- aspects of curriculum implementation;
- programme management;
- knowledge about children and their families;
- parent participation in programmes;
- classroom management; or
- observational techniques.

Objectives developed from self-evaluation can be private or shared with
trusted colleagues to discover common needs. These needs may then be used
as the basis for in-service training programmes and staff workshops.

The effectiveness of self-evaluation depends on how objective teachers are
in assessing their own performance and what specific actions are taken to
improve shortfalls in knowledge and competence. A summary of strengths
and weaknesses should be drawn up to create a plan of action. A sample summary follows.

Checklist for in-service training needs

Tick all subjects you think you need to know more about

Literacy

1. Current theory on young children's literacy development and integrating it across the curriculum
2. Current methods of teaching literacy
3. Diagnosing children's literacy abilities
4. Diagnosing children's language abilities
5. Encouraging self-expression
6. Assisting children with language and literacy problems

Numeracy

7. Current theory on young children's development of understanding about numeracy
8. Current methods of developing number concepts
9. Diagnosing children's number abilities
10. Integrating numeracy, literacy and other aspects of the curriculum

Child development

11. Information and understanding of child development
12. The relevance of developmental stages to the curriculum in a mixed-aged class
13. Observation of children

Teaching strategies and classroom management

14. Learning through activity-based integrated curriculum
15. Catering for children with special needs
16. Developing children's self-esteem
17. Classroom management and organisation
18. Child management

Family and community studies

19. Parent participation in school life
20. Making better use of community resources
21. The school as a community resource
22. The effects of disadvantages on children

Curriculum subjects

23. Art and crafts
24. Child protection and safety
25. Environmental studies
26. Health and physical education
27. Science
28. Music
29. Religion
30. Other

Curriculum design
Strengths:

Areas in need of development:

Curriculum implementation
Strengths:

Areas in need of improvement:

Other areas in which there is scope for improvement:

Objectives for self-improvement in order of priority
Knowledge or skill: Method of improvement to be adopted

Specific improvements to be accomplished

Priorities for improvements to be identified

Actions necessary to achieve these improvements

Problems to be overcome to achieve improvements

Help needed to achieve my objectives

Titles for further information on self-evaluation

Blount, G. (ed.), March 1974, *Teacher Evaluation: An Annotated Bibliography*. This provides 130 annotated references including a list of books, reports and journals, criteria for evaluation and processes of evaluation. Sections include observation techniques, self-evaluation and research on teacher effectiveness.

Catron, C.E. & Kendall, E.D., March 1984, 'Staff Evaluation That Promotes Growth and Problem Solving' outlines an approach to staff evaluation based on Gordon, T. 1974, Teacher Effectiveness Training, Wyden Books, New York.

Croft, D. 1976, Be Honest With Yourself. A Self Evaluation Handbook for Early Childhood Education Teachers, Wadsworth Publishing, Belmont, California.

Curwin, R. & Fuhrmann, B.S. 1975, *Discovering Your Teaching Self*. A general reference book for teachers containing many ideas, techniques and references for better self-understanding. Chapter 3, 'Examining Your Teaching Self', is particularly applicable.

Decker, C.A. & Decker, J.R. 1976, *Planning and Administering Early Childhood Programmes*. In particular, see pages 231ff., entitled 'Performance Evaluation for Improvement', in the chapter headed 'Leading and Managing Personnel'.

Hess, R.C. & Croft, D. 1972, *Teachers of Young Children*, explores 'The Challenge of Evaluation' in chapter 14.

Johnson, J.M., 1986, 'Improving the Quality of Staff Evaluations'. Intended for staff in daycare centres but some ideas are applicable to schools. Offers ideas for making evaluations more meaningful.

Kasindorf, M.E. 1979, *A Self-Evaluation Guide to Competencies in Early Childhood Education*. A handbook of resources for self-evaluation and improving performance and competence in early childhood programmes. Checklists may be reproduced.

Manning, R.C. 1988, *The Teacher Evaluation Handbook: Step-by-Step Techniques and Forms for Improving Instruction,*

New Zealand Educational Institute 1987, *Teacher Effectiveness and Accountability: A Guide for a School-based Programme to Enhance the Status of Primary Teaching and Teachers*. Wellington (10 pages) primary priorities, your priorities, an action campaign.

Old, R. 1973, *Self-Evaluation for Teachers and Administrators*. A handbook of methods of self-evaluation for teachers and administrators of programmes for children of all ages.

Radomski, M.A. 1986, 'Professionalisation of Early Childhood Educators: How Far Have We Progressed?'. Lists fourteen characteristics of a profession and asks questions related to each of these which deserve professional consideration.

Stanley, S.J. & Fopha, W.J. (eds) 1988, *Teacher Evaluation: Six Prescriptions for Success*. Ratings of teachers in the USA.

Takanishi, R. 1979, 'Evaluation of Early Childhood Programmes: Toward a Developmental Perspective', *Current Topics in Early Childhood Education*, vol. 2, Ablex, Norwood, NJ.

Glossary of terms

Acceleration: when a child is placed in a school year or grade level ahead of chronological peers in one or more academic subjects

Activity methods: where children's learning is encouraged by the provision of appropriate practical experience using specially selected materials for weighing, measuring, making, doing, building, pouring, creating, etc.

Affective education: underpinned by humanitarian priorities

Caregivers: persons who have responsibility for the care and education of other people's children, for example in daycare centres, family daycare, family centres and their own homes

Childcare: usually refers to daycare centres or family daycare, but this term is also used by British social workers for residential care and foster care

Childminders: those who look after other people's children, usually for payment. They may be registered with, inspected and approved by representatives of government departments, or they may be unregistered

Child sexual abuse: the use of children's bodies by others for sexual gratification

Creativity: ability to express novel and useful ideas, to sense and elucidate new and important relationships and to ask previously unthought of but crucial questions

Curriculum: the aggregate of programmes within the school

Denominational schools: pertaining to a particular religious body or sect

Divergent thinking: the ability to think across a range of possibilities and suggest several potential answers

Dramatic play: when children act out familiar situations in their play

Early childhood education: the education of young children under the age of eight years

Early childhood educators: people trained to teach children under eight years

Education authority: state, city, county or nationally provided government-funded department responsible for the provision of schools and employment of teachers

Educational priority programmes: programmes provided with special funding for schools in low socio-economic areas with large numbers of children from government-assisted families

Environment: the aggregate of surrounding things and conditions that influence personal development, for example work conditions, learning conditions, home conditions, etc.

Epistemology: the branch of philosophy which investigates the origin, nature, methods and limits of human knowledge

Ethics: the rules of conduct recognised in respect of a profession

Family daycare: where vetted, approved, registered and supervised adults accept responsibility for the care of other people's children in their own homes, for payment

Field experience: work undertaken in the field to gain experience as part of professional training, such as in schools. This may include teaching practice, also referred to as practicum

Fine motor skills: controlled movement of the small muscles, such as in fingers

Home-school co-ordinator: a member of staff or a parent who has responsibility for developing and improving all aspects of home-school relationships and possibly for promoting parent activities in school

Head teacher: principal or senior teacher and administrator in charge of a school

Home visiting: a representative of the school visits the homes of enrolled children as a matter of routine

Inclusive curriculum: sufficiently broad to enable every child to achieve his or her potential, irrespective of race, sex, socio-economic background, religion, etc.

Ideology: the body of doctrine associated with a social movement, a visionary theory, possibly of an impractical nature

Infant classes: catering for children aged five to eight years in infant or primary schools

Infant schools: catering solely for children aged five to eight years

In loco parentis: acting as a responsible parent of children in their care

Integrated curriculum: combining language, arts, maths, science, history, geography, music and creative activities or combinations of some of these to create a balanced experience

Junior primary schools: *see* infant school

Junior primary class: *see* infant class

Kindergarten: for the purpose of this book, a small school for furthering the development of young children under the age of five years, usually in the three- to five- year age group. In some states of the USA and in Western Australia, the first class in school is referred to as a kindergarten class

Language disorder: a lag in the ability to understand and express ideas that puts linguistic skill behind the child's developmental levels in other areas

Mainstreaming: the term used for the placement of disabled children in 'normal' classes

Mental retardation: a condition in which the individual has below-average intellectual functioning abilities. Both IQ and adaptive skills are considered as measures of retardation

Multi-Age Grouping: *see* vertical grouping

Nursery class: accommodates children aged three to five years within an infant or primary school setting (UK)

Nursery school: serves the same function as a kindergarten but consists of several or many classes catering for children in the two- to five- age year group (UK)

O.M.E.P: The world organisation for early childhood education

Orientation programme: a procedure to help individuals to adapt to a new environment

Pedagogy: techniques involved in teaching

Peer tutoring: a method based on the notion that children can effectively tutor one another

Perception: an individual's ability to process stimuli meaningfully; the ability to organise and interpret sensory information

Physically disabled children: those unable to perform significant physical activities required in everyday living that most children of the same age and sex can perform without special assistance

Physically handicapped children: those whose non-sensory physical limitations or health problems interfere with school life or learning to such an extent that they require special education

Play centre: provides preschool education similar to kindergartens, but with parents organising, leading and teaching children (NZ)

Playgroup: an informal gathering of preschool children with their parents, organised by families within a community to provide social contact and play experience for children

Practicum: refers to the periods of time when students are allocated to schools and pre-schools to practise teaching and acquire teaching skills

Pre-school child: the child before school attendance

Pre-school services: services for children under school age, including all forms of daycare, kindergartens, nursery classes and nursery schools

Pre-school teacher: qualified teachers working with children in pre-school classes and centres of all kinds

Primary school: catering for the education of children from about eight to twelve years, but may include the five- to eight- year age group

Principal: *see* head teacher

Reception class: the first year in the infant junior primary department or school

Streaming by ability: the grouping of children according to their perceived ability with 'top' and 'bottom' level ability groups

Stress: a disturbing physiological or psychological influence which produces a state of severe tension in the individual

Supervisory lecturer: the lecturer responsible for observing, assessing and diagnosing the needs of one or more students when they are practising teaching in school or pre-schools, etc.

Supervisory teacher: the teacher responsible for a student teacher who is practising teaching in that class

Teaching block: a period of unbroken time, such as a month or a term, during which students are working as trainee teachers in schools or pre-schools

Teaching practice: also referred to as field experience and practicum. The student works in the school or pre-school class, learning how to teach children, guided by the class teacher, the college or university lecturer and the course requirements

Tertiary education: all forms of formal education beyond secondary education including education at universities, colleges of advanced education and teacher training establishments

Tertiary institution: a college or university — *see* tertiary education

Vertical grouping: when classes contain children aged five, six and seven years who stay with the same teacher for the whole of their three years in the infant/junior primary school or department. This is also referred to as multi-age grouping.

References

Albert, R.S. 1989, 'Independence and the Creative Potential of Gifted and Exceptionally Gifted Boys', *Journal of Youth and Adolescence*, no.18, pp. 221–30.

Alberta Advanced Education & Manpower Social Services & Community Health Education, 'Now to Evaluate ECS Programme', undated.

Alberta Advanced Education & Manpower Social Services & Community Health Education, *Self-Evaluation, A Handbook for Early Childhood Services Staff*, undated.

Aliki 1989, *Feelings*, Australian Piper Press.

Allen, K.E. 1992, *The Exceptional Child: Mainstreaming in Early Childhood Education*, 2nd edn, Delmar Publishers Inc., USA.

Althea 1991a, *I Have Epilepsy*, Dinosaur, London.

Althea 1991b, *I Use a Wheelchair*, Dinosaur, London.

Andrews, G. 1982, *The Parent-Action Manual*, East Doncaster School Community Interaction Trust, Victoria.

Anon. 1985, *Daddy Doesn't Live Here Anymore—A Book About Divorce*, A Golden Learn Book, New York.

Anon. 1985, *Why did Grandpa Die?* A Golden Learn Book, New York

Appelbe, A., Sippel, J.E. & Smailes, C. 1984, *Trust Your Feelings*, CARE Productions Associations, BC.

Arthur, L., Beecher, B., Dockett, S., Farmer, S. & Richards, E. 1993, *Programming and Planning in Early Childhood Settings*, Delmar Publishers Inc., USA.

Augoustinos, M. 1987, 'Developmental Effects of Child Abuse: Recent Findings', *Child Abuse and Neglect, The International Journal*, vol. 11, no. 1.

Aylesworth, J. 1991, *The Bad Dream*, Chicago, Albert Whitman & Co., USA.

Balson, M. 1988, 'Understanding and Preventing Behavioural Problems in School', *The Practising Teacher*, vol. 10, no. 2.

Balson, M. 1994, *Understanding Classroom Behaviour*, 4th edn, Australian Educational Research Hawthorn, Victoria.

Bandura, A. 1969, *Principles of Behaviour Modification*, Holt Rinehart Winston, NY.

Barker Lunn, J.C. & Ferri, E. 1970, *Streaming in the Primary School*, NFER, Slough, Buckinghamshire.

Barry, K. & King, L. 1993, *Beginning Teaching*, 2nd edn, Social Science Press, Wentworth Falls, NSW.

Barry, S.L. 1986, 'Strategies for Success: From the Principal's Point of View', *The Journal*, no. 1, South Australian Junior Primary Principals' Association.

Berk, L.E, 1991 *Child Development*, 2nd edn, Allyn & Bacon, USA.

Blandford, J.S. 1958, 'Standardised Tests in Junior Schools with Special Reference to the Effects of Streaming', *British Journal of Educational Psychology*, vol. 28.

Bloom, B.S. 1972, *Taxonomy of Educational Objectives—the Classification of Educational Goals*, Longman, London.

Blount, G. (ed.) 1974, *Teacher Evaluation: An Annotated Bibliography*, Ontario Institute for Studies in Education, Toronto, March.

Bochner, S. 1987, 'Who Should Receive Special Education: Issues in Identification, Classification and Incidence?', in, J. Ward *et al.* (eds). *Educating children with Special Needs in Regular Classrooms*, Special Education Centre Special Education Centre, Macquarie University, NSW.

Borba M. & Borba, C. 1982, *Self-Esteem: A Classroom Affair*, Dove Communications, Melbourne.

Borg, W.R. 1966, *Ability Grouping in the Public Schools: A Field Study*, 2nd edn, Dembar Educational Research Services, Madison, Wisconsin.

Bornemann, K. 1992, *Everything You Need to Know About Incest*, Rosen Publishing Group, New York.

Bourgeois, P. 1987, *Franklin in the Dark*, Ashton Scholastic, Sydney.

Brady, L. 1985, *Models and Methods of Teaching*, Prentice Hall, Sydney.

Branscombe, F. & Newson, H. 1977, *Resource Services for Canadian Schools*, McGraw-Hill, Ryerson, Toronto.

Brassard, M. & Hart, G. 1987, *Psychological Maltreatment of Children*, Pergamon Press, NY.

Briggs, F. 1978, The Development of Nursery Nursing and the Changing Role of the Nursery Nurse 1870–1975, MA thesis, University of Sheffield, unpublished.

Briggs, F. 1984a, 'Streaming Rediscovered', *Set*, no. 2, reproduced from *Pivot*, vol. 10, no. 4, 1983.

Briggs, F. 1984b, 'The Organisation of Practicum: The Responsibilities of the Teacher and College Supervisor. A Pilot Study', *The Journal of Teaching Practice*, vol. 4, no. 2, Winter, pp. 15–26.

Briggs, F. 1986a, 'The Response of Teacher Education Curriculum to Teachers' Needs Relating to Child Abuse', *The Journal of Teaching Practice*, vol. 6, no. 2, pp. 5–15.

Briggs, F. 1986b, *Child Sexual Abuse, Confronting the Problem*, Pitman, Melbourne.

Briggs, F. 1988a, 'South Australian Parents Want Child Protection Programmes to be Offered in Schools and Preschools', *Early Childhood Development and Care*, vol. 34, pp. 167–78.

Briggs, F. 1988b, *Keep Children Safe*, Longman Chesire, Melbourne.

Briggs, F. 1989, 'Significance of Children's Drawings in Cases of Sexual Abuse', *Early Child Development and Care*, vol. 47, pp. 131–47.

Briggs, F. 1991, 'Child Protection Programmes—Can They Really Protect Young Children?', *Early Child Development and Care*, vol. 67, pp. 61–72.

Briggs, F. 1993 *Why My Child?* Allen & Unwin, Sydney.

Briggs, F. 1994, 'Keeping Ourselves Safe—A Personal Safety Curriculum Examined', *Best of Set*, NZCER/ACER.

Briggs, F. 1995a *Teaching Personal Safety Skills to Children with Disabilities*, Jessica Kingsley Publishers, London.

Briggs, F. 1995b *Victim to Offender*, Allen & Unwin, Sydney.

Briggs, F. & Hawkins, M.F. 1993, 'Children's Perceptions of Personal Safety Issues and their Vulnerability to Molestation', *Children Australia*, vol. 18, no. 3, pp. 4–9.

Briggs, F. & Hawkins, M.F. 1994, 'Follow Up Data on the Effectiveness of New Zealand's National School Based Child Protection Programme', *Child Abuse and Neglect*, vol. 18, no. 8.

Briggs, F., Hawkins, R.M. & Williams, M. 1994, 'A Comparison of the Early Childhood and Family Experiences of Incarcerated Convicted Male Child Molesters and Men Who are Sexually Abused in Childhood and Who Have No Convictions for Sexual Offences Against Children', Report for the Criminology Research Council, Canberra, University of South Australia, Adelaide.

Brindze, R. 1978, *Look How Many People Wear Glasses—The Magic of Lenses*, Atheneum, NY.

Brophy, J.E. 1981, 'Teacher Praise: A Functional Analysis', *Review of Educational Research*, vol. 5.1, no. 1, pp. 5–32.

Brown, M.W. 1979, *The Dead Bird*, Dell, NY.

Bruner, J. 1980, *Under Five in Britain*, Oxford University Press.

Burns, A. 1980, *Breaking Up*, Nelson, Melbourne.

Buschhoff, L.K. 1971, 'Going on a Trip', *Young Children*, March, p. 228.

Butler, S. 1990, *The Exceptional Child*, Harcourt Brace Jovanovich, Sydney.

Cahn, S. 1970, *The Philosophical Foundation of Education*, Harper & Row, NY.

Cartwright, C.A. & Cartwright, G.P. 1984, *Developing Observation Skills*, 2nd edn, McGraw-Hill, USA.

Catron, C.E. & Kendall, E.D. 1984, 'Staff Evaluation that Promotes Growth and Problem Solving', *Young Children*, vol. 39, no. 6, September.

Christensen, C. *et al.*, 1991, *Feeling Safe* (booklet & audio tape), Essence Publications, Adelaide, SA (Distributors).

Clarke, H. 1956, 'The Effects of a Candidate's Age', in B. Simon (ed.) 1964, *Non-Streaming in the Junior School*, PSW Educational Publications Forum.

Clay, M. 1990, 'A Portrait of a Five Year Old', *Independence*, vol. 15, June, no. 1.

Cleave, S. 1982, 'Continuity from Pre-school to Infant School', *Educational Research*, vol. 24, no. 3, June, pp. 163–77.

Cleave, S., Jowett, S. & Bate, M. 1982, *And So To School*, NFER–Nelson, London.

Cleaver, V. 1977, *The Mimosa Tree*, Oxford University Press, London.

Clegg, A.B. 1963, 'Children's Attitudes to Streaming', *Forum*, vol. 5, no. 2, Spring.

Cleverley, J. & Phillips, C.D. 1987, *Visions of Childhood: Influential Models From Locke to Spock*, Allen & Unwin, Australia.

Cohen, D. & Stern, V. 1978, *Observing and Recording the Behaviour of Young Children*, Teachers College Press, NY.

Cole, P.G. & Chan, K.S. 1987, *Teaching Principles and Practice*, Prentice Hall, Sydney.

Conant, J.B. 1963, *The Education of American Teachers*, McGraw-Hill, NY.

Congalton, A. 1969, *Status and Prestige in Australia*, Cheshire, Melbourne.

Connolly, J. 1983, *Stepfamilies*, Corgi Books, Australia.

Cooper, H. & Baron, R. 1977, 'Academic Expectations and Attributed Responsibility as Predictors of Teachers Reinforcement Behaviour', *Journal of Educational Psychology*, vol. 69, pp. 409–18.

Copeland, W.D. 1977, 'Some Factors Related to Student Teacher Classroom Performance Following Micro-Teaching Training', *American Educational Research Journal*, vol. 14, pp. 147–57.

Copeland, W.D. 1979, 'Student Teachers and Cooperating Teachers: An Ecological Relationship', *Theory into Practice*, vol. 18, no. 3, pp. 194–200.

Copeland, W.D. 1980, 'Teaching-Learning Behaviours and the Demands of the Classroom Environment', *The Elementary School Journal*, vol. 80, no. 4, pp. 163–77.

Council of Europe 1979, *Young Children in European Societies in the 1980s— From Birth to Eight*, a Council for Cultural Co-operation Conference organised by the School Education Division of the Council of Europe, published by NFER Nelson for the Council of Europe and National Foundation for Educational Research in England and Wales, part 2.

Cox, K.M. & Desforges, M. 1987, *Divorce and the School*, Methuen, NY.

Croft, D. 1976, *Be Honest With Yourself: A Self Evaluation Handbook for Early Childhood Education Teachers*, Wadsworth Publishing, California.

Curriculum Review Group 1969, New Zealand Post-Primary Teacher's Association, *Education in Change*, Longman Paul, Auckland.

Curtis, A. 1982, 'Continuity in Transition from Pre-School to School', paper presented to the 16th National Triennial Conference of the Australian Early Childhood Association, Hobart.

Curwin, R. & Fuhrmann, B.S. 1975, *Discovering Your Teaching Self*, Prentice Hall, Englewood Cliffs, NJ.

Daniels, J.C. 1961, 'The Effects of Streaming in the Primary School: 2. A Comparison between Streamed and Unstreamed Schools', *British Journal of Educational Psychology*, vol. 31, part 2.

Davies, M. & North J. 1990, 'Teachers' Expectations of School Entry Skill, *Australian Journal of Early Childhood*, vol. 15, no. 4, December.

Davies, M. & North, S. 1990, 'Teacher Expectations of School Entry Skills', *Australian Journal of Early Childhood*, vol.15, no. 4, December.

Dawe, L.C.S. 1973, 'The Professional Status of Teachers', *The Australian Journal of Teacher Education*, vol. 32, no. 1, March.

Dean, D. 1979, 'Emotional Abuse of Children', *Children Today*, July-August.

Decker, C.A. & Decker, J.R. 1992, *Planning and Administering Early Childhood Programmes*, Charles E. Merrill Publishing.

Dewey, J. 1963, *Experience and Education*, Collier Books, New York.

Dinkmeyer, D., McKay, D.S. & Dinkmeyer, D. Jnr 1980, *Systematic Training for Effective Teaching*, American Guidance Service, Circle Pines, MN.

Douglas, J.W.B. 1964, *The Home and the School*, Macgibbon & Keel, London.

Education Department of South Australia 1975, *Handbook for Teachers of Migrant Children in Infant Grades*, Adelaide.

Education Department of South Australia 1978, *Continuous Admission Resource Folio.*

Education Department of South Australia 1980, *Preparing for School.*

Education Department of South Australia 1981a, *Parental Involvement in Early Childhood Education.*

Education Department of South Australia 1981b, *Parental Involvement in Schools.*

Education Department of South Australia 1982, *Let's Get it Together*, R-7 Project Team.

Education Department of South Australia 1983a, *R7 Curriculum Management.*

Education Department of South Australia 1983b, 'Programming Guidelines for Teachers', in SA *Junior Primary Advisers.*

Education Department of South Australia 1984, *Close Encounters of the Parental Kind.*

Education Department of Victoria 1978, 'School Entry: Children's, Parents', Teachers' Expectations', Research Report 1/78, Curriculum and Research Branch.

Elkind, D. 1981, *The Hurried Child*, Addison-Wesley, Massachusetts.

Elliott, M. 1986, *The Willow Street Kids—It's Your Right to be Safe*, Andre Deutsch, London.

Essa, E. 1992, *Introduction to Early Childhood Education*, Delmar Publishers Inc., USA.

Essa, E. & Rogers, P. 1992, *Introduction to Early Childhood Education*, Delmar Publishers Inc. USA.

Fanshawe, E. 1975, *Rachel*, Bodley Head, London.

Farnette, C., Forte, I. & Loss, B. 1989, *I've Got Me and I'm Glad: A Self Awareness Activity Book*, rev. edn, Incentive Publications, Nashville, Tenn.

Feeney, S., Christensen, D. & Moravcike, E. 1983, *Who am I in the Lives of Children?*, Charles E. Merrill, Ohio.

Ferri, E. 1971, *Streaming: Two Years Later*, NFER, Slough, UK.

Fine, P.D. 1981, *Let's Remember Corky*, P. D. Fine, Ohio.

Finkelhor, D. & Browne, A. 1986, 'The Traumatic Impact of Child Sexual Abuse: A Conceptualization', *Journal of Annual Progress in Child Psychiatry and Child Development*, pp. 634–8.

Flemming, B., Hamilton, D. & Hicks, J. 1977, *Resources for Creative Teaching in Early Childhood Education*, Harcourt, Brace & Jovanovich, NY.

Flynn, H.E. & Munro, R.G. 1970, 'Evaluation of a Curriculum', *British Journal of Educational Psychology*, vol. 40, part 3.

Forman, G. & Kuschner, D. 1977, *The Child's Construction of Knowledge*, Brooks Cole, California.

Fox, A. 1971, 'Kindergarten: Forgotten Year for the Gifted?', *Gifted Child Quarterly*, vol. 15, pp. 42–8.

Fraiberg, S.H. 1959, *The Magic Years*, Methuen, London.

Freeman, L. 1984, *It's My Body*, Parenting Press Seattle, Wash.

Friebus, R. 1977, 'Agents of Socialization Involved in Student Teaching', *Journal of Educational Research*, vol. 70, pp. 263–8.

Gage, N.L. 1963, 'Paradigms for Research on Teaching', in N.L. Gage (ed.) *Handbook of Research on Teaching*, Rand McNally, Chicago.

Gallagher, Sister V. 1985, *Speaking Out, Fighting Back*, Madrona Publishers, Seattle, Wash.

Galloway, P. 1985, *Jennifer Has Two Daddies*, Women's Education Press, Toronto.

Garbarino, J., Guttman, E. & Seeley, J.W. 1986, *The Psychologically Battered Child*, Jossey-Bass Inc., San Francisco.

Gardner, D.E.M. 1942, *Testing Results in the Infant School*, Methuen.

Gardner, D.E.M. 1962, *The Education of Young Children*, Methuen, London.

Gessell, A., Ilg, F.L. & Ames, L.B. 1968, *The Child from Five to Ten*, Hamish Hamilton, London.

Girard, L.W. 1984, *My Body is Private*, Albert Whitman & Co., Chicago.

Girard, L.W. 1991, *At Daddy's On Saturdays*, Albert Whitman & Co., Chicago.

Gnepp, J. & Hess, D. 1986, 'Children's Understanding of Verbal and Facial Display Rules', *Developmental Psychology*, vol. 22, no.1, pp. 103–8.

Goldberg, J.J. 1962, The Effect of Ability Grouping. A Comparative Study of Broad, Medium and Narrow Range Classes in the Elementary School, Teachers College, Columbia University, NY.

Goldman, R. & Goldman, J. 1982, *Children's Sexual Thinking*, Routledge & Kegan Paul, London.

Goldman, R. & Goldman, J. 1988, *Show Me Yours*, Penguin Books, Melbourne.

Goldstein, M. 1975, *Teaching in the First School*, B.T. Batsford, London.

Good, T.L. & Brophy, J.E. 1978, *Looking in Classrooms*, Harper & Row, NY.

Gordon, A. & Browne, K. 1989, *Beginnings and Beyond*, Delmar Publishers Inc., USA.

Gordon, T. 1974, *Teacher-Effectiveness Training*, Wyden Books, NY.

Green, D. & Lepper, M.R. 1974, 'How to Turn Play Into Work', *Psychology Today*, vol. 8, no. 4, pp. 49–54.

Griffiths, A. & Hamilton, D. 1985, 'Parent–Teacher Cooperation Over Reading in a Junior School', *Early Childhood Development and Care*, vol. 20, no. 1, pp. 5–15.

Hadow Report 1931, *Report of the Consultative Committee on the Primary School*, London, HMSO.

Hains, A. *et al.* 1989 'A Comparison of Pre-school and Kindergarten Teacher Expectations for School Readiness', *Early Childhood Research Quarterly'*, vol. 4, no.1, March.

Halasz, G. 1988, Identification: Theoretical and Clinical Aspects, paper presented at the 1987 Australian Psychoanalytic Congress, University of Melbourne, *Papers of the Freudian School of Melbourne*, pp. 57–67.

Hallahan, D. & Kauffman, J. 1986, *Exceptional Children*, Prentice Hall, NJ.

Halsey, A.J. (ed.) 1972, *Educational Priority*, vol. 1, HMSO, London.

Harper, L.V. & Sanders, K.M. 1978, 'Preschool Children's Use of Space: Sex Differences in Outdoor Play', in M.S Smart & R.C Smart (eds) *Preschool Children: Development and Relationships*, Macmillan, New York.

Harris, J.R. & Liebert, R.M. 1992, *Infant and Child—Development From Birth Through Middle Childhood*, Prentice Hall, Engelwood Cliffs, New Jersey.

Hart-Rossi, J. 1984, *Protect Your Child From Sexual Abuse*, Parenting Press Seattle, Wash.

Hawker, F. 1979a, *With a Little Help from My Friends*, Jacaranda, Milton, UK.

Hawker, F. 1979b, *I Can Read in the Dark*, Jacaranda, Milton.

Hawker, F. 1979c, *Donna Finds Another Way*, Jacaranda, Milton.

Hazen, B.S. 1983, *Two Homes to Live In*, Human Services Press, NY.

Heim, A.W. 1964, 'The Appraisal of Intelligence', in B. Simon, (ed.) *Non-Streaming in the Junior School*, PSW Educational Publications, Leicester.

Hendricks, J. 1994, *Total Learning*, 4th edn, Merrill, NY.

Hess, R.C. & Croft, D. 1972, *Teachers of Young Children*, Houghton Mifflin, Boston.

Hessel, J. 1987, *What's Wrong With Bottoms?*, Century Hutchinson, London.

Hetherington, E.M. 1976, 'Divorced Fathers', *The Family Coordinator*, pp. 417–29.

Hewison, J. 1981, 'Home is Where the Help Is', *Times Educational Supplement*, vol. 16, no. 1.

Hitz, R. & Driscoll, A. 1988, 'Praise for Encouragement', *Young Children*, vol. 43, no. 15, pp. 6–13.

Holdaway, D. 1981, *Literacy and Early Childhood*, Ashton Scholastic, Sydney.

Huang, J. & Hatch, E. 1979, 'A Chinese Child's Acquisition of English', in E. Hatch (ed), *Second Language Acquisition*, Rowley, Mass., USA.

Hymel S., 1986 'Interpretations of Peer Behavior: Affective Bias in Childhood and Adolescence, *Child Development*, vol. 57, pp. 431–45.

Iannacone, L. 1963, 'Student Teaching—A Transitional Stage in the Making of a Teacher', *Theory into Practice*, vol. 19, pp. 73–80.

Jackson, B. & Marsden, D. 1962, *Education and the Working Class*, Penguin, Harmondsworth.

Jackson, B. 1961, 'Teachers' Views on Primary School Streaming', *Educational Research*, vol. 4, no. 1, November.

Jackson, B. 1964, *Streaming: An Education System in Miniature*, Routledge & Keegan Paul, London.

Jampole, L. & Weber, M.K. 1987, 'An Assessment of the Behaviour of Sexually Abused Children with Anatomically Correct Dolls', *Child Abuse and Neglect*, vol. 11, pp. 187–92.

Jencks, C. et al. 1972, *Inequality: A Reassessment of the Effect of Family and Schooling in America*, Basic Books, NY.

Jenkins, D. & Shipman, M. 1981, *Curriculum, An Introduction*, The Pitman Press, Somerset.

Jenkinson, J. 1984, 'The Integration Issue', *Set*, no. 2.

Jessel, C. 1975, *Mark's Wheelchair Adventure*, Methuen, London.

Johnson, J.M. 1986, 'Improving the Quality of Staff Evaluations', *Child Care— Information-Exchange*, no. 51, September, pp. 24–6.

Jones, E. 1973, *Dimensions of Teaching-Learning Environments*, Pacific Oaks College, Pasadena, California.

Joyce, B. & Weil, M. 1980, *Models of Teaching*, 2nd edn, Prentice Hall, NJ.

Kamien, J. 1979, *What if You Couldn't?*, Scribner, NY.

Kamii, C. 1984, 'Viewpoint Obedience is Not Enough', *Young Children*, vol. 39, no. 4, pp. 11–14.

Kasindorf, M.E. 1979, *A Self-Evaluation Guide to Competencies in Early Childhood Education*, Humanics Ltd, Atlanta.

Kast, F.E. & Rosenzweig, J.E. 1973, *Organization and Management*, 4th edn, McGraw-Hill, New York.

Katz, L.G & McClellan, D.E., 1991, *The Teacher's Role in the Social Development of Young Children*, ERIC Clearing House on Elementary and Early Childhood Education, Urbana, Ill.

Katz, L.G. 1988, Confessions—Reflections on the Problems of Teaching Undergraduates in Teacher Education, University of Illinois, Urbana, USA, paper presented at Early Childhood Education Conference, Dunedin, New Zealand, 1991.

Katz, L.G. 1991, 'Readiness: Children and Schools', *ERIC Digest*, ERIC Clearing House on Elementary and Early Childhood Education, Urbana, Illinois.

Keats, E. J.K. 1972, *Apt 3*, Hamilton, London.

Keller, H. 1987, *Goodbye Max*, Julia McRae Books, London.

Kelly, A. 1988, 'Gender Differences in Teacher–Pupil Interactions: A Meta-analytic Review', *Research in Education*, vol. 39, pp. 1–23.

Kenny, D. 1994, 'Is More of the Same Better? Studies of Grade Repetition and its Effects at Primary Level', *Best of Set*, Item II, NZCER/ACER.

Kesster, S. & Swadener, B. (eds) 1992, *Reconceptualising the Early Childhood Curriculum*, Columbia Teachers College, New York.

Kieslar, E.R. 1981, 'Attributions of Supervising Teachers for the Success and Failure of Pupils Taught by their Student Teachers', ED 199255.

King, R. 1978, *All Things Bright and Beautiful?*, John Wiley & Sons, Chichester, UK.

Kitano, M. 1982, 'Young Gifted-Children: Strategies for Pre-school Teachers', *Young Children*, May.

Klugman, R. 1988, 'Emotional Abuse', paper presented to the 7th Congress of the International Society for the Prevention of Child Abuse and Neglect, Rio De Janeiro.

Kounin, J.S. 1970, *Discipline and Group Management in the Classroom*, Holt, Rinehart & Winston, New York.

Kupersmidt, J.B. 1989, 'Socially Rejected Children: Bullies, Victims or Both?', paper presented to the Society for Research in Child Development, Kansas City, cited in Harris & Liebert 1992.

Kupke, D. 1987, *Just Me and the Kids*, Penguin, Melbourne.

Lapp, D., Bender, H., Ellenwood, S. & John, M. 1975, *Teaching and Learning. Philosophical, Psychological Curricula Applications*, Macmillan, NY.

Lee, C.M. 1977, *The Growth and Development of Children*, 2nd edn, Longman, London.

Leeper, S., Skipper, D.S. & Witherspoon, R.L. 1979, *Good Schools for Young Children*, Collier Macmillan International, New York.

Levine, E. 1974, *Lin and Her Soundless World*, Human Sciences, NY.

Lewis, D. & Greene, J. 1983, *Your Child's Drawings—Their Hidden Meaning*, Hutchinson & Co., London.

Lippett, I. 1990, *Trust Your Feelings: A Protective Behaviours Resource Manual for Primary School Teachers*, Essence Publications, Burnside, SA.

Litchfield, A.B. 1976, *A Button in Her Ear*, George J. McLeod, Toronto.

Locke, L. P. 1982, 'Research on Teacher Education for Physical Education in the USA. Part II: Questions and Conclusions', paper presented to the International Symposium on Research in School Physical Education, University of Jyvaskyla, Finland, November.

Lockheed, M. & Harris, A. 1984, 'Cross-sex Collaborative Learning in Elementary Classrooms', *American Educational Research Journal*, no. 21, pp. 275–94.

Lynch, M.A. & Roberts, J. 1982, *Consequences of Child Abuse*, Academic Press, London, pp. 99–108.

Maccoby, E.E & Jacklin, C.N. 1987, 'Gender Segregation in Childhood', in *Advances in Child Development and Behavior*, vol. 20, Academic Press, New York.

Maccoby, E.E. 1990, 'Gender and Relationships: A Developmental Account', *American Psychologist*, no. 45, pp. 513–20.

Main, M. & George, C. 1985, 'Responses of Abused Children and Disadvantaged Toddlers to Distress in Agemates: A Study in the Day Care Setting', *Journal of Developmental Psychology*, vol. 21, no. 3, p. 407.

Manning, R.C. 1988, *The Teacher Evaluation Handbook: Step-by-Step Techniques and Forms for Improving Instruction*, Prentice Hall, Englewood Cliffs, NY.

Martin, C.L. 1989, 'Children's Use of Gender Related Information in Making Social Judgements', *Developmental Psychology*, no. 25, pp. 80–8.

Mayeske, G.W. *et al.* 1973, *A Study of the Achievement of Our Nation's Students*, Washington DC, US Department of Health, Education and Welfare, Office of Education, DHE Publication no. (OE), pp. 72–131.

Mayhall, P.D. & Norgaard, K.E. 1983, *Child Abuse and Neglect: Sharing Responsibility*, John Wiley, NY.

McCracken, J.B. (ed.) 1986, *Reducing Stress in Young Children's Lives*, National Association for the Education of Young Children, Washington DC.

McInnes, L. 1988, *I'm a Walking Talking Miracle*, Cassette Learning Systems Pty Ltd, Melbourne.

McMillan, M. 1912, *Early Childhood*, George Allen & Co., London.

McMillan, M. 1919, *The Nursery School*, Dent, London.

McNamara, L. & Morrison, J. 1988, *Separation, Divorce and After*, 2nd edn, University of Queensland Press, St Lucia, Qld.

Mellonie, B. 1983, *Beginnings and Endings with Lifetimes in Between*, Hill of Content, Melbourne.

Midwinter, E. 1972, *Projections*, Ward Lock Educational, London, pp. 37–45.

Miller, P.H., Danaher, D.L. & Forbes, D. 1986, 'Sex-related Strategies for Coping With Interpersonal Conflict in Children Aged Three to Seven', *Developmental Psychology*, no. 22, pp. 543–8.

Morgan, V. & Dunn, S. 1988, 'Chameleons in the Classroom: Visible and Invisible Children in Nursery and Infant Classrooms', *Educational Review*, no. 40, pp. 3–12.

Morrison, G.S. 1978, *Parent Involvement in the Home, School and Community*, Charles E. Merrill, Columbus, Ohio

Moyer, J. 1986, 'Child Development as a Base for Decision-Making', *Childhood Education*, May/June, 1986.

Murray, S. 1987, *A Review of Research on Primary School Enrolment Procedures*, Australian Early Childhood Association Inc., prepared for the ACT Schools Authority, June.

National Association for the Education of Young Children (NAEYC) 1990, Position Statement on School Readiness, 1509 16 St., NW, Washington DC.

National Centre of Child Abuse & Neglect 1980, *Executive Summary: National Study of the Incidence and Severity of Child Abuse and Neglect*, Washington DC, Children's Bureau ACYF OHDS, US Department of Health & Human Services.

New Zealand Council for Educational Research (NZCER) 1984, 'To Stream or Not to Stream', *Set*, no. 2.

New Zealand Educational Institute 1987, *Teacher Effectiveness and Accountability: A Guide for a School-based Programme to Enhance the Status of Primary Teaching and Teachers*, Wellington, NZEI.

Nicolson, S. & Shipstead, S. 1994, *Through the Looking Glass: Observations in the Early Childhood Classroon*, McMillan Pub. Co., New York.

O'Brien, S. & O'Brien, T. 1988, *Teacher's Day: Diary and Program Planner*, Horwitz Graham, Sydney.

O'Neill, M. 1994, 'Dangerous Families', in F. Briggs (ed.) *Children and Families—Australian Perspectives*, Allen & Unwin, Sydney.

Oates, K. 1982, *Child Abuse—A Community Concern*, Butterworths, Sydney.

Oates, K. 1985, *Child Abuse and Neglect: What Happens Eventually?*, Butterworths, Sydney.

Oates, K. 1988, Keynote Address, 7th International Congress of the Society for the Prevention of Child Abuse and Neglect, Rio De Janiero, September.

Old, R. 1973, *Self-Evaluation for Teachers and Administrators*, School Management Institution, Worthington, Ohio.

Padilla, A. & Leibman, E. 1975, 'Language Acquisition in the Bilingual Child', *The Bilingual Review*, vol. 2, pp. 34–5.

Padoan, G. 1987a, *Remembering Grandad*, Child's Play International.

Padoan, G. 1987b, *Breakup*, Child's Play International.

Parr, J., McNaughton, S., Timperley, H. & Robinson, V. 1993, 'Bridging the Gap: Practices of Collaboration Between Home and the Junior School', *Australian Journal of Early Childhood*, vol. 18, no. 3, September.

Parry, J. & Hornsby, D. 1985, *Write On—A Conference Approach to Writing*, Horwitz Grahame, Sydney.

Perry, D.G., Perry, L.C. & Weiss, R.J., 1989, 'Sex Differences in the Consequences that Children Anticipate for Aggression', *Developmental Psychology*, no. 25, pp. 312–19.

Peters, T.J. & Waterman, R.H. 1984, *In Search of Excellence*, Harper & Row, Sydney.

Petersen, P. 1976, *Sally Can't See*, Black, London.

Pettman, J. 1992, *Living in the Margins: Racism, Sexism and Feminism in Australia*, Allen & Unwin, Sydney

Pithers, D. & Greene, S. 1986, *We Can Say No*, Beaver Books, in association with National Children's Home, London.

Plowden Report 1967, *Children and their Primary Schools*, Central Advisory Council for Education, HMSO, London.

Position Statement on School Readiness 1990, *Young Children*, vol. 46, November, pp. 21–3.

Potter, G.K. 1987, Environmental Influences on the Literacy Growth of Preschool Children, M. Phil. thesis, University of Nottingham.

Potter, G.K. 1989, 'Parent Participation in the Language Arts Programme', *Language Arts*, vol. 66, no. 1, January, pp. 21–8.

Purkey, W. 1970, *Self Concept and School Achievement*, Prentice Hall, Englewood Cliffs, NJ.

Quinn, P.E. 1984, *Cry Out!*, Abingdon Press, Nashville.

Radomski, M.A. 1986, 'Professionalisation of Early Childhood Educators: How Far Have We Progressed?', *Young Children*, vol. 41, no. 5, July, pp. 20–3.

Ramsey, P. 1984, 'Multicultural Education in Early Childhood', *Young Children*, vol. 37, no. 2, pp. 13–24.

Read, K. 1976, *The Nursery School*, Saunders, Philadelphia.

Reasoner, R.W. 1982, 'Building Self-Esteem', in *A Teacher's Guide and Classroom Materials*, Consulting Psychologists Press, Palo Alto, Calif.

Renwick, M. 1977 'Parent Involvement', a report from *Going to School*, presented to the Waikato Institute for Education Research, NZCER, July.

Renwick, M. 1984a *Going to School* (Guide for Parents), NZCER, Wellington.

Renwick, M. 1984b, *To School at Five*, NZCER, Wellington.

Renwick, M. 1994, 'Transition to School: The Children's Experience', *Best of Set—Families and Schools*, Item 6, NCZCER/ACER.

Ridgway, L. & Lawton, I. 1969, *Family Grouping in the Primary School*, Ward Lock Educational, London.

Roberts, M. 1981, 'Continuity of Experience in Early Childhood', *Early Childhood*, April, p. 15.

Roberts, T. 1983, *Child Management in the Primary School*, Unwin Educational Books, London.

Robertson, J. & Robertson J. 1967–73, *Young Children in Brief Separation*, film series, Tavistock Institute of Human Relations.

Robertson, J. & Robertson J. 1971, *Young Children in Brief Separation—A Fresh Look*, Child Development Research Unit, Tavistock, London.

Roeper, A. 1977, 'The Young Gifted Child', *Gifted Child Quarterly*, vol. 21, no. 3, pp. 388–96.

Rogers, R. 1982, 'Children, Separation and Divorce', *Where*, January, no. 174, pp. 23–9.

Ross, A.O. 1977, *Learning Disability: The Unrealised Potential*, McGraw-Hill, NY.

Routley, V. & de Lemos, M. 1993, 'Changing Trends in School Entry Age in Victoria', *Australian Journal of Early Childhood*, vol. 18, no. 2, June.

Rowen, B. 1973, *The Children We See*, Holt, Rinehart & Winston, New York.

Rubin, Z. 1980, *Children's Friendships*, Harvard University Press, Cambridge, USA.

Rule, S. *et al.* 1990, 'Preparation for Transition to Mainstreamed Post-Preschool Environments: Development of a Survival Skills Curriculum', *Topics in Early Childhood Special Education*, vol. 9, no. 4, Winter.

Russell, E. 1990, 'Teaching the Young Child to Draw and Paint', *Independence*, vol. 15, no. 1, June.

Sanders, P. 1991, *Let's Talk About Disabled People*, Franklin Watts, UK.

Saphira, M. 1985, *The Sexual Abuse of Children*, Mental Health Foundation, Auckland.

Saracho, O. & Spodek, B. (eds) 1983, *Understanding the Multicultural Experience in Early Childhood Education*, NAEYC, Washington DC.

Schiller, W. & Veale, A. 1989, *An Integrated Expressive Arts Programme*, Australian Early Childhood Association, Watson, ACT.

Schofield, G. 1986, 'All Things Being Equal', *Junior Education*, March, pp. 9–10.

Schickedanz, J.A. & Molina, A. 1979, unpublished data from the Boston University Pre-elementary Reading Improvement Project.

Shepherd, F., Cullen, M. & Moore, H. 1978, *School Entry: Children's, Parents', Teachers' Expectations*, Curriculum and Research Development Branch, Education Department, Melbourne.

Sherbourne, V. 1979, *A Matter of Confidence: Movement for Children and Parents*, Centre for Education Services, Bristol Polytechnic, Concord Video.

Sheridan, M.D. 1968, *The Developmental Progress of Infants and Young Children*, Ministry of Health Reports on Public Health and Medical Subjects, No. 102, HMSO, London.

Simon, N. 1991, *How Do I Feel?*, Albert Whitman & Co., Chicago.

Simon, B. 1964, *Non-Streaming in the Junior School*, Educational Publications, PSW Leicester,

Sisk, D. 1979, 'Giftedness: A National Perspective', *Science and Children*, vol. 16, no. 6, pp. 12–13.

Sivan, A.B., Schor, D.P., Koeppl, G.K. & Noble, L.D. 1988, 'Interaction of Normal Children with Anatomical Dolls', *Child Abuse and Neglect*, vol. 12, pp. 295–304.

Smith, A.B. 1985, 'Teacher Modelling and Sex-Typed Play Preference', *New Zealand Journal of Educational Studies*, vol. 20, no. 1, pp. 39–47.

Smith, S. 1978, *Happy Birthday, Antoinette*, Open Leaves Press Windsor, Vic.

Sonneborn, R.A. 1987, *Friday Night is Papa's Night*, Picture Puffin, New York.

Southall, I. 1968, *Let the Balloon Go*, Methuen, London.

Spodek, B. 1971, 'Alternatives to Traditional Education', *Peabody Journal of Education*, vol. 48, pp. 140–8.

Stallings, J.A. 1977, *Learning to Look—A Handbook on Classroom Observation and Teaching Models*, Wadsworth, California.

Stanek, M. 1991, *Don't Hurt Me Mama*, Albert Whitman & Co., Chicago.

Stanley, S.J. & Fopha, W.J. (eds) 1988, *Teacher Evaluation: Six Prescriptions for Success*, Association for Supervision and Curriculum Development, Alexandria, VA.

Stark, E. 1991, *Everything You Need To Know About Sexual Abuse*, Rosen Publishing Group, New York.

Steele, B.F. 1986, 'Notes on the Lasting Effects of Early Child Abuse Throughout the Life Cycle', *International Journal of Child Abuse and Neglect*, vol. 10, no. 3.

Stephens, L. 1974, *The Teacher's Guide to Open Education*, Holt, Rinehart & Winston, New York.

Stoneman, Z., Brody, G.H. & Mackinnon, O. 1984, 'Naturalistic Observations of Children's Activities and Roles While Playing With Their Siblings and Friends', *Child Development*, no. 55, pp. 617–27.

Stones, E. 1984, *Supervision in Teacher Education: A Counselling and Pedagogical Approach*, Methuen, London.

Stones, Rosemary 1992, *Children Don't Divorce*, Angus & Robertson Publishing, UK.

Stringer, B.R. & Hurt, H.T. 1981, 'To Praise or Not to Praise: Factors to Consider Before Utilising Praise as a Reinforcing Device in the Classroom Communication Process', paper presented at the Annual Meeting of the Southern Speech Communications Association, Austin, Texas, April.

Svensson, N.E. 1962, 'Ability Grouping and Scholastic Achievements: Report on a 5 Year Follow-Up Study in Stockholm' (abstract), *Educational Research*, Almquist & Wiksell, Stockholm, vol. 5, no. 1.

Takanishi, R. 1979, 'Evaluation of Early Childhood Programmes: Toward a Developmental Perspective', *Current Topics in Early Childhood Education*, vol. 2, Ablex, Norwood, NJ.

Taranaki Education Centre 1987, *The Mainstreamed Child*, New Zealand.

Thomas, D. 1986, 'Integration: To Begin at the Beginning', *The Journal*, no. 1, Junior Primary Principals' Association of South Australia.

Thomas, J.R. & French, K.E. 1985, 'Gender Differences Across Age in Motor Performance: A Meta-Analysis', *Pyschological Bulletin*, no. 98, pp. 260–82.

Tinning, R. 1984, 'The Student Teacher Experience—All that Glitters is Not Gold', *Journal of Teaching Practice*, vol. 4, no. 2, Winter.

Tizard, B. & Hughes, M. 1984, *Young Children Learning: Talking and Thinking at Home and School*, Fontana, London.

Tizard, B., Mortimore, J. & Burchell, B. 1981, *Involving Parents in Nursery and Infant School*, Grant McIntyre, London.

Tomlinson, J. 1968, *The Owl Who Was Afraid of the Dark*, Methuen, London.

Townsend, M. & Stern, R. 1980, *Pop's Secret*, Addison-Wesley, Reading, Mass.

Turney, C. et al. 1982, *Supervisor Development Programmes: Role Handbook*, Sydney University Press, Sydney.

Utech, D.A. & Hoving, K.L. 1969, 'Parents and Peers as Competing Influences in the Decisions of Children of Differing Ages', *Journal of Social Psychology*, no. 78, pp. 267–74.

Vellekoop, C. 1969, 'Streaming and Social Class', *Delta*, no. 5, August.

Vernon, P.E. 1964, 'Secondary School Selection', in B. Simon (ed.) *Non-Streaming in the Junior School*, PSW Educational Publication, Leicester.

Vigna, J. 1980, *She's Not My Real Mother*, Albert Whitman & Co., Chicago.

Vigna, J. 1991, *Mommy and Me By Ourselves Again*, Albert Whitman & Co., Chicago.

Waas, G.A. 1988, 'Social Attributional Biases of Peer-rejected and Aggressive Children', *Child Development*, no. 59, pp. 969–75.

Wachter, O. 1985, *No More Secrets for Me*, Penguin Harmondsworth, Middlesex.

Walker, R. & Adelman, C. 1975, *A Guide to Classroom Observation*, Methuen, London.

Watson, J. W. 1986, *Sometimes I'm Afraid*, Crown Publishers, NY.

Watson, J.E. 1969, *Intermediate School in New Zealand*, NZFER, Wellington.

Whelan, T. & Kelly, S. 1986, *A Hard Act to Follow*, Penguin, Ringwood, Vic.

Whitbread, N. 1972, *The Evolution of the Nursery-Infant School*, Routledge & Kegan Paul, London.

White, B.L. 1975, *The First Three Years of Life*, Prentice Hall, Englewood Cliffs, NJ.

White, B.L. & Watts, J.C. 1973, *Experience and Environment: Major Influences on the Development of the Young Child*, vol. 1, Prentice Hall, Englewood Cliffs, NJ.

Whitemore, J.R. 1979, 'The Etiology of Underachievement in Highly Gifted Young Children', *Journal for the Education of Gifted*, vol. 3, no. 1, pp. 38–51.

Whitemore, J.R. 1980, *Giftedness, Conflict and Underachievement*, Allyne & Bacon, Boston.

Wilby, P. 1982, 'The Belfield Experiment', *Educational Magazine*, vol. 39, pp. 5–9.

Wilhelm, H. 1985, *I'll Always Love You*, Hodder & Stoughton, Sydney.

Williams, H.G. 1983, *Perceptual and Motor Development*, Prentice Hall, Englewood Cliffs, NJ.

Willig, C.J. 1963, 'Social Implications of Streaming in the Primary School', *Educational Research*, vol. 5, no. 2, February.

Wilson, P. 1978, *Mummy Why Can't I Breathe?*, Nelson, Melbourne.

Winch, G. 1990, *Samantha Seagull's Sandals*, Childerset, Melbourne.

Woodhead, M. 1976, *Intervening in Disadvantage: A Challenge for Nursery Education*, NFER Publishing, Windsor.

Woodhead, M. 1979, *Preschool Education in Western Europe—Issues, Policies and Trends*, Longman, London.

Wragg, E. 1994, *An Introduction to Classroom Observation*, Routledge, London.

Yardley, A. 1971, *The Teacher of Young Children*, Evans, London.

Yardley, A. 1973, *Discovering the Physical World*, Evans, London.

Yardley, A. 1974a, *Reaching Out*, Evans, London.

Yardley, A. 1974b, *Senses and Sensitivity*, Evans, London.

Yates, A., Beutler, L.E. & Crago, M. 1985, 'Drawing by Child Victims of Incest', *Child Abuse and Neglect, The International Journal*, vol. 8, pp. 183–89.

York, S. 1991, *Roots and Wings: Affirming Culture in Early Childhood Programmes*, Toys 'n' Things, Minnesota.

Zill, N. 1982, 'Divorce, Marital Conflict and Mental Health of Children', in C. Baden (ed.) *Children and Divorce*, Wheelock College, Boston.

Index